Chanting in the Hillsides

To Les and Kyoko Gibson
and to
Soka Gakkai International members
Wales and the Borders
who made the writing of this book possible

Chanting in the Hillsides

The Buddhism of Nichiren Daishonin
in Wales and the Borders

Jeaneane and Merv Fowler

sussex
ACADEMIC
PRESS

BRIGHTON • PORTLAND

2 4 6 8 10 9 7 5 3 1

First published 2009 in Great Britain by
SUSSEX ACADEMIC PRESS
PO Box 139
Eastbourne BN24 9BP

and in the United States of America by
SUSSEX ACADEMIC PRESS
920 NE 58th Ave   Suite 300
Portland, Oregon 97213–3786

British Library Cataloguing in Publication Data
A CIP catalogue record for this book is available from the British Library.

Library of Congress Cataloging-in-Publication Data
Fowler, Jeaneane D.
Chanting in the hillsides : Nichiren Daishonim Buddhism in Wales and the
   Borders / Jeaneane Fowler and Merv Fowler.
p. cm.
Includes bibliographical references and index.
ISBN 978-1-84519-258-7 (p/b : alk. paper)
1. Soka Gakkai—Wales—History. 2. Soka Gakkai—Welsh Borders
(England and Wales)—History. 3. Soka Gakkai—Doctrines. I. Fowler,
Merv. II. Title.
BQ8412.9.W36F69 2009
294.3′92809429—dc22

                                                                    2008031386

Mixed Sources
Product group from well-managed
forests and other controlled sources
www.fsc.org Cert no. SGS-COC-2482
© 1996 Forest Stewardship Council

FSC is a non-profit international organization established to promoted the responsible
management of the world's forests. Products carrying the FSC label are independently
certified to assure consumers that they come from forests that are managed to meet
the social, economic and ecological needs of present and future generations.

Typeset and designed by SAP, Brighton & Eastbourne.
Printed by TJ International, Padstow, Cornwall.
This book is printed on acid-free paper.

Contents

List of Illustrations

Illustrations are placed after page 70.

1 Tsunesaburo Makiguchi, the first president of Soka Gakkai (photograph with kind permission of © *Seikyo Shimbun*).
2 Josei Toda, the second president of Soka Gakkai (photograph with permission of © *Seikyo Shimbun*).
3 President Josei Toda at the first general meeting of the Kansai General Chapter, April 1957 (photograph with permission of © *Seikyo Shimbun*).
4 Daisaku Ikeda, the current President of Soka Gakkai International (photograph with permission of © *Seikyo Shimbun*).
5 A young Daisaku Ikeda [left] walking with his mentor, Josei Toda [centre] (photograph with permission of © *Seikyo Shimbun*).
6 President Daisaku Ikeda with President Nelson Mandela at the Seikyo Shimbun Building in October 1990 (photograph with permission of © *Seikyo Shimbun*).
7 The marriage of Les and Kyoko Gibson in Japan.
8 Les and Kyoko Gibson at their home in Upper Cwm-twrch in the Swansea Valley of South Wales.
9 Taplow Court, Maidenhead, Berkshire, the headquarters of SGI-UK.
10 The library of the Institute of Oriental Philosophy European Centre (IOP) at Taplow Court with (left to right) the IOP-UK Director Jamie Creswell, librarian Sarah Norman, and Vice-General Director of SGI-UK and Secretary General of SGI-Europe, Kazuo Fujii.
11 Members from Pembrokeshire/Ceredigion chanting (left to right) Jo Ogilvie, Liz Moulson and Nick Dowsett.
12 The Dowsett family chanting (left to right) Nick, Hope, Mani and Tirion.

Preface and Acknowledgements

The third millennium dawned on the canvas of a world largely smudged by urgent global issues that will challenge humankind with its own destruction in the years to come unless radical change is affected. Ours is not a planet of peace and harmony: war, poverty and starvation are all too conspicuous in many corners of the globe. How, then, do we solve these crises? This book is about Nichiren Daishonin Buddhism, a branch of Mahayana Buddhism that believes it has answers for humanity's way forward – answers that not only provide a philosophy for life but, also, and importantly, pragmatic means by which that philosophy can be realized in daily existence.

We first came across Nichiren Daishonin Buddhism almost a quarter of a century ago when exploring dimensions of religion with our first year Philosophy and Religious Studies undergraduate students in the University of Wales. Study of Buddhism involved our students visiting different Buddhist communities – chanting at Lam Rim with the resident Tibetan monk and Tibetan Buddhist residents there, and practising *zazen*, the silent meditation of Soto Zen Buddhism, with another community. One student did a specialist dissertation based on her retreat at a Theravada Buddhist monastery, and several took up studies on Nichiren Daishonin Buddhism. It is in the context of this last branch of Buddhism that we met Les and Kyoko Gibson, the pioneers of Nichiren Daishonin Buddhism in Wales. They warmly opened their home to us and to our students, who enthusiastically joined in the chanting of *Nam-myoho-renge-kyo* – the central tenet of the practice. Les visited the university many times to talk to the students.

As authors and as human beings, we have always been interested in fundamental philosophical questions about life. Those who are familiar with some of our other books will recognize the same interest and exploration of the spiritual, scientific, cultural and religious expressions of cultures beyond our own, and the search for answers to the fundamental questions about our existence. What is our best purpose and function in life? How do we create the best balances in our lives? What are the ultimate goals of our existence? What are the proximate goals that will help us evolve towards our ultimate aim? Why do we suffer? What can we do to increase our personal happiness? And what can we do to increase the happiness of others and promote global harmony? These issues we have already explored in Hinduism, Taoism and Humanism (Jeaneane Fowler), and in mainstream Buddhism and Zen Buddhism (Merv Fowler). An independent study of Nichiren Daishonin Buddhism has long been an aim of both writers.

This book would not have been possible without the help of many people. We experimented with using our local library in Chepstow, Monmouthshire, South Wales, because we pass it so regularly, unlike the university library, and were delighted with the considerable help we received there and with the efficiency of the staff. Resources Manager, Anne Thomas, was very helpful indeed, and Claire Cross, who is in charge of inter-library loans, procured any texts we needed with remarkable speed. Annie Smalley, the Library and Information Assistant, was also extremely helpful in supplying contact information concerning statistics from the Welsh Office. Here, three people – Richard Matthews, Martin Griffiths and David Jones – provided a wealth of material, statistical websites and responses to many queries, without which some of the material in the book would have been rendered useless. We are extremely grateful to them for their patience and prompt responses to the many questions, and congratulate the Welsh Office on having such efficient staff. We have now had a long association with our publishers, Sussex Academic Press, who have always been available for discussion, advice and expertise. We are fortunate to have the experience of such a friendly and inspiring Press.

Finally, we have been humbled by the incredible response of the members of Nichiren Daishonin Buddhism in Wales and the Borders, who willingly filled in a lengthy questionnaire, giving us a wealth of information and very honest analyses of their beliefs and practices. This book is very much *their* book, *their* voices, *their* legacy. Half of the people contacted responded, and in comparison to other studies, this was a very good outcome. Three Headquarter leaders – James Rourke, Nick Dowsett and Chris Bradbury – took on the responsibility of distributing the questionnaires amongst their members, and we are very grateful indeed for their labours. They made a practical difficulty at the outset disappear. We are also very grateful for the assistance of Sarah Norman at the Institute of Oriental Philosophy European Centre at Taplow Court, near Maidenhead, Berkshire. Sarah has been a continued source of friendly help and support for all the books we have written. We would also like to thank Robert Samuels, the General Director of Soka Gakkai International – United Kingdom, for his sound advice during the preparation of the questionnaire, for his support in its distribution and for the very welcomed information on the structure of SGI in Wales and the Borders. It is thanks to Robert Samuels, also, that we were able to procure illustrations for the book. He supplied all but two, securing permission from the newspaper *Seikyo Shimbun* in Japan for the first six, and supplying high resolution photographs for printing of the majority. We are delighted that Nicky Delgado, a Welsh member of SGI, a writer and a poet, has allowed us to reproduce two of his poems from *Silence of the Raised Voice: If I Lie I Die*. One of the poems entitled "Repetition (But, Still, Yet)", begins the book and the other, "The Gauntlet", ends it.

The cover of the book was designed by artists Mark Medcalf and Masae Takeuchi, both of whom are members of SGI-UK Wales and the Borders and district leaders of Newport in South Wales. Mark's and Masae's work covers a range of media and creative ideas, which explore the spiritual nature of all phenomena. The work they produce is grounded in the rich tapestry of the philosophy of Buddhism and reflects their unique individuality and back-ground. Masae was born and brought up in Japan and has been practising Nichiren Daishonin Buddhism for thirty-three years. Mark, her husband, has been practising for twenty-three years. They were married in a Nichiren Daisonin Buddhist ceremony. We are extremely grateful for the energy and creativity they so willingly gave in designing such a beautiful cover at very short notice.

An *immense* gratitude is owed to Les and Kyoko Gibson, two very great individuals, who are the reason why this book is possible. They are also the reason why there are Nichiren Daishonin Buddhists in Wales and the Borders; they are the dedicated pioneers of Soka Gakkai International here. Their help in the preparation of this book has been so willingly given, with immediate responses to endless e-mails, editing of sections of text related to information on the history of Nichiren Daishonin Buddhism in Wales that has not hith-erto been documented – and all the time with a warmth and enthusiasm that have given us continued support. We hope the text is free from errors, but for any that are evident, we take sole responsibility.

JEANEANE AND MERV FOWLER
Summer, 2008

If the minds of the people are impure, their land is also impure,
but if their minds are pure, so is their land. There are
not two lands, pure and impure in themselves.
The difference lies solely in the good
or evil of our minds.
Nichiren Daishonin

To see a World in a Grain of Sand
And a Heaven in a Wild Flower
Hold Infinity in the palm of your hand
And Eternity in an hour.
William Blake

All the books in the world
Will not bring you happiness,
But they will quietly lead you
Back inside yourself.
There you will find all you need,
Sun, stars and moon,
For the light for which you search
Dwells within you.
The wisdom you so long sought in books,
Will then shine forth from every page –
For now that wisdom has become your own.
Herman Hesse

Life is dynamic; it is wisdom and compassion; it embodies the principle
of the indivisibility of life and death; it is a universal law. The cosmos
is not so big that life cannot embrace it, nor a particle of matter
so small that life cannot be contained within it. It transcends
words and thought and is truly unfathomable; it can only be
described as the Mystic Law. That is how
inscrutable it is.
Daisaku Ikeda

While life is eternal, it is the present moment that is crucial.
Each moment of our life is a summary of both
the effects from our past and the causes
for our future; our life is no one's
responsibility but our own.
Kazuo Fujii

We cannot be truly happy while others remain miserable. Nor is
the misery of another that person's alone. The more
happiness we bring to others, the happier
we ourselves become. As long as
one unhappy person remains,
our own happiness cannot
be complete.
Daisaku Ikeda

The same stream of life that runs through my veins night and day runs through
the world and dances in rhythmic measures. It is the same life that shoots
in joy through the dust of the earth in numberless blades of grass
and breaks into tumultuous waves of leaves and flowers.
It is the same life that is rocked in the ocean-cradle
of birth and death, in ebb and in flow. I feel my
limbs are made glorious by the touch of this
world of life. And my pride is from
the life-throb of ages dancing
in my blood this moment.
Rabindranath Tagore

If we can see ourselves as part of an eternal cosmos, as indeed we are, we
will be liberated from the anxieties that turn into fear of death and
greed. Then we can devote ourselves more faithfully to serving
others. The happiness of others will become our own
happiness. Whether we call this eternal spirit
Yahweh, Jesus, Allah, or Buddha, by
participating in the eternal, we too
become immortal.
Majid Tehranian

Peace cannot be a mere stillness, a quiet interlude between wars. It must be
a vital and energetic arena of life-activity, won through our own
volitional, proactive efforts. Peace must be a living drama.
Daisaku Ikeda

. . . if one with a joyful mind sings a song in praise of the Buddha's virtue,
even if it is just one small note, then all who do these things
have attained the Buddha way.
Shakyamuni Buddha

Repetition (But, Still, Yet)

Love dances in I,
But melody and rhythm
Cannot hide my fears.

Love dances in I,
But the raindrops on my face
Still taste like salt.

Love dances in I,
Yet my body
Shivers in the sunlight.

Love dances in I
And yet there is
Fear in the drumbeat.

Love dances in I
However, intoxication
Cannot set me free.

Love dances in I
But still yet I ache,
Just to be.

I don't wish just to be
An ache.
I wish – just to be;
A person who can truly say,
Love dances in I.

Nicky Delgado

Introduction

Soka Gakkai International, the lay movement of the religion of Nichiren Daishonin Buddhism, is perhaps a less well-known strand of Mahayana Buddhism than, say, Zen or Tibetan Buddhism. Yet it is remarkably prolific throughout the world – North and South America, Canada, Australasia, Africa and most of Asia and Europe – having spread to well over a hundred countries from its original home base in Japan, where its membership is accredited to be eight million households. Not only is it geographically prolific, but it is also becoming numerically prolific outside Japan, and has more members in the United Kingdom than any other Buddhist group. Within Soka Gakkai (Society for the Creation of Value) itself, there is an abundance of supportive literature and yet, outside that organization, world wide, there is very little, especially when one considers the amount of literature available on Zen and Tibetan Buddhism. We have long recognized the need for a comprehensive introduction to this unique strand of Mahayana Buddhism and it is hoped that this present book will go some way to addressing that aim.

In writing a comprehensive introduction to Nichiren Daishonin Buddhism, the aims have been historical, philosophical and sociological. The *historical* profile has been necessary in order to set the Buddhism of Nichiren Daishonin in the context of Mahayana Buddhism as a whole. The *philosophical* aim was necessary to assess the underpinning tenets that inform both its beliefs and its important practice. The *sociological* aim was designed to bring the research in line with other studies of Soka Gakkai International in different parts of the world. These have been undertaken in Canada,[1] the USA,[2] Great Britain,[3] Italy,[4] South-east Asia[5] and South America.[6] Apart from the study done by Wilson and Dobbelaere of Soka Gakkai Buddhists in the United Kingdom a decade and a half ago,[7] little has been done to assess the position in the UK at the present time, except for the doctoral research undertaken by Helen Waterhouse, also largely in 1994, who examined several Buddhist groups in Bath, of which Soka Gakkai International was one.[8]

Combining the dearth of works written by outsiders to the Soka Gakkai International organization itself and the need for a new sociological analysis of the movement, the time seemed apposite for this new venture. And since Nichiren Daishonin Buddhism has increased its membership in Wales, the country in which we, the authors, live, that membership has presented an ideal profile for research. However, while this book contains a sociological analysis in order to bring the material into line with other studies and facilitate research elsewhere, these are not its overriding aims, and dry statistics will not be a facet of its style. Rather, it is hoped that the personalities of the members themselves will speak through the pages and supply a degree of warmth to the academic research. The material ended up being very much in the ownership of the members from Wales and the Borders, whose views are articulated throughout. It is for that reason that their names are included wherever possible. It has been a privilege to conduct the first study of Nichiren Daishonin Buddhism in Wales and the Borders.

It should perhaps be made clear at this point that the authors are not and never have been themselves members of Soka Gakkai International and, while consulting the Wales and Borders area leaders and the Soka Gakkai International Directorate for advice on some matters of fact, and being given their full support and co-operation, there has never been any attempt at editorial censure by the movement, and there has been no suggestion of inhibiting the words of members in any way. All financial expenses for the research have been met by the authors themselves. Thus, the research is presented as an independent, academic study, bereft of influences from, or constraints imposed by, Soka Gakkai International.

Mahayana Buddhism evolved from the original Hinayana and has continued to evolve. Nichiren Daishonin Buddhism is part of that ongoing evolution. It is difficult to describe it as "new" when its roots are so clearly in the distant past, even if they were only to be accredited to the thirteenth century and the life of Nichiren Daishonin. Indeed, many of its tenets stand firmly in the mainstream tradition of Mahayana Buddhism that reaches well back before the advent of Nichiren. It is *Soka Gakkai* as a lay movement that is the true "new" aspect; the religious beliefs, and the practice, however, are anything but. In this sense, it would be impossible to call Nichiren Daishonin Buddhism a "cult", in whichever of the nebulous definitions the term might want to be interpreted. Indeed, our research has not found a shred of evidence that such an epithet might be applicable: Nichiren Daishonin Buddhists in Wales and the Borders are far too engaged in ordinary life and society, as we shall see as this book unfurls. Neither is the term "sect" an apposite one for, while there are some distinctive ideas in Nichiren Daishonin Buddhism, it nevertheless does not segregate itself wholesale from mainstream Buddhism, and has a healthy respect for its lineage from the Buddha, Siddhartha Gautama. The analogy is rather similar to the Methodists or Baptists within the Christian tradition. Nichiren Daishonin Buddhism is, therefore, more a *branch* or *school* of Mahayana Buddhism, though every care will be taken within this book to disclose where there may be differences between the two.

Apart from the historical and philosophical aspects of Nichiren Daishonin Buddhism in the pages that follow, the sociological analysis is based on responses to a questionnaire that was distributed to the 315 members in Wales and the Borders in 2007. With the exception of a short block at the beginning of the questionnaire that required information on gender, nationality and ethnicity, geographical location of each individual member, age, occupation, qualifications, chapter, district and divisional membership, the remaining questions were mainly open, encouraging more reflective response. The questionnaire can be found in Appendix A at the end of the book. Half of the members responded, many with very detailed comment, and it is their comments that have been the mainstay of several of the chapters of the book. Some commented on how useful they found the questionnaire. Debra Blakemore of Senghenydd, for example, writes: "Thank you for producing the questionnaire, it's been interesting completing it. It's made me examine my practice and how I've changed. It's given me precious insight, and thank you for that." Similarly, Suzanne Jenkinson of Cardiff says: "I found this questionnaire very helpful in clarifying my thoughts in relation to Nichiren Daishonin Buddhism and religion in general. Many thanks." In hindsight, however, it might have been wise to have devised a simplified questionnaire for younger people. Only two young people responded, in fact, and we are very grateful to Hope and Tirion Dowsett for attempting to respond to quite a taxing questionnaire.

Most of the questions on the questionnaire invited subjective responses. This was a deliberate intention on the part of the authors in order to avoid a dry and statistical account of the beliefs of the Nichiren Daishonin Buddhists in Wales and the Borders. Statistical tables, therefore, are nowhere evident, since this book is not a sociological study *per se*. Nevertheless, some objective statistics are included. In addition to the 150 questionnaire responses, Les and Kyoko Gibson provided anonymous information on the remainder, so that for objective material such as age, length of practice, occupation and location, we were able to have almost a hundred per cent return on which to work. *Notes to chapters* will detail such percentages in the appropriate chapters. So few of the Nichiren Daishonin Buddhists in Wales and the Borders have not received the *Gohonzon*, the initiatory object of devotion, that we have used the term "respondent" and "member" synonymously.

In terms of content, the book begins with an important *Prologue*, charting the beginning of Nichiren Daishonin Buddhism in Wales and the Borders with the incredible life of Kyoko Gibson. CHAPTER TWO sets Nichiren Daishonin Buddhism in its historical context, reaching right back to the life of the Buddha, Siddhartha Gautama, through to the instigators of Soka Gakkai. CHAPTER THREE takes up where CHAPTER TWO finishes, and examines the work of the current President of SGI, Daisaku Ikeda, the growth of Soka Gakkai to international status, and then turns to explore the fundamental concept of the "human revolution" in the context of adherents. It is in CHAPTER FOUR that a balance is set between an objective examination of the sociological profile of Wales and the Borders members and the more subjective accounts of the reasons why members were attracted to Nichiren Daishonin Buddhism, why they remain committed and what sort of prior beliefs they had. It is these kinds of factors that will be of interest to those who wish to make comparisons with the sociological profiles of members in other countries.

The religious and philosophical basis of Nichiren Daishonin Buddhism in the essential text, the *Lotus Sutra*, is the subject of CHAPTER FIVE, while CHAPTER SIX returns to the practice of Nichiren Daishonin Buddhism itself. Here, chanting, study and faith are examined in detail. The philosophy of Nichiren Daishonin Buddhism is explored in CHAPTER SEVEN, while CHAPTER EIGHT looks at how one would approach life-cycle rites in the tradition, as well as the attitudes of members to the religious celebrations of indigenous, and other, religions.

Respondents were invited to contribute their experiences to CHAPTER NINE. Some of these have been published previously in the SGI-UK magazine, the *Art of Living*, or the prior *UK Express*. Permission has been secured to reproduce these contributions in CHAPTER NINE. The experiences in CHAPTER NINE also include new, hitherto unpublished, accounts by members. The criterion for selection of these testimonies was purely pragmatic: respondents were invited to append an experience, or supply references to the appropriate *Art of Living*. It is these that are included; regrettably, some were not able to be traced. These personal accounts of life-situations will surely resonate with the lives of many readers, whether or not they are Buddhists. Nichiren Daishonin Buddhism is *engaged* Buddhism, and both undergraduate and postgraduate students will glean from this book what Nichiren Daishonin Buddhism means *in practice* and *experientially* to members, providing scope for mature engagement with this living and dynamic religion. It is the experiences of CHAPTER NINE, in particular, which translate academic analysis of the religion into the dynamism of everyday life by expressing how the tenets and praxis are effectuated in the kinds of situations that we all face. Having written a number of well-received textbooks for students, we both feel that the present work is the most valuable and worthwhile, for it approaches Nichiren Daishonin Buddhism in a personal, focused and utterly understandable way. The *Appendices* at the end of the book include the questionnaire, and the SGI Charter. Also at the end of the book is a *Glossary of Terms* and suggestions for further reading.

Chanting in the Hillsides is a book about people, people who live in Wales and the Borders and who are Nichiren Daishonin Buddhists. While it never strays from academic rigour, the comments of these Buddhists have provided a warm current that runs through its pages. It is hoped that they themselves will find in its pages a true expression of their beliefs. At the same time, *Chanting in the Hillsides* should place members in Wales and the Borders in the wider context of their place alongside adherents in other countries. Then, too, the rationale for the book has a broader academic aim in that the history and philosophy of Nichiren Daishonin Buddhism are of interest to the general reader, and to the student and teacher of other cultures and religions.

Nichiren Daishonin Buddhism has a wide appeal. Its practice is simple, the effects of which are hailed as profound and meaningful in daily life. It is pragmatic, world-affirming and positive in its aims. While beginning with change in the self, it aims for positive change and well-being in society, happiness for all, and world peace – these are hardly aims with which anyone would want to argue. Core concepts of Soka Gakkai International are :

- The inherent dignity and equality of all human life.
- The unity of life and its environment.
- The interconnectedness of all beings that makes altruism the only viable path to personal happiness.
- The limitless potential of each person to make a difference.
- The fundamental right of each person to pursue self-development through a process of self-motivated reform, or "human revolution".[9]

It is these principles that we now take up in the following pages.

CHAPTER ONE

Prologue

The atomic bombing of Hiroshima

On 6 August 1945, Colonel Paul Tibbets of the United States Air Force took off in his B-29 bomber, *Enola Gay*. His flight was from an air base in the West Pacific on a clear, sunny morning, chosen specially for the event: it was a six-hour flight. He was the commander of the 509th Composite Group, and would find his name immortalized following the USA's final offensive against the Japanese Empire – an offensive that ended World War II. He was heading for the Japanese city of Hiroshima – a target chosen not only for its military importance because it possibly housed 43,000 troops, but also for its urban population, its civilians, and the psychological impact it would have on them. Then, too, there was the international importance of using a new weapon. For Colonel Tibbets carried a nuclear, uranium bomb, nicknamed "Little Boy". At 8.15 on that clear morning, "Little Boy" was dropped on Hiroshima, a city that was home to at least 255,000 inhabitants.[1]

Although "Little Boy" was detonated nearly 2,000 feet/600 metres, above the city, the radius of its devastation was immense. Those within a mile of its epicentre were killed instantly, charred beyond recognition, while those that were spared instant death suffered horrendous burns, the white light from the bomb burning dark patterns from clothing indelibly onto the skin. Many were buried in collapsing buildings – few buildings survived intact in the whole city – or were caught in the firestorms that rose up in an area of about 4.4 square miles.[2] Then, radiation sickness set in, and many of those who survived the original blast found themselves dying several weeks later, others developing cancers at later stages of their lives. At least 90,000 inhabitants may have died in the first four months and possibly 140,000 during the year of 1945.[3] On 9 August, Major Charles Sweeney flew his B-29 with another nuclear bomb that was released over the sea port of Nagasaki.

Kyoko and Les Gibson

Those Japanese people who survived the bombings are known as "explosion-affected people" (*Hikabusha*). Kyoko Gibson is one such person. She was born three years after the bomb was dropped: "I was brought up in a community filled with families suffering tremendously from the effects of the bomb. One family I remember had had their whole skin burnt off by the heat. When you are skinless you are shiny and pink and in agony. It was horrendous to see. Some people managed to live on for years like this, but it was a living hell."[4] Like so many others, Kyoko suffers the effects of radiation: she has a mere fifty per cent effective immune system. Of life immediately after the bomb she says:

> After the bomb was dropped, no information was available as to the possible consequences, and the people were ignorant of the effects of radiation. They grew and ate vegetables from contaminated soil, and ate fish from the polluted sea . . . Even now, there is a lot of suffering behind closed doors. Marriage is very difficult as it may produce deformed children. People have lost hope and confidence for the future, because they feel they don't have the ability to provide for their families. There is a high suicide rate among victims and their families. This is an absolute land of hell – man-made hell! I remember when I was small, even though no-one told me, I knew I shouldn't stare or ask questions about people whose skin had melted with the intense heat.[5]

Kyoko points out that people like her, and those who continue to suffer right up to the present day, are not represented in the statistics of those with ongoing suffering as a result of the nuclear bombs.

Kyoko's mother became a Nichiren Shoshu Buddhist in 1956, and each time Kyoko became ill, she would encourage her daughter by saying: "How exciting! You have another opportunity to improve your physical *karma*."[6] While she rarely spoke about the bombing, Kyoko's mother would quote from the writings of Nichiren Daishonin, stressing how important it is for humanity to be happy, for human beings to aspire to Buddha-nature and not to be negative about life and its limited span. Encouraged by her mother, Kyoko, too, continued to practise the Buddhism of Nichiren Daishonin from the age of seven. By eighteen, she was also involved in the peace movement, carrying a placard to promote peace. But her mother would shake her head and say: "You cannot change people's hearts by carrying a placard." It was when, at the age of nineteen, Kyoko heard a non-Japanese statesman commenting that he was glad the horrors of Hiroshima and Nagasaki hadn't happened to white people, that she realized the full implications of her mother's words. Clearly, humanity needs a greater sensitivity to life, a new way of thinking, and a change of heart. This was a message that began to emerge more clearly after Kyoko heard Soka Gakkai President Daisaku Ikeda speaking in Tokyo, also when she was nineteen.

In September 2000, Kyoko returned to the hospital where radiation victims are treated in Hiroshima to nurse her dying mother: her mother was given only two weeks to live. In Kyoko's words:

> I heard a voice coming from the next room to my mother. I soon realized

that it was an elderly lady repeating over and over again: "Mammy, it hurts!" She was a survivor of the atomic bombing who had lived so long, and was ending her life in this way. When her voice stopped after two days, I wanted to scream on her behalf! Everyone knows that we should not destroy life, but many don't know how to actually treasure life. I used to feel overwhelming sorrow, but now I know how to transform the hunger, anger and stupidity that all human beings have into compassion, courage and wisdom, and I encourage others to do the same.[7]

In October 2006, Kyoko finally visited the atomic bomb museum in Hiroshima. She entered the building by herself and renewed her vow to work for world peace on behalf of her family, past and present, and for the people of Hiroshima. She does this as a Buddhist.

As a Nichiren Daishonin Buddhist, Kyoko is a pioneer of its international movement, Soka Gakkai, "Society for the Creation of Value", in the United Kingdom. She now lives in Wales. She is thoroughly positive about her life and her mission for the happiness of others: "My main message is not to concentrate on why something happens to you but on what you do as a result of it. You can never know why something happens. But you can use your experience for positive effect. All I can say is if I hadn't had this experience I wouldn't be the person I am today."[8] On fourteen occasions she had to have stitches following operations and falls from blackouts in her lifetime. But Kyoko remains inwardly strong. She says she can live her life "with or without" health, money, time. "I am not dependent on my circumstances", she says, "because I can bring out my Buddha-nature and use the problem, whatever it is, positively."[9] For Kyoko Gibson, practise of Nichiren Daishonin Buddhism is the means by which peace is created: "I am a wife, a human being, a mother and a grandmother. What I can do is teach people about fundamental respect for life and how to become a great human being. This is the result of my experience of war."[10]

As to her personal life, Kyoko was born into a fairly affluent family that originally practised Nembutsu Buddhism. When her father's first wife died, leaving him with two young infants, a marriage was arranged with a second wife, with whom he had three children, Kyoko being one. It was Kyoko's mother who began practising Nichiren Daishonin Buddhism – at first not seriously, but when her husband left her, and she became terminally ill with cancer with only three months to live, she began to chant *Nam-myoho-renge-kyo*. She lived until she was eighty five. Without a father, Kyoko, like others in the same position, would normally find it difficult to get a good job. However, she chanted so that she could have her own business – and succeeded. It was then that she met her future husband Les Gibson, and they were married six weeks later, neither speaking the other's language! Les, she thought, had promised to chant, and received his *Gohonzon*, the object of devotion, the day after their marriage. In fact, Les was not to practise at all for almost three years. Two months after their marriage, Kyoko joined Les in Newcastle in the

United Kingdom. They remained there for two years, returned to Japan briefly, then finally came to live permanently in the UK in 1977.

On their return to Japan after their two-year stay in the UK, a particular event was to change Les' life. It was New Year's Eve in 1971, and Les was living at the home of his mother-in-law in Hiroshima. Kyoko chanted daily, but Les had no inclination to do so. He says: "I believed that I could achieve anything in life with my own two hands and would be capable of overcoming any obstacle simply by meeting any challenge head on and dealing with it immediately. I was in reasonably good health, had a good job, a beautiful wife, and was quite content with life."[11] Then, Les had a telephone call from his mother to say that his father was very ill and was not expected to last the night. Thousands of miles away from the UK, this was a problem with which Les could not deal. Les takes up the story:

> Enter Kyoko! "If you chant these strange words (*Nam-myoho-renge-kyo*), your Dad will not die". What confidence! I immediately sat down in front of their *Gohonzon*, or object of worship, and began to chant. I did evening *gongyo* – reciting part of the *Lotus Sutra* – and again the next morning, and carried on chanting the next day. Then, I received another telephone call from England saying that Dad had mysteriously recovered, and no-one knew why. I knew, and Kyoko and her family knew! I carried on almost half-heartedly with the practice, half of me believing that this was coincidence. But I was having benefits; one of them being the disappearance of a minor stomach ailment that had troubled me for some years. I also had a promotion in my job with a lot more responsibility and, of course, a lot more money.[12]

In 1974, Les' parents journeyed to Japan for a holiday. While in the taxi from Tokyo airport, Les says his father announced that "the night he had been given up for dead, he had heard Kyoko singing as he drifted in and out of consciousness". For Les, "this was a turning point in my life and practice and I have devoted myself to the teachings ever since".[13] Les' mother died in 1976, but Les' father went on to live a healthy life for almost twenty more years; passing away peacefully of natural causes in 1993 at the age of eighty-four. Before that, he received his own *Gohonzon* in the North East of England, and he held regular discussion meetings about Nichiren Daishonin Buddhism at his home.

Chanting in Wales and the Borders

It was in 1977 that Kyoko and Les finally came to stay in the UK, with the goal of spreading the teachings of Nichiren Daishonin. Times were sufficiently hard and financially difficult for the first four years to be a considerable challenge not only to daily life but also to faith itself. It was the following passage from Nichiren's writings that enabled Kyoko to take charge of her own life in such a way that *she* controlled her reaction to circumstances rather than the other way around:

> ... even though you chant and believe in Myoho-renge-kyo, if you think the Law is outside yourself, you are embracing not the Mystic Law but an inferior teaching ... Therefore, when you chant *myoho* and recite *renge* [the Mystic Law], you must summon up deep faith that Myoho-renge-kyo is your life itself.[14]

The passage has inspired Kyoko's life to the present day. For both Kyoko and Les, every difficulty in life is seen as a benefit; just like Kyoko's mother had said each time her daughter became ill. As Les says: "Every benefit, incident, or problem in our lives has resulted in our becoming stronger. 'Benefit!' Because of the power of *Nam-myoho-renge-kyo*, we have never suffered. I am convinced that this is because we 'did the practice'!"[15]

By 1983, Les and Kyoko were settled in Bristol and were giving their support to other Soka Gakkai International members in Wiltshire, Devon and Reading. In Wales itself, there were only a scattering of members, and Les and Kyoko travelled from Bristol to lend their support to this tiny group. Nichiren Daishonin Buddhism in Wales began with a small group of six people meeting in a three-bedroomed, detached house in Cyncoed, Cardiff. It was the start of Soka Gakkai International in Wales. At the same time, a young married couple were chanting in Aberporth, West Wales, "not quite knowing what they were doing, but convinced of the power of the teachings of Nichiren Daishonin".[16] They were supported by members from Heathrow district – the closest district geographically to Wales! A "district" is a smaller unit within a "chapter", as we shall see in CHAPTER FOUR. These few members, representing all Wales, were known only as a single chapter. Three years later, in 1986, Les and Kyoko moved to Newport in South Wales, and by 1988, there were sufficient members for a general meeting to take place celebrating five years of the beginning of the spread of the movement in Wales. The event took place at Cardiff Castle, with some fifty people taking part. The practice of celebrating every five years is now well established; the twenty-fifth anniversary will be in Swansea, in November 2008.

By 1989, there were enough members for Wales to become a Headquarters with three chapters and sixty new members in Mid Wales, thanks to the efforts of a young mother-to-be, Soo Allan, who had moved from Southampton. Discussion meetings were extended throughout Wales and two new chapters were added in October 1991, one covering West and Mid Wales in Dyfed and Powys, and the other based around Cardiff in the East and West of the city. By the time of the ten-year celebration at the Civic Centre at Newport, numbers had doubled to a hundred. This general meeting was addressed by the late Richard Causton, the General Director of SGI-UK. Five years later, in 1998, the next celebration of fifteen years was held at Craig-y-nos Castle. At this meeting, Les and Kyoko handed over responsibility for Wales'

Headquarters to Nick and Mani Dowsett in a very emotional and joyful meeting. It left them free to oversee the whole of Wales and, later, the Borders.

By 2001, there were enough members in the various areas to form two Headquarters – South East Wales Headquarters, around Cardiff led by James Rourke and Kirsten Jones, and West and Mid Wales led by Nick and Mani Dowsett. Each of the Headquarters had two chapters. For both, however, some sixty members in each were spread out over large distances. This was especially so with Nick and Mani's western area, which ran from Bridgend, West to Pembroke and Aberporth and North to Powys. James and Kirsten's two chapters were scattered from Cardiff, Newport and Chepstow to the East, and Barry and the Western Valleys to the West. Les and Kyoko became the *area* leaders for the whole of Wales, including the English borders.

The year 2003 saw the anniversary of twenty years of Nichiren Daishonin Buddhism in Wales and the Borders with a general meeting in the City Hall in Cardiff – a glorious building and a glorious celebration. It was attended by almost five hundred members and guests. Judith Allan reported on the occasion: "The Assembly Room in Cardiff City Hall was filled to capacity for the SGI-UK Wales and the Borders Anniversary meeting. The two Welsh HQs worked together to create this colourful celebration. The 180 Welsh members were thrilled at the turnout, which exceeded expectations and showed the strong network of support that exists for our practice among our families and friends."[17] At this meeting, there was an exhibition dedicated to the work of Gandhi, Martin Luther King and President Ikeda, and memorable performances, including a rendition of *Shenandoah* by the magnificent bass baritone, Toby Hunt. By 2006, the Mid Wales chapter had grown sufficiently to form a third Headquarters, Mid Wales and the Marches, with two chapters, one based around Shrewsbury and Mid Wales and the other centred around Brecon, Hereford and Abergavenny. The new Headquarters is led by a husband and wife team, Chris Bradbury and Soo Allan, based in Newtown. Their first meeting was in November 2006 at Leominster Community Centre on the border of Wales and England, and began with more than seventy members spanning the two chapters.

At the time this book was commenced in 2007, there were just over three hundred members in Wales and the Borders. At the time of its publication in the summer of 2008, the number has risen to three hundred and ninety. For the last thirteen years, meetings have been, and still are, held every Monday evening at various locations to chant for peace. Wales and the Borders now have seven chapters and sixteen districts. It is anticipated that a new, fourth Headquarters centred around Swansea, Llanelli and Bridgend, will be announced in 2008, the year in which twenty-five years of SGI-UK in Wales and the Borders will be celebrated. Welsh/Borders members are hoping to set up a centre for the continued propagation of Nichiren Daishonin Buddhism and are hoping to have the opportunity to welcome President Ikeda to what Les Gibson describes as "this wonderful country".[18]

Paul Tibbets died in November 2007 at the age of ninety-two in Columbus, Ohio. Throughout his life, he defended his dropping of the atomic bomb on Hiroshima as necessary to bring World War II to a close. To the end, he remained tired of the criticism against him, and requested his family and friends not to hold a funeral for him, not to place a headstone at his grave. He wished to avoid creating a site at which people could continue to protest.

CHAPTER TWO

The Buddhism of
Nichiren Daishonin
Historical Perspectives

Neither the Buddha nor Buddhism began life in a cultural vacuum, having no roots and no substance. Both are the offspring of India. That country is without equal as a nation whose spirit of acceptance of all that is new and reluctance to discard that which is old have typified the very heart of its people in their search for the highest spirituality, their quest for ultimate reality. This is the essence of the Indian mind. Into an age of considerable social and political unrest, in the northern India of the sixth century BCE, the Buddha was born. It was a time when smaller tribes were being absorbed into larger monarchies and this brought about a period of insecurity that promoted a quest for personal identity, the purpose of life, and the meaning of ultimate truth and reality. Questions were being asked such as "What is the nature of eternity?", "What is real in a world of change?", "Why does humankind suffer?", and "What should we pursue as the spiritual goal of life?"

The life of the Buddha

Like other Indian religions, Buddhism accepts the doctrines of *karma* and *samsara*, rebirth, and the Buddha is believed to have been reborn over an incalculable period of aeons, each aeon being an unthinkably long period of time. The disciples and followers of the Buddha handed down their accounts of the Buddha's life and teaching, but often added their own thoughts and opinions; it is therefore difficult to abstract the historical events from the hagiographic nature of the material. When the Buddha realized enlightenment he became omniscient and was thus able to view his previous lives through all this vast period of time, recounting his past life experiences to his followers. Many of these stories are attested in what are called the *Jatakas*, one group of which relates, in particular, the lives of the Buddha in animal form. All these stories from past lives are said to have occurred in *cosmic* time, so called because they occurred in lives beyond the present *historical* time in which we live. The Buddha of this aeon, Siddhartha Gautama (Pali Siddhattha Gotama), is thus the historical Buddha and is distinguished so by being called *Shakyamuni*, the sage or *muni* of the Shakya tribe native to sixth-century India. The first complete biography of the Buddha is presented in the *Buddhacarita*, "The Life of Buddha", which was written by Ashvaghosha, an Indian poet of the early second century CE. The first thirteen cantos are extant in Sanskrit, the rest in the Tibetan translation.

The account of the Buddha's life in the Buddhacarita and other sources

Siddhartha was born the son of a *raja*, living in a luxurious palace. Buddhist tradition relates that miraculous, portentous events are associated with his birth; for example, he was born out of his mother's side. It seems that all Buddhas are characterized by unusual births. The purpose of such birth stories is to portray the birth of an exceptional being and, indeed, the *Buddhacarita* certainly does this, for Siddhartha was born in full awareness, able to walk immediately, and already in a high state of consciousness from the cumulative states of all his past lives.

His mother died seven days after giving birth, for the womb that had borne a Buddha could not then carry another ordinary mortal; she was reborn in a celestial realm. The capital city of the area was Kapilavasta, and this would have been Siddhartha's birthplace, from whence a forecast of the future enlightened life of Siddhartha was given to his father by the sage Asita. Alarmed by the sage's remarks, we are told that the *raja* imprisoned the growing boy within the boundaries of three palaces; one for the cold season, one for the rainy season and one for the hot season. He wanted his son to have a view of reality that was divorced from any concept of suffering or unhappiness. Without knowing of the natural state of humankind, Siddhartha would not need to embark on, or to proclaim any path to, something beyond it.

It was in these luxurious circumstances that Siddhartha grew up in a life of pure pleasure and indulgence, in which he married and had a son. We can call Siddhartha at this stage a *bodhisattva*. This word is used in Buddhism in two senses. In early Theravada Buddhism it means one who is on the way to enlightenment, but since Theravada Buddhism believes there can be only one Buddha in each aeon, there can be only one *bodhisattva* in this aeon, this historical time, and this would be Siddhartha when he was a Buddha-to-be. In Mahayana Buddhism generally, the term *bodhisattva* was used, as it still is, to depict someone who has attained enlightenment (*bodhi*) but who has delayed final enlightenment, full *nirvana*, in order to stay in existence and help others to reach enlightenment too. We shall see in later chapters how the term has evolved in Nichiren Daishonin Buddhism.

Despite his sheltered and luxurious life, we are told that Siddhartha heard about life outside the confines of the palaces and wished so much to experience the wider world, that he pleaded with his father to be allowed outside. The *raja* agreed, but all unpleasant sights, cripples, beggars and old people were hidden away. Yet it was Siddhartha's destiny to experience what are now called the four signs. It is likely that these were illusions, some sources suggesting that they were engineered by the gods. Whatever Siddhartha's experiences were, it seems they were shared only by his chariot driver and it is unlikely that they were factual experiences. On his first journey from the palace, Siddhartha saw, for the first time in his life, an old man. The *Buddhacarita* tells of the immense and violent shock that this caused the *bodhisattva*. His following excursion brought the experience of a sick man and we are told that his reaction was one of despair. It is a despair filled also with amazement and sadness that the world is surrounded with old age and sickness and yet each individual seemed not to face it at all, preferring to close his or her eyes. It is the third vision of a corpse that brings the strongest reactions that add the final and very poignant experience of the nature of reality and life. Again, Siddhartha is amazed that humankind closes its eyes to this fact of death. According to the *Buddhacarita*, he said: "It is a miserable thing that mankind, though themselves powerless and subject to sickness, old age, and death, yet blinded by passion and ignorant, look with disgust on another who is afflicted by old age or diseased or dead."[1]

Siddhartha's realization of the impermanence of all life and all the world was to be a very important one in Buddhism: because of the existence of old age, sickness and death, happiness, beauty and the many things that humankind cling to in life were seen by Siddhartha to be illusory and as things that should not inform the life of the high-minded. A final excursion is depicted as a visit to the forest in search of peace. Here, again, Siddhartha was filled with pity and remorse. He saw the plough overturning the soil, the ploughmen suffering in the dust and the wind, the weary oxen, and the insects and tiny creatures that the plough had killed. This is the sense in which he sees all life as *duhkha*, unsatisfactory and suffering in the sense of the disharmony of all existence.

Seeking solitude, Siddhartha gained his first insight into the three signs he had received. While reflecting in this way, he experienced his fourth illusion. It took the form of a mendicant, a homeless, wandering ascetic. This marked the final turning point from his former life and he saw clearly, at that time, the *dharma*, the true way, that he had to pursue. Accordingly, he decided to escape the palace in order to seek the state of deathlessness, to find the answers to the problems of old age, sickness and death in life. Siddhartha had experienced the disillusioning aspects of life, and he wished to seek liberation from them. What he had experienced was the predicament of humankind, the fact that humankind, placed in a temporal, materialistic existence, becomes intoxicated with diversions, and ignores the realities of ageing, suffering and death.

He said farewell to his stunned father who, on receiving the news, "shook like a tree struck by an elephant", pleading with his son not to go "in a voice choked with tears".[2] Then, Siddhartha summoned his faithful steed, Kamthaka, and prepared to forsake the palace. He had spent his youth and early manhood in extreme luxury; now he was to experience its very opposite in a life of total asceticism as a wandering recluse. For Siddhartha, the world became an illusion in which people chased happiness in things that were impermanent. Material existence could not possibly be reality, for reality, he thought, must be deathless. And so he tried to find the deathless state through extreme asceticism. For six years he became the most devoted of ascetics, eventually reducing his daily intake of food to one grain of rice. Although he was admired by five companion Hindu monks who accompanied him at the time, Siddhartha came to realize that he was nowhere near to finding the answers he sought in life through the yoga of the ascetic. And so he came to reject the ascetic path to enlightenment. Having regained his physical strength, he left his companions and journeyed to the holy town of Gaya, situated on a tributary of the Ganges. There, Siddhartha sat down under the shade of a great pipal tree and made a vow to remain there until he became enlightened.

He sat very quietly, very still, in the lotus *asana* position, and began to go through the traditional *dhyanas* of meditation, gradually allowing his thoughts to subside until no new thoughts arose, and a feeling of joyful elation, coherence and tranquillity remained. During the final stages, a state of perfect balance, perfect equanimity was experienced. It was an equanimity that allowed him to reach back through all time and, thus, through previous lives; it was the point at which *karma* is nullified. Although completely aware of his surroundings, Siddhartha was unaffected by them. His mind was free to travel in any direction and to any part of human experience past, present and future but without any conditioned emotion. And so Siddhartha proceeded through the final stages of meditation to the point of enlightenment. He perceived all his former births and his previous lives. He is said to have recalled a hundred thousand of his lives and all the pleasures and pains of each of them. He saw clearly the long thread that had brought him through countless generations to the present moment, and came to the conclusion that all that we view as real in the world is totally insubstantial. He was free: he had a knowledge of all that was to be known, free of the sense-pleasures, free of becoming and free of the ignorance that causes the individual to be reborn. Siddhartha had reached the state of *anatman* or "no self"; egoless, he had realized *nirvana*. As the dawn broke, Siddhartha became the Buddha, the Awakened One. At that moment, sources tell us that the blind could see, the deaf could hear, and the lame could walk; there was beauty and peace in the entire world.

For the next forty or forty-five years of his life, the Buddha travelled in the middle Ganges region as a religious wandering monk, a *sannyasin*, teaching and gathering disciples. Finally, some time towards the end of the fifth century BCE,[3] the Buddha felt his death approaching. As a *tathagata*, one who is fully awakened and is in a state of "suchness" or "thusness", the Buddha could have continued living until the end of the present aeon, the accounts inform us, but he relinquished this right to live longer. The realization that the Buddha was about to die was too much for his devoted disciple, Ananda, and the old man was reduced to tears. Tradition states that one morning, the Buddha gathered alms at Vaisali, gave the town one last "elephant look" by turning his whole body round, and then set his face towards Kusinagasa, quite near to his birthplace. There, surrounded by his disciples and local inhabitants, he entered into the stages of meditation and finally relinquished his body. No residue of *karmic* forces – negative or positive – remained that could bring about another birth. The Buddha was dead.

The development of Buddhism

Once the Buddha had achieved enlightenment, he began to attract a number of followers. This was the beginning of the *Sangha*, the community of monks, though it is doubtful if the Buddha had any idea how it would develop when he discharged his disciples with the words: "Go monks and travel for the welfare and happiness of the people, out of compassion for the world".[4] To become ordained it was normally accepted that a man (not a woman at first) should become an *arhant*, a perfected one who had reached the egoless state of *nirvana*. Having reached this state of perfection, the shaving of the head and beard followed, as did the wearing of yellow rags and abandonment of the home. Once ordained, these *arhants* were sent out by the Buddha to teach the *dharma*, the truth, and, as the *Sangha* grew in size, it became necessary for these ordained monks to ordain others rather than have everyone travel long distances for ordination by the Buddha himself.

After the Buddha's death, his disciples continued to travel widely, spreading the *dharma* of the Buddha and ordaining others as monks. It was essentially a monastic tradition. Approximately a century after the Buddha's death, in about 483 BCE, a Council was convened in order to formalize and authenticate the Buddha's teachings. Three collections or "baskets" of the *dharma* were identified – rules for the discipline of the *Sangha* (*Vinaya Pitaka*), the Buddha's teachings (*Sutta Pitaka*), and philosophical discussion of the teachings (*Abhidharma Pitaka*). Three subsequent Councils were held, one in 383 BCE, one in 250 BCE, and the last towards the end of the first century CE. Mahayana Buddhism was born sometime between the convening of the First and Third Councils because of the dissatisfaction of some monks with the rigidly orthodox interpretations of the old school. It was a development that was crucial to the future of Buddhism. Of the eighteen original Hinayana schools that comprised early Buddhism, Theravada is the sole survivor, while the more liberal strands blossomed into the many branches of the Mahayana.

The emergence of the Mahayana schools

From the time of the Second Council, the liberal strand was characterized by a more relaxed attitude to the rules of the *Vinaya*. The approach was more progressive and less exclusive and was very much favoured by the laity. Placing less importance on discipline, there was a tendency to stress meditation – something that the lay man and woman could practise in their own homes. Householders were not excluded from the *Sangha* so the monastic monopoly was diminished. Women, too, were more readily accepted. However, the most far-reaching expressions of the more liberal changes lay in the attitude to scriptures and the concept of the Buddha. With regard to the former, there was a willingness to accept scriptures that were composed at a later date, and this paved the way for the full flowering of the literature of Mahayana Buddhism. Concerning the concept of the Buddha, there was a general tendency to see the influence, power and essence of the Buddha as being *ever-alive* and *ongoing*. This made the Buddha supernatural and supra-mundane. There developed, too, the idea that, since the Buddha was always present, existing past, present and future, his teaching was also ongoing and would be expounded continually. It was ideas such as these that led to the different concept of *bodhisattvas* in Mahayana Buddhism; they were beings who had realized *nirvana*, like the Buddha, who shared his same essence, but who delayed their final *nirvana* to remain in the world and help all others to realize *nirvana* too.

The orthodox group, being less flexible, believed in strict adherence to the letter of the tradition and were the forebears of Hinayana Buddhism. *Hinayana* (a term avoided by most moderns who prefer "*early* Buddhism") was a derogatory term given to the older tradition by the descendants of the break-away monks, the Mahayana party. It means "Inferior Vehicle" (to salvation) as opposed to the name *Mahayana*, which means "Great Vehicle". As a result of this division, the common core foundations of the Buddha's teachings were developed distinctively and are preserved on the one hand in the sole surviving (Pali) canon, which still represents the orthodox scriptures of Southern Buddhism (Theravada), and on the other in classical Sanskrit scriptures which became the canon of Northern Buddhism (Mahayana).

The *dharma* of the Buddha

The Sanskrit word *dharma* (Pali *dhamma*) has different meanings in Indian thought: here it is used in the sense of "right" as opposed to "wrong". The basic teachings of the Buddha are the *dharmas*, the right ways or teachings about life. Indeed, Buddhists in Asia do not use the term "Buddhism", preferring to speak of the *dharma* of the Buddha. Before the Buddha's first teaching and after his enlightenment, he drew a wheel on the ground. This symbolized the starting of the wheel of order, law or *dharma,* the wheel being an ancient Indian symbol. After drawing attention to the wheel of *dharma*, the Buddha expounded the importance of realizing the need for *dharma*. He taught the *Four Noble Truths*.

The Indian mind has long been tormented by the problem of *duhkha*, the realization that humankind will have to endure the suffering experienced not just in one lifetime, but in virtually countless lifetimes. Such a treadmill was seen by Indian philosophers as an aimless wandering through eternity, a continuous cycle of death and rebirth, repeated *ad infinitum*, appropriately termed *samsara*, "that which turns around forever". It was to the problem of suffering that the Buddha turned his attention. Because the Buddha recognized the problem, identified the cause of the problem, affirmed that there is a cure, and prescribed a remedy, it comes as no great surprise to find that his *dharma* is often compared to that of a medical practitioner, who writes a prescription for treating the human condition. This is why the Buddha is known as "the great physician". In his very first sermon in the Deer Park at Ishipatana, the Buddha set out the kernel of his *dharma*, as found in the *Four Noble Truths*:

- All life is suffering (*duhkha*) or, more accurately, unsatisfactory, dis-ease, disharmony.
- The root of the problem is the false notion that we have a permanent self (*atman*) that has to be appeased, which introduces a craving (*tanha*) to satisfy this supposed self.
- Suffering may be terminated by the cessation of craving (*nirodha*).
- Cessation of craving can be effectuated by following the *Noble Eightfold Path* – *right understanding* of the impermanence of all things in life, including the egoistic "self"; *right thought*, suggesting that in order to change one's understanding of life, there must be a change in the way we think. Similarly, there must be *right speech*, *right action*, *right livelihood*, *right effort*, *right mindfulness* and *right meditative concentration*.

There can be no concept of a first cause in Buddhism since everything is said to depend on something else. This cyclic concept, one of the cornerstones of Buddhist philosophy, is known as *Dependent Origination*, *Conditioned Genesis* or *Conditioned Arising*.

The Buddha's legacy

Even if there is a tendency amongst the laity to regard the Buddha as the object of devotion, the Buddha was never considered to be in any way divine by the Theravada monastic tradition. He is not thought to have lived on after his death in some miraculous way, nor was he resurrected, since there is no concept of a permanent unchanging *atman*, self, spirit or soul in Theravada Buddhism. So the Buddha could never be a cosmic soul or spirit of the universe. After his death, his final or *parinibbana*, he simply ceased to exist. Yet in Pali and Sanskrit commentaries there are times when the Buddha is given a cosmic dimension that suggested his ongoing nature.[5] This suggests that the trend to give the Buddha some kind of absolute and permanent essence in the cosmos was a conspicuous need, an idea appropriated by later Mahayana Buddhism. Moreover, while it is generally accepted that the old school recog-nized only one Buddha in this aeon, there are occasions in the early texts when the *arhants*, the perfected ones, were also called *buddhas*. Indeed, the Buddha himself said that the only difference between him and other enlightened monks was the fact that he was a teacher. Such a concept of a wider possibility of Buddhahood for many was also something taken on board by the Mahayana tradition. It is these two factors of the different concept of the Buddha and the lack of exclusivity of Buddhahood that underpins much of the Mahayana tradition.

The two centuries that acted as bookends to the turn of the millennium appropriately bore witness to an India that was changing from an oral to a written culture, a change that would give a hitherto unknown finality to a standardized form of the Buddha's *dharma*. The most important literature for Mahayana Buddhism is called the *Prajnaparamita* literature. It began as a basic text formulated in the last century BCE and the first century CE, and was later expanded into a number of *sutras*. *Prajnaparamita* means "Perfection of Wisdom". Mahayana *sutras* were still being composed as late as the eighth century CE and their development is a complicated one. The *Lotus Sutra* is one of the most influential in the whole of Mahayana literature, attesting that all of the Buddha's previous teaching was provisional, since humankind could not have coped with being taught the highest truths in one fell swoop. The *dramatis personae* of the *Lotus Sutra* include buddhas and *bodhisattvas* as well as humans, and its message is unequivocal: Buddhahood is for all humanity, indeed, it is humankind's natural state. The great drama played out in the *Lotus Sutra* finds Shakyamuni Buddha as the cosmic Buddha in human form helping others on the same path to enlightenment that he himself treads. We shall explore the *Sutra* fully in CHAPTER FIVE.

The doctrine of the Trikaya

The *Yogacarins* are credited with the development of one of the most important concepts in Mahayana Buddhism, the doctrine of the *Trikaya*, or three bodies of the Buddha. The theory was formulated in answer to a paradox that confronted Mahayana Buddhism. Whereas the true ideal of early Buddhism was the *arhant*, this was replaced in the Mahayana by the *bodhisattva*. Yet if this were the true ideal, why did Siddhartha Gautama not become a *bodhisattva*, rather than a Buddha who selfishly passed to *nirvana*? Such an objection was addressed in the Yogacarins' concept of the *Trikaya*. The Buddha was held to have three bodies – the Body of Essence (*Dharmakaya*), the Body of Bliss (*sambhogakaya*), and an earthly emanation (*nirmanakaya*). The earthly emanation of the Body of Bliss was Siddhartha Gautama, but the Body of Bliss was in turn the emanation of the Body of Essence, the cosmic and eternal Buddha, who dwelled forever in the universe. The doctrine of the *Trikaya* was given a particularly distinctive interpretation in the Buddhism of the Far East in the *Tathagatagarbha* school of thought. The teaching that Buddha-nature is the hidden essence within all sentient beings is the main message of the *Tathagatagarbha* literature, the earliest of which is the *Tathagatagarbha Sutra*. This short *Sutra* says that all living beings are in

essence identical to the Buddha regardless of their defilements or their continuing transmigration from life to life. Thus, all sentient beings are capable of
full Buddhahood, and later *sutras* were keen to express this theme.

Buddhism reaches Japan

In Central Asia, the exportation of silk from mainland China to north-west
India lent its name to an international trade route to the north of Tibet. Along
the Silk Road, as it was called, Buddhist merchants from India, together with
wandering monks, disseminated the Buddha's *dharma* along the route,
carrying it into the heartland of China; consequently, Buddhism was known
in Central Asia from the second century BCE. In the fourth century, Mahayana
Buddhism spread from China to Korea first and then Japan. It was the
Mahayana that had the greater missionary success. With its more liberal attitude towards the *Vinaya*, it was possible for Mahayana missionaries to
condone the eating of fish by the Japanese, for example, which would never
have been tolerated by early Buddhism. Nor would the *Vinaya* accept that
monks could practise medicine, an edict that the Mahayanists readily overlooked since these acts of healing, which they saw as great compassion, were
found to win the hearts of many grateful listeners at home and abroad. The
adaptability and tolerance of Mahayana was particularly conspicuous in
China as well as Japan.

The earliest period of recorded Japanese history attests to the initial appearance of Buddhism there, and an image of the Buddha (Jap. *Hotoke*) arrived
from Korea shortly afterwards in the year 552. Initial opposition to this new
religion was soon overcome, and by the time of prince-regent Shotoku Taishi
(572–621), the primitive *kami* cults of Shinto had become dominated by
Buddhism. The prince-regent devoutly promoted Buddhism, and found the
spirit and doctrine of the Mahayana to be crystallized in the *Vimalikirti Sutra*,
otherwise known as "The Way of Enlightenment for All". The *Sutra* itself
emphasizes right meditation, though meditation was forced to play second
fiddle to the philosophical speculation and magical extravagance of Tendai
and Shingon.

It is well said that no one can step into the same river twice. This should
be borne in mind in any study of that stream of Mahayana philosophical
thought that has flowed throughout East Asia. The rise of the Buddhism of
Nichiren Daishonin in Japan is a tradition that did not allow itself to be swept
mindlessly along by the current, and was not afraid to depart from mainstream
Buddhism, or to evolve from its own early teachings. Its founder, Nichiren
Daishonin, like other schools of the Mahayana, ignored many of the fundamental principles of early Buddhism, such as the Four Noble Truths and the
Noble Eightfold Path, but retained much that was thoroughly in the tradition
of Mahayana Buddhism. We must turn, now, to plot the history of Nichiren
Daishonin Buddhism, beginning with the Chinese school of T'ien-t'ai.

The Tendai (Chin. T'ien-t'ai) school

The Chinese T'ien-t'ai school proposed an immense philosophical system known as *ichinen sanzen* based on the *Lotus Sutra*. It is a doctrine central to the Buddhism of Nichiren Daishonin and is treated in full in CHAPTER SEVEN. It is basically an explanation of the unity and interconnectedness of the universe. The establishment of the supremacy of the *Lotus Sutra* amongst all Shakyamuni Buddha's teachings is directly attributable to the work of this sixth-century Chinese Buddhist school. Appropriately known as the "Lotus school", the Chinese name literally means "School of the Celestial Platform". Together with the Hua-yen school, the T'ien-t'ai tradition forms one of the two major doctrinal systems of Chinese Mahayana Buddhism.

The fundamental problem facing Chinese Buddhist thinkers of the fifth and sixth centuries was how to reconcile a plethora of doctrinal differences presented in a vast collection of texts favoured by a variety of schools. The T'ien-t'ai school, the first of the great multi-system schools, addressed this problem, emphasizing, among others, meditation techniques, using both *mandalas* and *mudras* (symbolic signs and gestures made with the hands). Its aim was a synthesized, unified system of belief for many of the different teachings of Buddhism, melding all the divergent views of the other schools. Hui-ssu (515–76) is said to be the founder of the school, which takes its name from its place of origin on a mountain in Chekiang in south-east China. However, it is Hui-ssu's student, Chih-i, also known as T'ien-t'ai, who is credited with being the school's first great systematic architect and eponymous figure.

In one of his letters, Nichiren himself makes the salient point that Japan is but "a tiny island country in the east separated by two thousand *ri* of mountains and seas from the country of the Buddha's birth".[6] Having hardly any direct contact with Indian monks, Japanese Buddhists had to depend entirely on Chinese translations of Indian *sutras* and commentaries, as well as writings germane to China. The sheer volume of such literature was overpowering, as was the influence exerted on the Japanese mind by these writings.[7] In order to give itself credence by way of Indian pedigree, as was common in East Asian traditions, the T'ien-t'ai school in China took the Indian Buddhist philosopher, Nagarjuna, as its first patriarch. As the founder of the *Madhyamika* system of Mahayana Buddhism, Nagarjuna was arguably the greatest of all Buddhist thinkers and is often referred to as "the second Buddha". T'ien-t'ai derived its doctrine of the Three Truths (Jap. *santai*) from Nagarjuna's thesis that all *dharmas* are empty (*shunya*) of inherent existence. While ultimate reality is one, it is nevertheless informed by three perspectives of the same reality, *ke*, *ku* and *chu*, which will be examined in detail in CHAPTER SEVEN. An enlightened person experiences the perfect unity of these three. With the benefit of Chih-i's thrust of thought, the T'ien-t'ai school proposed that the teachings of Shakyamuni Buddha be classified into five periods and eight teachings. Although modern scholarship no longer accepts Chih-i as the author of the final synthesis, it has never denied that it was Chih-i that gave the system definition. For the T'ien-t'ai school, this synthesis advocates the important point that the words of the Buddha were carefully chosen to suit the level of consciousness of his audience, and that his teaching was evolutionary in nature, being directly proportional to the increased consciousness of his listeners.

In this light, Chih-i's system opens with the assertion that, in chronological sequence, the Buddha's teachings that occupied the three weeks following his enlightenment were incomprehensible to his listeners. Accordingly, in the second period that lasted twelve years, the Buddha reappraised his teaching and taught only what his students could understand: this included the Four Noble Truths, the Noble Eightfold Path and the theory of Dependent Origination. The third period lasted eight years and introduced the fundamental teachings of the Mahayana, including the twin pillars of wisdom and compassion. A twenty-two year long fourth period embraced the teachings of the *Prajnaparamita sutras*, including the concept of *shunyata* (emptiness) and the false notion of all opposites.

On Chih-i's view, it would have been entirely inappropriate for Shakyamuni to present his teachings in the same way to different audiences with different levels of consciousness. As surely as no responsible mother would dream of giving the same answer to a question from her four-year old as she would to her eighteen-year old child, neither did the Buddha give the same response to audiences with differing levels of consciousness, even when their questions were identical. Appropriately, on one occasion, we find him assuring a Hindu audience at their first meeting of the existence of a permanent soul or *atman*, which was total anathema in relation to his other teachings. Had he expounded his views on *anatman* (no soul) at their very first encounter, his audience would have simply evaporated into the mist of day. Accordingly, it was not until the last eight years of the Buddha's life (Chih-i's fifth period) that the Buddha expounded the complete and perfect truth in the *Lotus Sutra*.

Nevertheless, it is not suggested that the Buddha's teaching was purely one of chronological progression. Indeed, Shakyamuni is depicted as having taught his truths contemporaneously throughout his life. The T'ien-t'ai school has identified four teaching methods – the sudden method for the most receptive students; the gradual method for those less gifted; the secret method whereby many hearers would be present though only one would comprehend the teaching; the intermediate method wherein the teaching would have different meanings for different students, though all would hear the same words. Additionally, four different categories of teaching have been isolated, again delivered by the Buddha throughout the course of his ministry. These include the teachings of early Buddhism, teachings of both early and Mahayana Buddhism, teachings aimed particularly at *bodhisattvas*, and what are described as "round" or "complete" teachings found only in the *Lotus Sutra*. Nevertheless, as Yampolsky points out: "It was, however, only one of a number of different theories regarding the relative superiority of the various sutras and, as Nichiren's writings reveal, was disputed or rejected outright by many of his contemporaries, a fact that was a source of unending distress to him."[8] Nariyoshi Tamaru, too, reminds us that not all thirteenth-century Buddhist schools in Japan thought the same way: "Thus, the Tendai school regarded the Lotus Sutra as the final message of the Buddha (for this reason it was called the Tendai-Hokke school); the Pure Land school replaced it with the Three Pure Land Sutras; the Zen group went even further and insisted on 'a direct transmission outside the scriptures'".[9]

However, for T'ien-t'ai, and certainly for Nichiren Daishonin Buddhism, not only does the *Lotus Sutra* represent the culmination of the Buddha's thoughts, but, as noted above, all of Shakyamuni's earlier teachings are regarded as provisional, merely a "skilful means" (Skt. *upaya kaushalya* Jap. *hoben*), entirely appropriate to the unevolved levels of consciousness of his audience at any given time, but never intended to be regarded as ultimate truth. According to the T'ien-t'ai school, it is the *Lotus Sutra* alone that contains the ultimate truth of Shakyamuni's teaching, a truth that at one and the same time transcends all his earlier teachings, and yet unites them. This ultimate truth affirms the existence of the inherent Buddhahood in every sentient being, and the consequent assurance that all sentient beings can become Buddha. Moreover, this scripture presents the nature of Shakyamuni as ongoing.

The decline of Buddhism in China and the consequent demise of the *Lotus Sutra* saw the sixth T'ien-t'ai high priest, Miao-lo, reaffirm the efficacy of the *Lotus*, and it was returned to pre-eminence. T'ien-t'ai's teachings were brought to Japan, where the school was known as Tendai, through the direct result of the efforts of Saicho (Dengyo Daishi, 767–822), a student of one of the disciples of Miao-lo. Saicho founded the Tendai school of Buddhism in Japan in the eighth century. There are no fundamental doctrinal differences between the Chinese and Japanese forms of the school, though Saicho refuted the teachings of all the other Buddhist schools.

The Shingon school also had been introduced to Japan from China by Kukai (774–835). Like Tendai, it, too, stressed that the attainment of Buddhahood was a possibility open to everyone in a single lifetime, provided one followed the correct beliefs and ritual practices. But by the middle of the twelfth century, Japanese Buddhism had all but lost touch with its people. The old schools of Tendai and Shingon, together with Hosso and Kegon, had become totally power conscious, with incomprehensible (to the laity) magical rites seen by the monks as being far more important than any quest for enlightenment. Moreover, as the days, as well as the charisma, of Shakyamuni Buddha began to distance themselves in time from the memory of Buddhist minds, the path to enlightenment became increasingly difficult. Certain texts espoused a declining view of history, where *mappo* marked the third and most degenerate stage of the Buddha's *dharma*, when no individual could attain enlightenment in a single lifetime. Appropriately named "The Latter Day of the Law", all that remained of the Buddha's memory were his teachings; practices were a thing of the past and "enlightenment" a mere word. From the Kamakura period (1185–1333) came a cry for help, "a cry from a burning house", to use the imagery of the *Lotus Sutra*. Clearly, the time was ripe for a Buddhist revival; gone were the days when a plurality of approaches was acceptable, and towering personalities began to emerge, each stressing his own single doctrine or practice to replace all others. Through the mist of this confusion, appeared Zen and Pure Land masters, and onto the stage of thirteenth-century Japan's history strode Nichiren Daishonin.

The life of Nichiren Daishonin

On 16 February 1222, a baby boy was born in the south-eastern corner of Japan to two poor fisherfolk, Mikuni no Tayu and Umegiku-nyo. The name of the small fishing village was Kominato in the province of Awa; the name of the baby boy was Zennichimaro, which means "Splendid Sun". At the age of twelve (in Japanese chronology a child is deemed to be one year old at birth), the boy was sent to Seicho-ji, the local temple on Mount Kiyosumi. In those times it was commonplace to send teenage boys to monasteries and no exceptional circumstances are attributed to Zennichimaro's departure.

Throughout the days of his novitiate, Zennichimaro was an earnest seeker of the truth, who directed his mind towards becoming a Buddha with a dedication that won the admiration of the temple's master, Dozen-bo. The boy became an ordained monk at the age of sixteen and was given the name Zesho-bo Rencho. Rencho means "Lotus Growth". In his quest for enlightenment, Zennichimaro became confused by the diversity of beliefs and practices of the various Buddhist sects in Japan, and he resolved to study them all fastidiously in order to reach his goal. He even embraced the practice of the Jodo sect by chanting *Namu Amida-butsu*. This resolve he later regretted deeply, as his "Letter from Sado", written in 1272, attests: "Since Nichiren himself committed slander in the past, he became a Nembutsu priest in this lifetime, and for several years he also laughed at those who practiced the Lotus Sutra, saying, 'Not a single person has ever attained Buddhahood through that sutra,' or 'Not one person in a thousand can reach enlightenment through its teachings.'"[10] However, several years of praying to the Bodhisattva Kokuzo, whose statue was enshrined at Seicho-ji temple, gave Zennichimaro what he later termed a "jewel of wisdom" – an appropriate term since his prayers to Kokuzo were that he should become "the wisest man in Japan". With increasing confidence, the young priest, still only eighteen, left for Kamakura and the Kyoto-Nara area to study Buddhism for three years, determined to find the truth.

The truth for Rencho (as Zennichimaro was now known) was to be found in the *sutras*, and he scoured the libraries of the temples that proliferated these great centres of learning, ever searching for documentary evidence of what could justifiably be called "the true Buddhism". His constant concerns were: "Which of the Buddhist schools is the true one?", "What are its beliefs and practices?", and "How do these relate to my own enlightenment?" Initially, he believed that the truth was to be found in the teachings of both the Tendai Hokke and Shingon sects, an opinion he committed to writing during a brief return to Seicho-ji.[11] However, after considerable deliberation and further reading, Rencho concluded that, not only were Tendai Hokke and Shingon far removed from the truth of Buddhism, but so was every other Buddhist sect!

The more he travelled and studied, the more Rencho became convinced of a truth that he had first realized before the Bodhisattva Kokuzo – that among the vast libraries that comprise the Theravada and the Mahayana *sutras*, the *Lotus Sutra* alone contains the true teachings of the Buddha. In due course, the now thirty-two year old priest returned to the Seicho-ji temple at Kasagamori and, after a week's meditation, it was with great anticipation that the assembled company, comprising priests and students at the temple, as well as locals from nearby villages, awaited his revelations. Thirteenth-century Japan was a particularly poignant time and place to await declarations on how to achieve enlightenment, for at this time the attainment of enlightenment through one's own efforts was considered to be well-nigh impossible. It was generally considered that it was an age of despair, the evil period called *mappo*, "the end of the *dharma*", or "Latter Day of the Law" – a time so decadent that the Buddha's teachings were considered to be in their death throes. This was the political backdrop to the revelations at Kasagamori.

With growing expectancy, the crowd assembled in the priests' lodging at Seicho-ji temple, waiting for the return of Rencho, not from Kamakura but from a nearby hilltop. There, Rencho had proclaimed to the heavens, but not within human earshot, that the supreme law of life is the very title of the *Lotus Sutra*, *Myoho-renge-kyo*; this he chanted at sunrise on 28 April 1253. A stunned audience listened as Rencho first proclaimed this chant (that they had not heard previously), to be the true essence of Buddhism, and then proceeded to denounce those very forms of Buddhism that the assembled audience had cherished since childhood. He castigated the very foundations of Zen, and reviled the proponents of Nembutsu[12] for encouraging belief in a Western Paradise, which, claimed Rencho, does nothing to encourage people to establish peace in their present lives. These were not the revelations the assembled audience wanted to hear, as John Strong shows: "Reciters of the nembutsu (Pure Land Believers), he declared, would go to hell; advocates of Zen were devils; Shingon, with its dependence on esoteric rituals, would destroy the nation; proponents of the Vinaya rules for ordination were enemies of the state; the Tendai sect, founded by Saicho, was outdated."[13] Were this not enough, Rencho next attributed the decadence of the times to those very heresies that he had just castigated. Forsake these and accept *Nam-myoho-renge-kyo* as the supreme law of life, and not only will the age of decadence come to an end, but Japan will become a Buddha Land. This was the message he gave first to the assembled company and, later, to the Japanese government.

Rencho had reached his conclusions through researching the *sutras*. For him, there was unequivocal evidence that all teaching prior to that contained in the *Lotus Sutra* was simply provisional and should be discarded. The reason it was there at all was because of *upaya kaushalya*, the Buddha's "skill-in-means" (Jap. *hoben*), whereby the Buddha, the Great Physician, would prescribe only the medicine appropriate to the level of response of his patients or, in Buddhist terms, the *dharma* the audience was ready to receive in terms of their levels of consciousness. Interestingly, if Watanabe Hoyo is correct, this could well have been a method later employed by Rencho as Nichiren himself: "An integral aspect of his method of conversion (*shakubuku*) was the condemnation of the popular sects of Buddhism. Nichiren held that by deliberately provoking people and raising their anger he would cause them to evaluate their beliefs. Anger and hatred, in Nichiren's system, were productive and creative emotional states."[14]

Furthermore, Rencho then informed the startled assembly that in future he was to be called not Rencho, but Nichiren, "Sun Lotus", reflecting the fact that there is no light in existence brighter than the sun and the moon, and there is nothing purer than the lotus flower: "Giving myself the name Nichiren signifies that I attained enlightenment by myself."[15] His words were later interpreted by the Nikko school to mean that Nichiren was claiming to be the original Buddha. The new *mantra* that revealed the eternal truth was the title of the *Lotus Sutra*, with the addition of the prefix *nam* ("devotion" or "homage to"), and the direct path to enlightenment that would reveal the Buddhahood inherent within every human being. However, the level of consciousness of his audience was unprepared for this panacea, for though Nichiren certainly raised their anger it did nothing to cause them to revaluate their beliefs, and Nichiren was fortunate to escape with his life.

Undaunted, he soon converted his parents, and then a stream of disciples; nothing could shake the conviction of Nichiren in the efficacy of the *Lotus Sutra*. In his treatise, "On Attaining Buddhahood in This Lifetime",[16] Nichiren echoed the theoretical analyses evident in the writings of T'ien-t'ai, but he went much further than this; his was a practical application to the teachings of the *Lotus Sutra* – a point fervently believed by devotees today. Convinced that the *Lotus Sutra* was *the sutra* for the age of *mappo*, and that the Buddha's teachings therein were the universal remedy for this evil and decadent period in Japan's history, Nichiren next turned his attention to the Japanese government. He pointed to the aforementioned Buddhist sects that he had earlier castigated as "heretical", and laid the blame for the demise of the nation firmly on their doorsteps. Searching for documentary evidence to support his claims, Nichiren concluded that various *sutras* attest to the fact that the slandering of the Mystic Law of cause and effect, as exemplified in the *Lotus Sutra*, would bring a series of disasters on the nation. These were already in evidence in thirteenth-century Japan, as Kirimura has noted: "The seven disasters differ according to the sutras. The *Yakushi Sutra* defines them as pestilence, foreign invasion, internal strife, extraordinary changes in the heavens, solar and lunar eclipses, unseasonable storms and typhoons, and unseasonable droughts."[17] Internal strife and foreign invasion were yet to come; as for the others, Nichiren firmly pointed the finger of blame at those who were slandering the teachings of the *Lotus Sutra*.

In one of his most famous writings, *Rissho Ankoku Ron* ("On Establishing the Correct Teaching for the Peace of the Land"),[18] Nichiren associated true Buddhism with national peace. He laid the blame for the series of disasters currently besieging Japan firmly at the door of a government that steadfastly refused to acknowledge the supremacy of the *Lotus Sutra*. The treatise, written in 1260, reminds the Kamakura officials of the dire state of the nation, extols the efficacy of the *Lotus Sutra*, and berates other Buddhist sects, particularly proponents of the Nembutsu belief in Amida Buddha – all of whom Nichiren believed to be responsible for the nation's downfall. With the notable exception of the Tendai school, all of the Buddhist schools in Japan in those times were founded on the teachings delivered by Shakyamuni *prior* to those expounded in the *Lotus Sutra*. The treatise ends with a traveller forsaking his previous convictions and resorting to the one true Buddhism by following the teachings of the *Lotus*. This ideal ending did not materialize, however, and for the second time Nichiren narrowly escaped with his life.

The next year, the full fury of the Nembutsu priesthood descended on him and, in collusion with an enraged government, its priests and adherents had Nichiren banished to the Izu Peninsula, where they held the ascendency. A determined Nichiren, far from being downcast, once again resorted to studying the *Lotus Sutra*, where, to his immense solace, he found that he was living out its predictions. Nichiren saw his life unfolding before him in the thirteenth (*Kanji*) chapter of the *Lotus*. There, the *bodhisattvas* are found reassuring the Buddha that all will be well after his death, for they will disseminate the *dharma* far and wide, despite the attentions of an ignorant laity, a presumptuous priesthood, and priests with friends in high places – all of whom will revile the votary of the *Lotus Sutra*: "It is already twenty-four or twenty-five years since I began studying Buddhism . . . Now, however, for a period of more than 240 days – from the twelfth day of the fifth month of last year to the sixteenth day of the first month this year – I think I have practiced the Lotus Sutra twenty-four hours each day and night."[19] Nichiren believed that it was for the sake of the *Lotus Sutra* that he was undergoing the Izu exile. Throughout the exile, Nichiren was attended by one Nikko Shonin, a sixteen-year-old priest, who would become Chief of Doctrine and succeed the Daishonin[20] twenty years later. In 1263, the now forty-two year old Nichiren was pardoned by Hojo Tokiyori and returned to Kamakura.

His exile had done nothing to cool his fervour, however, and he continued to denounce both the government and all other sects of Buddhism, particularly Pure Land, with the same energy that he had shown both before and throughout his exile in Izu. In 1271, having incurred the fury of the Japanese court, the Nembutsu priesthood, and the nation at large, Nichiren was summoned to explain himself in court. Undaunted, Nichiren repeated his accusations against all rival forms of Buddhism and delivered to one of his chief accusers and Amida devotee, the major-domo Hei no Saemon, his treatise *Rissho Ankoko Ron*. At the same time, he reminded the government of the impending Mongol invasion in the light of his previous warnings.

His declaration: "The Pillar of Japan is now falling" was the last straw, and Nichiren was brought before the Supreme Court and charged with high treason. Sentenced to exile on Sado Island, Nichiren was placed in the charge of Hei no Saemon, who had other plans for the Daishonin. Escorted to the execution ground at the behest of Hei no Saemon, Nichiren paused at the Hachiman shrine at Tsurugaoka. Before his startled bodyguard he prayed:

> Bodhisattva Hachiman, are you truly a god? . . . I, Nichiren, am the greatest votary of the Lotus Sutra in Japan, and entirely without guilt . . . the Lord Buddha urged each Buddhist god to pledge to protect the votary of the Lotus Sutra at all times. Each and every one of you Buddhist gods made this pledge . . . If I am executed tonight and go to the pure land of Eagle Peak, I shall report at once to Shakyamuni Buddha that Tensho Daijin and Hachiman have broken their oath to him. If you feel this will go hard on you, you had better do something about it right away.[21]

The escort party continued its mission of death, and eventually arrived at the Dragon's Mouth on Tatsunokuchi beach, the place of execution. Seated on a straw mat before the executioner and the official witness, Hei no Saemon, Nichiren uttered the invocation of the *Lotus Sutra* – *Nam-myoho-renge-kyo* – for what should have been his last time. As he stretched out his neck for the blow that would never come, "a brilliant orb as bright as the moon burst forth from the direction of Enoshima, shooting across the sky from southeast to northwest. It was shortly before dawn and still too dark to see anyone's face, but the radiant object clearly illuminated everyone like bright moonlight."[22] With a now-blinded executioner and a panic-stricken bodyguard both incapacitated, the execution was terminated before it had begun. The incident at Tatsunokuchi was a turning point in his life, but not in the way Hei no Saemon and his fellow conspirators intended, and Nichiren Daishonin walked out of the Dragon's Mouth and into history.

When, in his writing "The Opening of the Eyes",[23] the Daishonin later claimed that he had died on Tatsunokuchi beach, he was not echoing the claims of Christianity for the events at Calvary, nor those that occurred on the road to Damascus. His message was that the prisoner escorted to the place of execution was one whose sole function was to teach the true Buddhism by disseminating the message of the *Lotus Sutra*, one who functioned in the role of the Bodhisattva Superior Practices (Jap. Jogyo-bosatsu), the votary predicted in the *Lotus Sutra*, the eternal Buddha, whose existence has been, and always will be. Furthermore, in "The True Object of Worship", the Daishonin is also believed to have identified himself with the eternal Buddha, coexistent with the eternal Law expressed in the invocation *Nam-myoho-renge-kyo*. Thus, in the background notes to this letter, we find: "Nichiren Daishonin embodied the condition or state he attained as the original Buddha within the object of worship so that people could reach that same condition of enlightenment."[24]

Exiled to Sado Island, after his supporters had been accused of arson and murder, he somehow survived in a bleak hut. A half-starved Nichiren crystallized his philosophical and spiritual beliefs in what was to become a period of great creativity.[25] Nichiren never shifted from his conviction that Buddha-nature exists within every human being, no matter how low the level of consciousness. Time and again, his writings stress that this is no elitist dogma, for every being has Buddha-nature within. The problem is that, though *everyone* has it, not everyone knows *how* to realize it. It was to this problem that Nichiren turned his attention on Sado Island. Accordingly, he designed an object of worship in the form of a *mandala*, known as a *gohonzon*, thereby encompassing his philosophical beliefs in graphic form. It is before a copy of the *Gohonzon* that followers of the Buddhism of Nichiren Daishonin chant *Nam-myoho-renge-kyo* to this day, convinced of its efficacy to assist the realization of Buddhahood.

After two and a half years on Sado, Nichiren was mysteriously pardoned, perhaps as the result of events at home and abroad. With an impending Mongol invasion and internal strife in the form of a failed coup very much in people's minds, it may have been that Nichiren's earlier predictions were recalled. Any thoughts of advising the Japanese people to turn to the Buddhism of Nichiren Daishonin was far from governmental minds, however, for they looked to the Shingon priests to help first with a drought and then with the Mongol invaders. A saddened Nichiren sought solace in retirement at Minobu, near Mount Fuji, having failed to convert the nation to his form of Buddhism. There he was attended by Nikko Shonin, the young priest who spread Nichiren's message at every opportunity.

On 12 October 1279, three years before his death, Nichiren fulfilled what he considered to be the purpose of his appearance in this world, by inscribing not individual *gohonzon*, as he had done hitherto, but the Great or *Dai-Gohonzon*, the very embodiment of the Daishonin, the efficacy of the *Lotus Sutra*, and Nichiren's legacy to mankind:

> A sword will be useless in the hands of a coward. The mighty sword of
> the Lotus Sutra must be wielded by one courageous in faith. Then he will
> be as strong as a demon armed with an iron staff. I, Nichiren, have
> inscribed my life in *sumi* [black Chinese ink], so believe in the Gohonzon
> with your whole heart. The Buddha's will is the Lotus Sutra, but the soul
> of Nichiren is nothing other than Nam-myoho-renge-kyo.[26]

Nichiren devoted his remaining years to the training of young priests and the writing of letters to lay followers. The profusion of writing that had been the hallmark of his life began to diminish as death approached, and his energies became focused on words of encouragement in times of political turmoil, rather than innovation. On 8 September 1282 Nichiren wrote the "Document for Entrusting the Law which Nichiren Propagated throughout his Life", in which his devoted disciple Byakuren Ajari Nikko (Nikko Shonin) was named as his successor. One month to the day later, Nichiren appointed six priests as elders – Nissho, Nichiro, Nikko, Niko, Nitcho and Nichiji. Five days afterwards, the life of one of the most powerful personalities in Japanese thought ended.

With the notable exception of Nikko Shonin and his immediate disciples, particularly Nichimoku Shonin, these elders were not prepared to toe the party line. Nikko had a difference of opinion with the other elders over the legitimacy of worshipping at Shinto shrines. The resulting rift saw the evolution of a number of schools. Entrusted by Nikko to keep watch in turn over Nichiren's tomb, they neglected this duty, departing instead to their respective temples. Separated from the Daishonin in his closing years, they entirely missed the kernel of his message as his embodiment in the *Gohonzon* and *Nam-myoho-renge-kyo*. They instead interpreted his teaching as an inferior form of Tendai Buddhism, belittling his works because they were written in the lowly Japanese *kana* alphabet, rather than the educated classical Chinese used by T'ien-t'ai himself. Ignoring both the object of worship and the invocation, they dispatched their disciples to the headquarters of that sect on Mount Hiei. Others forsook the Buddhism of Nichiren Daishonin for Shinto and Nembutsu, as well as setting up a statue of Shakyamuni, to the chagrin of Nikko Shonin. Nikko dedicated his remaining years (he died in 1333, aged eighty-eight), to the precise preservation of Nichiren's teachings, which he named *Gosho* (honourable writings). In 1298, he established a seminary in Omusu and appointed six disciples to guard the *Dai-Gohonzon*. Utterly frustrated with the events that followed his master's death, Nikko departed from Minobu, taking with him his loved one's ashes, letters and the *Dai-Gohonzon*, before establishing a small temple, called Dai-bo, near the foot of Mount Fuji – hence the origin of the Fuji school.

Nichiren Shoshu

The Fuji school[27] was the former name of Nichiren Shoshu, one of the many subschools subsumed under the Buddhism of Nichiren Daishonin. The lodging temples established by Nikko's disciples surrounding Dai-bo formed the roots of the Taiseki-ji head temple. A year before Nikko died, while chief priest at Taiseki-ji, he appointed Nichimoku as his successor. Shortly before his death, he wrote *Twenty-six Admonitions of Nikko*, attesting to his warnings that the teachings and practices proposed by Nichiren are not to be tampered with but must be preserved and followed to the letter. This edict was assiduously kept by Nichimoku, who took responsibility for the observance of daily prayers as well as for the widespread dissemination of the *Gosho*. Like his two predecessors, he extended this propagation of Nichiren Buddhism to the shogunate – a system of military government headed by a Japanese general. Tragically, when the shogunate fell, Nichimoku lost his life in the same year as Nikko, while making a hazardous journey attempting to deliver a letter of remonstration to the succeeding imperial court in Kyoto.

One of the fundamental aspects of Nichiren's teaching was his categorization of the second half of the *Lotus Sutra* into what he termed the Three Great Mysteries – *honzon*, *daimoku* and *kaidan*. *Honzon* is Japanese for an object of worship (*Go* is an honorific prefix), and *daimoku* strictly refers to the title of a *sutra*, particularly the *Lotus Sutra*, though in Nichiren Daishonin's Buddhism it came to mean the invocation of *Nam-myoho-renge-kyo*. A *kaidan* is an ordination platform, though Yampolsky suggests that "this latter term was not defined precisely by Nichiren and various interpretations of its meaning have been put forward".[28] Nariyoshi Tamaru traces an interesting development of thought in the minds of devotees with regard to the Three Great Mysteries:

> Nichiren Shoshu may be regarded as the most radical among the subschools of Nichiren Buddhism in terms of doctrine . . . Nichiren himself saw the *honzon*, the first of his Three Mysteries, in the eternal Buddha as revealed in the Lotus Sutra. Later on, however, there arose a tendency among his disciples and followers to accord central significance to the unique mandala that he made toward the end of his life showing the sacred title of *Nam-myoho-renge-kyo* surrounded by the names of a few buddhas and bodhisattvas. Since it was in the possession of Taiseki-ji, the school insisted on its supremacy over other groups. The emphasis on this object of worship at the same time induced people to think of Nichiren, its author, as a manifestation of truth even greater than the historical Buddha Shakyamuni. Chanting the *daimoku*, too, came to be interpreted as the realization of *jyobutu* (enlightenment).[29]

Nichiren's teachings occupy a unique position in the history of Japanese Buddhism at several points. To begin with, Nichiren Buddhism is the only extant major Buddhist school germane to Japan, others making their way to the islands from China.[30] Nichiren was much more than a theorist, however, for his central position was that the *Lotus Sutra* is the ultimate message of the Buddha, and hence not only must be studied but *lived*.[31] This conviction induced Nichiren to style himself a "prophet of the *Lotus Sutra*" and to give his position political orientation in an attempt to persuade society at large of the truth of his message. Although suppression at the hands of religious and political opponents in 1537 took its toll, Tamaru affirms that Nichiren eventually was largely successful in his efforts: "The teachings of Nichiren, which started as a new movement outside the established schools, gradually took root in Japanese society and have by now become firmly institutionalised. In fact, it constitutes one major sector of Japanese Buddhism together with the earlier groups of Tendai and Shingon, and the Pure Land and the Zen groups, which rose almost simultaneously."[32] As the centuries after Nichiren rolled by, however, the prediction of an age of *mappo*, when the teachings of the Buddha would be in decline, certainly seems to have taken place, and it was not until modern times that the Buddhism of Nichiren Daishonin was to emerge in vibrant form.

Tsunesaburo Makiguchi (1871–1944)

Although Nichiren Buddhism in general had enjoyed an upsurge in popularity during the late nineteenth and early twentieth centuries,[33] by the time Tsunesaburo Makiguchi had become interested in Nichiren Shoshu (1928), it was no more than an obscure seven-hundred-year-old sect. Claiming to be the only orthodox expression of Nichiren's teachings, its doctrines, rituals and institutions were not always to Makiguchi's liking. Interestingly, despite Nichiren's conviction of the merits of stringent proselytizing (*shakubuku*), the laity to that day had made little attempt to increase membership.[34]

Makiguchi had spent a lifetime as an educator, urging the development of the creative potential of every student. Ever aware that it is the child, not the system, that is at the heart of the educational process, he decried the burdensome chore of book reading and deplored learning masses of meaningless material by rote – soon to be forgotten, since it is unrelated to the pupils' lives. This copycat method of force-feeding children, he argued, was proving injurious to the development of both child and society alike. He described the rote-learning process as "that uneconomic method of education taken for granted the world over. It is surely one of the oldest and most primitive schemes ever invented by humans. Each student copies exactly what the teacher does. It is the very image of fishing peoples who have always fished with poles and know nothing of nets; farmers who continue to work the soil with a spade and hoe passed down from previous generations, never thinking to improve their tools."[35]

Makiguchi was one of a number of dissident scholars singularly unimpressed by the legacy of educational practices that were bequeathed by the Industrial Revolution in Europe. As his words above show, he was not slow to condemn poor teaching, or to give examples of the type of responses that we have all suffered at some time:

> Suppose a pupil asks his teacher: "What is this?" If the teacher scolds him and says: "Do you mean to say you still don't know what it is?" he is definitely confusing the process of cognition and evaluation. The pupil who asked the question was not asking for a judgment on his own competence. He was seeking information. The teacher who does not answer the pupil's real question but diverts his attention to something else

> is intimidating the child. If he thinks he is helping the child's
> comprehension he is mistaken . . . With a teacher of this kind, a poor
> pupil cannot help becoming an even poorer pupil.[36]

According to Makiguchi, one of the problems with the Japanese educational system was that educational policies were formulated by those "high up" who had little experience of the teaching situations "below" on which they purported to give advice. Makiguchi argued that every child has the potential for both goodness and greatness, in fact "in the beginning of life there is very little difference between people".[37] One of Makiguchi's strongest convictions was that, if one becomes a slave to books, even after reading thousands of books, one's true potential will never be realized. The greatest resource that teachers worldwide have at their disposal is the curiosity of the child, and Makiguchi's philosophy of education, which stressed the role of creative thought and personal experience, centred on what he termed *Value Creation* (Jap. *Soka*).

For Makiguchi, the creation of value is integral to what it means to be a human being. He distinguished between "gain" and "goodness" by holding that, whereas some thought or action may well bring *gain* to an individual, it can only be described as *goodness* when it is of value not only to the individual but also to the group and the welfare of society. Makiguchi was passionate in his conviction that only by developing an awareness of their interdependence and interconnectedness with the natural world and their social environment could persons truly be described as being of good character. As Dayle Bethel explains: "In Makiguchi's thinking, a fully alive, happy, fulfilled person is a person whose existence centers in creating value that enhances to the fullest both personal life and the network of interdependent relationships that constitutes the individual's communal life."[38] The central aim of education for Makiguchi was to develop the potential of those persons capable of recognizing and acknowledging these and related concepts. In 1930, like-thinking educators formed the Academic Society for Value-Creating Education – the Soka Kyoiku Gakkai – to this end. Makiguchi advocated a three-way educational partnership amongst the school, the home and the community, with the children spending only half days in school. One cannot overestimate the influence that the home has on the child's upbringing, nor on the expectations of the parents on the school.

Makiguchi's revolutionary thrust of thought was on direct collision course with the Japanese educational establishment, where rote learning and repetitive exercises were the order of the day. Accordingly, his contract as an elementary school teacher was terminated on more than one occasion, before he was forced into early retirement. Following his first dismissal, he sought to support his family by writing, his first book being published in 1903.[39] Appropriately named *A Geography of Human Life*, the work set out to examine human life in its relationship to the earth. Field trips and hands-on experiences are advocated as opposed to learning geography from books. This is far more than a methodology manual, however, for it depicts Makiguchi's future vision for the world condition.

Not without his critics, Makiguchi has been described by some as naïve, having a simplistic understanding of the relationship between the individual and society, particularly in regard to his attitudes towards race, modernization, technology and international relations.[40] Yet his world vision portrays an alarming understanding of what will happen (indeed, is happening today!) if humankind continues to abuse nature and the environment. His farsighted ecological vision is what today would be termed a holistic approach to understanding life. Nature is not "an object waiting to be exploited", as Alvin Toppler recognized, for to live as a human being is to love nature and live in harmony with the earth.[41] In this light, regardless of its authenticity, it is worth pausing to consider the sentiment expressed in a speech, as well as in a letter allegedly penned in the 1800s by Chief Seattle, Patriarch of the Duwamish and Suquamish Indians of Puget Sound, in response to the American Governments' request to buy land:

> The President in Washington sends word that he wishes to buy our land. But how can you buy or sell the sky or the land? The idea is strange to us. If we do not own the freshness of the air and the sparkle of the water, how can you buy them?

> Every part of the earth is sacred to my people. Every shining pine needle, every sandy shore, every mist in the dark woods, every meadow, every humming insect. All are holy in the memory and experience of my people.

> We know the sap which courses through the trees as we know the blood that courses through our veins. We are part of the earth and it is part of us. The perfumed flowers are our sisters. The bear, the deer, the great eagle, these are our brothers. The rocky crests, the dew in the meadow, the body heat of the pony, and man all belong to the same family.

> This we know: the earth does not belong to man, man belongs to the earth. All things are connected like the blood that unites us all. Man did not weave the web of life, he is merely a strand in it. Whatever he does to the web, he does to himself.[42]

The impact that these words have is considerable, though critics will argue that they probably were never spoken or written by a Red Indian chief, and hence have no warrant.[43] Perhaps the same critics would like to visit the Millennium Stadium in Cardiff, next time the Welsh Rugby Union team wins the Triple Crown, and remind the crowd that this, too, is a mythical trophy that has never existed and hence has no value whatsoever![44]

Humankind's talk should not be of *conquering* mountains or *harnessing* the waters, but of entering into dialogue with nature, understanding and appreciating it, and recognizing that we have so much to learn. As Makiguchi illumined: "The natural world can inspire us, foster our wisdom, and family, friends, neighbors, and community groups can nurture us in so many ways".[45] A man decades ahead of his time, Makiguchi had already anticipated the effects of atmospheric pollution that nowadays we are reminded of daily:

> In our time, the wireless telegraph . . . has resulted in the atmosphere's becoming a part of our human communication network. Moreover, a machine with the ability to fly, a long-time dream of humankind, has nearly been realized. Thus we can expect that at some time in the near future, this atmospheric region will become another busy traffic network. Still, compared to land and water, both of which are being used widely for transportation, the atmosphere is far less tangibly entwined with human life. Why is this? It is because the atmosphere is an invisible, gaseous substance which we can neither see, feel, nor touch. This may be why most people are oblivious to the atmosphere and the important role it plays in our lives.[46]

Makiguchi wrote these words in 1900, yet, almost a century later, a publication entitled the *World Scientists' Warning to Humanity* advised that: "Human beings and the natural world are on a collision course . . . A great change in our stewardship of the earth and the life on it is required, if vast human misery is to be avoided and our global home on this planet is not to be irretrievably mutilated."[47] The summer of 2007 found campaigners warning "Cheap flights cost the Earth!" It is perhaps not without significance that the self-same day President Bush promised there would be worldwide discussion on greenhouse gas emissions within eighteen months. On 8 August of the same summer, the Yangtze River porpoise was pronounced extinct. Four days later, conservationists were expressing concern that speedboats and water skiers were responsible for the deaths of scores of turtles off the Greek islands.

With unconfirmed reports linking the unprecedented 2007 UK summer floods in Hull, Gloucester and Tewksbury with climate change, 16 August found ten protesters claiming to have closed Biggin Hill airport by chaining themselves to the gates. The same day, concerns were being expressed about tourists abroad purchasing keepsakes made from endangered species of animals, while Chinese medicines were said to contain animal parts. On 1 November, it was affirmed that there remain just thirteen hundred tigers in the wild. August 19 in the same year saw hundreds of environmentalists concerned with climate change ensconced at Heathrow airport, protesting against proposals to build a third runway with accompanying air pollution. Some four thousand campaigners repeated the protest on 31 May 2008. This said, it is sobering to remember that the strongest human emotion is fear and that, after whipping up terror for months on end in anticipation of the emergence of the so-called Millennium Bug, the media were curiously silent when it failed to come out of hibernation. Similarly, the sighting of a Yangtze River porpoise on 29 August, just four weeks after it was declared extinct, was an item of news that proved far less attractive to the media.

In 1928, shortly before his enforced retirement as head teacher of Shirogane Primary School in Tokyo, Makiguchi was introduced indirectly to Nichiren Shoshu by a news reporter who was visiting his school. Having shown no more than a passing interest hitherto in Nichiren Shu (a related but different sect, and the religion of his parents), and Christianity, several reasons are oft-adduced for his move towards religion, though it is worth noting that "no specific statement has come to light in which Makiguchi recognized and acknowledged this shift in his thought and outlook".[48] Be this as it may, the fact remains that, for whatever reason, the closing years of his life saw Makiguchi's mindset gradually turning towards Buddhism. The distressing fact that four of his five children had been lost to disease could have been a contributory factor, since personal misfortune is often responsible for attracting people to religion. Also, by this time, at the very end of his teaching career, he would have recognized that his strident efforts to transform a society set in a rigid culture and dominated by the military through educational means, had come to nothing, perhaps because he lacked a university education – a sobering thought indeed, as Dayle Bethel notes:

> Makiguchi was a man ahead of his time. The general climate of Japanese society during the period in which he lived was not right for the kind of educational and societal reforms that he advocated. Neither on a theoretical nor on a practical level can it be claimed that Makiguchi's educational ideas have taken over Japanese education. The fact is that few teachers in Japan, even today, know who Makiguchi was nor what he stood for. However, Makiguchi did influence Japanese education indirectly in that both Toda and Ikeda picked up and rewrote his major ideas and incorporated them into the thought and practice of the Soka Gakkai organization. It can also be said that Makiguchi did influence Japanese education in that Soka Gakkai is today attempting to implement his ideas by establishing formal educational institutions based on those ideas. In addition, Makiguchi's influence can be seen in Komeito's concern with educational issues and problems.[49]

Makiguchi may have found the persuasive influence of *shakubuku* in the Nichiren Shoshu sect a more compelling vehicle to disseminate his ideas and hence effectuate reform, particularly in light of his strong will. Given his uncompromising nature, not to mention the frustration he must have felt because of the futility of his efforts, it is also conceivable that Makiguchi would have felt comfortable in an atmosphere generated by "perhaps the most militantly exclusivist of the Nichiren sects, its very name proclaiming that it is the True Religion".[50]

Some of these factors, or indeed all of them, may well have influenced Makiguchi's thinking, though it is worth considering two fundamental principles that possibly informed his beliefs. According to the T'ien-t'ai (Jap. Tendai) school, the *Lotus Sutra* alone contains the ultimate truth of Shakyamuni's teaching affirming that Buddhahood is universally accessible to all; each sentient being can become a Buddha. This is an assurance given to *everyone*; it is not an exclusive message to a chosen people or a select body of disciples. Given Makiguchi's aversion to elitism and his conviction that every child has the potential for goodness and greatness, the message of the *Lotus Sutra* – and hence the attraction of Nichiren Buddhism – must surely have influenced him.

Additionally, in Nichiren Buddhism, ultimate reality is the Mystic Law that ensures the interconnectedness of all manifest phenomena. Recognizing this interconnection, and living one's life in harmony with the rhythm of life, is central to Nichiren Buddhism's philosophy, the realization of which reveals one's Buddhahood; the Mystic Law is Buddhahood.[51] The teaching of the *Lotus* is that the true Buddha is awakened wisdom. The *Lotus'* teaching would have appealed greatly to Makiguchi, given his deep conviction that one cannot realize one's full potential as a human being unless one develops a sense of interrelatedness and interdependence with the natural world. Makiguchi's, "theory of value" set out in 1931 "stipulates that values, like scientific truth, should first and foremost rest on reason and evidence. Second, values should have the form of 'law' instead of 'person'. And third, religious value should also comprehend morality and science"[52] Given these criteria, Makiguchi became convinced that Nichiren's teachings represent ultimate truth.

What began as a small educational reform movement with the formation of the Soka Kyoiku Gakkai (Value Creating Education Society) on 18 November 1930, became fused with religious thought by 1936. After the inaugural meeting in a Tokyo restaurant in 1938, it was clear that the main function of the Society would be to spread the message of Nichiren Shoshu. Testimonial meetings were held in members' homes to this end, and by 1941 membership had increased to some three thousand nationwide. Wartime Japanese government policy, however, was to consolidate religious groups, hence increasing government control for the war effort, and moves were afoot to meld Nichiren Shoshu with the much larger, and consequently more influential, Nichiren Shu sect – a move that was successfully resisted by Makiguchi.

Although Makiguchi won the day in his determination to maintain independence from Nichiren Shu, resisting a religiously intolerant government's policy on State Shinto proved to be an entirely different matter, leading to Makiguchi's downfall. Since the 1890s, expressing loyalty to a civil religion that dutifully paid homage to a succession of Japanese emperors had become custom and practice. Japan's entry into World War II intensified the government's resolve to enforce this nationwide, uniting the war effort behind the emperor in the nation's bid to defeat a common enemy. A decree was issued that required each family to demonstrate its allegiance to State Shinto – and hence the emperor – by accepting into its home a talisman from the main

Shinto shrine. On 6 July 1943, the seventy-one year old Makiguchi rejected the emperor's decree outright, inducing the charge of *lèse majesté* (insulting a sovereign or ruler), and bringing to an end his freedom. His life ended on 18 November of the following year, when he died of malnutrition in prison.

Josei Toda (1900–1958)

Tsunesaburo Makiguchi is generally credited with being the founder of Soka Gakkai in 1930, and the current SGI President, Daisaku Ikeda, pays tribute to the dedication to which he applied his studies of the *Gosho*:

> There is a book that made a lasting and indelible impression on my life: the Gosho that belonged to Soka Gakkai founding president Tsunesaburo Makiguchi . . . I saw in it solemn evidence of his fervent dedication to study. Opening the worn and tattered cover, I discovered page after page filled with red lines and pencilled comments. Some passages were underscored twice, and others were marked with dotted lines for emphasis. Important passages were outlined by boxes. There were numerous comments written in pen, and on some pages, in the margins near difficult passages, he had inscribed : 'Study' or 'Study further'. Clearly, Mr Makiguchi had read the Gosho over and over again . . . From the time he first took faith at the age of 57, Mr Makiguchi studied Nichiren Daishonin's Buddhism with tremendous dedication.[53]

Scholars are not of one mind on this view, however, and those such as Daniel A. Métraux point out that initially, and certainly prior to 1937, Makiguchi was interested primarily not in religion but in educational reform, leaving pre-war Soka Kyoiku Gakkai bereft of a spiritual vision. Accordingly, it may not have been Makiguchi, but his educational colleague and disciple, Josei Toda who, in deleting the word *Kyoiku* from the title in 1946, just eight months after his release from prison, removed vestiges of education from the Gakkai at the time. Soka Gakkai was then a lay organization of Nichiren Shoshu, which Toda had joined with Makiguchi in 1928. On this view, it is Toda who is responsible for giving Soka Gakkai its present character and direction. In the words of Métraux: "The real foundation period of the Soka Gakkai is not the 1930s, but 1943–51. Between the years 1943–45, Toda, while in prison, redefined his religious ideas and decided to devote his life to the spread of these ideas. From 1945–51, Toda reconstructed the Soka Gakkai to conform to his own beliefs."[54] Métraux is unequivocal that, though little is said about it openly, Toda actually reversed the emphasis given to the Soka Gakkai by Makiguchi: "Although religion was becoming increasingly important to Makiguchi and his followers, the small movement was still anchored to the educational aims of its founder. The old SKG died with Makiguchi. It was Toda who removed education and "value creation" from center stage and who launched the Soka Gakkai as a strictly religious movement that only much later would develop an interest in such things as education."[55] It is as well to remember that Métraux wrote these words in 1988, and though there may have been a measure of truth in them then, twenty years later, Soka Gakkai International has developed its vision considerably.

Josei Toda was born on 11 February 1900, the eleventh son of a fisherman. When he was four years old, the family moved to Hokkaido and it was there, many years later, at the age of seventeen that Toda qualified as a supply teacher in the primary sector of education. In 1920, he moved to Tokyo and taught in the same school as Makiguchi. Eight years later, both Makiguchi and Toda joined Nichiren Shoshu. Toda followed Makiguchi into prison, as much out of respect for his mentor, as for his own uncompromising principles. Arrested on the same day as Makiguchi, and incarcerated for two years in the same prison, Toda had an intense religious experience in his small dark cell. Nichiren Buddhists take this to be an enlightenment experience. Indeed, Ikeda says: "President Toda battled difficulties head-on and was imprisoned. It was there that he attained enlightenment."[56] Given this, albeit unwelcome, solitude to reflect on life, Toda devoted his time to fastidious study of the *Lotus Sutra*, Nichiren's writings and other *sutras*. Chanting the *daimoku* two million times convinced Toda that all life and the universe are fused as one and that in this revelation he had discovered the meaning of life itself. At the heart of Nichiren Buddhism today lies the threefold application of faith in the power of the *Gohonzon*, practice, and study, and Toda emphasized that study alone is insufficient. Mindful of this contingency, he puzzled over the precise meaning of the sixteenth chapter of the *Lotus*.[57] Perplexed by such complex issues as the eternal Buddha's role in the *Lotus*, the nature of life itself, and what is meant by Buddha-nature, after much deliberation, Toda came to the realization that the eternal Buddha as revealed in the *Lotus Sutra* is the cosmic life-force (Jap. *seimei*) that equates with the universe. He emphasized the view of the *Lotus Sutra* that Buddha-nature is not the preserve of an elite few or of a chosen people, but the inherent nature that we all have – we simply need to be aware of how to realize it. With this ever in mind, Toda set about reshaping Soka Gakkai as he reinterpreted Makiguchi's thoughts.

Toda's vision rose from the ashes of a defeated and war-weary Japan, subjected in 1945–52 to American occupation. General Douglas MacArthur demilitarized the nation and steered a new constitution. Japan no longer was able to dictate what it considered to be an acceptable state religious belief system. State Shinto was abolished, and the divinity of the sacred Shinto priest – the emperor of Japan no less – annulled, thereby separating religion from state in a stroke. Religious freedom was now the constitutional right of a desperate and disorientated people, who poured into the fire-ravaged cities in search of work, leaving their roots and their kinship groups far behind. This newly-found freedom of the individual conscience did not chime with Japanese collectivism. The response of a dislocated people has been described by one writer as "the rush hour of the gods",[58] with new religions springing up like lotus flowers on a hot day. Soka Gakkai was one among many; other Nichiren groups included Rissho Kosei-kai and Reiyukai. New religious movements came to be regarded with suspicion, but the opportunities offered by these sociological developments were not inconsiderable. Nor did they escape the attention of Josei Toda, whose zeal for the *Lotus Sutra* induced him to compare MacArthur with Bonten, a helper of the Buddha attested in the *Sutra*. Richard Hughes Seager summarizes the results this had on Soka Gakkai:

> Toda's Buddhism was both a restatement of and an expansion upon Makiguchi's hybrid philosophy. He deepened its traditional aspects by an increased dependence on the Lotus Sutra, Nichiren's *Gosho*, and Nichiren Shoshu doctrine. He also strengthened its modernistic elements by identifying the Buddha with the life force and by teaching Buddhism as a transformative force in culture and politics. These teachings had popular appeal, as evidenced by the Gakkai's rapid growth from a few thousand in the late '40s to 70,000 families by 1953, 160,000 the following year, and 300,000 the next.[59]

This said, Toda was not without his critics, who saw in his commitment to the furtherance of Soka Gakkai a flagrant violation of the new constitution at several points. Toda's devotion to Nichiren's treatise *Rissho Ankoku Ron* ("On Establishing the Correct Teaching for the Peace of the Land"), and his insistence on the exclusive truth of Nichiren Buddhism, brought intense criticism of Soka Gakkai. Nichiren's treatise castigated the state for colluding with what he described as heretical religions, blaming this act on the demise of the country and urging the state to turn to the "true Buddhism". Toda's continued support of the treatise implied state support for Soka Gakkai, an implication that was magnified by his calling for the construction of the ordination platform (Jap. *kaidan*) prophesied long ago by Nichiren. Toda went so far as to describe this as a *kokuritzu kaidan*, "an ordination platform established by the state",[60] thus fusing the efficacy of Nichiren's Buddhism with the state rebuilding of Japan. Toda combined his proposal to establish a national *kaidan* with the doctrine of *obutsumyogo* (the union of worldly matters and Buddhist teaching). This doctrine drew fierce opposition from many quarters and was later withdrawn, though Toda's other vision of a "philosophy of life" lies at the heart of Soka Gakkai activities to this day.

Toda equated the life-force that we all possess with happiness – happiness not simply for certain individuals, but for everyone. In this light, it is members' *duty* to realize the Buddha-nature that we all have, and to help others realize it also. Tamaru writes: "Happiness was none other than a harmonious relation between us and the Buddha-life, and it could be achieved by sincerely believing in the Three Great Mysteries as formulated by Nichiren and by the chanting of *daimoku*."[61] In making *life-force* a key term in his understanding, Toda modified his thinking on Nichiren Buddhism, and in so doing developed the teachings of Makigichi. Makiguchi certainly used similar terms in his vocabulary; equally certainly they were never his focus. Faith, practice, and study were now the means by which to change one's *karma*, thus enabling a distraught and war-torn people to become masters of their own destiny, at the same time affecting others around them in a positive light. Chanting, further-more, could be for spiritual and this-worldly benefits.

A term of particular significance to, and ubiquitous amongst SGI members is "the human revolution". It is a concept that will be taken up for detailed analysis in the following chapter. The words refer to a positive inner trans-formation that takes place within members, which can be effectuated by assiduous practice. Shigeru Nambara, president of Tokyo University, who used the term in a not dissimilar way, coined the phrase at a 1947 address. However, a nervous Japanese government, already suspicious of Toda's plans for the future of the movement, became increasingly suspicious when the term became associated with Soka Gakkai, and they feared a planned *coup d'état*.

Undaunted and convinced of the truth of Nichiren Buddhism, religious tolerance was not in Toda's vocabulary. *Shakubuku* ("break and subdue"), was the driving force by which membership could be, indeed should be (*and was*), increased – to three-quarters of a million members within his lifetime! At his presidential inaugural address in 1951, Toda bade his audience "all of you take on evil religions and convert everyone in the country".[62] This driving force was steered by a militant, militaristic stance. Soka Gakkai youth divi-sions were designated using military terminology, and Kisala notes that comparisons with the military did not end there: "At a rally on 31 October 1954 Toda even mounted a white horse as he addressed the assembled columns with the following words: 'In our attempts at *kosen rufu* [propaga-tion of Buddhism], we are without an ally. We must consider all religions our enemies and we must destroy them.'"[63] It will be seen later that, though the word *shakubuku* still obtains in SGI parlance today, it is now used in a far more conciliatory, recruiting sense, as we shall see in CHAPTER THREE, and Toda himself later modified his understanding of *shakubuku*. Nevertheless, it is Toda's original use of the term that still informs sections of Japanese public opinion about Soka Gakkai to this day, and none of these activities did anything to endear him to his critics.

In August 1947, Daisaku Ikeda formally joined Soka Gakkai. A special rela-tionship soon developed between mentor and disciple, with the young Ikeda acting as personal assistant to his mentor. The disciple had both the trust and the confidence of Toda, and was given responsibility for editorial and finan-cial matters. He was also privy to Toda's vision for Soka Gakkai, particularly his development of a systematic organizational structure for the movement. Older departments and divisions such as the Youth Division and the Women's Division were revitalized and new ones inaugurated. Ever mindful of the soci-ological situation that had arisen in Cold War Japan, Toda ensured that Soka Gakkai appealed to the needs of the ordinary person rather than those profi-teers that had benefited from both Japan's war effort and Japan's capitulation.

Toda gave meaning and purpose to lives that saw little point in continuing. Members were encouraged to chant and recite *gongyo* themselves rather than turning to the priesthood for this assurance, though the priesthood and Soka Gakkai held each other in mutual respect, each benefiting from the other's strengths. Before he passed away on 2 April 1958, Toda saw Soka Gakkai becoming a nationwide lay movement informed by a communicating network of districts. With Tokyo as its hub, and the Study Department at its heart, study courses were developed and distributed via newspapers, and an examination system was introduced. The means by which his aims were fulfilled, as well as an exploration of Soka Gakkai International itself, will feature in the following chapter.

Finally, we should remind ourselves of the legacy bequeathed to Nichiren Buddhism by the various sources. All agree that it is the *Lotus Sutra* alone that attests to the ultimate truth of Shakyamuni's teachings – Buddhahood is universally available to everybody, rather than being the preserve of a select or chosen people. All prior teachings of the Buddha, compiled over many sacred texts and commentaries, failed to attest to this revelation because they were simply provisional teachings, excellent examples of his "skill-in-means" – eminently appropriate to the varying levels of consciousness of his audience at the time, but never intended to be revelations of ultimate truth. This was affirmed by T'ien-t'ai who, amongst deeply profound theoretical analyses, added an immense philosophical system known as *ichinen sanzen*. Based on the *Lotus*, it is basically an explanation of the unity and interconnectedness of the universe.

Nichiren echoed the teachings of the T'ien-t'ai school, and he made *ichinen sanzen* central to the Buddhism of Nichiren Daishonin. He inscribed individual *gohonzon* as the object of worship, as well as the Great or *Dai-Gohonzon*. He exalted the Mystic Law of cause and effect, but his overriding contribution is that, in declaring *Nam-myoho-renge-kyo* to be the true essence of Buddhism, Nichiren added a practical application to the philosophical speculations of the *Lotus Sutra*. Makiguchi's educational background gave him a deep belief that developing a sense of interrelatedness and interdependence with the natural world is the only way to realize one's full potential as a human being. With this in mind, Makiguchi became convinced that Nichiren's teachings represent ultimate truth, and he founded Soka Kyoiku Gakkai. In deleting the word *Kyoiku* (education) from the title, Josei Toda made the Soka Gakkai a lay organization of Nichiren Shoshu. Consequently, it was Toda who gave Soka Gakkai its present character and direction, and he emphasized the threefold application of faith in the power of the *Gohonzon*, practice and study. Philosophically, Toda identified the eternal Buddha of the *Lotus Sutra* with the cosmic life-force that is the universe. Practically, he advised that since this life-force that we all possess is Buddha-nature and the realization of true happiness for all, it is members' *duty* to realize not only their own Buddha-nature, but to assist everyone in revealing theirs.

CHAPTER THREE

The Human Revolution for a Universal Humanity

The Buddhism of Nichiren Daishonin is a belief system that focuses on the evolution of each individual self, the evolutionary progress of the individual in the societal framework in which he or she lives, and the evolution of all humanity in all its possible dimensions. Like all evolutionary processes, discovery and release of positive potential, improvement of attitudes, positive development of socio-economic well-being, and increase in social and global responsibilities are ones of progression that take place in the daily existence of each person. The Buddhism of Nichiren Daishonin does not focus on rewards in a future life, but on the quality of life in the present, and how that quality can pervade humanity through compassion and responsibility for all living beings as well as the planet on which we live. It is Soka Gakkai International – SGI – that is the means by which such goals are articulated in Nichiren Daishonin Buddhism.

Soka Gakkai International

Soka Gakkai (SG), as we saw in CHAPTER TWO, is a Japanese term meaning "Society for the Creation of Value". It is sometimes known as the Gakkai, though Soka Gakkai tends to be the Japanese phenomenon and Soka Gakkai International, SGI, the world-wide phenomenon. SGI is the name given to a federation of organizations throughout the world, each one essentially, and importantly, a *lay* organization. As was also seen in CHAPTER TWO, it was Tsunesaburu Makiguchi who founded the movement and who became its first president. Today's honorary president, Daisaku Ikeda, refers to SG as "a new Mahayana movement", and one that is a global manifestation.[1] From its inception under Makiguchi, the movement grew in Japan, and when Daisaku Ikeda became president of SG in 1960, that expansion continued.

It was in January 1975, at a conference held in Guam, that SG became *international*, SGI, with Ikeda as its first president. Indeed, it is Ikeda more than any other who is responsible for the spread of Nichiren Daishonin Buddhism throughout the world today. Daniel Métraux, who has studied the growth of the movement in Canada, considers Ikeda's great leadership skills to be the reason for its outstanding expansion: "He is a brilliant bureaucratic manager fully capable of developing an able staff and delegating authority and is a very capable and careful planner who has laid a strong foundation for the vast growth and expansion of the Soka Gakkai from a strictly religious movement into one with strong social, cultural and political concerns."[2] Estimates suggest about twelve million members in and outside Japan,[3] with eight million in Japan alone.[4] Richard Hughes Seager, indeed, describes SGI as "a classic case of modern Buddhism on the move in the age of globalization, having found its way to more than a hundred nations".[5] While, at first, the movement had to grow through direct connections with Japan – Japanese immigrants, servicemen and businessmen in Japan, who married Japanese women, for example – direct or even indirect contact of members with Japan now no longer obtains, as is the case with most of the members from Wales and the Borders.

Fundamentally, however, SGI seeks to bring about in each of its members a *human revolution* – a change of being, of attitude, of potential, of social and global responsibility, of value. The means by which such inner and outer revolution is brought about is *kosen-rufu*, "wide propagation" or "wide proclamation", literally, "to declare and spread widely", and is a term used in the *Lotus Sutra*, the primary text on which Nichiren Daishonin Buddhism bases its teachings. Propagation of the teachings of the *Lotus Sutra* and those of Nichiren Daishonin are the means by which the human revolution can occur. They are points that will be taken up in detail below. Peace, culture and education are the media by which the humanism of Nichiren Daishonin Buddhism is to be spread throughout the globe, but it is with the individual self, as we shall also see later in this chapter, that the process begins. In Ikeda's words: "The goal of the SGI movement is nothing less than this: to instill an ethos of worldwide citizenry. . . . by defining ourselves as citizens of the world, we can revitalize the now almost faded virtues of courage, self-control, devotion, justice, love and friendship, and make them vibrantly pulse in people's hearts."[6]

So what makes SGI attractive to new converts? It has to be said that it is, again, the work of Ikeda that has made its expansion possible. SGI is *modern*: it is not a religious movement that is so rooted in past tradition that it has no relation to the age in which we live. Indeed, it is very much associated with present-day social, economic and global problems while maintaining certain basic beliefs that stem from its more ancient past. Its modern nature encourages a humanism that is associated with the very best of ideals for living. In the context of the movement in Japan, Seager's research suggests that "the Gakkai seems to represent much of what is quintessentially modern and Japanese – diligence, activism, energy, idealism, individualism within a strong group orientation, and great success – a modernist humanist movement for Japan's globalizing century."[7] These are aspects that might well be taken up as goals by any modern society. And not only does the movement accept and adapt to change, it actually advocates it. Such a characteristic has enabled it to be attractive and not antagonistic to a variety of different cultures. Its goals are the same but the means for each culture to realize those goals are expressed differently according to the nature and needs of each environment. At an individual, societal and global level, the goal of increased levels of happiness for all is a fundamental reason for the success of SGI, while daily chanting turns vicissitudes into positive aspects and revolutionizes the way life is lived.

For its goals to be realized, SGI has not been able to divorce itself from the political agenda of Japan specifically and the world stage more generally. Again, Seager points out that "there is a strong pragmatic streak in Gakkai spirituality that does not shrink from the fact that a movement needs dedicated members, a strong motive, solid doctrine and practice, focused leadership, social awareness, money, and political will to transform the world".[8] Such pragmatic spirituality has necessitated varying degrees of political involvement. The very fact that its founders were imprisoned for their pacifism and anti-nationalism suggests that their belief in peace, culture and education for all cannot be secured without considerable political struggle.

For SGI, political struggle, however, should be set against a foundational policy of pacifism, though perhaps not absolute pacifism. SGI has been very active in campaigning against nuclear weapons both by petitions and by extensive literary effort. The women's division, for example, produced more than a hundred volumes of anti-war documentation of stories from those who had survived World War II. Massive respect for all life is informed by the belief that the same Mystic Life-Force exists in all things, so all beings are valued with the same respect, and have the same rights to peace, stability and happiness. The search for peace, then, transcends the national and cultural boundaries that overlay the hidden equality of the same Life-Force in all.

The political involvement of the Gakkai and SGI has had both negative and positive outcomes. Makiguchi was critical of the political leaders of his time in the same way that Nichiren was in his day. Both saw establishing the correct form of Buddhism as a political issue. It was Toda who first advocated local and national political engagement and this led to the formation of a political party, which eventually became known in 1964 as Komeito. By 1969, its success was sufficient for it to have become the third largest party in the Japanese House of Representatives. The dangers of a religious group being so closely aligned with a political party are perhaps all too obvious, and controversy surrounded both Komeito and the Gakkai, especially because of stringent recruitment of new converts to the movement by the process known as *shakubuku*. Each new member, of course, would lend an additional vote for political candidates. Criticism by other groups and the media was legion. In fact, Ikeda was at one time imprisoned, though after a lengthy trial, all charges against him were dropped. Events such as these led Ikeda to separate Komeito from the Gakkai in 1970, though Komeito continued to be supported by Gakkai members. Thus, there is no doubt that the early years of the Gakkai were witnessed by pronounced political involvement, particularly amongst youth division and student members. However, the separation was the beginning of a more open and less activist approach to dissenting and differing viewpoints, as well as an important softening and moderating of the *shakubuku* principle that was less exclusivist, and that was to have remarkable effects in the further evolution and growth of SGI.

That the Gakkai does not entirely shake off its political associations is not surprising, given its aims of education, culture and world peace for all the citizens of the planet. It would be impossible to achieve these aims without some political involvement, so SGI has to be socially and politically engaged. There are tensions, too, between the pacifist stance of SGI and the pseudo-pacifist one of Komeito.[9] Outside Japan, however, overt political activity in the form of an associated party is entirely absent, and even in Japan itself, Komeito gained the freedom as a non-religious party to appeal to the wider Japanese populace: the separation from SGI has been a healthy one.[10] Nevertheless, there is still regular contact between the two,[11] and SGI is supportive of the party, but each is able to engage in open dialogue with those who would, in the earlier days, have been seen as antagonists. Makiguchi had wanted a fusion of religion and politics (*obutsumyogo*) and the conversion of a whole nation. Those aims are modified under Ikeda as part of a necessary process of change and adaptation in a more tolerant and global perspective. But total separation from the political scene is impossible for any individual or movement that seeks to engage in the crises we face for peace in the world, for ecology, for the fight against poverty, and world aid.

Members of Soka Gakkai International are fully aware of its fundamental aims and the ways in which it strives to fulfil them. While members all around the world meet to chant and discuss in a wide range of individual divisions such as professional, women's, men's, youth and the like, all such groups are parts of the whole federation that is informed by the same basic beliefs. The Japanese newspaper *Seikyo Shimbun* is underpinned by the Nichiren Daishonin Buddhist humanistic philosophy while, for members in Wales and the Borders (as, indeed, for all UK members), SGI-UK at Taplow Court in Berkshire publishes the monthly magazine *Art of Living*. Whoever a member is, and wherever he or she may be, SGI's beliefs and values in relation to human existence and the planet on which that existence is dependent are disseminated. Ikeda points out that the teachings today are so very relevant in that they deal with deeper issues like the meaning of human existence and the kinds of values and world view necessary in today's world. Then, too, Ikeda points out that the Buddhist principles of the past are not rooted in antiquated ideas, but are transformed in the light of contemporary science, and are specifically concerned with the problems facing humanity at this moment in time. Nor are they isolated from everyday life, for the depth of the universe itself is present in each moment of the living day.[12]

The schism

While Nichiren Daishonin Buddhism is usually portrayed as a "new" movement, its religious traditions, as was seen in CHAPTER TWO, stretch back to the early Mahayana, to the teachings of the Tendai school, and to the life and teachings of Nichiren Daishonin. Since the time of the Daishonin, a lineage of priests has existed to maintain the original teachings and to preserve the major focus of worship, the *Gohonzon*. There were many other schools, too, that rose from Nichiren Buddhism, perhaps the most well known being Reiyukai and Rissho Koseikai, but it was to the Nichiren Shoshu priestly order that Soka Gakkai allied itself. While Nichiren Shoshu has a long history and is not at all "new", it was Makiguchi's inception of Soka Gakkai as a lay organization attached to Nichiren Shoshu that was a new element, along with Toda's enlightenment while in prison. That said, Soka Gakkai members carefully followed advice from the Nichiren Shoshu headquarters in respect of its religious beliefs and its praxis, and both are anything but new.

Relations between the priesthood and Soka Gakkai were mutually productive in the early years. As membership of SG and then SGI increased enormously, financial support for the priesthood was massive, leading to the building of many new temples. In return for financial support, Nichren Shoshu priests issued *Gohonzon* to new members, who received them at a *Gojukai* ceremony. Since the *Gohonzon* was the focus of chanting, its production was seen as a crucially important function that the priests provided. Priests also conducted marriage and funeral ceremonies, led ritual on special occasions, and produced a number of writings aimed at interpreting the teachings of Nichiren Daishonin. For most of these services, the laity had to pay.

The harmony and symbiosis between the Nichiren Shoshu priesthood and Soka Gakkai was not to last. The basis for the rift was probably due to the lay character of SGI. As the movement spread around the world, it was exigent to adjust to changing times, to a modernized world, to make the teachings of Nichiren Daishonin Buddhism relevant to modern life in a variety of cultures as well as to present-day global problems. Then, too, the lay members of SGI looked not to the priesthood for their guidance, but to their SGI leader who, in turn, elevated lay members as spiritual equals to priests. Thus, while the priests had always taught that the Three Treasures of Nichiren Daishonin Buddhism were the Buddha Nichiren Daishonin, the Law, and the High Priest, Soka Gakkai accepted the first two, but substituted lay members as the third, while emphasizing that it was to the first three priests of the lineage to whom they looked for correct beliefs, interpretations and praxis. What was beginning to emerge was a belief that the priesthood was not a necessary intermediary between a believer and his or her experience of life lived in the Law, particularly because all – high priest, president and individual member – are equal in the light of that Law. It has to be said that such a belief is certainly in accordance with the egalitarian teachings of the *Lotus Sutra*. The

priesthood, however, firmly maintained its hierarchical tradition of the superiority of high priest and priesthood.

The direction in which the third president of SG, Daisaku Ikeda, was taking
its members alarmed the priesthood, who saw the deference due to them
constantly being eroded. Tensions were very evident in the 1970s, even
resulting in a formal criticism of Ikeda by the priesthood in 1978. While Ikeda
apologized for any offence he might have inadvertently caused, and his
apology was accepted, tensions never healed. Ikeda had resigned as president
of SG in 1975, though he became its honorary president; the move left him
free to concentrate on his role as president of SGI. The rift culminated in
November 1991 with the Nichiren Shoshu high priest's excommunication of
Soka Gakkai and all its members world-wide. These members would receive
no *Gohonzon*, could not expect priests to conduct marriage or funeral rituals,
and were literally banned from all Nichiren Shoshu temples. It was an attempt
to cut off the millions of SGI members from the high priest, who was believed
by the priesthood to be equal to the *Dai-Gohonzon* and to the essence of
Nichiren Daishonin himself. It was, thus, an attempt to remove the ground
completely from underneath every lay believer, severing them from the very
spirit of the Daishonin himself, and making enlightenment for each SGI
member impossible.

In 1972, with the finances supplied by SGI, the Grand Main Temple, the
Sho Hondo, which became the high sanctuary or *Kaidan* of Buddhism, was
built at Taiseki-ji, the priestly headquarters, to house the *Dai-Gohonzon*. The
building of it was believed to have been prophesied by Nichiren. Yet, in 1998,
despite a world-wide outcry, the high priest of Nichiren Shoshu ordered its
destruction and, after removing the *Dai-Gohonzon*, the magnificent structure
was levelled. No longer was it an external sanctuary to which pilgrims flocked.
However, SGI members were encouraged to internalize the symbolism of the
sanctuary in their own beings. For many outside Japan who never had or never
would visit it, such internalization was not too difficult. For those who knew
it, the destruction was the final cut of the ties with the priesthood. Ultimately,
the event was a liberating one.

The matter did not end with excommunication and destruction of the
temple, because spurious allegations – all finally castigated by the Tokyo
District Court in May 2000 – had considerable adverse effects on the Gakkai,
the Komeito and on President Ikeda himself. The tabloid media the world over
has a lot to answer for in terms of its general ethics, and negative media
coverage of Ikeda and of the Gakkai have been difficult to shake off, despite
the main culpable newspaper, *Shukan Shincho*, being twice successfully sued
by SG. Allegations against Ikeda of rape in the Japanese press were repeated
in the British newspaper, *The Times*. The plaintiff, however, was later thoroughly discredited, but, as in many cases world-wide, it is so often the spurious
headlines that make the news while apologies, if they occur at all, are reduced
to the short sentences hidden in the depths of the publication.[13] The British
Broadcasting Corporation even linked SGI with the gas attacks on the Tokyo

underground – an act committed by a completely separate group, Aum Shinriko.[14]

However, it has to be said that some stringent criticism of Ikeda still obtains in Japan – accusations of cult status, personal aggrandizement and financial scandals, together with the sexual harassment noted above. One Japanese psychologist in conversation with the writer Daniel Métraux alleges that Ikeda is a cult figure worshipped as a virtual deity.[15] If this were the case, it would not seem unreasonable to find Ikeda the centre of focus in members' chanting. Yet, there is scant evidence for such in our survey. In fact, from the evidence of members from Wales and the Borders,[16] only 3% so much as mentioned Ikeda, and none in the sense of cultic or deified language. Clearly, he may be a revered and respected figure, but there is no evidence from the present research to suggest he is a cult figure, and he is certainly not conceived of as a deity.

For those far away from Japan, the schism may not have been felt as seriously as by those in Japan itself. In the UK, Wales and the Borders, as in other countries, the lay people themselves began to take over the fundamental functions of the priesthood. Writing in the *UK Express*, the precursor of the *Art of Living* in 2000, Kazuo Fujii, now Vice-General Director of SGI-UK and Secretary General of SGI-Europe, says that lay people, even from the beginnings of the Gakkai, were beginning to take charge themselves of the three main functions of the priests – "mastering the correct teachings, refuting incorrect teachings and guiding people to enlightenment . . . These days, therefore, we have to reconsider and re-establish what the function of 'priest' really means. The Soka Gakkai has been practising correctly, but the priesthood has lagged behind. They have just kept following the old traditions – fixed, feudal traditions."[17] Importantly, Kazuo Fujii encapsulates the spirit of Nichiren Daishonin Buddhism in today's world, and certainly one of the hallmarks of Ikeda's presidency, when he writes that "Buddhism is always evolving and developing":[18] that is exactly what the priesthood would have feared the most. Nevertheless, there is always present a desire to convey the true spirit and teaching of the Daishonin's message.

Precisely because the Gakkai has always been a lay organization, it has had the space and freedom to evolve; as Seager puts it "always oriented to a shifting landscape of social realities that challenge ordinary people. Created in tandem with the rise of the Japanese middle class, unencumbered by the institutions and traditions of Buddhist monasticism, the Gakkai has a natural affinity for the needs and aspirations of regular working people in nations around the world."[19] Thus, the energy and enthusiasm of its members was sufficient to ride the storm of schism without too much disruption to its daily practice wherein lay its strength. The practice of study meetings, including regular monthly ones, where the beliefs of Buddhism and of Nichiren Daishonin are studied, has brought about a body of members who are highly informed about the roots and beliefs of their faith and has also absolved the need for priestly mediators. The *Lotus Sutra* teaches that all beings have

Buddhahood; each can realize it within his or her self without the need of a priest. Daily practice of chanting to the *Gohonzon* democratizes and empowers all members to seek in themselves the path of evolution: it is with individuals that power resides.

For members of Soka Gakkai International, the schism has had its positive results. In 1993, SGI decided to issue a *Gohonzon* from one transcribed in 1720 by Nichikan, the twenty-sixth high priest. The SGI-USA Study Department says of this momentous decision: "It was one of the defining moments of SGI's lay Buddhist movement because it signalled the return of the object of devotion from the hold of clerical authority to its rightful heirs – ordinary people who practice the Daishonin's Buddhism."[20] A new book for *gongyo* was produced by SGI entitled *The Liturgy of the Buddhism of Nichiren Daishonin*. In it there are additions to the former priestly version, as well as extractions. No longer does the third prayer offer praise to successive high priests; only the first three in the lineage from Nichiren Daishonin are mentioned. There are amendments to the fourth and fifth prayers, prayer for *kosen-rufu*, prayer for the work of SGI in activating *kosen-rufu*, and expressions of gratitude to Presidents Makiguchi and Toda.

Importantly, Soka Gakkai now refers to its religion as the *Buddhism of Nichiren Daishonin*, in contradistinction to the Nichiren Shoshu Buddhism of the priests. Nichiren Shoshu *also* produced a new *gongyo* book, removing any mention of Soka Gakkai from it. As we shall see, the freedom of SGI from its early traditionalist partner enabled it to reach out to others and embrace *world* citizenship, enabled it to accept cultural and religious diversity, and to take a modern, adaptable Buddhism and face the global challenges of the third millennium. The goals of peace, culture and education for all humanity and a living Buddhism that could reach out to all were possible once the break with the priesthood occurred. The individual who has made this possible is Daisaku Ikeda, the President of Soka Gakkai International.

Daisaku Ikeda

As the third, current, president of Soka Gakkai International, Daisaku Ikeda is known to everyone in Japan, is highly respected by many Japanese people and yet, to quote one author "has been a lightning rod for both harsh criticism and high accolades".[21] The successor of Josei Toda, Ikeda was his disciple, and stood firmly in the mentor–disciple relationship, choosing to follow the principles and vision of his mentor. The bond between the two men was considerable though permitting personal evolution and individuality. Seager comments that: "The spiritual bond that exists between mentor and disciple is so intimate that to make a fast distinction between his [i.e. mentor's] inspiration and one's own accomplishment is not viewed as particularly relevant."[22] In the same way, Ikeda is mentor to the many members of SGI, and a charismatic mentor at that, referred to frequently as *Sensei*, "Teacher". It seems, however, that there are no arrangements for anyone to succeed him; perhaps he believes that a human successor is not necessary given the strength of the communities of the movement world-wide, and the more open-minded approach to cultural diversity.

Ikeda first met Toda in 1947 and joined Soka Gakkai in the same year, assisting Toda in building the movement with the aims of establishing peace, education and culture for society. As his mentor, Toda educated Ikeda in a wide variety of scholastic disciplines – philosophy, literature, science, politics and economics, for example. Anyone reading Ikeda's copious works cannot fail to be impressed by the breadth and depth of Ikeda's understanding of so many subjects, especially in his dialogues with eminent scholars. Ikeda refers to Toda as the "most deeply influential person in my life".[23] He says also: "Throughout my work for Buddhist-inspired world peace and along all the uncharted paths I have followed, Josei Toda has never left my thoughts for a moment."[24]

Ikeda was born in Tokyo on 2 January in 1928. He came from a large family, being the fifth of eight children. His family were seaweed farmers. In his youth, he lived and worked in an intensely militarist Japan and suffered the vicissitudes of war, like so many Japanese people of the time. His health was poor, and he suffered from tuberculosis and pleurisy. His father's health was also poor, and when his four older brothers were conscripted, it was the very young Ikeda who had to care for his parents. He married Kaneko Shiraki in 1952, by which time he was working indefatigably for the Gakkai in a number of leadership roles.

In 1960, two years after the death of his mentor, Josei Toda, Ikeda became President of Soka Gakkai. In his diary for Thursday, 14 April 1960, the day he accepted presidency, Ikeda wrote:

> It rained in the morning but cleared up later, although the forecast said it would rain all day.
>
> Left home at 8:30 a.m., my feet feeling heavy.
>
> In reception room #1, the general director and three other directors conveyed their desire for me to become third president. It was 10:10 a.m. Could not refuse, and they naturally took my inability to decline as an acceptance. So this is my destiny. A wave of joy washed over everyone. Everyone seemed to dance with delight.
>
> The directors said they had been waiting, along with President Toda's family and everyone else, for me to accept. Now, it's finally over. This will be a great turning point in my life.
>
> It can't be helped. There is no other choice. Thought of President Toda and made a solitary determination.[25]

In 1975, as we have seen, Ikeda resigned the presidency to take up that of Soka

Gakkai International. But as honorary president, he remains the spiritual leader of the Gakkai. Daniel Métraux, reporting on a conversation he had with Ikeda about his role in life after taking up the presidency of SGI, says Ikeda "saw himself as a teacher whose goal was to offer religious guidance to Soka Gakkai faithful and other interested persons. He also said that he could be helpful as an informal ambassador for peace and human justice".[26] As a leader, and as teacher, Sensei, Daisaku Ikeda guides SGI members by teaching them how to apply the teachings of Nichiren Daishonin in everyday life, and how to spread peace to all humanity through the spread of Nichiren Daishonin Buddhism (*kosen-rufu*). Akemi Baynes, in an article in *Art of Living*, believes that by studying the monthly speeches of Ikeda to Leaders of Headquarters in Japan "we put ourselves in rhythm with his life and the movement for kosen-rufu and from that basis are able to discern what action we should be taking to further our own human revolution and kosen-rufu".[27]

From his writings and from those who have written of him both within and without the Gakkai, Ikeda comes across as a man who enjoys interaction with people on a personal level, and also on a cultural and spiritual level. While he is certainly not devoid of political acumen, political activism is tempered by spiritual ethics. Such spiritual ethics are grounded in a deep respect for life, for humanity, for human dignity, irrespective of culture, gender, nationality, and race. His beliefs are epitomized in his following words:

> Differences of race, nationality, or culture do not of themselves create division or confrontation. It is people's hearts and minds that supply the energy that tears people apart. It is the task of religion to control the heart and mind and, while glorying in these mutual differences, to direct them towards the source from which all values are born. To fix one's eyes on the eternal, the universally valid, and in this way to bring about a revival in human values – this, it seems to me, is the prime requirement of the kind of world religion demanded by our present age.[28]

But it is the spread of the teachings of Nichiren Daishonin that is at the heart of the work of Ikeda and of those who follow him; the recognition of *kosen-rufu* as "the driving conviction of the three founding presidents . . . The spirit of selfless devotion – of not begrudging our lives and of giving our lives to propagating the Law – is the pride of the Soka Gakkai".[29]

As a staunch pacifist, like most SGI members, Ikeda's belief in the sanctity of life prevents any acquiescence in support of war, capital punishment, physical retaliation or revenge: "I am determined to fight against anyone who supports or advocates war", he writes. "I will fight the dark, demonic forces of destruction! And I am joined by an impressive force of close to twelve million people who, armed with brilliant strength of spirit, are powerfully committed to the cause of genuine lasting peace."[30] His experiences as a child and youth watching his brothers go off to war and, in the case of one, to death, had a lasting effect on his adult psyche. His efforts for world peace are a major facet of his work and we shall return to them below. First, we need to examine some of the key characteristics of the presidency of Daisaku Ikeda.

Dialogue

One of the most important policies that Daisaku Ikeda has applied to his presidency is that of dialogue. Unless there is conversation and discussion between individuals or parties, there can be no effective communication. There can be no progression in a positive and democratic way without effective dialogue, and aspirations cannot be fully realized without it. Anyone analysing the character and work of Ikeda cannot fail to recognize the immense contribution to the growth and progression of Soka Gakkai International through his dialogues with others world-wide. Just how crucial dialogue is for world peace is put masterfully by Majid Tehranian:

> Dialogue is both an end and a means to human understanding. In dialogical communication, we engage others as different but equal. We try to enter their world of meaning through an open-ended process of communication and exploration. Dialogue is premised on mutual respect and learning. In dialogue, we change through mutual appreciation, sympathy, and empathy. This is not the easiest method of human communication, but it is the most fruitful. That is why dialogue is the most meaningful path to negotiating a new global civilization based on the contributions of all past human civilizations.[31]

These wise words clearly demonstrate how dialogue needs to inform all other aims. Indeed, Ikeda himself makes the equally wise point that: "Without dialogue, humans are fated to walk in the darkness of their own dogmatic self-righteousness. Dialogue is the lamp by which we dispel that darkness, lighting for each other our steps and the path ahead."[32] Notably, in the context of Wales and the Borders, is Daisaku Ikeda's dialogue with the internationally renowned astronomer Chandra Wickramasinghe, Professor of Applied Mathematics and Astronomy at the University of Wales, Cardiff, published as *Space and Eternal Life*.[33]

Ikeda's concept of this necessity for dialogue was gleaned from his mentor, Josei Toda, who believed that was the method by which humanity could be connected.[34] And the greater the differences between people, the greater the need for dialogue as a means to lasting peace. Moreover, dialogue recognizes that truth and wisdom are not the prerogative of one person. Thus, Ikeda says: "I hold and publish dialogues with persons who represent the wisdom of the world because I believe it is possible that the truth disclosed therein, transcending time and space, will shake people to their very souls and continually provide those in the vanguard of the times with fresh suggestions."[35] These words might be said to be the rationale on which Ikeda bases much practical endeavour, particularly in the desire to prevent the kinds of divisiveness in human existence that thwart the progress of peace. Dialogue is an essential ingredient of our common humanity, and if it could take place in a genuine fashion between the world's leaders then peace processes would stand a chance of being furthered: even a little dialogue can go a long way:

> It is only within the open space created by dialogue – whether conducted with our neighbors, with history, with nature, or the cosmos – that human wholeness can be sustained. The closed silence of an autistic space can only become the site of spiritual suicide. We are not born human in any but a biological sense; we can only learn to know ourselves and others and thus be "trained" in the ways of being human. We do this by immersion in the "ocean of language and dialogue" fed by the springs of cultural tradition.[36]

Global symbiosis

It is clear from the words of Shakyamuni Buddha as depicted in the *Lotus Sutra* that the spread of the *Sutra*'s teachings was of paramount importance. Similarly, Nichiren Daishonin said: "The moon appears in the west and sheds its light eastward, but the sun rises in the east and casts its rays to the west. The same is true of Buddhism. It spread from west to east in the Former and Middle Days of the Law, but will travel from east to west in the Latter Day."[37] Makiguchi had taught how important it is to see one's own culture from the point of view of the world perspective and *vice versa*, and Toda also believed in a global community in which common humanity transcended differences of race and nationality. Toda particularly wanted the Buddhism of Nichiren Daishonin to be spread throughout the world. As soon as Ikeda became president of Soka Gakkai in 1960, he began his overseas travels, first to Hawaii, then to Brazil and then to North and South America – the first moves towards opening up dialogue and *kosen-rufu* on a truly global scale. In 1961, he was off to south-east Asia, to India and to Europe. In anticipation of opening up Nichiren Daishonin Buddhism globally, before his travels, he set up the Overseas Affairs Section. New chapters and districts were established outside Japan, usually with Japanese leaders. Importantly, Ikeda himself maintained supportive contact with all groups, even with members he did not know personally, as he does today. During this global expansion, members everywhere were encouraged to overcome the religious misconceptions of others and replace such erroneous views with those of Nichiren Daishonin Buddhism – the process called *shakubuku*.

However, with the changing times and Ikeda's increasing dialogue with other cultures, a more liberal attitude began to set in. Transcending ethnic, racial and national boundaries is not a vision that excludes the diversity of humanity but one that recognizes the differences while respecting the rights of a global civilization: there can be diversity but also unity. For Ikeda, the key is to have core values for all humanity, values that encompass respect and tolerance and, above all, positive dialogue. Such a policy will offset any selfish individualism and encourage harmony of existence – a symbiotic universalism. Members are encouraged to engage with the world as much as Ikeda does.

The university addresses of Ikeda reveal how well-informed he is about a variety of cultures. These geographically wide-ranging addresses – Institut de France, Ankara, Peking, Bologna, Moscow, the Philippines, Guadalajana, Sofia, Bucharest, Macau, Fudan, California, Harvard, Shenzhen, Buenos Aires – all relate remarkably well to the particular culture and country in question, singling out its artists, philosophers, educators but, at the same time, emphasizing Soka Gakkai beliefs. The knowledge he gained and his global openness were passed on to members of all countries as part of the Gakkai policy of education. Ikeda met many world leaders as part of his commitment to dialogue, his networking policy, and his belief in the interconnectedness of all human beings.[38]

The success of Ikeda's networking was a main contribution to the continued success of SGI after the schism, as well as to the modern and liberal Buddhism that taught of personal empowerment, development of personal potential and yet social and global responsibility. Members could feel that they played an important part in the move for world peace and in solving global problems. All such success, however, was rooted in practice, harnessing power in the self through *daimoku* to the *Gohonzon* and meeting together as members, as professional groups, as women, men, youth, for a cultural occasion, a festival, musical performances – all these were provided by SGI as part of the networking interconnection of groups throughout the world, with a motto of "world peace through individual happiness".

Ikeda's mission to convert new members globally has certainly been fulfilled. It was a success that both preceded, and was concomitant with, Japanese economic expansion. Such success is likely to have been hampered by association with the priesthood, which was far less open to the global scene, so the break from the priesthood was essential for the Gakkai's globalization. Underpinning all is *dialogue* – among individuals, in groups, in societal intercourse, between races, religions, cultures and civilizations. The goal is world-wide citizenry, cultural internationalism or "cultural interpopulism, a movement for cultural interaction in which ordinary citizens are the protagonists".[39] A certain degree of ability to transcend closed partisanship, ideologies and national identity for a global humanism is exigent and, Ikeda believes, "the establishment of principles and ideals that are at once universal in orientation and global in scope is an inescapable necessity if we are to cope successfully with this new century's challenges".[40]

A much greater cooperative ethos is essential to create a compassionate global society but that ethos begins with the individual. In Ikeda's words: "Nichiren said that the inherent dignity of one person serves as an example of all, meaning that all human beings should be regarded as equal. The idea of the absolute equality and the sanctity of all human beings expressed here is the product of the unrelenting inward exploration of life itself as manifested in the individual. Because this view of the human being is internally generated, it leaves no room for the distinctions based on such external factors as nationality and race."[41] Ikeda calls this idea "inner universalism". It is discovered and revealed through dialogue on the one hand, and by education on the other. We have seen how essential dialogue is to inner change and global exchange, now we must turn our attention to the concept of education as the facilitator that gradually turns people into world citizens.

Education

Education at all levels of society is a lynch pin for the practical outcome of SGI's aims: it is the key that overcomes ignorance, prejudice and intolerance. Apart from education in the Buddhism of Nichiren Daishonin, SGI has established educational institutions at all levels of education from kindergarten and infant to university level[42] as well as launching cultural and artistic events and setting up museums. In 1971, Ikeda founded Soka University in Tokyo. The aim of the University is a secular, rather than a religious one – to encourage fulfilment of the innate potential and creativity in all individuals – and non-SGI children and students are accepted in all the educational institutions, though teaching staff are normally SGI members. Soka University is not, however, a Buddhist institution *per se* but holds its own in the wider secular academic world.[43] Values taught are Buddhist, but the contributions to society of great thinkers, intellectuals, sportsmen and women and artists past and present, reflect the global outlook of education. Echoing the views of Makiguchi, Ikeda writes: "I believe it is vital that education be reoriented to its prime objective, namely, the lifelong happiness of learners."[44] Where full potential and creativity is not being realized, true education is not occurring. However, education on a global scale is not directed solely to ending illiteracy (though SGI has established literacy courses in Brazil, Mauritius, rural Japan and remote islands of Japan). Rather, bringing out the latent abilities of individuals and directing those abilities towards global harmony is seen as the way forward to a universal humanity and a global community.[45] Thus, the aim is education for the individual *and* for humanity – education for global citizenship and a greater understanding of the problems we face in today's world.

Learning is the key to life, and education begins with a stable family where harmony in relationships is important for the growth of respect for individuals, for the ability to share, to sympathize and to empathize, but at the same time, for the development of free and unique individuals. We develop physically, psychologically, emotionally and spiritually in the home environment, and it is to the wife and mother that Ikeda places "the role of imparting the culture of humankind to children".[46] He writes too: "Saplings grow into strong trees only if they are rooted in good earth. The loving, harmonious family is the good earth of human physical and spiritual development. Its lack causes warped, twisted growth that contributes to social malaise and eventually threatens the achievement of lasting, universal peace."[47] It is in the home that the "human revolution" can begin with each individual and the relationship of each to others. No individual can achieve such an inward revolution without some degree of harmony with others: change does not mean aggressive lack of respect for the welfare of others. One of Nichiren's parables states that when you bow respectfully facing a mirror, the image in the mirror likewise bows to you. In recognizing and creating value within ourselves, in turn we create value in society.

The emphasis in educational policies is on the development of potential within each student, but with global links with other countries and races through exchanges of students and staff at Soka University, conferences, discussion forums, seminars and intercultural events. By developing inner potential and critical thinking, like Makiguchi, Ikeda hopes that people will be released from confined and myopic attitudes that bind them to narrow parochialism, nationalism and ethnicity, all of which prevent a more open view of humanity as a whole. Nichiren Daishonin said that: "To teach another something is like oiling the wheels of a heavy cart so that they will turn, or like floating a boat upon the water so that it may move ahead without difficulty."[48] Exploration of, and dialogue in, social issues such as AIDS, societal violence, problems of age, human and children's rights, world peace, ecology, global economics, are ongoing educational policies. They are policies that embody Ikeda's view that "education imbued with true humanism is absolutely essential to peace".[49] When Soka University was opened, Ikeda set three ideals for it:

> Be the highest seat of learning for humanistic education.
> Be the cradle of a new culture.
> Be a fortress for the peace of humankind.[50]

The ideals are aimed at fostering world citizens, at education for a universal humanity, at respecting diversity but recognizing a fundamental equality, and at establishing creative coexistence.

To promote education, the *Institute of Oriental Philosophy: European Centre* (IOP-UK) was inaugurated at Taplow Court in Berkshire, UK, in 1989. It is a centre for international academic discussion in seminars, symposia and congresses as well as for culture, with open days and exhibitions. It has an excellent library with texts not only on Buddhism but also on other Eastern religions. Set in exquisite surroundings, the IOP is a magnificent setting in which scholars of world stature are periodically invited to share their knowledge with SGI members and the general public. Dialogue is an essential facet of its agenda. In June 2008, for example, the IOP joined forces with the Network of Buddhist Organizations (NBO-UK) to explore the development of Buddhist traditions in the UK in a conference entitled *The British Buddhist Landscape – Transplantation and Growth*. The aim for each Buddhist organization was to explore and understand the views of the other groups.

Taplow Court is an important venue for practitioners in Wales and the

Borders. Each year the Taplow Court Festival of Arts with theatre, opera, classical and modern music and poetry readings, attracts a large number of people from the region. Liz Moulson is one member from Cardigan who was there at the opening of Taplow Court. She writes: "I attended its opening and stayed on for a few days to volunteer my help as there was a week for events. Japanese, European and UK members were invited."[51] Such volunteer work at Taplow is called *keibi*, which involves members staying at Taplow to support the centre. A good proportion of members from Wales and the Borders have engaged in this kind of activity on more than one occasion. *Gohonzon* receiving ceremonies take place at Taplow Court and are attended not only by those receiving *Gohonzon* but also by many who wish to support the new members.

At least 18% of the members from Wales and the Borders have attended so many courses and functions at Taplow Court that they could not possibly list them all. Others attest to attendance at general meetings, leaders' meetings, divisional, chapter, men's, women's, youth and professional meetings, as well as attendance at day events for youth and youngsters. There are also residential courses specific to Wales and the Borders. The Centre caters not only for the groups in its organizational structure but also provides a forum for those who wish to focus on their own specific interests. Suzanne Jenkinson, for example, a semi-retired Reiki teacher, attends "social and medical meetings, that is, topics concerning sociology and medical ethics". Many of the courses held there are occasions for study, with educational seminars, workshops and courses for students. Family events are also a feature of the Taplow programme with children's fun days. Every year, an All Wales Course is held at Taplow Court. The course lasts from Friday afternoon until Sunday afternoon. Each morning and evening the members chant together. There are also study lectures, discussion meetings in small groups, videos of SGI events such as meetings of Headquarter leaders with Daisaku Ikeda in Japan. A pronounced feature of all such occasions is the sharing of experiences. A senior leader will also be available to give guidance if needed. There is also free time, and on the Saturday evening, entertainment by the members themselves.

Fifteen per cent of the members from Wales and the Borders have also attended courses at the European Centre at Trets in France. One member from Swansea, Anny Pritchard, has also attended a study course in Hong Kong, another member, a youth conference in Auckland, New Zealand, and Carol Brown, also from Swansea, writes: "I have attended courses at various venues in England, at our UK centre, Taplow Court, and at our European Centre in Trets. I have attended meetings or visited members when I am travelling to other countries, for example, I attended the AGM of SGI in South Africa when I was in Johannesburg. I set up the first discussion meeting in Vilnius, Lithuania and I set up an introductory meeting in Addis Ababa." While there are only a few people practising in Lithuania, Carol still visits them to offer her support. The point here is that, wherever a person may be, there is usually a group of practising individuals, and if there is not, as in the case of Carol's experiences, it is always possible to start one, but for most, Taplow Court provides an educational and cultural focus, as well as a centre for study.

Culture

Education is the key to promoting culture and the key to appreciation of artistic expression. By culture, here, SGI concentrates on *cultivation*, that is to say, the cultivation of the best kind of inner attitudes and spirituality, and it is perhaps the artist in whatever medium – literature, poetry, art, music, philosophy – that comes some way to fulfilling this. The way in which this is promulgated globally in SGI is by exhibitions and cultural events. In 1995, in collaboration with UNESCO, a collection of children's paintings from around the globe became the focus of an exhibition in Tokyo, from where it was taken world-wide. The theme was peace and friendship, and the educational aspect was enhanced by seminars on this theme. Ikeda also set up the Tokyo Fuji Art Museum. "Art," says Ikeda, "is to the spirit what breath is to the body; through art we find oneness with a transcendental entity, breathe its rhythm, and absorb the energy we need for spiritual renewal."[52] Music, also, is part of the cultural emphasis of SGI, and in 1965, Ikeda founded the Min-On Concert Association, the cultural organizational centre of the Gakkai. This large organization sponsors world-wide musical concerts and performing arts. Underpinning its cultural programmes is the aim of social and global interrelation and harmony.

While cultural events take place within the Welsh/Borders region itself, particularly at the periodic five-year celebrations of Nichiren Daishonin Buddhism in the region, Taplow Court is very much a focal point for such events for Wales/Borders members. The annual Taplow Court Festival is popular, with some members participating in its organization, and one Welsh member, Ben Davies, having produced the event. The choir at Taplow is a numerically large one, as anyone who attended the thirtieth anniversary of the SGI, celebrated in the Royal Albert Hall in May 2005, will affirm. Some Welsh/Borders members sing on such occasions, travelling to Taplow Court once a month for practice. They also sing at other concerts and recitals.

Peace

> The crisis modern humanity faces is not imposed from without. It is as if, in the name of selfish advantage, dwellers were destroying their own house by fighting for furnishings, ripping out ceilings, tearing up floors, and pulling down pillars. Conflicts of emotion and interest engender hatred inspiring these dwellers to devise and store weapons powerful enough to blow the whole house away. Madness is the only way to describe a situation in which people in a cramped, frail building threaten each other with bombs of tremendous destructive force. But such is the

world crisis today, as the environment is being polluted, natural resources are being exhausted, and all humanity lives under the threat of war.[53]

The Nichiren Daishonin Buddhist is very much aware that these words are a graphic analogy of the state of the world in which we live. The lack of peace at all levels – in the individual self, society, nations, with the environment, with the earth, the seas and the whole planet – must surely be close to its nadir. Peace is not just the cessation and absence of war; it is fundamental harmony of living at every possible level with humanity and with all nature. The important message of the Buddhism of Nichiren Daishonin in the present day is that all existence is interconnected and that we need to rise above the "selfish advantage" noted above and to broaden consciousness to concern for the whole globe. Many of the exhibitions mounted by SGI in various parts of the world serve to highlight this fundamental drive towards world peace and a universal humanity. Petition drives, like the "Petition for the Abolition of all Nuclear Weapons and for the Elimination of War" of 1973–5, and the "Abolition 2000 International Petition" of 1998 requesting governments to get rid of nuclear weapons, are huge movements for peace. The SGI's Women's Peace Committee produced a twenty-volume work entitled *In Hope of Peace*, which told the stories of women in World War II. There have also been important seminars, lectures and symposia directed towards dialogue about means to peace.[54]

Daisaku Ikeda's brother was killed in action in Burma in 1945: it was two years before his family was officially notified. In conversation with Chandra Wickramasinghe, he writes: "I shall never forget the sight of my mother, her back turned to us in sorrow. I found myself hating war and the foolish leaders who instigate it."[55] It was Makiguchi's and Josei Toda's anti-militarism and suffering in prison that entrenched Ikeda's anti-war stance, and his hope for a humanity that would transcend nationalistic differences. In 1957, Toda had pressed for the abolition of all nuclear weapons, and Ikeda followed suit. In 1993 he set up the Boston Research Centre for the 21st Century, and in 1996, the Toda Institute for Global Peace and Policy Research. Both are dedicated to the establishment of world peace. Above all, Ikeda believes that peace should stem from a fundamental belief in the sanctity of all life,[56] and an expansion of consciousness towards the cosmos and eternity and away from "small egos".[57] His premise is that aggression and war stem from humanity, not from something extraneous to it: therefore, peace can equally be the product of humanity. But his peace proposals – brought out each year on SGI Day, 26 January – are meant to be concrete proposals for change and action rather than theoretical considerations.[58] He writes: "Peace cannot be a mere stillness, a quiet interlude between wars. It must be a vital and energetic arena of life-activity, won through our own volitional, proactive efforts. Peace must be a living drama . . ."[59] The idea of peace as a drama, an *active process* that needs effort and cultivation, places the emphasis for it on every individual. His peace proposals, therefore, address many concerns, for example, social and economic peace, as in the Proposal of 1996. For his own efforts, Ikeda was awarded the United Nations Peace Medal in 1982.

In addresses to the United Nations General Assembly, Ikeda is keen to express how dialogue and negotiation are the means for overcoming national and international crises. Utterly in favour of universal disarmament, Ikeda is thoroughly pacifist in that he does not accept any military presence that might be part of future aggression, such as United Nations peacekeeping forces, though he accepts that there may be some need for multinational force for security reasons on occasions.[60] Ikeda's words on peace have been gathered together into a volume whose English title is *A Lasting Peace*.[61]

SGI is a non-governmental organization (NGO) of the United Nations (UN), as also are the Toda and Boston peace research centres noted above. Both of these centres have been set up to *unite* discussion about world peace throughout the world. It is in conjunction with the UN that exhibitions such as "Nuclear Arms: Threat to our World" and "War and Peace: From a Century of War to a Century of Hope" and "Toward the Century of Life: The Environment and Development" have circulated across the globe. In conjunction with the UN, SGI organizes global humanitarian aid with money, food, medical supplies and teams, clothing, bedding – in short, wherever there is any kind of disaster or suffering in the world and wherever the protection of human rights is necessary. It is in the United Nations, albeit its need for more expansive concerns, and particularly the NGOs, that Ikeda puts his hopes for future change. It is in these bodies that Ikeda finds the best outlets for Buddhist principles. Members of NGOs, especially, can act as altruistic *bodhisattvas* for the peace, welfare and dignity of all humanity. The *non-governmental* nature of the NGOs is especially important in having a non-partisan view of the problems facing humanity.[62]

If we turn to the members of SGI-UK in Wales and the Borders, at least half of the respondents express concern about global issues of war, conflict, the need for peace, the problems of poverty and famine, the trade in arms, and the political machinations that cause suffering in the world.[63] The specific practices will be examined in CHAPTER SIX, but relevant here is the point that Nichiren Daishonin Buddhists chant *Nam-myoho-renge-kyo* daily and, while doing so, chant *for* goals that are important in their own lives or in those of others. Interestingly, only a quarter of the respondents chant for the cessation of such global problems.[64] The same might be said about concerns about the environment such as global warming, energy, and climate change. While just under half of the respondents find environmental issues a global concern, only three chant for solutions to them. While chanting is a topic that will be taken up in CHAPTER SIX, a few points are relevant in the context of the present chapter.

First, overwhelmingly, it is personal aspects of life about which respondents chant. Such a statement is not meant pejoratively in view of the second point that many respondents considered that the priority is to change the self first and, by so doing, the first ripple in wider change can take place. Indeed, this is what the "human revolution", which we shall be examining below, is all about. Sarah Crowley from Cilgerran, for example, says: "I chant to achieve certain goals in my life, and for happiness and contentment in my own self. I often chant for my family and friends, for their happiness and well-being, and for any conflicts they have to be resolved." When asked specifically to list ways in which areas of concern in society and the world could be addressed,[65] changes in one's own personality, living by example, as well as Buddhist practice, particularly chanting, are seen to be the ways forward. Liz Moulson from Cardigan puts the point rather well when she says: "I like the phrase: 'Think globally, act locally.' Because I believe in the interconnectedness of all life, I also trust that by making positive inner changes in my life and then acting on them in my daily life, I can not only affect those close to me, but those whom I'll never meet, and also the natural environment." Similarly, Louise Squire from Lampeter writes: "In the same way that my behaviour affects and changes those around me, my deep desire for the resolution of the world's troubles, I do believe, seeps out somehow into the wider consciousness." It would have to be said that it is in the context of the family, the home and personal relationships that the emphasis on enhanced living is the most important, judging by responses, but mainly at the level of each individual. Thus, Sriram Vaidyanathan of the Cardiff East Chapter writes: "Of course, one cannot ignore poverty, global warming, violence among youth and religious intolerance. However, these issues cannot be resolved merely by social, political or economic change. Ultimately, changing the human heart is the only way to change these external issues."

Cultural pluralism

The early history of Soka Gakkai was characterized by a strong missionary flavour, originally in Japan itself, and then globally, beginning with expansion to the USA in 1960, before spreading elsewhere. Nichiren Shoshu Buddhism was exclusivist, following the nature of Nichiren Daishonin's Buddhism of the thirteenth century in Japan. But if there was anything exclusivist about Nichiren Daishonin Buddhism in its developing phase, it is surely Ikeda who has emphasized the necessity of acceptance of the diversity of human life and belief, dialogue in and about such diversity, and tolerance as a means to global peace and harmony. Even Nichiren himself commended study of other traditions of Buddhism, of Confucianism and of Classical Hinduism.[66] The break from the Nichiren Shoshu priesthood served to free SGI from the shackles of exclusivism, permitting a broader outlook on religious diversity that is an ongoing development.

While in the past it seems the acceptance of diversity existed alongside the concept that the Soka Gakkai's religious beliefs were superior to others, it is diversity that seems to win the day rather than superiority. Acceptance of diversity is based on a growing and profound belief in the need for *deep* respect for all people. For nearly half a century gay Nichiren Daishonin Buddhist members have often formed their own divisions, with complete acceptance by SGI, and ceremonies to celebrate same-sex partnerships have been in place for well over a decade. Chapter 5 of the *Lotus Sutra* contains a beautiful passage that talks of different trees, shrubs and herbs on which the same moisture falls. Each is different but united by the same life-giving moisture. Given, too, a profound theory of the interconnectedness of all life and all things, mutual, yet diverse, relationships are of the essence of existence. There is diversity but there is also commonality: there is diversity, but interconnected unity. These are concepts that we shall explore fully in CHAPTER SEVEN. Cultural exchange is integral to the present policies of SGI: "The SGI promotes cultural exchange and seeks to advance the search for common values, such as tolerance and coexistence, which are present in different forms in all cultures and traditions. These activities are based on the premise that through direct interactions with people from different cultures – whose backgrounds and assumptions about life may differ greatly from our own – we strengthen our sense of common humanity.[67] Again, it is out of respect for each human being that such "direct interactions" are applauded.

Thus, there has been a marked development in inter-faith dialogue, though with the acceptance that it is imperative that a religious belief system contributes to individual value and global harmony. For global peace to be enhanced it is necessary to advance beyond narrow sectarianism. Ikeda writes: "Similarities provide a basis for cooperation, but we must also be aware of our differences, ready to respect each religion's role and the strengths of the other. Then we will find ways we can each contribute to the world."[68] Because of belief in the interrelation and interdependence of all things, tolerance between individuals and cultures, between races and nations should be a common denominator along with, and recognition of, our dependence on others for our own well-being. Again, Ikeda writes: "Tolerance is more than just a mental attitude; it must grow out of a sense of larger order and coexistence, a cosmic sensibility that issues up from the wellsprings of life."[69] Just how far SGI has come in terms of religious tolerance and inter-faith dialogue is exemplified in the truly remarkable appointment in 1996 of a Sufi Muslim from Iran, Majid Tehranian, as the founding director of the Toda Institute for Global Peace and Policy Research. The Institute sponsors inter-faith dialogue through conferences and symposia, while its charter emphasizes tolerance and respect for other religions.

The openness to other religious beliefs is very evident in the responses of members in Wales and the Borders.[70] With the exception of only three individuals, there was overwhelming evidence of religious tolerance. If there were critical comments, they were qualified by provisions that religions should not justify violence, fundamentalism, dogmatism, fear, bigotry, subjugation of women, intolerance, extremism and the like – in short, very much the kind of caveats that most people, whether religious or not, might support. Let us look now at some of the views of the respondents, which will demonstrate rather well how religious tolerance pervades SGI. Anlya Zahabian from Haywards

Heath sees religions as "different ways of finding the unified essence of life", while an anonymous respondent comments that: "It all comes from one source but we all have many ways of getting there". A large number believe in the right of each individual to choose his or her religious path; this from Jenny Bartlett from Leominster: "People are entitled to their own beliefs and this should be respected. All religions provide positive spiritual and practical help. The key is freedom of choice not coercion or imposition of religion." Roger Langford of Hereford writes: "I respect those who profess other religious beliefs. Religious freedom is another human right."

The word "respect" chosen by Roger is crucial to the view of so many of the respondents. Some, like Carole Gell from Newport in South Wales says that she has more respect for other religions *since* becoming a Buddhist, and Adrienne O'Sullivan from Cardiff echoes the same sentiment: "Years ago, before I started practising, I was very anti-religious: I thought it was the cause of most of the major world conflicts. Since my practice of Buddhism, I have become more tolerant of other religions and now respect people who have a faith." Adrienne's words are indicative not only of enhanced religious tolerance but also of a greater broadmindedness brought about by her practice. Ikeda writes a good deal about the congruence that there is in much religious diversity. So, in the words of Jill Sutton from Drefach: "What has been a positive step for me is that through practising Nichiren Buddhism I have found a greater interest, tolerance and common ground with all types of religion." Such congruence is noted, too by Nick Sherwood from Westhope, who says: "There are many points of convergence between Nichiren and other faiths. Anyone who has a faith based on respect for life in all its forms has my sympathy and respect."

One of Ikeda's key concepts, as we have seen, is that of dialogue, and it is in the spirit of such that his engagement with other faiths is forwarded. Nick Dowsett from Dinas Cross makes the point that: "It is very important to engage in dialogue with people of all (and no) faith. How else can we progress humanistic ideas." Preference for one's own faith does not seem to deter dialogue with that of others. Harry McIver from Cardiff says: "The primary importance is to be a person of faith and to support others in that. Discussion and encouragement and example may bring others to my faith, but if they have a strong faith, we already have common ground." Harry's words will be important to bear in mind when we look at the concepts of *kosen-rufu* and *shakubuku* below. Finally, in the words of Peter Grayer of Beacons and Borders chapter: "I believe that all faiths have a place and function to fulfil and should work together for the good of all humanity." All these ideas are resonant amongst the vast majority of respondents and are indicative of a thorough openness and tolerance to other religious traditions.

Kosen-rufu and shakubuku

Two important concepts that are very relevant to the concept of cultural pluralism are *kosen-rufu* and *shakubuku*. The first of these is *kosen-rufu*. It is a term used in the twenty-third chapter of the *Lotus Sutra*, "Former Affairs of Bodhisattva Medicine King", and means to propagate, proclaim, declare and spread widely – namely the *Lotus Sutra* itself and, in SGI belief, the teachings of Nichiren Daishonin based on the *Sutra*. The *Lotus Sutra* expresses concern that its teaching should not be lost, and prophesied the dark age of our present time when, without those dedicated to its spread, it would disappear. How, then, does the mission to spread such teachings correlate or conflict with the clear interreligious dialogue that is a key feature of the presidency of Daisaku Ikeda? To begin with, SGI-UK adds to the definition of *kosen-rufu*: "To secure lasting peace and happiness for all humankind through the propagation of Nichiren Daishonin's Buddhism."[71] The words are indicative of a wider interpretation of *kosen-rufu* to encompass broader agendas that move towards world peace. Such aspects as inner revolution of each individual are part of what *kosen-rufu* now means, with engagement in the world in a modern rather than religiously radical way. This makes *kosen-rufu* more of a *process of living* than an end product. Thus, the positive way in which Soka Gakkai International members conduct their own lives is in itself an example that may attract others to the movement. However, the desire to build a global society based on the principles of Nichiren Daishonin Buddhism remains the overarching goal and priority. Ikeda wrote the following poem about *kosen-rufu* in 1970:

> What the people long for
>> to carry them through the twenty-first century
>> is no reorganization of external forms alone
> They desire a sound revolution
>> carried out within themselves
>> gradually and in the atmosphere of peace
>> founded upon the philosophy and beliefs of each individual
> This calls for farsighted judgments
>> and a profound system of principles
> This is what I would name a total revolution
>> and it is this
>> we call *kosen-rufu*.[72]

Kazuo Fujii, interviewed in 2000, defines *kosen-rufu* as: "Practice for oneself and others", at the same time keeping the goal of propagation in mind when he adds: "We really have to push forward as individuals and as a movement for *kosen-rufu*. We have to establish Nichiren Daishonin's Buddhism as the religion for the twenty-first century, for the happiness of the people."[73]

As to *shakubuku*, the official definition is: "A method of expounding Buddhism, the aim of which is to suppress others' illusions and to subdue their attachment to error or evil. This refers to the Buddhist method of leading people, particularly its opponents, to the correct Buddhist teaching by refuting their erroneous views and eliminating their attachment to opinions they have formed. The practice of *shakubuku* thus means to correct another's false views and awaken that person to the truth of Buddhism."[74] The language here is strong – suppress, subdue, correct, eliminate – appropriate for the time in which Nichiren lived, but less so in a world in which tolerance and understanding of others is essential for world peace. Contrasting with *shakubuku* is the less confrontational term, *shoju*, a term also used by Nichiren Daishonin, which emphasizes leading someone to the correct teaching *gradually*, according to the level of consciousness of the individual, and without any refutation of mistaken views. Here, there is dialogue rather than overt attempts at conversion. Generally, the former is considered the method used for those who persecute or strongly contest the tenets of Nichiren Daishonin Buddhism, while *shoju*, the gentler method, is for those who are ignorant of Buddhism. Toda, especially, successfully evoked *shakubuku* as a means to expand the Gakkai, and it is difficult to see how he might have embraced the more thorough respect for inter-religious dialogue and global expansion that characterizes Nichiren Daishonin Buddhism today. Indeed, in the early days to be fiercely and aggressively "*shakubukued*" was something of an alarming experience.[75]

Today, the aggressive tactics have almost disappeared and have given way to greater tolerance to, and interest in, other religious viewpoints. Jane Hurst makes the point that: "The practice of *shakubuku* itself has changed, and should take place on the basis of pre-existing relationships or natural affinities with other people. This has made the group more genuinely open to friendships with outsiders, who in the past might have been seen only as 'potential members'. The model for understanding is to engage in dialogue, to talk as equals and to respect differences, while focusing on the common cause of making the world a better place."[76] As Jane Hurst points out in her paper, the change in focus has a good deal to do with the more liberal attitudes engendered by the split with the priesthood: the split led to a more liberal, open and international movement.

Nevertheless, *shakubuku* remains a critically important concept in the Buddhism of Nichiren Daishonin. Thus, Ikeda says: "*Shakubuku* is a practice that is a concrete expression of our belief in the Buddha nature within ourselves and others; it is a humanistic act of the highest respect for others."[77] The very title of the article in which these words appear, "The Practice of Respecting Others", indicates clearly how aggressive practice has given way to gentle and appropriate discussion. Ikeda goes on to say: "Fundamentally, *shakubuku* may be thought of as a battle between the inclination to respect human beings and the tendency to diminish them. Buddhism enables people to develop a solid character and self-identity."[78] The goal of *shakubuku* is still the sharing and speaking of the truth of Nichiren Daishonin Buddhism with others, but has become expanded to encompass compassion for others, the end of human suffering, as well as joy and peace for all people. Ikeda adds: "It definitely is not, and must not become, narrow-minded sectarianism."[79]

The greatest quality of the Buddha Shakyamuni was his immense compassion, and it is this quality too, that is now at the heart of *shakubuku*. In the *Lotus Sutra*, he asks his multitudes of followers to keep the spirit of the *Sutra* alive, and to perpetuate the teaching about the true path to Buddhahood in all the ages to come. To become compassionate, to experience joy and peace, is about realizing *shakubuku* within one's own self, as much as being made aware of it from without: both are engendered by respect – for oneself and for all others.

How, then, do the SGI-UK members in Wales and the Borders understand these two concepts of *kosen-rufu* and *shakubuku*? To begin with, there is a considerable overlap in the responses to definitions of both terms.[80] While 66% of respondents understand *shakubuku* as introducing others to Nichiren Daishonin Buddhism, 42% of respondents hold that *kosen-rufu* has the same meaning. A good number of respondents find introducing others to Nichiren Daishonin Buddhism a difficult process. Helen Delingpole from Cardiff very sensitively exemplifies what many members feel. She writes of *kosen-rufu*: "I am chanting to engage in it more and more. I'm chanting to overcome my inhibitions about telling others about the practice. I find that the more I engage in *kosen-rufu*, the happier I feel about my life: synchronicity happens more and more." And of *shakubuku* Helen writes: "I understand it to mean introducing others to the practice and supporting them in any way possible. I have been reluctant to do this for fear of scaring people off, or 'coming on too strong'. I'm finding my own way with it and I'm chanting to meet people who are ready to meet the practice. I bought my first *shakubuku* some beads, a *gongyo* book and a silk envelope, and gave them to her yesterday." Helen's words are echoed frequently in the responses by those who feel somewhat inhibited about talking freely to non-members about their faith.

While so many respondents understand *kosen-rufu* and *shakubuku* to be involved in gaining new members, others had a totally different view. Equating the living of life itself with *kosen rufu* was the answer given by at least 20% of respondents. Here, every action engaged in is *kosen rufu* and, indirectly, if done well, it encourages others to ask questions about the success of an individual's happiness and the ability to deal with life. Thus, Nicky Delgado from Cardiff writes of *kosen-rufu*: "My life is *kosen-rufu*, all my work – inspiring, educating, supporting, learning from others, developing young people, children, adults. Buddhism directs my life's goals and purpose . . . my behaviour towards others, and challenges faced (and often overcome). Some people view my Buddhism as very positive, enlightening and reflecting my/their Buddhahood. What I do now is just a precursor of what I will achieve and am currently achieving." Another sensitive response is that of Adrian Hardinges from Godrergraig in Swansea: "The most fundamental way I engage in *kosen-rufu* is through my *daimoku* – by putting it in my heart. If I can do this first thing in the morning, I can contribute to *kosen rufu* throughout the day by revealing my Buddhahood in working life, through conversations and just by giving someone a smile. I try to engage with every person with whom I come into contact to create peace and happiness in my environment. Quite often, my Buddhist practice will come up in conversation, so I may find myself talking about fundamental principles of Buddhism like having respect for other human life."

Kosen-rufu for these members is life, is living. Jenny Nicholson from Fishguard, Pembrokeshire takes the view that it is: "In everything I do: it is in no way different to daily life. It is in my action as a human being, which helps create world peace." Similarly, Amy Milton from Newport, South Wales says: "Buddhism is life, so I try to make positive causes for myself and others as much as possible: then, there's nothing that you or anyone else can't achieve." What we have here is the spreading of Nichiren Daishonin Buddhism *by example*, by living life with positivity and with intention to change. Jodie Allinson from Grangetown, Cardiff writes: "I see every action I take as contributing to *kosen rufu* in the sense that if I can create happiness and value in my interactions then I am contributing to *kosen-rufu*. More specifically, I see my participation in Buddhist activities as engaging in *kosen-rufu*." Jodie's point is an important one, for many respondents understand *kosen-rufu* to be Buddhist practices such as chanting, study, weekly and/or monthly group practice specifically for *kosen-rufu* and, significantly, arranging and attending meetings, supporting SGI activities, supporting and encouraging fellow members and participating in, even arranging, courses. At a more personal level, a member might use his or her home for meetings, host friendship meetings, conduct home visits, invite people to discussion meetings, and lend books. Some donate money to the *kosen-rufu* fund. On an inner level, some believe *kosen-rufu* to be concerned with inner change in the self – the "human revolution" that will be dealt with below. Life in the community, too, whether in one's occupation or with old and new friends, or in general interaction, is also evident from the responses.

Clearly, while there are overlaps between the understanding of *kosen-rufu* and *shakubuku*, it is the latter that is conceived of as introducing, telling about, sharing, explaining or raising awareness of Nichiren Daishonin Buddhism to others, but there is little mention of the aim of refuting and suppressing other religious views. The expression "where appropriate" occurs on a number of responses, in the context of spreading Nichiren Daishonin Buddhism, and many see such appropriate occasions as when a person is suffering through illness, has relationship problems, financial difficulties, low self-esteem and the like.[81] However, there is nothing forceful about the process. According to Lynne Hayes from St Dogmaels, Cardigan: "My understanding is that I pass on my beliefs to as many people as I can, as often as I can, but not in an intrusive way: if they're not interested, I don't force it on them". It is worthy of note here that we, the present authors, while not Nichiren Daishonin Buddhists, have had considerable contact with SGI locally, and at Taplow Court in the context of introducing university students to Buddhism. Some students continued their interest sufficiently to undertake undergraduate or postgraduate study of Nichiren Daishonin Buddhism. To our knowledge none has been subject to *shakubuku*, nor were we, the authors, during more than two decades of contact. In her study of SGI-UK members in Bath, Helen Waterhouse found that the term *shakubuku* persisted, rather than the term *shoju*, and that it was unpopular because of its connotations of militancy and compulsion. She notes that members "still speak in terms of 'who *shakubuku*d whom when they discuss introductions to SGI and its practices."[82] This is certainly not the case in Wales and the Borders, as far as the written evidence is concerned. Indeed, the present research has found that the term "to *shakubuku*" someone is rarely mentioned, despite being a focused question of the questionnaire.[83]

So, while *shakubuku* is essential to Nichiren Daishonin Buddhism, there is no forceful proselytizing. Nor, it seems, are members forced to engage in it in ways they cannot handle. Phil Luffman, recently of Usk and Wye district, says of *kosen-rufu*: "I *like* to talk to people about Nichiren Daishonin in the hope that they will be interested enough to pursue greater understanding." However, for *shakubuku*, he writes: "I am not particularly active in bringing others to the practice. I can understand the importance of *shakubuku* but I have a more laid-back approach to it than some of my Buddhist colleagues." Judging by the responses in general, Phil's actions for *kosen-rufu* would be seen by many as very good *shakubuku* too. Stephen Millson from Abergavenny reflects admirably the more liberal stance now given to the term *shakubuku* when he correctly defines it as "to refute erroneous teachings". He adds: "I am not sure I like the term, or the way in which it can be interpreted. I am not sure it is relevant to this time in a mainly non-Buddhist country. I prefer to practise *shakubuku* by spreading the benefits of the practice." In fact, very few respondents mentioned *shakubuku* as refuting the beliefs of others: the overriding impression was one of too much respect for others to engage in such praxis. Liz Moulson expresses these points well when she says:

> Just as seeds blossom at different times, so will some people want to practise quite soon after hearing about *Nam-myoho-renge-kyo*, while others take many years or maybe will not practise at all in this life. Someone I introduced Buddhism to ten years ago has started practising in the last year and is just about to get her *Gohonzon*. I feel being a good friend and gaining people's respect and trust is also important. I often have to find the courage to overcome my inhibitions or shyness. I don't try and convert people of other religious beliefs but I try and have a fruitful dialogue so that we can understand one another better. Over the years, a lot of people I've introduced have received *Gohonzon* and it gives me tremendous joy and pride to see how their lives have developed. You never know where telling someone will lead.

It seems, then, that in the context of Nichiren Daishonin Buddhism in today's world, *shakubuku* has changed focus. Mark Radcliffe makes the point neatly when he defines the term as: "*Strictly*: to refute erroneous Buddhist practice. *Practically*: to introduce others to Nichiren Daishonin's Buddhism."

1 Tsunesaburo Makiguchi, the first president of Soka Gakkai.

Photograph with kind permission of © *Seikyo Shimbun*

2 Josei Toda, the second president of Soka Gakkai.

Photograph with permission of © *Seikyo Shimbun*

3 President Josei Toda at the first general meeting of the Kansai General Chapter, April 1957.

Photograph with permission of © *Seikyo Shimbun*

4 Daisaku Ikeda, the current President of Soka Gakkai International.

Photograph with permission of © *Seikyo Shimbun*

5 A young Daisaku Ikeda [left] walking with his mentor, Josei Toda [centre].

Photograph with permission of
© *Seikyo Shimbun*

6 President Daisaku Ikeda with President Nelson Mandela at the Seikyo Shimbun Building in October 1990.

Photograph with permission of
© *Seikyo Shimbun*

7 The marriage of Les and Kyoko Gibson in Japan.

8 Les and Kyoko Gibson at their home in Upper Cwm-twrch in the Swansea Valley of South Wales.

9 Taplow Court, Maidenhead, Berkshire, the headquarters of SGI-UK.

10 The library of the Institute of Oriental Philosophy European Centre (IOP) at Taplow Court with (left to right) the IOP-UK Director Jamie Creswell, librarian Sarah Norman, and Vice-General Director of SGI-UK and Secretary General of SGI-Europe, Kazuo Fujii.

11 Members from Pembrokeshire/Ceredigion chanting (left to right) Jo Ogilvie, Liz Moulson and Nick Dowsett.

12 The Dowsett family chanting (left to right) Nick, Hope, Mani and Tirion.

It is a view supported in general by the responses from the questionnaires. Interestingly, Louise Squire from Lampeter *internalizes shakubuku*, at the same time reflecting the respect with which most respondents engage in *shakubuku*: "*Shakubuku* is simply the understanding that all people/life have Buddhahood and are worthy of respect. Also it is *living* this understanding. I have brought a good number of people into this practice, but I do not consider *shakubuku* something that you "do": it is not as vulgar as that. That attitude generally leads to a dead end." The same emphasis on respect is clear from Stephanie Bond, also from Lampeter: "*Shakubuku* only means to lead people to happiness. To me, it's more important that people are happy and fulfilled in what they do and how they live than if they get a *Gohonzon* – that's completely up to them. If they do, I'm delighted though! It's all about mutual respect and knowing what each individual needs or wants: we are all unique."

For many Wales and Borders members *shakubuku* is spreading Buddhism by one's example in life, as in the case of *kosen-rufu*. James Donson from Cardiff writes: "It is a concept that can be put into practice in many ways. I often talk about Buddhism with friends but mainly I believe that Buddhism is best portrayed through my behaviour: often, you don't even need to mention Buddhism whilst still engaging people in its practical elements." Clearly, then, refutation of the religious views of others has given way to sharing Nichiren Daishonin Buddhism with others but not in a real proselytizing way. Interested people might be encouraged to chant, invited to meetings, loaned books or engaged in dialogue, while for some, *shakubuku* is more about reflecting one's own awakening out into the world as an example of Nichiren Daishonin Buddhism. Ben Davis from Cardiff describes it as "a way or state of life borne out of compassion and a desire to relieve suffering and to enable myself and others to perceive and realize their own Buddhahood and greater potential". Likewise, Teresa Kean from Lilleshall in Shropshire says: "It is a way of life and it is about our behaviour as human beings."

The human revolution

The "human revolution" (Jap. *ningen kakumei*) is the inspiration of Daisaku Ikeda and has become an attractive feature of SGI. While the word "revolution" conjures up impressions of violence, of the overthrowing of structures and institutions, here, revolution is meant in an *inward* sense. It is indicative of the inward change of human beings, the revelation of their *bodhisattva-hood* and Buddhahood, *and from that change*, a change, too, in the wider environment, in moves for peace, happiness, stability, responsibility for others, compassion, willingness to share – in short, creative value for a universal humanity. But it all begins with the individual. The way to change the world is to begin with personal change. It is a view that is consonant with the philosophy of Nichiren Daishonin Buddhism that the whole cosmos is a unity of its diverse parts, and that each action in one moment has an effect on everything else in a mutually interdependent universe. These are ideas we shall take up in detail when we look at the philosophy in CHAPTER SEVEN. The more individuals are able to, and the more individuals who operate from, an enlightened inner self, the greater the impetus for environmental and global harmony. "A tide culminating in the reformation of humanity and our planet is the ultimate goal of the human revolution", says Ikeda.[84]

Nichiren had a vision of infinite peace, *rissho ankoku ron*, and it is this vision that is maintained by Nichiren Daishonin Buddhism – a difficult aim in the age of *mappo* in which we live, and one to be achieved by each individual *thinking* not selfishly, but globally, and inspired by holistic fairness and justice. Mahayana Buddhism in general accepts that three poisons affect the way in which we live. They are greed, anger and delusion, ignorance, or foolishness, and they inform selfish living at all levels. The human revolution is designed to change not only the present thinking that perpetuates such selfishness, but also the negative *karma* accrued from selfish thought, word and action. By changing individual *karma* there is the potential to change general human *karma*. And SGI regards it as *essential* to change not just the self, but also social, educational, economic, governmental, national, cultural and global perspectives. As has been pointed out above, Nichiren Daishonin Buddhism is not, as many religions, rooted in a changeless tradition, but is one that can move with the challenges and trends of the time. This may involve engagement in struggles for agendas such as human rights, anti-war and the environment, for example.

Self-transformation and realization

Nichiren Daishonin Buddhism teaches that the human revolution involves *transformation* and *change* of each individual through faith in the *Gohonzon* and regular practice, so that one changes adverse *karma* – negative causes made in the past that reap negative effects in the present and future – to more positive causes for *benefits* in the future. At the same time, each person evolves through lower states to higher ones, that is to say, to states of *bodhisattva* and Buddhahood, filtering all life's situations through these evolved conditions. What is involved is a reformation of one's own character that, in turn, will have an effect on the immediate and wider environment. It is a process of empowerment of individuals – not the violent power unleashed by historical revolutions, but a "soft power" encompassed by positive change within each human being. Responsibility for change is placed squarely on the shoulders of each individual and in pursuit of such self-realization there is less likelihood of imposition of our own values on others.

Self-revolution is a search for the truth within the self and the means to becoming a new, stronger and more fulfilled person. It is a process of self-mastery and revelation of inner potential through an elevation of one's present life-condition to a higher one. Each person's transformation is a unique mission, personal to his or her own self. Eighty per cent of the Wales and the

Borders respondents to the questionnaire[85] understand the term "human revolution" to be concerned with transformation and change. Liz Mitchell from Cardiff sums up what most people understand by the term when she writes: "Once we change ourselves – and we understand we always start with ourselves – then these changes in us affect others around us, together with the environment." Josei Cousens, also from Cardiff, says the term means for her: "Constantly working to reveal my Buddhahood, Looking honestly each day at my life and always striving to bring about positive change to create happiness for myself and all others. The term also means tackling the stuff I'd rather shy away from!" An anonymous respondent writes: "I understand this to be a commitment to transforming your inner world for the benefit of yourself and others around you. For me, it has been connected to deconstructing my social conditioning."

The goal for each individual is victory over the challenges and struggles that life presents so that inner potential is realized and peace and happiness experienced. The means to these goals are Buddhist practice. In Ikeda's words: "What we in the SGI have been doing is trying to stimulate this kind of "human revolution" in people all over the world, trying to help them build their own inner peace. I will always have faith that humanity can extricate itself from the conflicts and violence imposed by the vicissitudes of fate when the internal change in human lives, coming like wave upon wave on the shore, turns into a swelling tumult of people with the wisdom of inner peace."[86] It is a noble aim, and might seem an idealistic dream, though we are certainly seeing how individuals are beginning to change consumer trends by their demands for additive free and organic foods, for example. It is individuals here who are dictating change by the changes they wish to make in their own lives.

The human revolution is not a move towards the fulfilment of egoistic, selfish goals for the pursuit of happiness. A necessary corollary is the perception of the interconnectedness of all life and the related perception that negativity in the individual has a wider consequence for those around, like the ripples of a pebble thrown into a pond. It is mutual happiness for the individual and all humanity that is at the heart of the inner transformation of the human revolution. The transformation of the self is one from a lesser self (Jap. *shoga*) to a greater one (Jap. *taiga*), from a self that is concerned only with its own interests to one that recognizes connection to, and an effect on, all others. Each individual has to come to know that how he or she thinks and behaves has wider consequences, and that changing positively the way one sees oneself and the way one thinks and behaves will have wider positive effects. Sriram Vaidyanathan, a respondent from Newport in South Wales writes: "Human revolution is an inner transformation based on the understanding of the workings of life, one's great inner potential and the relation of life to its environment. Then, we must be prepared to take full responsibility for our lives and for the societies in which we live." Life will never be trouble free. But Nichiren Daishonin Buddhist practice is aimed at giving the kind of inner strength that is robust and courageous enough to withstand adversities.

The greater self coexists with the force of the universe itself; a fact that wisdom acquired through practice allows the individual to perceive. Ikeda writes: "This wisdom is not to be sought in some distant place, but can be found within ourselves, beneath our very feet as it were. It resides in the living microcosm within and wells forth in limitless profusion when we devote ourselves to courageous and compassionate action for the sake of humanity, society and the future."[87] In each individual are the darker forces that create traits such as selfishness, greed, prejudice, intolerance, pride, arrogance and ignorance – particularly the three poisons of greed, anger and delusion, ignorance or foolishness. Many respondents to the questionnaire expressed their understanding of the human revolution as reflecting this transformation of negative traits to positive ones. An anonymous respondent defines the human revolution as: "Fighting my inner negativity, doubt, prejudice, hurt, annoyance, arrogance etc., so that I can approach myself and others in a higher life-condition."

For Nichiren Daishonin Buddhism, conquering such negative forces – and each of us has them – is what the human revolution is all about, producing the "soft power" that is enduring and all-encompassing rather than the "hard power" that soon spends itself out: all that needs to happen is the polishing of the dust and grime to reveal the Buddhahood within. It is, as Joanne Roxburgh from Dinas Powys says: "A personal and unique struggle to overcome the negative forces that cause self and others to suffer." Developing wisdom, compassion and courage within empowers the individual in a way that engenders greater positive expansiveness and openness of self into the world beyond: imagine, for example, how different the world would be if we just eradicated human greed. Marc Lister from Bridgend describes the process as: "Taking small steps outside your own comfort zone in order to grow as a being. The human revolution is about developing myself into the best human being that I can be." The philosophy relating to such a process we shall leave until CHAPTER SEVEN. But all that is really needed to begin with is the chanting of *Nam-Myoho-Renge-Kyo*.

Chanting *Nam-Myoho-Renge-Kyo* reveals the Buddhahood within, and many respondents understand this to be the purpose of transformation in the human revolution. Hideko Nakatani from Bridgend writes: "We all have Buddhahood, the highest condition of life, and we can reveal it. We can change our lower life-states into positive states through our daily practice." As Hideko says, Buddhahood is the highest potential for any person even if the path to it is not easy; so Carol Brown from Swansea points out: "For me, human revolution means struggling to become the best person you can be, revealing your courage, wisdom and compassion as often as possible. It is the understanding of your life patterns and working hard to polish your character so that it doesn't cause pain or problems to yourself and others." What is involved is a change in *karma*, and a removal of the darkness within over the course of a lifetime. Peter Baker-Jones from Solva describes this very well when he says that the human revolution is: "Using our prayers and desires to fuel a process of self-purification by drawing out our negative *karma* that manifests as an obstacle or as suffering. Repeating this action time and again helps us change our negative tendencies. This process is a lifelong commitment to self-growth." Similarly, Nicky Delgado from Cardiff sensitively describes human revolution as: "Continuing deep and sometimes painful change that is necessary if you want to encourage and support others. I have no enemies but the dark side of my own *karma* – that is the one thing to change. The only real revolution is your own human revolution." It is, as S. Lewis from Brecon says: "Breaking through your own insecurities and *karmic* barriers to grow spiritually."

According to Nichiren Daishonin Buddhism, the greater self exists in all individuals because all are united by the same essence, the same Law of the universe: the same universal principle underpins all things. Thus, reality is humanity, its environment and the cosmos itself unified as one in a creative, pulsating and dynamic symbiosis. Its many parts may be richly diverse like the varied vegetation given life by the same rain, but all is interdependent: in line with the basic Buddhist doctrine of Dependent Origination (Jap. *engi*), nothing can exist independently of anything else. Once this is recognized – and Nichiren Daishonin Buddhism teaches that chanting and practice can bring this about – then it is possible for the individual to transcend the lesser, egoistic self and see his or her interconnection with the rest of humanity and the mutual reciprocity of all activity, at the same time not annihilating the lesser self, but filtering its desires and aversions through the greater one. Enlightenment in Nichiren Daishonin Buddhism is not the suspension of desires, but *involvement* in the world, *engaged* living – in the true spirit of the *bodhisattvas* of Mahayana Buddhism. It is those who can experience their greater selves who can effectuate greater global peace and harmony, and have the wisdom to engage in tolerant, unprejudiced and non-aggressive dialogue with mutual respect. In the words of Steffan Ellis from Cardiff, the human revolution is: "A transformation of the self that contributes to lasting happiness and the development and transformation of society towards understanding, civilization, harmony and peace."

The bodhisattva life

In the *Lotus Sutra*, the Buddha speaks of *bodhisattvas* rising from the earth. In Mahayana Buddhism in general, *bodhisattvas* are those who vow to delay final enlightenment to be reborn in order to help the rest of living beings on their path to enlightenment. Nichiren Daishonin Buddhism interprets "rising from the earth" as the rising life-condition of Buddhahood within each being concomitant with increasing compassion for all. It is a personal and individual awareness of the Buddha-nature that is inherent in the cosmos and all things. The human revolution is the path to the development of the full potential of Buddha-nature that is buried deep within the self. "In its essence", says Ikeda, "this nature is adamantine and indestructible, pure and undefiled. When it is revealed, it becomes the core of life which, by enabling us to master ourselves, determines our happiness."[88]

It is through the revelation of the Buddha-nature in each individual that the scope for societal and global harmony and peace can begin. Social responsibility is a corollary of personal inner evolution. Three-quarters of the members from Wales and the Borders are engaged in voluntary works *outside* SGI activities and nearly half of all respondents in more than one way.[89] In a quiet way, SGI members are engaging in their communities in all sorts of charitable activities (apart from such things as projects for humanitarian relief, campaigns for the environment, reforestation projects and research provided officially by SGI itself). But with individuals, it is the adage of one first step, one individual's efforts that is the beginning of far wider consequence. In Ikeda's 1998 Peace Proposal, he writes:

> It is my belief that we can foster, in the depths of each individual human life, the kind of active, independent basis for altruistic behaviour exemplified in the bodhisattva's vow, we can establish the fundamental basis for an ethic of responsibility and commitment, upon which a genuine culture of human rights can flourish. This is because the inner motivation that spurs people to act in the face of threats to human dignity is, for human rights, the most crucial supporting and sustaining force.[90]

Struggle against any kind of injustice has been a hallmark of SGI, but its means begin with the human revolution that creates a "Treasure Tower", to use a figure from the *Lotus Sutra*, that is the Buddha-nature, within each person. There is no withdrawal from the world for the *bodhisattva* who "plunges into life's turbulent waters in the effort to help each person drowning in suffering onto the great vessel of happiness".[91] And each follower of Nichiren Daishonin Buddhism acts as a *bodhisattva*. The *bodhisattva* can only be truly happy when all others are happy, too, expanding his or her own life through altruistic devotion and compassion to others – an ideal human being. The *Bodhisattvas of the Earth* in the *Lotus Sutra* are those who have courage in the face of difficulties, wisdom to know what is right, knowledge of how to adapt that wisdom into the best kind of action for humanity and against evil and, above all, boundless compassion. Their role is the creation of value in the lives of all other beings, inner peace and harmony within their own selves and within all humanity, and peace and harmony with the universe itself, their lives an expression of the universal Law of Buddhahood in all things.

CHAPTER FOUR

Nichiren Daishonin Buddhism in Wales and the Borders

Many studies of SGI in various countries throughout the world have been undertaken. This chapter is designed partly to place SGI-Wales and the Borders in the context of some of these studies and, also, to examine the sociological and demographic nature of the phenomenon of Nichiren Daishonin Buddhism in Wales and the Borders. Both aims will seek to discover how far the adherents are similar to, or different from, the general population in Wales, and adherents of Nichiren Daishonin Buddhism in other countries with respect to themes like gender and age of members, nationality and ethnicity, occupations, general qualifications and marital status. These are more objective considerations, but subjective themes such as previous religious beliefs, reasons for initial and continued attraction to Nichiren Daishonin Buddhism, and the reactions of friends and family, are also relevant in our enquiry. The personal views of members of SGI-Wales and the Borders will be an important facet of this chapter. To begin with, however, we need to know something about the geographical spread of the members and the organization of the movement throughout Wales.

Geographical spread of members

Geographically and economically, the population of Wales is mainly concentrated in the South, in the major industrial city and capital of Cardiff and, though to a much lesser extent, Swansea. Welsh area authorities like Rhondda Cynon Taff, Carmarthenshire and Caerphilly also have high population figures.[1] It might be expected that the capital would have the major part of the total number of SGI-Wales/Borders members and, indeed, this is so: Cardiff alone has 93 members – almost a third of the total number. However, while Swansea has about 19 members, once Cardiff is discounted, it is not the highly populated areas that have high percentages of members. Both Pembrokeshire and Ceredigion, for example, have 13% and 11% respectively of the total membership. Since Ceredigion is one of the least populated authorities in Wales, this is quite surprising. Perhaps, as Les Gibson suggests, "a lot of people escaped from London and large cities to the far West of Wales and were ready for the practice".[2] Smaller percentages come from Monmouthshire, the Vale of Glamorgan, Powys and Carmarthenshire, this last authority being the best represented of these. Areas such as Blaenau Gwent, Neath Port Talbot, Rhondda Cynon Taff, Bridgend and Merthyr Tydfil have a handful of members each. On the border of Wales in England, Shropshire and Herefordshire have about 24 members.[3]

Thus, as far as Wales is concerned, there is little correlation between highly populated authorities and membership numbers.[4] With a collective population certainly greater than Ceredigion, Camarthenshire and Pembrokeshire, the counties of North Wales – Conwy, Flintshire, Gwynedd and Denbighshire – do not appear to have any members, and may well be areas into which Welsh Soka Gakkai might expand in future. SGI-Wales / Borders has also made no inroads on the Isle of Anglesey. We can say, then, that it is mainly a phenomenon of South and Central Wales, stretching East to the borders of England and beyond, and West to the coast. Traditionally, there has been, and still exists to some extent, a tacit, and sometimes overt, division between North and South Wales.[5]

Organization

A brief explanation of the current structure of SGI-UK Wales / Borders might be appropriate at this point.[6] The UK is divided into **areas**, of which Wales is one. From October 1, 2007, the area of Wales was officially extended to Wales *and the Borders* to reflect more accurately the actual geographical membership. As its name suggests, "Borders" encompasses areas of England like Herefordshire and Shropshire that border Wales. At present, this whole area is divided into three **Headquarters**. Each of the Headquarters is responsible for a number of **chapters**, which are themselves divided into **districts**. The structure in the area of Wales and the Borders, then, is as follows:

Mid Wales and the Marches Headquarters
  Chapters
  • *Beacons and Borders* with two **districts** – Abergavenny, and Usk & Wye
  • *Mid Wales and Shropshire* with three **districts** – Cambrian, Shrewsbury, and Upper Severn

South and East Wales Headquarters
  Chapters
  • *Cardiff East* with four **districts** – Cathays Heath, Newport, Roath/Penylan/Lakeside, and Splott/Adamstown
  • *Cardiff West* with three **districts** – Canton/Llandaff, Croeso, and Grangetown/Riverside

West and South-west Wales Headquarters
Chapters

- *West Wales* with two **districts** – Cwm Rheidol, and Treasure Tower
- *Eagle Peak* with three **districts** – Dragon Gate, Friendship, and Preseli
- *Unoliaeth* with four **districts** – Llanelli & Amman Valley Red Dragon West Wing, Bridgend, Gower & Swansea West Dragon's Tail, and Central Swansea Morriston & The Valleys

The HQ/chapter/district organization here is mainly geographical and locational. In addition, there are **divisions**, which are mainly groupings according to gender and age. Thus we have *Men's*, *Women's*, *Young Men's* and *Young Women's* etc. As far as age is concerned, however, there is no strict limit on movement between divisions, so the age criterion is very flexible. There is also a Future Group for young people aged 13–18, Mimosa for girls aged 7–12, and Young Eagles for boys 7–12. Gender divisions probably reflect the single sex meetings characteristic of the original movement in Japan. Divisions may also arise (and disappear) for other reasons, such as ethnicity and profession, though while a student division is embryonic in Wales and the Borders, there are no other divisions at present. Districts are usually subdivided into local groups of a smaller number of people who can easily meet together for discussion meetings called *zadankai*. At these meetings they can give mutual support, exchange experiences, and engage in study, and it would be to these local groups that newcomers might have their first experiences of Nichiren Daishonin Buddhism. Districts have monthly meetings in which they explore *Gosho*, the teachings of Nichiren Daishonin, and such texts as the commentaries of Daisaku Ikeda on the *Lotus Sutra*.

The important point about the organization is that, at the local and small group level, encouragement and support of new members is established policy. Regular meetings mean that social contact, interaction and engagement are core aspects of SGI life, not only in Wales and the Borders but in any country where Nichiren Daishonin Buddhism obtains. It is not only newcomers who are offered support, but also longstanding members. Adherents are encouraged to take responsibility for their own lives and for wider social and global concerns. David Chappell found in his study of SGI in America that such social development is essential to SGI and that it is this aspect that is quite different from other forms of Buddhism like Zen, Tibetan or Vipassana, because it is socially engaged – "socially transforming at the very core", as Chappell puts it.[7] The same importance of self and societal transformation is the case with SGI-Wales/Borders. And as Chappell also says of the American scene, which is also true of SGI-Wales/Borders, there is an "expression of social connectedness and social responsibility" that is part of the life of the *bodhisattva* that each member strives to be.[8]

Leaders, now called leaders in faith, are essential to the social transformation of the members of the different groups. They are often individuals who have been members for many years and who have considerable experience in the movement. It is they who offer guidance and act as counsellors at divisional, district and chapter levels. Wilson and Dobbelaere, in their analysis of SGI in Britain, suggested that, without being in any way regimental, leaders provided "a systematic diffusion of certain values throughout the entire organization".[9] Leaders also assist each member's fluidity of experience of local, district, chapter, Headquarters and national levels. Since there is no priesthood and no religious intermediaries in Nichiren Daishonin Buddhism, and each person is responsible for his or her own personal development, leaders provide advice where it is needed, but only because they are more experienced in the self-evolving process and in the foundations of Nichiren Daishonin Buddhism. It would be naïve to expect that every leader has the kind of outstanding qualities that demand total respect from general members, and some respondents to the questionnaires are, indeed, critical of leaders. These, however, are few and the overall picture is one of a fairly successful leadership arrangement. From the Young Men's division comes what used to be called the *Value Creation Group* (VCG), but is now simply *Soka*, and from the Young Women's, *Lilac*. Both tend to have genderized functions at special occasions, where Lilacs are responsible for such activities as serving refreshments and caring for people, and Soka takes on more intentionally "masculine" roles of directing traffic and parking, laying out furniture, and the like. There is also the volunteer work known as *keibi*, noted in CHAPTER THREE.

The largest chapters are, as might be expected, those of Cardiff East and Cardiff West with 43% of members being represented within them.[10] Unoliaeth, however, with its four districts, also has a sizeable representation (16%) of the total number of members. The Women's Division has most members (52%), a point that will be explored fully in the following section concerning gender and age. The Men's Division accounts for just over a quarter (27%), while there are clearly fewer in the Young Women's Division (14%) and fewer still in the Young Men's (7%).

The questionnaire invited members to cite their chapter and district.[11] It was clear that there was some confusion concerning the overall organization, not only in the correct naming of chapter and district, but also in the ability to differentiate between chapter and Headquarters. This was particularly so with regard to areas of Wales, when respondents cited Mid West Wales, South West Wales, West Wales and the Borders, and South East Wales, for example, none of which is official terminology. While some respondents were clearly citing Headquarters rather than chapters, others had combinations that bore no resemblance to either. Perhaps, too, those who omitted to respond to the chapter/district rubric (yet often filled in other sections fully), were not themselves sure of the correct names. A glance at the dates when members joined SGI-Wales/Borders suggests that mistakes are not only being made by newcomers. Helen Waterhouse found a similar lack of clear ideas about the structure of SGI in her study of members in Bath.[12] Perhaps it is an area that SGI-Wales might want to address in future.

Gender and age of members

Women outnumber men by almost 2:1 – a factor that is consonant with Nichiren Daishonin Buddhism in all other countries, too. Wilson's and Dobbelaere's 1994 study of SGI in the United Kingdom as a whole, for example, also found that 60% of adherents were women,[13] slightly lower than the 65% of women in SGI-Wales and the Borders. Similarly, Hammond and Machacek's study in America, researched in 1997, found the same 2:1 ratio of women to men,[14] and Macioti's study in Italy in 1998 found 67% of members to be female.[15] Such a high percentage of women in SGI probably reflects religious movements and established religious gatherings outside Nichiren Daishonin Buddhism: perhaps women are more inclined to explore the diversity of life's pathways. In Japan, where Soka Gakkai began, the same phenomenon is evident.[16] The women's division dates back to 1940 in Japan and the first women's division chapter leaders' meeting there was held in 1951. As in so many cases world-wide, Soka Gakkai facilitated the personal and social empowerment of women, and President Toda encouraged women as "the foundation of the Soka Gakkai",[17] though generally as the foundation of the family. In the post-modern world, the idea of self-transformation, of chanting for success *in* life and not being disengaged from it are particular attractions for the woman of today.

Out of the total Wales and Borders membership, 36% are in the 41–50 age range.[18] A further 22% are in the 51–60 age range. Thus, the majority of the members, 58%, are in the 41–60 age range: adding the over-sixties, that percentage rises to 68% over 40 years old. While, as we have seen, women outnumber men by almost 2:1 – a factor evident in the age ranges 31–40, 41–50, and 61–70, the ratio is a little more balanced between the genders in the 21–30 age range, and also in the 51–60 age range, but more especially in the former. It was noticeable that females in the 21–30 group were those from whom the least number of responses to the questionnaire were received (7 responded, 23 did not). In comparison, half of the men in the same age range did respond. In fact, exactly half of the men overall responded to the questionnaires in comparison to only 46% of the women. Across the total membership, it was only in the age range 51–60 that responses to the questionnaire were a good deal greater than non-responses. While the members are mainly over 40, the fact that there are more members in the 21–30 age range than the 31–40 group, albeit fractionally (51 in the former as opposed to 47 in the latter), suggests that there is a thriving youth movement in Wales and the Borders and, as noted above, the ratio of women to men is much reduced here. With the exception of Japanese Soka Gakkai, where the structure is more male-dominated in the higher echelons, women in SGI have equal leadership to men at all levels. Like the Canadian members, there are fewer elderly practitioners in SGI-Wales and the Borders.[19]

Nationality and ethnicity of members

The overwhelming majority of members are white UK Caucasian, mainly Welsh or English, with a tiny number from Irish and Scottish backgrounds.[20] Only 7% have non-UK nationality and ethnicity.[21] It is significant that, while the percentage of members not ethnically from the United Kingdom is very small, the proportion of Japanese amongst this group is considerable (9 out of a total of 26). The non-Japanese are spread across a wide ethnic range with only a few members from each.[22] There is not, then, a highly multi-ethnic character in SGI-Wales/Borders, unlike, for example, the members in Canada,[23] or in the USA, where, Chappell believes, a significant reason for the success of SGI is its ability "to organize individuals from a wide variety of ethnic and cultural backgrounds into an organic whole".[24] In the UK as a whole, Wilson noted that members came from 40 different countries:[25] as many as 28.7% were born outside the UK.[26] Since, however, such studies report that SGI is mainly an urban phenomenon – two thirds of the members studied by Wilson and Dobbelaere came from London, for example[27] – it is perhaps not surprising that a high multi-ethnic presence is not evident in Wales and the Borders. It was noted above, for example, that Ceredigion is the third least populated area authority in the whole of Wales: yet it has a very healthy percentage of members.

Soka Gakkai, of course, began in Japan and it was usually the Japanese wives of foreign business men who left their native land to settle elsewhere, and who continued their practice of Nichiren Daishonin Buddhism in their new homes, combining with other adherents in order to maintain a sense of identity. They encouraged their husbands, and brought up their children, to chant, and it was in such ways that Soka Gakkai took hold in countries outside Japan. The exception was the incursion of Soka Gakkai into south-east Asia where it attracted ethnic Chinese communities in Hong Kong, Thailand, Malaysia and Singapore. Here, many of those attracted to Soka Gakkai were already Buddhists or had a Buddhist background.[28] Of the nine ethnically Japanese members of SGI-Wales and the Borders, all are female and all have been practising for a considerable length of time. Kyoko Gibson, who brought Nichiren Daishonin Buddhism to Wales, has been practising for 52 years, but following her closely is a housewife who has been practising for 51 years and a retired Japanese member (in the age range 61–70), who has been practising for 48 years. Another female of Japanese ethnicity has been practising for 34 years. Clearly, these are Japanese members whose roots are deep in Nichiren Daishonin Buddhism. There are a number of younger women of Japanese ethnicity who are maintaining the tradition. One was born into Nichiren Daishonin Buddhism and has been practising now for 41 years. Four women of Japanese ethnicity in the 30–40 age range have also been practising for 12, 20, 20 and 26 years respectively. Japanese members in Wales and the Borders, then, are longstanding adherents.

It might be expected that, since Soka Gakkai originated in Japan, has its overall centre at Tokyo, and has the towering, charismatic figure of Daisaku Ikeda at its head, that most adherents would have some contacts with Japan. Wilson and Dobbelaere found that most UK members did not even perceive Nichiren Daishonin Buddhism as being Japanese and were mainly not interested.[29] While a few of the Wales/Borders members have friends or family who are Japanese, or are familiar with Japan through travel, culture and the media, over two thirds (69%) have no contacts with Japan or anything Japanese.[30] In the USA, in contrast, Hammond and Machacek found that 47% of SGI-USA members had a prior interest in Japan or Japanese religion.[31]

Some countries felt the schism between SGI and the priesthood very keenly. Macioti, for example, found that this was the case in Italy.[32] The same can be said of places like Singapore.[33] In contrast, Métraux says of Canadian SGI: "The fact is that SGI Canada has been a lay movement from the start and that it has never had any direct connections with the Nichiren Shoshu priesthood."[34] The same may be said of SGI-Wales and the Borders, where the schism had little impact. Canadians, like the Welsh and Borders members, are not culturally used to having priests conduct their ceremonies. While, in many countries, there may be some opposition to customs such as segregation of the sexes or stereotypical genderized roles in the Lilac and Soka groups,[35] Ikeda's global policy has encouraged adaptation, a policy known as *zui ho bini*, so that members do not now have to kneel to chant, but may sit on chairs. One of the major reasons for the success of SGI anywhere is its accommodation to the host culture without departing from basic tenets of belief and praxis. Another is the extent of inter-personal and social engagement that does not necessitate looking too far beyond local, district and own nation to Japan, even if Tokyo remains a centre that unites all nations.

Occupations and qualifications of members

Studies of Nichiren Daishonin Buddhism throughout the world have demonstrated that, in comparison to the rest of the population, SGI has a very high percentage of middle-class, well-educated and professional men and women. This is certainly the case in the USA.[36] Japanese immigrants to other countries like the USA naturally found a sense of identity through grouping together with other members where possible. They were mostly housewives, and not well-qualified women who did not have professional occupations.[37] All this is now changed in the USA today, where American members are more likely to be better qualified and seekers of occupational status.[38] In places like Hong Kong and Malaysia, too, members are proving to be well-educated, professional and free-thinkers. Malaysia, in particular, has a high number of graduates amongst its members.[39] It is this kind of changed scene that is reflected more accurately in Wales/Borders SGI, though far more radically.

Self-realization and self-development alongside thorough engagement in society are some of the foundations on which Nichiren Daishonin Buddhists make successes of their lives. There is no exclusivity from society in SGI, and Bryan Wilson made the point that: "The impression of independent people standing on their own feet and expressing individual personality dispositions is altogether at variance with the blanket image of members of new religions (of 'sects' or 'cults' as the media often choose to call them), who are depicted as virtually brainwashed zombies."[40] Similarly, Wilson and Dobbelaere referring to the same study of UK members, comment on the "unusually high proportion of what might be termed independent people – people who were engaged in full-time education, or people who had, as they themselves would like to put it, taken responsibility for their own lives".[41] How, then do the occupational profiles of members in Wales and the Borders compare with these comments?

Overall, the number of SGI professional people is high – 54%,[42] and is a figure much higher than the 40% found in the comparable study done of the UK over a decade ago,[43] though the difference is sure to reflect the changing economic and social movements of society. What is very interesting is the percentage of members who are in the caring professions and in creative arts. In the general population of Wales as a whole, the number of people in the caring professions is about 16%.[44] With the exception of female SGI-Wales/Borders members who are in the 21–30 age range, in most other age ranges, the percentages of those in the caring professions are much higher:

21–30	females 10%	males 20%
31–40	females 27%	males 25%
41–50	females 32%	males 18%
51–60	females 38%	males 19%

Clearly, there is an increasing trend for women members, in particular, to take up the caring professions, and the overall percentage of members in caring professions is, at 23%, higher than the national average. It is also higher than that in the study of SGI-UK members over a decade ago.[45] It is in the case of creative arts, however, that the figures are most dramatic. We should remember that Daisaku Ikeda encourages the arts and cultural activities, and this seems to have spread into the ethos of the working ethic of SGI members. In Wales as a whole, the percentage of individuals in the world of art, acting, music, writing and the like is very small, a mere 0.7% of the whole working population.[46] Indeed, Martin Griffiths of the Welsh Office comments: "I'm afraid the figures for actors, entertainers, dancers, choreographers and chiropodists were below the publication threshold for the Annual Population Survey so we had to group them together."[47] In comparison to these low, or almost non-existent, national percentages, the percentages of SGI members in the artistic professions in Wales and the Borders are, according to age range and gender, as follows:

21–30	females 17%	males 25%
31–40	females 30%	males 17%
41–50	females 14%	males 18%
51–60	females 5%	males 19%

This is quite a remarkable contrast to the national trend in Wales with an average of 18% employed in creative arts as opposed to the national average of 0.7%, though it is lower than the 21% in the study undertaken by Wilson and Dobbelaere in the UK.[48]

Other characteristics concerning occupations deserve comment. There is a high percentage of students in the 21–30 age range (33% of women and 20% of men). The highest percentage of housewives occurs in the 31–40 age range (27%), perhaps indicative of the period in which women are raising young families. This percentage then declines in the 41–50 age range (25%), and further in the 51–60 age range (20%, including some retired women). Unlike UK members, however, there is no marked evidence of a high number of self-employed individuals. The current unemployment rate for Wales is 5.1% of the economically active population.[49] The unemployment rate amongst SGI-Wales and the Borders members is only 3%.

As far as qualifications are concerned, the statistics are impressive indeed. Like the emphasis on culture and performing arts in SGI, education is also at the core of its international profile. Looking at the statistics for Wales as a whole, the Welsh Assembly's most recent document on levels of highest qual-ification of working-age adults in Wales assesses qualifications in the light of the *National Qualification Framework* (NQF). The interest here lies in the highest levels. Just over 5% of the Welsh adults of working age have post-graduate degrees (NQF levels 7–8), and 26% have qualifications at levels 4–6. These latter levels include such qualifications as degrees, Higher National Certificate, Higher National Diploma, BTEC (Business and Technician Education Council Award), and appropriate qualifications in teaching and nursing.[50] In comparison to the 5% with higher degrees in Wales as a whole, 18% of the SGI-Wales/Borders members have a postgraduate degree. Similarly, in comparison to the 26% in Wales with levels 4–6 NQFs, 27% of members are graduates, with a further 23% possessing other professional qualifications equivalent to NQF levels 4–6. Only 29% of all members have no qualifications beyond school-leaving age; 67% of the members have qual-ifications at or above levels 4–6, and 44% are graduates or postgraduates. In each age range and irrespective of gender, over half of the respondents have professional qualifications. Outstanding is the 83% of women in the 41–50 age range who have professional qualifications.[51]

Such results are also markedly different from those of Wilson's and Dobbelaere's UK study of SGI members in 1994. Here, and even though they proved SGI members were more highly qualified than the national averages, only 12% had a degree, a further 4% a higher degree, and a further 7% a degree and a further professional qualification. Fifty per cent were, it seems, educated beyond the age of 18.[52] Wilson's comment concerning UK members that: "The proportion of the highly educated may well exceed that of any other sizable spiritual movement in Britain"[53] makes the scale of educational achievement amongst members of SGI-Wales and the Borders all the more remarkable. Hammond and Machacek found, in their USA study that "the education and occupation profile of SGI-USA members shows them to be in social positions with the greatest *potential* for upward mobility".[54] It would seem from the occupations and qualifications of SGI members from Wales and the Borders that occupational, professional and educational opportunities are being explored to the full. Members are overwhelmingly educational achievers.

Marital status of members

Wilson and Dobbelaere's study of UK-SGI members found that there were more single individuals than married, or living with a partner.[55] Hammond and Machacek also found that in Soka Gakkai in America, members are less likely to be married.[56] In Italy, too, according to Dobbelaere, members are mostly single, a smaller number are married or widowed and a greater percentage is divorced.[57] However, in SGI Wales/Borders, only 21% are single. In fact, most are either married[58] (38%, which is about the same percentage as in Wales as a whole), or living with a partner (a further 16%, again, close to the percentage for Wales as a whole.)[59] 18% are divorced, which is lower than the average divorces in Wales at 22%.[60]

Previous religious beliefs and knowledge

In general, most of the members of SGI-Wales and the Borders had some kind of previous religious beliefs, 77%, in fact.[61] Fifty-five per cent had belonged to the Christian faith, whether Anglican (most), Roman Catholic or Non-Conformist. Such figures are considerably in contrast to those gleaned from UK members over a decade ago, where only 19% belonged to the Christian religion prior to joining Nichiren Daishonin Buddhism.[62] Wilson thought UK members were *not* specifically religious or religious "seekers", but this does not seem to be the case with Wales/Borders members. Many expressed dissatisfaction with Christianity. Debra Blakemore from Caerphilly echoes the thoughts of many members when she says: "I grew up Christian and attended church until I was about fourteen. I stopped believing in God around the age of twenty. I was not looking for a new religion when I met the practice, but was looking for spirituality."

The issue of a "God" seems to have been a difficulty for many Wales and the Borders members, too. Chris Bradbury of Newtown in Powys writes, for example: "I had looked for 'something' in the Christian Faith. I got baptized at thirty-two, but soon lost interest. I couldn't come to terms with a superior being 'up there'". Christianity for many members did not fulfil expectations about life. In the words of James Rourke: "I was brought up as a Christian, but lost faith at the age of sixteen when questions I asked about the nature of life went unanswered, or were unsatisfactory." Similarly, Nick Dowsett from Dinas Cross in Pembrokeshire says: "I was christened and confirmed in the Church of England, but in adult years became more drawn to eastern philosophy as the idea of 'God' became increasingly fanciful and lacking in daily 'engagement'". Nick's term of "engagement" here, expresses rather well the ideas of many members who saw a gap between a theistic and anthropomorphic "God" and the daily lives and inner natures of human beings today.

Only 5% of members claim to have been previously atheist or agnostic, though many passed through periods of atheism or agnosticism while experimenting with other beliefs or, as is more often the case, transitionally between Christianity and the Buddhism of Nichiren Daishonin. Margaret Sadler of Chepstow left Christianity and, like about 9% of members, explored other aspects of Buddhism before finding Nichiren Daishonin Buddhism. She writes: "I was sent to a Methodist Sunday School when a child, but Christianity seemed to have too many contradictions and hypocrisies which, as I got older, turned me away from the Church of England. So I was an atheist, or at best, agnostic. I had read widely about Buddhism and the philosophy seemed to make sense to me, though most of the things I had read centred on Tibetan rather than Japanese Buddhism." What is evident from members' responses is that there was clearly not so much a predisposition to religious ideas as a healthy enquiry into both philosophical and pragmatic belief – perhaps more so the former – that informed their lives. Bridget Keehan of Barry writes: "I had been brought up (not strictly) in the Catholic faith but had not practised since my teens. I would describe myself as 'spiritually curious'". It is well to remember that we are dealing with a highly intelligent group of people, given their educational achievements noted above, and that there is likely to be a strong element of intelligent questioning of traditional and new values by members. Adrian Hardinges from Godrergraig, Swansea, puts this point admirably:

> I was baptised as a child into the Church of Wales and raised by my mum
> to believe in God. I remember going to Sunday School and midnight
> mass. As a teenager and during my twenties I began to question
> Christianity and found the belief of a God difficult to accept; it appeared
> to me like life's last fairy tale – the tooth fairy, Santa Claus, God . . .
> However, I still longed to have the answers to the big questions in life
> answered: why are we here? What is life all about? Where did we come
> from? The idea that a God created us and had influence on our lives was

unacceptable, and science, too, only seemed to provide some of the answers. During college and university, I seemed to find truth in the existential philosophies of Albert Camus and Sartre, even though their view of the world was slightly pessimistic. Buddhism seemed a natural progression, though all that seemed available was Tibetan Buddhism – some of which made sense to me while other things seemed nonsensical and steeped in ritual. The Buddhism of Nichiren Daishonin seemed to hold all the answers at last.

Adrian's words are interesting because, while it is quite usual for young people in their teens to question belief in God, most turn away entirely from religion. What seems to be the case with people like Adrian and other members of SGI-Wales/Borders, is that they continue to journey, continue to explore, and have arrived at Nichiren Daishonin Buddhism mainly through informed choice.

The overall picture is of members who have explored many different religions as well as Christianity. While only 9% had previously been members of other Buddhist movements, and so had reached Nichiren Daishonin Buddhism from outside Buddhist tradition, almost the same percentage had embraced other eastern religious beliefs. Sixteen per cent had tried a number of beliefs. Wilson's and Dobbelaere's study of SGI in the UK suggested that rejection of Christianity by members came about because of its acceptance of suffering as a saintly way of life and the trials of life as a test of worthiness.[63] "Christianity", wrote Wilson, "never assumed that human happiness in this life was in any sense a laudable or worthwhile goal."[64] Wilson thought that the climate of economic change in Britain left a vacuum ready to be filled by the spiritual humanism of Nichiren Daishonin Buddhism because it endorsed the pursuit of happiness through taking responsibility for one's own life. We shall see below how far such an idea is relevant to reasons why members of SGI-Wales and the Borders began to chant, but it has to be said here that in terms of previous religious belief, there seems to be a pre-existent healthy enquiry and testing of religious belief amongst the Welsh/Borders members.

Seventy-six per cent of the SGI-UK members studied by Wilson and Dobbelaere had previously belonged to no religious group at all,[65] contrasted with (and including self-designated atheists and agnostics) 22% of Welsh/Borders members. Similarly, the study done of Canadian members found that very few had previous strong religious beliefs.[66] Wales has always had strong religious traditions, even if they are somewhat in decline now but, given that Wilson and Dobbelaere's study was undertaken almost a decade and a half ago, the profile for previous religious beliefs of Welsh/Borders members is all the more remarkable. Hammond and Machacek's study of members in the USA is more in line with the Wales/Borders profile. They, too, found there were a negligible number of American members who were not previously religious.[67] They also discovered that many members had previously been interested in other new movements like Transcendental Meditation, Christian Science etc., so, they conclude that "conversion to Soka

Gakkai is best understood as giving expression to previously held values rather than a dramatic transformation of world-view. Those who convert are not randomly drawn from the population at large but come out of a sub-population who, metaphorically at least, 'demand' a religion reflecting transmodern values".[68]

However, our study of Welsh/Borders members does not suggest quite the same inference. Certainly, a number of the Welsh/Borders members have belonged to religious movements like New Age – and these movements range from Druidism, Sai Baba and Yoga to Wicca – but there are only one or two individuals who belonged to each. Taken altogether, these amount to 13%. From the comments of members like those above it would perhaps do them an injustice to say that they were drawn to Nichiren Daishonin Buddhism as some kind of collective "sub-population". In the 2001 census, the population of Wales was 2,903,085, 72% of whom declared themselves to be Christian (2,087, 242). Only 15% belonged to religions like Buddhism, Hinduism, Judaism, Islam and Sikhism or "any other" religion. Rather than being recruited from this "sub-population", it seems more likely, as previously stated, that we have a highly intelligent group of adherents here, which is informed by natural enquirers. In Hammond and Machacek's survey most American members said they were spiritual but not religious[69] whereas only 7 Wales/Borders members mention the word "spiritual", so there are certainly differences in religious outlook. Hammond and Machacek do, however, say that most American members were originally "curious" about Nichiren Daishonin Buddhism, and it seems that this a term that reflects the attitudes of Wales and the Borders members in their rather wide experience of religions before encountering Nichiren Daishonin Buddhism. This will become clearer when we look at their experience and knowledge of eastern religions prior to encounter with SGI.[70] It would be true to say, however, that, like their American counterparts, Welsh/Borders members are more "predisposed" to alternative religions.

From responses to the questionnaires concerning knowledge of eastern religions prior to encounter with Nichiren Daishonin Buddhism, 26% had no experience of them at all. Of the remainder, 43% had some knowledge of other forms of Buddhism such as Zen, the Friends of the Western Buddhist Order and Tibetan Buddhism. Twenty per cent had knowledge of Hinduism and 7% of Islam, including Sufism. Some had read about eastern religions (8%) and some were familiar with meditation (9%) and Yoga (7%). However, more had gained knowledge through the media like films and novels (7%) and travel (5%) than through academic study (4%). Given this lack of *academic* knowledge of other religions, the percentages here are quite pronounced, revealing a general interest in religions, particularly eastern religions. In our experience of teaching world religions in university courses over a quarter of a century, it would be unusual for students entering university wishing to specialize in Religious Studies to have such a *wide* knowledge of world religions. None of our students in the University of Wales, for example, knew anything of Taoism before beginning the university course, yet some of the Wales/Borders members (5%) had knowledge of Taoism. These findings are quite the opposite to those of Helen Waterhouse's study of SGI members in Bath: "All the local members to whom I have spoken express a respect for other religious paths although none of them claims to have much academic or experiential knowledge of any except for the past experience of several members of the Christian churches in which they were brought up."[71] Her finding, too, that: "There is a lack of accurate knowledge about other schools of Buddhism which members readily acknowledge", is not conspicuous in Wales/Borders members, particularly since 43% of them claimed such knowledge. Wilson and Dobbelaere found that only 20% of SGI-UK members had some knowledge of eastern religions and 19% had knowledge of religions like Hinduism, or even Taoism:[72] the evidence from Wales and the Borders members suggests a much wider knowledge.

What seems to be evident, then, is a marked interest in eastern religions in particular, enough to suggest that Wales/Borders members are quite well-informed about eastern religious beliefs: many had knowledge of more than one eastern religion. Actual attitudes of members to other religions were examined in the previous chapter, CHAPTER THREE, where it was found that members were overwhelmingly tolerant of religions outside Nichiren Daishonin Buddhism. From the evidence of CHAPTER THREE, it was found that joining SGI increased respect for other beliefs – something which many members may already have had. Thus, as an anonymous member says regarding familiarity with eastern religions before encountering Nichiren Daishonin Buddhism: "I had basic knowledge of religions; however, since practising [Nichiren Daishonin Buddhism], my knowledge and understanding of other religions has increased." While no member described him or her self as a "seeker", they might well be described as "explorers" with the same kind of openness to alternative religions that Hammond and Machacek found in their American study.[73] Hammond and Machacek found that many (38%) had experienced Buddhism or other eastern religions before converting to Nichiren Daishonin Buddhism, many of whom (25%) had been very interested in eastern religion and philosophy. Like Wales and the Borders members, they were open to alternative religions.[74]

When asked if they were members of SGI *and* another religion,[75] four members still retain other beliefs (1 Quaker, 1 Sufi, 1 "non-Buddhist" and 1 Christian). Most suggest that Nichiren Daishonin Buddhism is a fulfilling faith. Thus, Stephanie Bond of Lampeter replies: "No, not now. At first I found it hard to let go of my other practices, but after studying Nichiren Daishonin's writings, I realized all the answers I was looking for were there." Similarly, Carol Brown from Swansea writes: "Just Nichiren Buddhist: it's a very pure and complete teaching that I don't want to water down or mix up with anything else." Jo Ogilvie is definitive in stating "No: if I were, I would not be practising correctly," and Mark Radcliffe makes the same point: "To practise another religion means one is not practising Nichiren Daishonin's

Buddhism properly!" In short, most members would agree with James Rourke, who says: "The philosophy and practice of Nichiren Daishonin Buddhism is complete and so, no, I don't practise anything else in addition." Of those who claim some affiliation to another faith, Suzanne Jenkinson makes the very honest admission: "It's difficult to answer this because, as you must know, Nichiren Daishonin Buddhism states that all other religions are regarded as provisional teachings, which suggests I am a Nichiren Daishonin Buddhist. However, I was confirmed into the Christian faith as late as *ca.* 1977/78 and still celebrate Christmas!" Suzanne's comments reflect what must be the official position more than any other, but at the same time reflect the fact that *most* members, right across the board, still celebrate Christmas, so Suzanne can relax about any misgivings she may have.

Absolutely no pressure is placed on any member with the intention of inhibiting engagement in other faiths, nor is any vow of commitment expected prior to, or at, a *Gohonzon* receiving ceremony. Indeed, the only preparation for becoming a member of SGI and receiving a *Gohonzon* is the individual's own chanting. In Les Gibson's words: "We don't insist on people abandoning other faiths when they receive *Gohonzon*, though we would encourage it simply because it can cause a lot of mental confusion. The only preparation they receive is through their own *daimoku*, and it is explained that this is a commitment for life."[76] In the light of these words, it is all the more remarkable that the majority of members, of their own volition, find Nichiren Daishonin Buddhism sufficiently complete in itself not to need other religions.

Encounter, engagement and commitment

First encounters with Nichiren Daishonin Buddhism[77]

Most of the Wales and the Borders members first encountered Nichiren Daishonin Buddhism through a friend or friends (38%), or acquaintances (12%).[78] Some first became acquainted through someone at work, a colleague or a fellow student (14%). Taken together, then, it seems that friends, acquaintances and the work or student environments are the means of first encounter by the majority, 64%, of the members – a fact reflected in studies elsewhere.[79] Only 13% encountered Nichiren Daishonin Buddhism through family members. The incidents of *shakubuku* are much vaguer, though being introduced to Nichiren Daishonin Buddhism through a therapist, a teacher, a patient or the postman, might amount to *shakubuku*, but such cases are few (5%), and the term itself is rarely mentioned. Very few (4%) claim their first encounter to have been via the media or an advertisement. Some encounters can be quite unusual. James Rourke from Cardiff writes of his first introduction to Nichiren Daishonin Buddhism: "In a London restaurant, my partner and I were having a heated political debate when the wine waiter commented: 'Everyone wants change, the question is how?' A good question!"

Reasons for initial attraction

One reason for initial attraction (21% of members) to Nichiren Daishonin Buddhism was the observation of the vibrant, positive and joyful character of practitioners who were first encountered. Their genuine nature, respect and enthusiasm were something to be admired and emulated. In the words of Carol Brown from Swansea: "I was attracted by the way the person who introduced me led his life . . . the way he was. I felt that whatever he was in to must be good for him to be the way he was." Carol remains attracted because she finds the practice faultless: "I am constantly amazed at how great it is and how I keep learning more and more how to be deeply happy." Nicky Delgado from Cardiff says:

> I was first attracted by how genuinely caring and supportive people were. I thought, 'I want some of that'. I had experienced various growth methods, but saw this as the full bottle. . . In the first five to seven years, I tried to see if there was a crack in the practice, in which case it would be flawed. I finally gave up the search for the non-existent crack. I still tell others, if you find something better let me know and I will examine it. But no one has returned with a suitable answer, perhaps because this Buddhism is the real thing.

Liz Jenkins from Goodwick in Pembrokeshire was at an outward bound field-study centre when she first encountered Nichiren Daishonin Buddhists. Liz writes: "Members on the summer course at Morriston seemed different to any other group – happier and more open with each other, so I had to find out why. What did they have that other people did not? They were not pushy, and I had to summon the courage to ask about the practice."

Attraction to Nichiren Daishonin Buddhism because of the quality of lives of its members was one reason why Canadians joined SGI,[80] but, while clearly an important factor, it is not the main reason for attraction for Wales/Borders members. Indeed, the percentage of members attracted through admiration of SGI individuals is much lower (21%) than the 37% given by Wilson and Dobbelaere in their study of UK members,[81] and the 52% in the study of USA members.[82] What, then, is the major factor that attracted Wales and the Borders members? It has much more to do with the *philosophy* of Nichiren Daishonin Buddhism than tangible outward indicators. Being attracted to the philosophy is sometimes cited alongside respect for the character of the members, but more often is the reason for attraction *per se*, and this is a unique characteristic in comparison to results in other studies. Some examples from the respondents will make this clear.

Debra Blakemore from Senghenydd combines both praise of the adherents she first met and the consonance of ideas in Nichiren Daishonin Buddhism with her own as what attracted her: "It was amazing to find a group of people who all had the same thoughts/ideas that I had already concluded by myself.

I was also attracted by the people, who were all in an amazing life force and had amazing vibrancy. I remain attracted because of my progress as an individual, which is proof of the power of practise. The more I read/study, the more I am attracted because it fits so much of what I already believe and understand." Like Debra, who found the beliefs of Nichiren Daishonin Buddhism complementary to her own, many other members were attracted by its philosophy because it seemed packed with common sense, and to be reasoned and logical. In fact, 31% were attracted by the teachings. Adrienne O'Sullivan from Cardiff writes: "It has always answered my questions about life and death. It makes common sense and has reason in it. I feel happy and strong and motivated when I practise and the people that practise are all wonderful, interesting and diverse. I continue to practise because it works for me, it gives me a sense of connectedness, and I have a practical tool to move my life forward. What I love most is the non-judgemental tenets of Buddhism and its strict laws of cause and effect." David Moy from Bridgend says, too: "The philosophy or theory of Buddhism itself first attracted me as it seemed so logical and in line with reason. I remain committed because it generally gives me a positive outlook on my life and I feel a better person."

The humanistic aspect of Nichiren Daishonin Buddhism was what attracted some. Thus, Roger Langford sensitively responds: "I saw it as the ultimate expression of humanity, as a real humanism. It is honest and realistic about human nature and has compassion at its core. It seems a commonality amongst all things. This still attracts me." Similarly, Richie Turner says: "I have always held humanistic views. Nichiren Daishonin Buddhism corrects many perceived errors in Buddhism, such as the idea that only men can reach *nirvana*! Taking total personal responsibility for my actions, recognizing everyone's Buddhahood, and realizing through this practice that we can achieve world peace are what attracts me."

Nick Sherwood from Westhope in Herefordshire is one of a number of members who felt comfortable and at home with Nichiren Daishonin Buddhism from the beginning. Nick writes: "I had decided to reject Christianity after some bad experiences with 'Christians'. I had a feeling Buddhism was interesting but it always seemed too complex, almost 'antiquarian'. I met someone in Cardiff and just decided to try Nichiren – it immediately made sense to me in a number of ways. I liked the people as well as the beliefs." A few members reiterated the instant attraction to Nichiren Daishonin Buddhism. Robert Cook from Pontfaen describes a dramatic reaction to chanting: "I was not attracted at all but when I first chanted I knew (like a memory) that this was the fundamental truth of life. I experienced tremendous joy and personal power and meaning."

In the same sensitive vein, Rose York from Lampeter writes: "I chanted one evening and felt and experienced a revelation. This was one reason that made me carry on, and though in the first six months there were days when I didn't chant, I always went back, and have seen my life change in its scope, breadth and depth; so it would be stupid not to carry on!" Like Robert Cook's experience of a "memory", Amy Milton from Newport describes experiencing the same kind of sensation when she began to chant: "I believe in my heart that I did this practice before because when I read the card for the very first time, I felt that I was being re-introduced, not introduced! So, I think that I will always remain attracted to it until I die because it feels right and is so natural to me, to my life and for my family. It has brought growth, health and joy to my life and to others and nothing will ever change that. It's constant, even when you feel low; other people see your high life-state." Nichiren Daishonin Buddhism seemed to be the right path for Auriole Herriott, from Pembrokeshire too: "I found a newspaper article and was instantly drawn to find out more. The strange thing was that afterwards, I kept coming across many more things that pointed to this practice." Jenny Nicholson from Fishguard in Pembrokeshire also found that something seemed to take place immediately she started chanting: "It is hard to express. My first prayer was for my brother. I had just been given a card with *Nam-myoho-renge-kyo* on it, so I tried it. I felt an immediate change in myself. My brother's life has changed for the better (over time), but, mostly, my heart feels it to be right."

Apart from feeling at home with the practice, a few members found that Nichiren Daishonin Buddhism confirmed and articulated some of their own beliefs and that it was this, also more philosophical, factor that attracted them. So Jane Grayer from Market Town comments: "The more I read, the more I found that the ideas of Buddhism tied in with the ideas I had but in greater depth. I remain attracted because I can see the effect it has on my life and other people's lives. I believe I can affect everything." For Hannah Chivers: "It was a way of explaining what life is all about that matched with what I thought." Those who were attracted primarily by the beliefs feel that Nichiren Daishonin Buddhism answered their questions about life. "It seemed to put life into perspective", writes Jill Sutton of Drefach. "It gave me answers about how life and relationships work and illustrated a pathway to overcome problems. Even though happiness may not happen overnight, there is a course of action. There is not a higher being to answer all your problems; it is down to me. This is what attracts me; the answers are in my hands and heart." A few members say they were attracted by Daisaku Ikeda's teachings, like Jenn Carter from Whitland, who writes: "I admired the things Daisaku Ikeda was doing – especially his peace work. I thought, here, at last, is someone I would like to have as a mentor."

From their responses above, the reason why many of the members of Wales and the Borders remain committed to Nichiren Daishonin Buddhism is because of the changes practice has made in their lives. Twenty-two per cent of members found this to be the attraction of Nichiren Daishonin Buddhism in the first place, mainly the fact that one has to take responsibility for one's own life, as Jill Sutton said, above. Thus, Jodie Allinson from Grangetown, Cardiff was attracted primarily "by the idea that I am totally responsible for my life and that I can impact on *anything*. The more I study the philosophy, the more I support it. I also like the community aspect of it – being so connected to other people and supporting each other in our practice. And I like the chanting! It sounds and feels beautiful!" For Mairead Knell from Baschurch, also, the idea of individual responsibility and its humanist philosophy were attractive. She writes: "It's very humanist – no rules or religion. It's more of a philosophy than a religion. I'm attracted by the fact that we and no one else are responsible for our actions, for the way things are. It's easy to blame others, but it's only us that can change things." Liz Court from Cardiff echoes the same point. She, too, was attracted by "the focus on taking responsibility for your own life", but found "the belief that we can all ultimately be happy, and that we can start from this moment on", attractive.

Liz's phrase, "from this moment on", is important because mistakes of the past, guilty consciences and negative baggage are overridden by the positivity of responsible change in the present, *"from this moment on"*. Nicky Delgado points out that there are "no morals, rules or regulations in Nichiren Daishonin Buddhism. Wisdom brings continuing guidance and guidelines to find your own based on continuing faith. As we are all Buddhas, we possess the internal knowledge to create individual morals in accordance with Life: Life is Buddhism, Buddhism is Life." Sally Thomas from Swansea says: "I don't have to rely on others to reveal my Buddhahood. Nichiren Daishonin says we all have Buddhahood. I feel better, more grounded and content the more chanting I do. I feel in control of my destiny." Jane Timmins of Glanaman, too, was attracted by the same idea of self-responsibility, the idea "that we are each solely responsible for our own lives and reactions and that we can make a difference positively, however small." Jane was also attracted by the point that "people who had practised for a long time were deeply contented and calm whatever life threw at them." Deeper self-awareness continues to attract Tessa Waite from Brecon, who writes with considerable beauty: "It enabled me to see a deeper, richer part of myself, an expansive self. This is why I continue to practise, to deepen, enrich and expand my inner life and connect to the universe around and in me." And from a true Buddhist perspective, Peter Baker-Jones of Solva says he was attracted and continues to be attracted because: "It gives you the tools to change your life. The journey to the originally inherent Buddha within is the only worthwhile endeavour in life. All else is constant change or non-substantial. Ego-driven goals do not bring lasting happiness on their attainment."

The idea of change beginning with the individual, that is to say, change of oneself *and* concomitant change in one's environment is clearly important for Wales and the Borders members and the concept comes up again and again in the context of responses to other questions posed on the questionnaire. The reasons why there is such a congruence between self-change and the environment will be left to CHAPTER SEVEN, when the whole philosophy underpinning Nichiren Daishonin Buddhism is examined, but if we cast our minds back to the previous chapter, CHAPTER THREE, and the "human revolution", that term is all about creating change and transformation in the self, creating, what Peter Baker-Jones above described as "the tools to change your life".

A few, like Ilona Bailey, mention that they found the idea of changing their *karma* attractive: "I liked the fact that Nichiren Daishonin Buddhism gave me the means to directly challenge my *karma* (or, causes that I have made and repeated in the past that had the effect of making me suffer). *Karma* runs deep, so I continue to chant to change "poison into medicine". Sharing her very personal experiences, in the context of *karma*, Jo Ogilvie says she was attracted to Nichiren Daishonin Buddhism because: "I saw that there were like-minded people. It also answered the questions as to why I had a handicapped child, why her *karma* was to suffer in this lifetime, but why I had good fortune to meet this practice and aide her to change her *karma*."

About 12% of respondents focused on the chanting itself as the reason why they were attracted to Nichiren Daishonin Buddhism, some because it was a means to happiness, and some because it was a means for prayers to be answered – even for quite mundane things at the start. An anonymous respondent says: "I was attracted because I thought I could chant for anything and I would become rich. I am no richer, but some of my prayers have been answered along the way." Others were attracted because they saw chanting as a means to promote world peace and harmony. It was a point particularly pertinent to Desmond Connell, in his first encounter with chanting: "The first meeting I went to there were people there from all over the world chanting for peace in Ireland (my country of birth) and South Africa. My aim is world peace." Others were attracted because they loved the sound of the chanting, like an anonymous woman, who lists this as one of the reasons why she was attracted. Chanting *per se* is not usually the only reason why people were attracted, but one of the reasons. Another anonymous woman puts the point graphically when she writes that she was attracted because of: "Initially the character and general 'amazingness' of a woman . . . but I had no idea she was a Buddhist. Then, the SOUND of chanting – which was like 'positive machine-gun fire'. When I asked about it, the whole concept made sense to me. I am still attracted because I see and feel the benefits to myself and others, and have (now) complete confidence and trust in the SGI."

Surprisingly, only six members were attracted to Nichiren Daishonin Buddhism because they believed chanting worked. Antony Owen Hicks from Cardiff was one such individual. He writes: "I was attracted to Buddhism, though not specifically Nichiren Buddhism. But when I first tried chanting, the results were immediate, so I kept going to see if it kept working. I remain attracted because of the results I have achieved, because of the examples of other members, and in particular, because of Daisaku Ikeda." Of course, members are hardly likely to continue if they do not perceive any benefits from the practice. Moreover, as Frances Brett points out, Nichiren Daishonin Buddhism "works *within* society and does not require separation from society". That was one reason that attracted her. Chanting is easy to do, is personal, practical, can be related to everyday problems and one's family and yet is dynamic and profound. Stephen Millson of Abergavenny says he was attracted because: "It was a way to personally practise, a route to enlightenment and happiness based on something solid in you, rather than transient and external. It was simple to do, was not corrupted by priests or religious leaders for their own glorification. It suits my lifestyle and I can practise anywhere." Phil Luffman of Usk and Wye district gives three reasons why he was attracted: "1. Initially, it fitted with my beliefs for a more peaceful, loving, tolerant world. 2. It is pro-active Buddhism, not retreat, withdrawn-from-life Buddhism. 3. It is revolutionary, but non-violent: few organizations can maintain this fine balance." Phil's words demonstrate the pragmatism of chanting as being *engaged* in life and society.

Out of all the respondents from Wales and the Borders, only 11% said they were attracted because they were in an unhappy time of their lives – break-up with a partner, depression, illness, death of someone close, fear, or because they were spiritually adrift. Douglas Angus, for example, writes: "My life was in a state of decline. I was in pain and nothing was working. I read some wise words from Nichiren Daishonin and tried chanting, and things keep on improving." From the responses of members it seems it does not matter at what point an individual is in life, positive outcomes reinforce the practice. Liz Mitchell from Cardiff says:" I have been depressed most of my life and made wrong choices often. I heard an experience at an introductory meeting, together with a friend, who *shakubukued* me, and promised me that things would change with *Nam-myoho-renge-kyo* and she gave me a few examples of how much changed for her." Liz continues to be committed to Nichiren Daishonin Buddhism because, she says: "I'm much happier while chanting, more focused; things fall into place easier, my mind is clearer. All around me, things are changing." These reasons for attraction reflect members' views in south-east Asia (Malaysia, Singapore and Hong Kong) where, apart from the main attraction through family members, the other major reasons were because of personal or family illness, lack of direction in life, financial problems and family disharmony.[83] In Italy, too, 80% of members had personal problems before they joined Soka Gakkai.[84]

It is interesting that Liz is the only individual that mentions *shakubuku* in the context of initial attraction to Nichiren Daishonin Buddhism. As a process, in even a mild, form it seems unnecessary on the whole, at least from the evidence of Wales/Borders members. They were much more attracted by the rational beliefs of Nichiren Daishonin Buddhism, by the personal example of those SGI people they met, and by the idea of taking responsibility for their own lives. Finally, in this section, we can include Rob Woodfall's reason for being attracted to SGI: "I fell in love with one of the members!"

The reasons Wales and the Borders members put forward for being attracted to Nichiren Daishonin Buddhism are, then, proportionally different to those of members in other countries. In Canada, for example, *psychological* reasons are very prominent – the need to live a more meaningful life despite economically advantaged living, and the need for better relationships with others.[85] In the study of UK members,[86] hardly any mention is made of the *philosophical* attraction of Nichiren Daishonin Buddhism as a viable rationale for life. It is surprising that Wales/Borders members were attracted so much by philosophical tenets and ideas of Nichiren Daishonin Buddhism when these hardly feature in other countries. Perhaps the reason is, again, due to the explorative, enquiring minds of a higher than average intelligence amongst members. The philosophy of Nichiren Daishonin Buddhism is, therefore, clearly critical to membership and will warrant an independent chapter, CHAPTER SEVEN, later in this book.

Reasons for remaining committed

So what about commitment? Why is it that individuals remain in SGI? Obviously, there must be perceived *benefits* for each member to remain attracted, and some of these reasons have been seen above. While a number of respondents simply state that *it works* (9%), a further 50% give ways in which it is felt to do so. Put basically, David Harris from Barry, who was originally attracted by Ikeda's book *The Human Revolution* writes: "It works – I'm no fool – if it didn't work, I'd stop!" Many say they are happier and that there is more joy in their lives. Importantly, the process is ongoing, so that individuals continue to improve. Adherents remain committed because the practice is thought to be life-supporting and protective and because of the benefits to the self. Josie Cousens from Cardiff finds that: "It seems a profoundly humanistic faith. It offers a mode of organizing together as people and of conducting supportive relationships and of bringing out the best in oneself and others, which accords with my desires and beliefs. It does not impose modes of behaviour or rules. It is built on trust in each person."

Members say the practice gives vitality, confidence, strength, maturity, wisdom, positivity and optimism, hope, a purpose in life, and is empowering. As Lynette Rowlands from Cardiff says: "I like me when I practise," and Edward Thomas from Swansea, who finds that the philosophy of Nichiren Daishonin Buddhism "fitted with what I had come to regard as my way of looking at the world", writes, too: "It still does, plus it enables me to cope with what life throws at me." Elissa Lewis, also from Cardiff, is committed partly because she is able to go some way to solving that old Buddhist and eastern problem of controlling the mind: "I'm a better person now", she writes "I'm excited about the possibility of each new day. I'm in control of my mind in a way I never used to be. I'm not a victim of circumstances."

Because the results of practising are ongoing, a process of change is evident in what these adherents say – change in the way life is lived, of *karma*, of individual character – it facilitates a growing process. Jonathan Davies puts this well when he says: "I needed to find a way of dealing with life, of overcoming the fear within. Every day, I am grateful for it saving my life. Every day, it gives me strength, wisdom and reason to grow." Such an idea of personal growth and evolution is reiterated by Kirsty Foster, of Roath, Lakeside, Penylan district. She writes: "I was attracted by the idea of being enabled to create your own change for happiness in your life. I am a strong character who likes challenge, to learn and continue to develop, so this Buddhism suits me well!"

Some (7%) claim the communal support within SGI to be the reason why they remain committed. While initially attracted by the chanting, Suzanne Jenkinson from Cardiff says: "The social interaction, and the friendship that grows from a united desire for a better world now and for future generations, sustained the initial attraction." Ann Shabbaz from Cardiff also likes the communal nature of SGI. She was sceptical and wary of religion at first, but now writes: "I liked the basic principle of doing your best, the non-judgemental people, the wide age range, wide range of ability, of colour, and gay and lesbian people, and that is why I stay – it's diverse! Many in body, one in mind." The communal aspect of SGI-Wales and the Borders, is clearly critical to Lillah Cottier, now in her nineties, and the oldest member in Wales: "I was going through a bad patch, one of my daughters had died. Buddhism opened a door for me. I have met some nice friends who have cared for me, and at my time of life I would be lonely without them. I feel I am getting back some of what I have put in over the years."

Others (11%) remain attracted because of the focus Nichiren Daishonin Buddhism has on societal and global issues and the possibility of creating change in such spheres as well as the life-changing possibilities for their individual lives. In Katherine Kingston from Newport's words: "I was looking for a daily practice – something like meditation – to relax and improve my concentration. I was also unemployed and was told I could chant for a job. I liked the aspect of working towards world peace and the belief that every single person has massive potential and can bring out their Buddha-nature. I continue to practise because it works very strongly as a positive force in my life." Louise Squire from Lampeter also incorporates a wider focus in her commitment:

> Initially, I was attracted by the idea that I could take part in the world I saw around me and make a difference, and that change was possible. Why I remain attracted is for the same reasons, plus the ongoing human revolution, which I feel is immensely important. And [I remain attracted] because the practice is a 'tool' that is useable by anyone – with positive benefits to them and others. I have studied many paths and I believe this one is very valuable in today's world.

Terence Murphy of Treharris says: "I watched my wife join SGI and measured SGI members' words against their actions for over two years before I joined. I remain a member because I know how important the ideas of SGI are for the future of the world."

As was noted above, there is a high percentage of members who were attracted by the philosophy and beliefs of Nichiren Daishonin Buddhism, particularly the lack of rules and regulations, and this is what attracted Liz Moulson from Cardigan initially. Liz gives a very full account of her first attraction to Nichiren Daishonin Buddhism and the eventual acceptance of it after asking two basic questions of a member – questions that anyone newly interested in Nichiren Daishonin Buddhism might also want to ask:

> I asked what rules and regulations there were as I am quite a free spirit. I was told there were none. However, by doing a regular practice, people developed their own wisdom as to how to direct their lives. This both surprised and appealed to me. I then asked how much money was asked for. I was told no money was demanded. This allayed my fears about joining a money-grabbing organization. My ex-husband also decided to join me, which was a huge bonus, and I shall be forever grateful to him. When I started attending meetings, whether large or small, I gained even more trust in SGI. It comprised of a broad cross section of people. Everyone seemed friendly and had vibrancy about them. Twenty-six years later, I still feel this way, and have made wonderful friends. For me, SGI has more than lived up to the ideals and hopes for creating a better world, which I had in my youth.

The reasoned beliefs, common-sense views, profound but accessible philosophy, humanism and flexibility and adaptability of Nichiren Daishonin Buddhism are the reasons why some have committed themselves to the practice. But while the philosophical ideas attracted so many in the first place, they are by no means the reasons why people stay committed. In fact only about 8% give the teachings as the reason for commitment. And only 6% give the desire to make a difference in society and the world as their reason. The high percentage of people who were attracted to Nichiren Daishonin Buddhism by the vibrant characters of those members with whom they first came into contact, hardly mention such a factor as the reason why they remain committed – a factor evident also in the UK study.[87] It is the more immediate *effects*, the *pragmatic outcomes* and *self-change*, which are the major reasons for commitment, a point also reflected in the wider UK study,[88] though the motivating "intellectual considerations" noted for *commitment* by Wilson and Dobbelaere seem to be the reason for *attraction* amongst members in Wales and the Borders. In conclusion, members seem to find Nichiren Daishonin Buddhism attractive for a variety of reasons, perhaps because it is intended to be a complete philosophy and practice. As Hideko Nakatani from Bridgend says: "I thought Soka Gakkai's way of having regular meetings and of encouraging each other, was good, and then, I was attracted by the teaching. This religion contains everything we need as religion – good organization, ease of practice and sound philosophy." According to all the members, once practice begins and outcomes are increasingly evident, evidence of the efficacy of the practice speaks for itself.

Reactions of families and friends

The reaction of family, friends and associates to each member's affiliation to Nichiren Daishonin Buddhism[89] seems, with not too many exceptions, to be positive – anything from passive acceptance to being very supportive. Most respondents give a mixture of responses they had had from people. However, the term mostly used is "supportive" (26%), also "very supportive" (16%), and "respectful" (20%), but also "interested" (22%). A few (13%) had positive reactions because of the noticeably positive changes that had taken place in their lives. Hope Dowsett from Dinas Cross, who is in her teens, says: "I get fairly good reactions from most people. My relatives already know quite a lot about Buddhism and my friends ask me lots of questions about it." Again, it is often the good example of a vibrant and well-balanced individual that elicits support and respect from those outside the movement: "I think they respond to who I am, rather than what I believe or practise", says Louise Squire of Lampeter. "If I receive any negative reactions, then I use my practice to help me tackle them with wisdom, courage and compassion. Nobody has ever given a negative response to my practice."

One reason for acceptance of the practice by non-members is that, apart from chanting, members live very ordinary existences. Liz Moulson puts this point across very well when she writes:

> Initially, people are a bit wary, so I often focus on trust and friendship. I think people have often been surprised at how normal I am and how much I enjoy life. I love socializing, walking, music, including live music, eating out with friends and family, films, gardening and reading. My family and friends are incredibly supportive, even though my parents are Catholic. I get on very well with the people in my local community. Even though I am a Buddhist-style mother, I feel they trust and respect me through observing my behaviour and attitude. . . I feel that it is a part of my function or mission to demonstrate to people that practising Nichiren Buddhism is about playing an active part within society rather than escaping from it and that it's possible to become happy in a way that's not dependent on circumstances alone.

Some members note the initial scepticism of people that is then followed by positive interest and support. An anonymous writer says: "They were initially sceptical – my parents, certainly – with anxiety and concern. Now, most of my friends have become Buddhists. My mother requested a Buddhist funeral, my partner has begun to practise and many people seek my point of view or encouragement." The change from scepticism to support is reflected in the responses of many members. Thus, James Donson from Cardiff writes: "My friends are supportive and most are interested. Many see positive changes in me. Some take the mickey, but in good jest. My parents and my brother are very supportive – Mum and brother have chanted. My mother often tells me to chant when I go to her with problems!" Nick Dowsett finds people very supportive, even though "some may challenge my commitment to the SGI and the practice, believing it takes too much of my time and energy, but they accept that it gives meaning to my life."

A few members find that they are able to offer advice to others or are a positive influence when others have problems and that this is another reason why their practice is accepted. "My family and friends are very supportive", writes James Rourke from Cardiff "and often come to me with their problems. I offer them my Buddhist understanding of the situation – but without mentioning Buddhism." Elissa Lewis, also from Cardiff, says her friends, family and associates react positively: "They often tell me I bring calm to difficult situations and respect everyone". Elissa warmly adds in parentheses: "It's hard graft!" Clearly, such responses are good examples of respondents' *engagement* in daily life, and it is this engagement, alongside positivity of personality, which ultimately shifts scepticism to positive support. Sriram Vaidyanathan from Newport certainly holds such a view: "I always believe that one cannot progress in life without constantly communicating with others. Because of this attitude, most of my family, friends, relatives and associates view this Buddhism, and my practice, in a very positive manner."

On the other side of the coin, some members have encountered negative attitudes. Gillian Gregory from Shrewsbury says: "Most of them respect my choice and are curious, but so far, are not rushing to join. Some are very sceptical and quite rude at times." Gillian's response is a good example of a number of others who have had more mixed reactions. Katherine Kingston from Newport notes the same mixed, though changing, response: "My parents find it difficult but are starting to understand more. Friends and associates generally are very interested and respectful even though they may find it strange. Most of my friends have seen evidence of the practice working in my life." Nichiren Daishonin Buddhism is far removed from being a "cult", but it is perhaps natural for parents to show some concern about something they do not initially know anything about. When life proceeds normally, when positive attitudes to life develop, and where there are advantageous changes in character, the practice is viewed with a lot less suspicion by families. This seems to be the trend of many respondents' experiences. So Sally Thomas from Swansea says: "At first they were waiting for the orange robes! Now they say we have a happy glow and make comments like, 'You're always so nice' and show some interest in what we do." Amy Milton from Newport gives a warm account of her experience:

> At first, I think that my family thought I was mad, especially when my mum tried to do *gongyo* and burst into tears: it was unusual for her, but that was early on in my practice. Now they know that it is part of me. We were at a gathering, meeting family that we had never seen before, and a week later my dad said that the way me and my sister were made

my parents very proud. I sang for all of them as well, which, years ago, would have been a no no! So their relationship with the practice has changed, hopefully because of my behaviour and I hope to have at least my sister getting a *Gohonzon* at some point next year – who knows, even this year.

There is a good percentage (41%) of negative comments, though they are usually contained in those members' responses who find there are mixed reactions to their practice. Apart from negative reactions to begin with, some friends, family and associates have reservations about Buddhism, are nervous and wary of it, or are afraid they would be targeted to become involved. Tim Galloway from Blaina says people "smile, nod, smile", obviously with some concern! Harry McIver from Cardiff says that he finds people are "generally very supportive and some are more interested", though he adds: "Occasionally it's a case of have a few drinks and start arguing – something I now refuse to do." But while such negative responses exist, they are in the minority and, like Harry, few have experienced such negativity devoid of some kind of support. When compared with their American counterparts, 60% of whom had negative responses from family and friends to their practice,[90] members from Wales and the Borders have very positive feedback.

Chanting and membership

The time between the first encounter with Nichiren Daishonin Buddhism and actually beginning to chant[91] varies only slightly between women and men. At least two-thirds of the women and 60% of the men began to chant on their first encounter or a short time afterwards. Of those who took longer than a year, women were more reticent (39%) than men (30%). [92]A few individuals say that they stopped and started chanting, perhaps several times. Judith James from Cardiff, for example, says: "I began chanting in 1986 and stopped the same year, then started and stopped a few times after that. I began in earnest on 1 January 1997." As to the interim period between chanting and receiving a *Gohonzon*, thus taking up membership of SGI-Wales and the Borders,[93] it is men who are the quicker to do so. Thirty-three per cent of women became members of SGI and received their *Gohonzon* within a year of beginning to chant compared with as many as 46% of the men. For both genders, a further 22% became members after twelve months had elapsed and it seems that, on average, one year after first chanting is the time when most take up membership. Sometimes, an individual is abroad when introduced to the practice. David Harris from Barry, for example, says: "I met the practice in Tokyo and read for a year about Buddhism. Whilst in Tokyo, non-Japanese were advised to wait at least six months to practise properly [before receiving the *Gohonzon*]. Also, many people were only in Tokyo temporarily and it was wiser to receive it in their home countries."

While the majority of members (62%) have been chanting for six or more years, the remainder (38%) have only been chanting between one and five years, indicating a very healthy influx of new members and growth of the Wales/Borders area in recent years, even more so since, of these, 15% have been chanting for just one or two years. Many individuals in SGI Wales/Borders – almost a third, in fact – have another member of their family who is also an SGI member, and about the same number have individuals in their family who chant, but who are not members. A third of the men actually live in the same household as another SGI member,[94] though fewer of the women do.[95] Far more men than women[96] have a partner or spouse who practises. As with the study of Canadian members, the research here shows that most members are the only practitioners in a household.[97] In the UK, study,[98] like Welsh/Borders members, the majority (54% in both cases) had no one in the family practising, but in both cases this still indicates a good percentage of people practising with other members of the household or wider family.

General attitudes

In CHAPTER THREE, we saw how SGI-Wales and the Borders members were very concerned about human rights and environmental issues, seeing the goal of personal human revolution as the first step in the means to change the environment and, indeed, the world. Here, in this chapter, such general views are extended to a few other areas that will exemplify the attitudes of members to societal issues. Three areas were included on the questionnaire – abortion, euthanasia and homosexuality.[99]

Abortion

In relation to abortion, 11% declined to comment perhaps, as a few say, it is too emotive a subject. But, of the remainder, 60% state that it is the woman's right to choose (hardly anyone mentions the father), and a further 11% have no problem with abortion. However, it is clearly a sensitive issue, and Peter Baker-Jones displays such sensitivity rather well when he writes: "While (as a vegetarian) I believe all life is worthy of respect, and I would not wish to deliberately terminate a life, I accept that this decision must rest with the mother carrying the child. Her mental state and financial security is a factor in making such a difficult decision. We must not judge harshly but have compassion." Like Peter, many had personal feelings about the issue but could still engage with the broader picture, or could balance one principle of life with another. Jane Robbins from Caerphilly says: "Although I consider life itself to be of the utmost value, I would not want to generalize or take away freedom of choice." Similarly, Peter Grayer of the Beacons and Borders chapter says: "I believe in the sanctity of life, but I also believe in individual choice and do not feel that

I can judge any other person's life." Even many who are against abortion personally (10%) accept the right of freedom of choice.

Most members have the same kind of sympathetic response, suggesting, like Adrienne O'Sullivan that: "It is the right of the individual to choose. Everyone has a unique set of circumstances and they must make the best and most informed choice for their life and the unborn life." The general impression is one of situational ethics in which the circumstances will dictate the right kind of choice. An anonymous writer points out that abortion is part of the issue of human rights, and that "it often requires deep wisdom and respect, also great confidence, that a decision to abort is needed." Sriram Vaidyanathan from Newport deals fully with the wider concepts of abortion, both from a Buddhist and a pragmatic point of view:

> Every Buddhist upholds the dignity of life: however, abortion is a personal matter. First, one must consider why the young woman or woman is going for abortion. The social, educational and psychological issues surrounding such a decision must be taken into consideration before either condemning or condoning it. Secondly, one must refrain from passing judgement as, ultimately, the decision is that of the mother's. Thirdly, better educational initiatives, advice on contraception and social support might help reduce the number of abortions taking place due to poor planning.

As stated above, few mention the role of the father in any decision-making: indeed, some of the men feel that the question is not particularly relevant to them because they are male. A few of the men and women respondents (7%) feel that abortion should be a last resort, should be strictly controlled, or only an option in extreme cases where the mother's life is in danger or in cases of rape. Only 7% are totally against abortion so, in the final analysis, the majority of SGI-Wales and the Borders members believe in the freedom of the individual to choose in the case of abortion.

Euthanasia

Clearly, euthanasia is a more difficult issue for SGI-Wales and the Borders members. Thirteen per cent declined to answer. However, the same consideration for personal choice as in the case of abortion is evident from the responses, with 48% of respondents expressing this, though, equally clearly, less than in the case of abortion. A further 11% are also supportive of euthanasia. Of those who feel that it is a matter of personal choice, some comments are noteworthy. Allison Bridger says: "If someone has a serious or incurable illness, of course I wouldn't want to see myself or others suffer. After all, what we want in life is the quality not quantity of years. So, in my opinion, it's okay for the patient to choose euthanasia." Some are more specific about the circumstances. Mike Bridger from Hengoed writes: "When life would naturally have ended were it not for modern medical science, if the person who is suffering cannot face living any more, then I think he or she should have the right to die." And Kim Rees from Pembrokeshire reiterates what many people often believe: "It's okay if someone is really suffering and it is his or her wish. We don't let animals suffer, but sometimes we let people suffer."

As in the case of abortion, balancing the principle of the value of life with suffering is what is important to a number of respondents. Thus, Linda Owen Hicks from Cardiff believes: "People should have the choice, but I would always promote the idea that life is more valuable. But who am I to say when someone is in utter agony? It's case by case, without judgement." And Jane Grayer from Market Town says: "The important thing about life is to create value – we can't judge other people's decisions because we are not living their lives." At the end of the day, most, like Ann Shabbaz, also from Cardiff, say that it comes down to "respect and dignity for human life as defined by the individual." Jayne Timmins from Carmarthenshire has a very informed opinion as a nurse and psychotherapist. In her experience: "Individuals have the right to die in the manner they choose, in the way they choose at the time they choose. I have been with many, many people in my job who are dying and who have expressed the wish to be allowed to die quickly and painlessly and I feel it is an infringement of their *rights* to have this denied." Respect for the wishes of others is paramount in Nick Sherwood's view: "We should all take full responsibility for our lives – if a person feels it right or necessary to end his or her life at a certain point that is a way of taking responsibility, which deserves respect. No one should be made to suffer against his or her will."

Others find the issue of euthanasia much more difficult. Adrienne O'Sullivan from Cardiff writes in a very positive tone: "Life is precious and we can experience the preciousness of it whatever our health. Again, I think it is the individual human being's choice. I would hope that whatever my challenges with my health that I will be able to transcend the suffering through my practice. However, this is a very difficult subject and raises many questions." While Kirsty Foster of Roath, Penylan, Lakeside district thinks it is a question of the personal choice of others, as far as her *own* life is concerned, she thinks differently: "Through my practice, at the end of my life, I hope to have lived an amazingly fulfilling and happy life, and be ready to pass my amazing life-force on to another existence – through natural means!"

For many respondents, euthanasia is certainly a grey area and they are undecided about their own attitudes to it, or how they would react to such a difficult issue personally. In the words of Katherine Kingston from Newport: "I believe in completely respecting everybody's life; whether this means I would always want to keep someone alive I'm not sure. Sometimes it may be more respectful to let someone die; it would depend on the individual." On a philosophical angle, Peter Baker-Jones comments:

> I believe in the eternity of life and in the importance of having a death
> free of regret. To end one's own life seems to me to be an expression of

despair for which I have great sympathy. I would try to persuade someone in this situation to fight that despair and make a great transition to the next phase of life (ku), neither being nor non-being. I would chant to support him or her and pray the pain would go to give clarity at death. Once a law allowing euthanasia were passed, those with a superficial view of death might get into a position to end a life before a change of heart might have taken place.

Amy Milton from Newport is also philosophical and apprehensive about euthanasia. When asked for her view she responds: "I honestly don't know. I really think that it should be up to the individual and the family as to how to progress with the decision. If I were in pain myself, and there were no way back to health, then I guess I would just chant, but for people who have no philosophy like ours, then their decision would depend on their life-state at the time."

Like Howard Leah from Cardigan, who finds euthanasia "tricky", because it is "against the grain of our life", Ilona Bailey from Fishguard says: "This really worries me. It could open the door to killing off old people for convenience." In a very reflective response, Amanda (Mani) Dowsett from Dinas Cross believes: "We all have the right to die with dignity: we also have the right to live to our fullest until the last moment. If people are choosing to die before the natural moment comes, we need to look at how people's lives are supported at this time of their life and what needs to be done to improve the circumstances around the death of an individual human being."

A good number (17%) were decidedly against euthanasia, usually for well thought out reasons. Steven Harris thinks it "should not be supported as it could be highly open to abuse". And a very informed opinion from a professional community carer, Liz Moulson from Cardigan, is the following:

> I feel many ill and elderly people would feel they were a burden and feel obliged or pressurized into asking for euthanasia. I feel it is better to create better care, pain relief and quality of life for such people. I care for the sick, elderly and disabled and each is a unique and irreplaceable individual. Life is the most precious treasure. I do not like the new law that says people can sign to be withheld food and water, as this is a painful, distressing way to die. A doctor often increases morphine to a person who is dying anyway, to ease the pain and suffering. This, I feel, is far better.

Another highly informed opinion comes from a doctor herself, Anny Pritchard from Swansea, who says of euthanasia: "I am totally against this. As a GP, I have experience of helping my patients to die with dignity, to lessen their pain and suffering, reduce their fears, and *not* need euthanasia."

The evidence from the responses of the Wales/Borders members suggests that many see the dangers acceptance of euthanasia could incur and feel that possibilities for quality of life – no matter what health condition one might be in – are still in need of exploration. However, most still maintain that it is matter for personal choice. As Phil Luffman puts it: "The quality of life and the quality of one's departure from life is an individual decision/issue."

Homosexuality

In response to a question on attitudes to homosexuality, the vast majority of respondents are supportive, 92% in fact. Some members themselves are gay or lesbian and many say they have friends who are homosexual, like Stephanie Bond from Lampeter: "Some of my dearest friends of both sexes are gay. I fail to see what someone's sexual preference has to do with anything or anybody as long as it's between two consenting adults." Sally Thomas from Swansea says a similar thing: "Fine, if that's your thing. I have many homosexual friends and family members. It doesn't bother me: I respect people's choices." Elissa Lewis from Cardiff says: "Human beings loving other human beings can't be wrong," and another Cardiff respondent, James Rourke writes: "I find it difficult to understand why people talk about it any more. A person's sexuality, to me, is irrelevant." An anonymous respondent reiterates James' view here when he or she says: "I think it's sad that in the twenty-first century it is still a question that is being asked. It shouldn't be an issue any more: nor should it ever have been."

These, then, are some of the typically positive attitudes of SGI-Wales/Borders members to homosexuality. The same kind of freedom of choice for individuals is evident as in the case of abortion and, though to a lesser extent, euthanasia. Sriram Vaidyanathan puts such freedom of choice in the wider context of human rights when he says: "Some of my best friends, greatest supporters and more sensitive human beings are homosexuals. It has never bothered me, and I don't see this as an issue while interacting with them. Each person has a right to choose the life he or she wants, and has an inalienable right to happiness in a manner which he or she chooses." Louise Squire from Lampeter also views the issue from the wider perspective: "My life is my life and yours is yours. That is a cultural/social issue. We should look far beyond such differences, deal with our own stuff and leave others alone." And from a psychological view, Jodie Allinson from Cardiff says: "Sexuality is much more complex than the reductive terms of heterosexual or homosexual, and all people should have the right to express their sexuality as long as it does not harm others or is non-consensual."

A superb comment on homosexuality comes from Jane Grayer, whose attitude is: "Fine! I would class myself as being bi-sexual – this lifetime I'm married to a man, next lifetime, who knows?" The lack of prejudice, acceptance and respect for homosexuals is very evident indeed. It is beyond the scope of this study to discover how far such acceptance reflects the general attitude of Welsh or English people, but clearly, SGI-Wales/Borders members regard homosexuality as "fine, natural, and should be accepted as part of the human condition and its variations", as Stephen Millson from Abergavenny puts it. So "whatever floats your boat", as Jonathan Davies from Haverfordwest says, rather reflects the general attitude of members, despite a minority who find homosexuality difficult to understand, or who responded with less positive comment. Amanda (Mani) Dowsett perhaps supplies the best overall conclusion when she writes: "Sexuality is a wonderful and varied aspect of life. I feel we should celebrate differences and not treat them as problematic." It is a view that most of her fellow Welsh/Borders members would endorse.

CHAPTER FIVE

The *Lotus Sutra*

Background to the *Lotus Sutra*

. . . a person of wisdom,
hearing how keen are the benefits to be gained,
after I have passed into extinction
should accept and uphold this sutra.
Such a person assuredly and without doubt
will attain the Buddha way.[1]

These words attest to the immense importance of the *Lotus Sutra* in the whole of the East Asian Mahayana Buddhist tradition. Highly revered, highly influential, it is believed by many to contain the pinnacle of the Buddha's teachings that are believed to be ultimate truth, and to supersede all his previous doctrines. More than any other Buddhist *sutra*, the *Lotus* has been the subject of prolific commentaries. While other *sutras* contain some of its teachings, the *Lotus* is thought to encapsulate all teaching in its twenty-eight chapters. What adds to its importance, however, is the point made by Ruben Habito that "it weaves these various elements to present a grand and compelling picture of the continuing dynamic activity of the Buddha, in a way that invites the devoted reader to enter into this very activity itself, as one's response to the reading of the sutra".[2] Such words are thoroughly relevant to the beliefs and practices of Nichiren Daishonin Buddhism. It was the sixth-century major architect of T'ien-t'ai Buddhism, Chih-i, who first acknowledged this *Sutra* as containing the Buddha's ultimate teaching, but it was Nichiren Daishonin who made the title *Myoho-renge-kyo* indicative of the universe and the Buddhahood of each being, and critical to the faith of Nichiren Daishonin Buddhism. Nichiren Daishonin believed that three proofs were necessary for establishing the validity of religious teaching. These three are documentary proof, theoretical proof and actual proof. It is the *Lotus Sutra* that provides the documentary proof.

The date of the *Sutra* is uncertain. It was certainly in circulation by the mid-third century when a text, now lost, was translated from Sanskrit into Chinese, though even Sanskrit may not have been the language of its original text.[3] A tentative dating would be somewhere in the first century, long after Shakyamuni Buddha had died. It is more than likely, too, that it was transmitted orally before being committed to written form. In 406 it was translated into Chinese by Kumarajiva,[4] who hailed from the small state of Kucha in Central Asia, and it is his text that has become the most authoritative. Later Sanskrit copies that have been found have additions to the text, so Kumarajiva's still commands the greatest respect. Manuscript fragments of the *Lotus Sutra*, dating from the fifth or sixth centuries, and written in Sanskrit, were stored for some time at the Lüshun Museum in China. Examination of these texts has led to the conclusion that Kumarajiva's text is highly reliable. Discrepancies in later Sanskrit versions contain copying errors that Kumarajiva's work does not have. It is, then, probably the most reliable.[5] As to the author of the written text, there is no evidence; but its words are said to be those of Shakyamuni Buddha, indicated by prefacing the content with the words "Thus have I heard", that is to say from the Buddha himself. Whoever wrote it must have been aware that its content was radically different from the teachings of orthodox, early Buddhism.

Structurally, the *Lotus Sutra* is written in prose and then the content is repeated in verse form. It is likely that this verse form was the earlier layer, because it is briefer than the prose parts and because its language suggests an earlier date. The verse form is easier to commit to memory and may represent an early, oral transmission, though given the respect for oral tradition, both verse and prose may have been transmitted in this way. Later chapters (23–28) are likely to be an addition and show that the *Lotus Sutra* is not a unified text but a collated one. The whole *Sutra* divides into two parts – a division made by T'ien'tai – the first fourteen chapters dealing with the teachings of the historical Buddha who was born, became enlightened and then passed out of existence, and then the last fourteen important chapters dealing with the eternal Buddha. The first fourteen encompass the *provisional* or *theoretical* teaching and the last fourteen the *essential* or *true* teaching. The transition from the first to the second is dramatic, representing a total change from the accepted views to revolutionary new ones and a revelation of the true nature of the Buddha.

The *Lotus Sutra* is a devotional text that, Burton Watson aptly says, "calls upon us to act out the sutra with our bodies and minds rather than merely reading it".[6] Such, indeed, is how Nichiren Daishonin Buddhism understands it. In the words of Daisaku Ikeda:

> The Lotus Sutra has the drama of fighting for justice against evil. It has a warmth that comforts the weary. It has a vibrant, pulsing courage that drives away fear. It has a chorus of joy at attaining absolute freedom throughout past, present and future. It has the soaring flight of liberty. It has brilliant light, flowers, greenery, music, paintings, vivid stories. It offers unsurpassed lessons on psychology, the workings of the human heart; lessons on life; lessons on happiness; and lessons on peace. It maps out the basic rules for good health. It awakens us to the universal truth that a change in one's heart can transform everything.[7]

The purpose of this *Sutra*, then, is manifold in relation to the benefits of its outcomes, but in essence it presents the Buddha's wisdom as available to all – the awakening to Buddhahood by all humanity.

These manifold outcomes of the *Sutra* are a result of the variety of meanings that can be extracted from the text. Some of its teachings could well be written in tablets of stone; others are vaguer, but permit many meaningful interpretations even for the modern age. A first reading of the *Sutra* might leave one with an expectation that is never actually fulfilled: much is said about the *Lotus Sutra* that is to be taught but it is not really expounded! We are left with a feeling that it is *about* to be preached, but when the final word is reached, we are left thinking what exactly *is* the *Lotus Sutra*? What it *is* is the whole wisdom and ultimate truth of an eternal Buddha, and ultimate wisdom, ultimate truth cannot really be taught or put into words. Indeed, the Buddha says in chapter 10 that "this Lotus Sutra is the most difficult to believe and the most difficult to understand".[8] One aspect of its style that stands out is the use of parables and similes. There are seven important parables in the text, which, on the one hand provide profound teaching through graphic imagery, but serve on the other to give us an insight into the Buddha-mind to which the *Lotus Sutra* draws all beings. Parables, says Ikeda, "are wisdom and compassion distilled to their most fragrant essence"[9] and that essence is, for Nichiren Daishonin Buddhism, equated with the Mystic Law itself.

We are told by the Buddha in the *Lotus Sutra* of the great benefits to be gained for those who venerate it. In chapter 10 it is said that those who hear just one verse or one word, or who delight in just one thought of the *Lotus Sutra* will be assured of enlightenment. This will be particularly so in a "latter-day existence".[10] Since the *Lotus Sutra* is the mystical teaching of the Buddha, *hearing* the *Sutra* is very important. Indeed, chapter 10 is an important one in the light of praxis for Nichiren Daishonin Buddhism. Wherever the *Lotus Sutra* is taught, read, recited, copied or venerated, the Buddha will be present and Buddhahood will be the outcome. Those who hear it, understand it, think about it and practise it are like a man digging for water on a hill: after a long time the dry mud becomes damp and he knows he is on the right path, "if they hear this profound sutra which defines the Law of the voice-hearer, if they hear this king of the sutras and afterward carefully ponder it, then you should know that such persons are close to the wisdom of the Buddha".[11]

In chapter 18 of the *Sutra*, we are told that benefits await those who encourage others to listen to the Law that is the *Lotus Sutra* – a factor that has importance for the propagation (*kosen-rufu*) of Nichiren Daishonin Buddhism, for SGI members become teachers of the Law. The importance of transmission of the *Sutra* is especially emphasized in chapters 17–19, particularly in the difficult centuries of the Latter Day of the Law when the teaching is threatened with loss and persecution. Ikeda goes so far as to say that *kosen-rufu* "is itself the heart of the Lotus Sutra. It is the rhythm of the cosmic life that is Nam-myoho-renge-kyo. It is the endeavour to elevate the life-state of all humanity to the world of Buddhahood".[12] Reading, accepting, upholding, explaining, sharing, repeating, copying, memorizing and especially preaching of the text are powerful means to Buddhahood, and chapter 19 depicts miraculous benefits for those who do these acts. Thus, chanting the title of the *Sutra* (*daimoku*) and chanting parts of certain chapters of the *Sutra* (*gongyo*) are integral to the praxis of Nichiren Daishonin Buddhism and designed to resonate with the Buddha, the Law, the Buddha-nature of all Buddhas and Buddhahood within.

Faith in the *Lotus Sutra* is essential; it amounts to faith in the Buddha himself and his power to bring enlightenment to all – a major tenet of Mahayana Buddhism in general. It is through faith that the individual life can be transformed in order to reveal its higher natures and let its lower natures be channelled through the medium of Buddhahood. When, in chapter 2 of the *Lotus Sutra*, the Buddha says that he is about to reveal his ultimate teaching, those who believed themselves to be already enlightened left the assembly: those who had real faith in the Buddha stayed to hear what he would say. Malcolm Eckel describes rather well the difference that faith in the *Lotus Sutra* brings when he says: "One sees oneself as part of an enormous process of salvation, much larger than a single life or world-system, and recognizes that one is, has been, and will be sustained in that process by the power of innumerable buddhas in the past, present, and future."[13]

Buddhahood is the ultimate outcome of faith and faith is, at the same time, the cause of that Buddhahood. There is a theory in Nichiren Daishonin Buddhism known as the Ten Worlds. It accepts that all our states of mind – Hell, Hunger, Animality, Anger, Tranquillity, Rapture, Learning, *Bodhisattva* and Buddhahood – exist *simultaneously* within us. It is a concept that we shall be examining in detail in CHAPTER SEVEN of this book. If the Ten Worlds' theory is accepted, it is the Buddhahood world within that enables faith to occur in the first place: then, reciprocally, faith reveals Buddhahood. Thus, the *Lotus Sutra* cannot be understood without faith, for only great faith in the *Sutra* will permit transformation into the Buddhahood within that is the mind and wisdom of the Buddha revealed in the *Lotus Sutra* itself. Faith in Nichiren Daishonin Buddhism is *active* faith in the Law to the extent that one's whole life is an expression of both. The *Lotus Sutra* suggests that it will be difficult but exigent to propagate the Law, that is to say, the *Lotus Sutra*, in times when the Buddha will no longer be present. Then, it will be important to preserve and teach the *Lotus* as the means to Buddhahood. It will be the Buddha's multitudes of *bodhisattvas* who will have the task of ensuring that the Law and the *Lotus Sutra* as the means to enlightenment are permanently available to all. But they will need faith to embrace it.

The cosmic canvas

The *Lotus Sutra* opens with a scene of incomprehensible magnitude. Multitudes of enlightened beings and those not yet enlightened – monks, nuns, *bodhisattvas*, *mahasattvas*, deities, dragon kings, beings from all sorts of realms beyond the human (beings more numerous than the dust particles of thousands of worlds) gather to hear the teaching of the Buddha. A great beam of light shines from the tuft of hair between the Buddha's eyebrows and lights up all the Buddha lands, heralding that the Buddha is about to preach the *Lotus of the Wonderful Law*, the *Lotus Sutra*. He will "rain down the rain of the Law to fully satisfy all seekers of the way".[14] The whole of the universe is displayed under the power of the light – thousands of worlds, upwards to the heavens, downwards to the hells and in all possible directions, a "panorama of unlimited universes, all of them ever-changing manifestations of the All-Buddha, of whom Sakyamuni is but one expression in one of infinite worlds".[15] In each world, a Buddha exists teaching his disciples. Each of the infinite worlds is born, flourishes and dies in perpetual cycles stretching into infinite space and time. Later in the *Sutra*, the Buddha will lift the entire assembly into the air, transcending space and, indeed, time, for the *Sutra* is presented over aeons, though, to the participants, the teaching seems to last for only a few hours. Later still, there are other worlds that are revealed.

Despite the vastness of the universes portrayed, the centre of events is *this* world, the *saha* (suffering) world, and it *is* a world of suffering rather than of enlightened beings. The cosmic backdrop to the *Lotus Sutra* links this world as the microcosm with the vast macrocosm of the multiple universes not as a plurality of realities but as a single unity: each individual is at one with the whole cosmic macrocosm, is affected by it and affects it reciprocally. The whole cosmos is symbolized by the lotus flower. The gathered assembly represents all aspects of existence – all the Ten Worlds – that can be present in the microcosm of the human self. Each being has the capability of existing in any of the realms of the hells, of ghosts, of beasts, demons, humanity, deities, voice-hearers (those who have heard the teachings of a Buddha), self-enlightened beings, *bodhisattvas* and Buddhas, because he, she or it contains the Ten Worlds. The unity between the self and the entire cosmos is beautifully portrayed by Ikeda when he says that faith in Nichiren Daishonin Buddhism "is the recognition that the infinite horizon of the cosmos exists right here within the self. One's life opens out toward the cosmos and is enfolded in it; at the same time, one's life encompasses the entire cosmos. We are in constant exchange and communication with the cosmos, our lives reverberating with it as one living entity."[16]

Expedient means

In their daily practice of *gongyo*, Nichiren Daishonin Buddhists recite parts of the *Lotus Sutra*, part of the *Juryo* chapter and a small part of chapter 2, the title of which in Sanskrit is *upaya kaushalya* "skilful means" and in Japanese, *hoben*. The idea of "skilful means" has a nuance of *expediency*, like the sort of skill we use to coax someone into doing something. But to understand its meaning and use in the *Lotus Sutra* we have to look back a little at the history of Buddhism that was explored in CHAPTER TWO.

When, somewhere in the sixth or fifth century BCE the prince Siddhartha Gautama of the Shakya tribe (hence, often referred to as Shakyamuni Buddha), left his royal home to pursue a spiritual path, his journey ended under a *bodhi* tree when he realized enlightenment and became the Buddha. After his death and final *nirvana*, the disciples that followed him believed that he had passed out of existence completely leaving only his teachings as a pathway for others to gain the same kind of release from the endless cycle of rebirth and the concomitant suffering in life after life. Those who followed him aimed at stilling their desires and aversions to the point of equilibrium so that there would be no *karma* necessitating their rebirth. As was seen in CHAPTER TWO of this book, rules of conduct and strict scriptures were drawn up to assist the disciples on their path to enlightenment, and it was only the dedicated monk that could hope to realize his aims. The Buddha's teachings became the *dharma*, the truth, the Law, that he had left for those that followed him.[17] Centuries after his death, however, there were those who questioned the exclusive nature of this monastic path and it is here that we have a division of belief and practice between the conservative and orthodox *Theravada* tradition and a more fluid and liberal *Mahayana* tradition.

Two outstanding differences marked Mahayana from its conservative origins. The first was its concept of a more universal salvation in that it was felt that the orthodox idea of individual salvation was somewhat self-centred: what was the point of salvation when it left behind countless other suffering souls? Secondly, the nature of the Buddha was understood not as a limited existence but as an eternal and ongoing essence. Different schools varied these themes, but essentially, Mahayana Buddhism has a much more universal view of enlightenment and a generally non-monastic stance to life. However, the problem remains as to which view of Buddhism – the conservative or the liberal – is the right one. The *Lotus Sutra* encapsulates an answer for us, despite giving radically opposite views to the orthodox school.

The way in which the *Lotus Sutra* solves the difficulty is to say that the earlier teaching of the Buddha is *provisional* and the Mahayana teachings revealed in the late stages of the Buddha's life his true teachings, so solving the difficulties of contradictory texts. But not only were the earlier teachings provisional, but the life of Shakyamuni Buddha was also a provisional life, that is to say, not the true one – it was a mere shadow of his real nature. Good teachers use a variety of means to put across their points and they often have to adjust their teaching according to the level of understanding and consciousness of their pupils. It is this kind of teaching that is a *skilful* or *expedient means*. One of the ways in which the Buddha explains such expedient means in the *Lotus Sutra* is through the medium of parables. For example, in chapter 4 we have the tale of a young man who abandoned his father and lived a life of poverty in consequence. Although lowly, he was honest and trustworthy, but aspired only to his humble life. When he found himself one day at the gate of a wealthy man, he did not recognize the owner sitting like a lion on a throne as his father, who had done very well indeed in life. His father, however, recognized his son but knew that he could not reveal the real relationship to him since his son's humble mind was not ready. So for many years the father used expedient means to help his son gradually and to broaden his mind. He withheld the truth until the right time, when he could also bestow on him all his treasures. The father is likened to the Buddha and the son to all those who believed they had become enlightened. As the *Lotus* says: "The Buddha is like this, resorting to a rare course of action. Knowing that some have a fondness for the petty, he uses the power of expedient means to mold and temper their minds, and only then teaches them the great wisdom."[18]

Another parable in chapter 3 of the *Lotus Sutra* brings us even closer to the essence of expedient means and the differences between the beliefs of early Buddhism and the Mahayana. An old and rich man sees his dilapidated house, to which there is only one entrance and exit, on fire. His sons, engaged in games, take no heed of his cries for them to leave, so he resorts to expediency to tempt them out with promises of goat, deer and ox-drawn carts outside the gate. By this expedient means he saves their lives, and gives them not small carts but each has exactly the same sumptuously handsome carriage. The dilapidated house represents the world and the suffering of birth, old age, sickness and death. The sons are like humanity caught up in the desires of the world and ignorant of suffering. The old man is the Buddha and the three carts are usually depicted as representative of the three ways in which one could become enlightened according to the provisional teachings of the Buddha. These three ways are the way of the *shravaka*, the "voice-hearer", who seeks to become an enlightened *arhat* (Pali *arhant*) through the aid of the direct teachings of a Buddha; the way of the *pratyekabuddha*, who achieves enlightenment by self-effort without the aid of a Buddha; and the *bodhisattva* path[19] where salvation for others as well as personal salvation is the goal. According to the Buddha's words in the *Lotus Sutra* he taught these three paths as expedient means to rescue people from their ways.

While most of the components of the above parable have clear allegorical representations, and the meaning of the three carts is reasonably clear, the same magnificent chariots given to each son, instead of the carts, are open to a number of interpretations. Perhaps the magnificent chariots represent the truth that is given in the *Lotus Sutra*. But does the replacement of the three carts with better ones simply represent a replacement of the old teachings for something better? Or are the more magnificent chariots symbolic of all paths being subsumed into one ultimate truth? Nichiren Daishonin Buddhism interprets the three carts as the three vehicles above but also equates the *shravaka* path with Learning, the *pratyekabuddha* path with Realization and the *Bodhisattva* path with the *Bodhisattva* state of the Ten Worlds. The tenth world of Buddhahood is representative of the true teachings of Buddhahood in the *Lotus Sutra* – the One Buddha Vehicle.[20] The Buddha makes it clear that the number of carriages is not the important point, for he refers to them as the *Great Vehicle*. In the words of the *Lotus Sutra*: "First he preaches the three vehicles to attract and guide living beings, but later he employs just the Great Vehicle to save them."[21]

Like the promise of three carts to his sons, the Buddha's earlier teachings are expedient or skilful means by which he prepares them for his greatest teaching of all. What is important, too, about the One Vehicle is that it is open to all and is not an exclusive path to enlightenment as the *shravakas* and *pratyekabuddhas*, who had no thought of helping others, believed. Indeed, as noted above, many of those who believed that they had already achieved the ultimate goal of enlightenment left the gathering. One purpose of the *Lotus Sutra* is to awaken and change those who had achieved an isolated, imagined, lesser, so-called enlightenment to a *real* enlightenment that would enable them to work for the salvation of all others – in other words a radical change from the orthodox idea to the Mahayana and a response to the wrangling between different Buddhist sects concerning the right path. The *only* way to enlightenment is through Buddhahood, according to the *Lotus Sutra*. And that Buddhahood is one that aims at enlightenment for *all* people. Such, indeed, is one of the central messages of the *Lotus Sutra*. It is what Chappell refers to as the "outreach of the Dharma". He writes, "the Lotus Sutra shows that the Buddha-path means not just that everyone will receive buddhahood, but that buddhas and those on the Buddha-path must actively share it with others by adapting it to their needs and helping them to grow".[22]

The One Vehicle, Great Vehicle, Buddha Vehicle, *bodhisattva* Vehicle, unique Vehicle, to give it some of its names from the *Lotus Sutra*, is the ultimate teaching understood only by Buddhas, and experienced through Buddhahood. All Buddhas, therefore, have to use provisional, expedient means to adapt the ultimate truth for their different audiences through parables, similes and provisional teachings. Thus: "In the Buddha lands of the ten directions there is only the Law of the one vehicle, there are not two, there are not three, except where the Buddha preaches so as an expedient means, merely employing provisional names and terms in order to conduct and guide living beings and preach to them the Buddha wisdom."[23] Despite what seems to be a nullifying of the three paths by the One, the *Lotus Sutra* also says that "the Buddhas, utilizing the power of expedient means, apply distinctions to the one Buddha vehicle and preach as though it were three".[24] This statement may suggest that the One Vehicle was divided into three types of teaching that are really subsumed into the One and unified as a result of the revelations in the *Lotus Sutra*. If this is so, then the *Lotus Sutra* serves to integrate the different main streams of Buddhism. It is interesting that there are parts of the *Lotus Sutra* that praise devotional veneration of *stupas*, the relic mounds visited by the populace, and those that pay homage to Buddhas, thus also suggesting that all practices are integrated into the One Vehicle. Clearly, too, the *bodhisattva* way is taken up and extolled by the *Sutra*, albeit with new perspectives. However, each of the *distinctions* of the One Vehicle represent only a partial view. When unified, they permit a higher view of the ultimate goal of

Buddhahood; segregated they are helpful, albeit unequal, expedient means to the goal.

The point about teaching by expedient means is that those who are taught do not have the mental capacity as yet to understand the full truth. They need steps on the way to that truth. It is a point brought out well in the parable of the phantom city in chapter 7, in which a guide leads thousands of people on a long, difficult and dangerous road. When they become tired and want to turn back, he conjures up a phantom city as their goal. Then, after rest in the phantom city, he places the true goal – the true end of the journey – in front of them. The Buddha does the same:

> I see the seekers of the way
> growing disheartened in mid-journey,
> unable to pass over the steep road
> of birth and death and earthly desires,
> and therefore I use the power of expedient means
> and preach nirvana to provide them with rest,
> saying, "Your sufferings are extinguished,
> you have carried out all that there is to be done."
> When I know they have reached nirvana
> and all have attained the stage of arhat,
> then I call the great assembly together
> and preach the true Law for them.[25]

So even *nirvana*, the end goal of extinction of all desires and total equilibrium and a central doctrine of Buddhism, is stated here as an expedient means! *Nirvana* is presented as only part of the journey, not the culmination of it: ultimate wisdom is yet to come for the many in the multitudes present in the *Lotus Sutra* setting that believe they have realized *nirvana*. But the *Lotus* does not seem to negate *nirvana*; rather, it presents it as a stage, part of the process, the means to a more ultimate level. A constant criticism by Mahayana Buddhism of the goal of *nirvana* and extinction of the self, is that what is the point of it when so many others are left to suffer in the world? Once those who had realized *nirvana* could turn round to help humanity, then true *bodhisattva* and Buddhahood are experienced instead. All expedient means in the *Lotus Sutra* are for the *benefit* of humanity and this is perhaps why the word "skilful" is often used instead of "expedient", for the means stem from the skill of the Buddha in knowing exactly what was right *and ethical* at a particular time and for particular people. The same skills also characterize *bodhisattvas* according to the *Lotus Sutra*, and, therefore, become critical in the expression of Buddhism.

The many parables of the *Lotus Sutra* are the means of portraying the Buddha's expedient means as a way of helping people to awaken to the path of truth. Like so many parables, they present truth in story form and are a marvellous facet of the *Sutra*. One of the central messages of the expedient means chapter, chapter 2 of the *Lotus Sutra* is encapsulated in the Buddha's words "at the start I took a vow, hoping to make all persons equal to me, without any distinction between us".[26] The words suggest that Buddhahood is the goal of Buddhism and a universal possibility and, since it is the *Lotus* that purports to express the mind and wisdom of the Buddha, it is itself a means to Buddhahood. This Buddha wisdom, described at the beginning of chapter 2 of the *Lotus Sutra*, provides part of the content in the practice of *gongyo*, the recitation of parts of the *Sutra* by Nichiren Daishonin Buddhists. Thus far, then, the *Lotus* teaches a higher *dharma* of Buddhahood for all and the responsibility of all who experience it to assist others to do so also. Concomitant with such a message is the compassion for humanity that makes such responsibility a reality. Gene Reeves rather pertinently makes the point that: "It is in this sense that appropriate means is an ethical teaching, a teaching about how we should behave in order to contribute to the good. It is prescriptive not in the sense of a precept or a commandment, but in the sense of urging us, for the sake both of our own salvation and that of others, to be intelligent, imaginative, even clever, in finding ways to be helpful."[27]

The nature of the Buddha

The truth to which Shakyamuni Buddha awakened was and is *the* eternal truth, *the* Law, *the* dharma. Awakening to the Law is what it means to be a Buddha. Since that Law transcends space and time, so does the Buddha. One of the other pivotal themes of the *Lotus Sutra* is the Buddha's revelation in chapter 16 that he has been a Buddha for infinite, incalculable, millions of aeons of time. He is the eternal, omniscient and omnipresent Buddha, himself transcending space and time like the Law with which he is one, but transcendent from, and immanent in, the universe. This suggests, in the words of Yoichi Kawada: "The idea of the Eternal Buddha makes it possible to integrate the present moment and eternity, thereby dialectically sublating historical and suprahistorical time onto a higher plane."[28] And his sole function is to bring all other beings, even those in the hells, to the same state of Buddhahood as himself. He is often called the *Tathagata*, the "Thus Come One". He is the very nature and life-force of the universe itself. At the same time, we are not given the impression that the Buddha had never been human: his compassionate humanity seems to be paramount, despite the fact that he is also supramundane. It is an important point that supports the idea of Buddhahood as the true nature and life-force of all who reside in the present world.

A part of chapter 16, "The Life Span of the Thus Come One", is recited daily during *gongyo* by Nichiren Daishonin Buddhists. This chapter reveals that, for all the eternities of time the Buddha has existed, he has been teaching the Law for the benefit of incalculable numbers of beings. The account of his birth and enlightenment under the *bodhi* tree was an expedient means for the benefit of all people: "I appear in different places and preach to them under different names, and describe the length of time during which my teachings will be effective."[29] Sometimes, the Buddha says, he finds it necessary to disappear in order to strengthen people's resolve to enter on the path to Buddhahood, and to encourage a longing for it, though in reality he is always present. Another parable is found in chapter 16 to explain this. A physician finds that his children have consumed a poison and are out of their minds, but when he wants them to take an antidote some do, but others will not. So the physician goes away and sends back word that he has died. This brings the children to their senses so that they drink the antidote. Only then, can the father return. The father is like the Buddha, his children, humanity. The poison is the sufferings of the world; only some will readily accept the antidote, and the antidote is the *Lotus Sutra*, the Law. His feigned death represents his feigned *nirvana*.

Particularly important for Nichiren Daishonin Buddhism is the eternity of the Buddhahood in all, as much as in the Buddha himself. Eternal life is the Buddha, Buddhahood, the Mystic Law, and *Nam-myoho-renge-kyo*. It is in the hidden depths of the "Life Span" chapter of the *Lotus Sutra*, chapter 16, that T'ien-t'ai brought out the theory of *ichinen sanzen*, three-thousand realms in a single moment of life, which we shall be examining in CHAPTER SEVEN of this book. Thus, in Ikeda's words: "To study the 'Life Span' chapter is to study the very essence of Buddhism. It is to deepen one's understanding of the essence of life and of the true nature of the self."[30] It is to know that Buddhahood is without beginning and end, and in all beings, as with the Buddha.

With the Buddha's revelation of his immeasurable existence, we also have to raise again the question of how far his provisional teachings and the causes of enlightenment he set out in that teaching can be given any credit – even if they are considered as expedient means. Nichiren Daishonin Buddhism accepts that the denial of the effect of Buddhahood in his historical existence is a denial of the causes of it as well. It is a denial of the causes and effect of enlightenment as far they were understood before the *Lotus Sutra*. It is the "Life Span" chapter that begins for Nichiren Daishonin Buddhism the *essential* teaching of the nature of all as Buddhahood, as opposed to the earlier provisional teaching.[31] Importantly for Nichiren Daishonin Buddhism, too, is the implication that eternal life is universal. In chapter 16 the Buddha says: "There is no ebb or flow of birth and death, and there is no existing in this world and later entering extinction."[32] This suggests to Nichiren Daishonin Buddhists that there are phases of life and death, but they are without end.

The power of the Buddha is evident throughout the *Sutra*. The very setting of it with multitudes gathered from countless Buddha worlds, all summoned by the Buddha, evokes the image of the Buddha's boundless power. In chapter 26, this is also the case with Buddhas, *bodhisattvas*, celestial kings and even female demons, all of whom cast spells, *dharanis*, which will guard and protect all those who teach the *Lotus Sutra*. Chapter 21, especially, is devoted to the "Supernatural Powers of the Thus Come One" and in the following chapter it is through his supernatural power that the Buddha places his hands on the multitudes of *bodhisattvas* to entrust them with the *Lotus Sutra*.

Emanations of the Buddha

Since countless other Buddhas are present at the gathering, the question of their status alongside Shakyamuni Buddha is a pertinent one. Nichiren Daishonin Buddhism accepts these other Buddhas as emanations of Shakyamuni. Indeed, given his power and prominence in the *Sutra*, it is not an unreasonable conclusion. Thus, all Buddhas are at one with Shakyamuni Buddha. The Buddha in Mahayana Buddhism was believed to have three bodies, the *Dharmakaya* or Law body, the *sambhogakaya* or enjoyment, bliss, transcendental body, and the *nirmanakaya*, the physical body that he takes when fully manifest. This idea of three bodies is known as the *Trikaya* doctrine, which we met in CHAPTER TWO of this book. Most Mahayana sects view the *Dharmakaya* as absolute, infinite and ultimate, and superior to the other two. Nichiren, however, endowed the Buddha with all three properties. He brought the absolute into the world itself as the medium for the actuality of the Buddha, bringing Buddhahood in all its dimensions into the heart of life. Mahayana Buddhism had, and has, numerous branches that accept one or more Buddhas as superior and as the objects of devotion. The suggestion that all Buddhas are emanations of Shakyamuni Buddha integrates and unifies them, as well as perhaps attempts to unify the varied strands into which Mahayana Buddhism had diversified.

The emanations of the Buddha are sometimes described as his "provisional aspects", rather like a shadow is to the body, or the moon in the sky and its reflection in a pond. Such emanations are, thus, replicas and partial expressions of the eternal, fundamental Buddha. So the provisional teachings of the first half of the *Lotus Sutra*, in which the Buddha realized enlightenment under the *bodhi* tree, speak of a provisional Buddha, while the essential teaching of the latter half refers to the true and eternal Buddha.[33]

Another central message of the *Lotus Sutra* – one that can hardly be separated from any facet of the text – is the *empathetic compassion (karuna)* of the Buddha and of the *bodhisattvas* who turn their attention to the suffering in the world. Compassion is paramount in the parable of the father whose wayward son returns (chapter 4) and in that of the physician who needs to save the lives of his children (chapter 16), or the father whose children will not leave the burning house (chapter 3). In chapter 5, the Buddha is likened to rain that waters every kind of plant, tree and herb:

> I appear in the world
> like a great cloud
> that showers moisture upon

> all the dry and withered living beings,
> so that all are able to escape suffering,
> gain the joy of peace and security,
> the joys of this world
> and the joy of nirvana.[34]

The *Lotus Sutra* shows that the Buddha's compassion is never ending, never ceasing, and it reveals that the true path to enlightenment is also utter compassion by all to all. The Buddha's compassion is a result of his infinite wisdom (*prajna*); indeed, the two go hand in hand, for wisdom brings compassion and compassion brings wisdom. It is out of compassion that the Buddha is portrayed as teaching the *Lotus Sutra*, and the same compassion promotes his concern to ensure that it will be taught in the ages to come. The Buddha is portrayed in the *Lotus* Sutra as a compassionate father to all living beings and to the vast assembled company with promises of Buddhahood and Buddha lands for each of them in the future. Thus, the *Lotus* depicts all sentient beings as children of the Buddha. However, if the Buddha rains down nourishing water on all plants and herbs, each remains different, and sentient beings have the free will to choose to hear the truth or to disregard it.

Bodhisattvas

The Buddha reveals to the assembly his presence as *bodhisattvas* in the distant past. He was, for, example, the Bodhisattva Never Disparaging, who used to bow to all people in reverence of their future Buddhahood even though he was subjected to abuse and sometimes physical violence for doing so. As he was about to die, he heard the *Lotus Sutra* preached by the Buddha of the previous age, and this increased his life span into immeasurable aeons, during which time he, himself, preached the *Sutra*. However, the Buddha is portrayed in the *Lotus Sutra* as remaining a *bodhisattva*, because he continues to undertake *bodhisattva* practice – he assists all others to Buddhahood: such indeed, is the definition of a *bodhisattva* in the Mahayana tradition.[35] It is an important point, too, that the salvific activities of the Buddha as a *bodhisattva* are concentrated on *this* world.

The *Lotus Sutra* abounds with *bodhisattvas* from all directions of the universe. All are dedicated to assisting beings to Buddhahood. Chapter 14, "Peaceful Practices", lists the many virtues of a *bodhisattva* like perseverance, gentleness, non-violence and possessing a calm mind. The chapter even gives advice concerning with whom a *bodhisattva* might avoid intimacy, like kings, butchers, heretics, fishermen and women.[36] The *Lotus* is full of stories about *bodhisattvas* because it is their lives that reveal true Buddhahood through their tireless devotion to all beings. Stories are told of great *bodhisattvas* – Bodhisattva Medicine King; Bodhisattva Wonderful Sound, who has the power to transform himself into any form needed; Bodhisattva Universal

Worthy, who will be with any person who recites the *Lotus*. All the *bodhisattvas* vow to preach the *Lotus Sutra* in the ages to come.

Many well-known *bodhisattvas* are mentioned in the text. Manjushri, "He Who is Noble and Gentle", is the *bodhisattva* of wisdom, prominent in Buddhism in general. Maitreya, "Loving One", is the Buddha of the future, the fifth and last of earthly Buddhas. In chapter 25 we find one of the most important *bodhisattvas* in Mahayana Buddhism, the *bodhisattva* of compassion and mercy, Avalokiteshvara. This chapter contains the oldest reference to him. In Chinese he is known as Kwan-yin/Guanyin and in Japanese as Kwannon. His Chinese and Japanese forms are often regarded as feminine. Avalokiteshvara appears as Bodhisattva Perceiver of the World's Sounds, who can help anyone who calls on his name. His presence in the chapter is as a stimulus for *bodhisattva* practice to all who hear the *Lotus Sutra* for it is he (or she) that hears all the cries for help that emanate from the world of suffering.

Of specific importance in the *Lotus Sutra* are the *Bodhisattvas of the Earth*. While all those present vow to preserve and preach the *Lotus Sutra*, their services are not needed in this world, for the Buddha calls forth multitudes of *bodhisattvas* and *mahasattvas* – each one also a leader of multitudes – from Earth itself, and it is they who will read, expound and teach the *Sutra* to humanity in the ages to come. It is they who will enliven the seeds of Buddhahood in beings through keeping the *Sutra* alive. Shakyamuni Buddha reveals that he himself has been instructing these *bodhisattvas* for aeons. As far as Nichiren Daishonin Buddhism is concerned it is the Bodhisattvas of the Earth who will be responsible for the propagation (*kosen-rufu*) of the *Lotus* in the Latter Day of the Law. They will be *active* in the world by alleviating suffering, and acting as an inspiration they will bring out the *bodhisattva* in, and Buddhahood of, other beings. Nichiren Daishonin Buddhists see themselves as fulfilling such a role. Ikeda writes: "The Bodhisattvas of the Earth are eternal activists who base themselves on the Mystic Law; theirs are lives of eternal progress. Our summoning forth the boundless energy of these bodhisattvas constitutes the "emergence of the Bodhisattvas of the Earth" within our own beings. When we do this, we can break through the shell of the lesser self that has constrained us."[37]

The Buddha and the Law

The wisdom and compassion of the Buddha are rooted in the *dharma*, the Law to which he became enlightened myriads of aeons ago. That is why he is *Dharmakaya*, "Law Body", as much as present in physical form (*nirmanakaya*), at various times. Since the Buddha wants all beings to awaken to the *same* wisdom, the same Law as himself, the potential for Buddhahood that is at one with, indeed, *is* the Law, is present in all living beings. Buddhahood is transforming oneself into the eternal Buddha and into the Law. And without a Buddha present in any age, the Law becomes the medium for

Buddhahood. The urgency with which the Buddha encourages the assembly to uphold the Law as grounded in the *Lotus Sutra* reflects this need for the ages to come. In Nichiren Daishonin Buddhism, that Law is embodied in the very title of the *Lotus Sutra*, *Myoho-renge-kyo*. The Law is the eternal Buddha, eternal wisdom, the essence of the universe and the Buddhahood of each being. Shakyamuni became enlightened to the Mystic Law and knew that this Law could be the teacher, the mentor that is, in the end, his very self, and the self of all others. Buddha-nature is without mention in the *Lotus Sutra*, but if we think of the nature of the Buddha as the Buddhahood within all, then Buddha-nature abounds in the *Sutra*. The nature of the Buddha is the Law, is universal life, is the true self: all has Buddha-nature within. Ikeda says that those who cherish the *Lotus Sutra* are able to say: "I am a child of the Buddha, and therefore I can inherit in its entirety the wisdom that is the Buddha's legacy."[38]

Buddhahood

The Theravada tradition accepts that there can be only one Buddha in any aeon and that, for this age, it was the enlightened Siddhartha Gautama. The best others could do was aim for an enlightened state through stilling the ego and becoming free of all desires and aversions. Those who did this directly through the Buddha's teachings became *arhats* (Pali *arhants*) though others, as we saw earlier, became enlightened through their own efforts. The *Lotus*, however, addresses all such beings with the message of Buddhahood – the same status as the Buddha's. This is the truth that the Buddha wants his hearers to understand; *this* is the *Lotus Sutra*. It is an awakening to the truth of one's own reality as ultimately one with the Law and with the Buddha. In the *Record of the Orally Transmitted Teachings*, the *Ongi kudan*, Nichiren is reported as saying concerning the "Life Span" chapter of the *Lotus Sutra*: "You should understand that the ultimate meaning of this chapter is that ordinary mortals, just as they are in their original state of being, are Buddhas."[39]

Buddhahood is there as the potential in each being. It does not have to be reached for, or achieved as the end product of a goal or journey; rather it has to be realized within. This is the message that Nichiren Daishonin Buddhism wishes to spread – the encouragement of the state of Buddhahood in all beings. Thus, Ikeda writes:

> This world is like a dream one dreams in a brief nap. From the standpoint of eternity, there is hardly any difference between a 'long' and a 'short' life. Therefore, it's not whether our lives are long or short but how we live that is important. It is what we accomplish, the degree to which we develop our state of life, the number of people we help become happy – this is what matters.

Those who firmly establish the state of Buddhahood in their lives will enjoy this state of life eternally. This is what attaining Buddhahood means.[40]

It is the *manifestation* of Buddhahood through the trials and vicissitudes of ordinary life that is important in Nichiren Daishonin Buddhism, that is to say, filtering all the lower nine of the Ten Worlds through the tenth state of Buddhahood. Chanting *daimoku* with faith is a means to realize Buddhahood in Nichiren Daishonin Buddhism. Chanting *Nam-myoho-renge-kyo* is at once the cause of realization of Buddhahood *and* the simultaneous effect of being Buddhahood, the Mystic Law, the essence of the Buddha itself. Buddhahood is, therefore, not a static state. In containing the other nine worlds it contains the dynamism and reverberations of all life's intricate patterns as they are worked out in human life: the other nine worlds themselves all have the same potential for Buddhahood and are the means by which Buddhahood can be revealed and made manifest. These Ten Worlds will be explored fully in CHAPTER SEVEN of this book.

The importance of the *Lotus Sutra* as the medium for Buddhahood is described in chapter 14 in the parable of the king who shares his treasures (the Buddha's provisional teachings), with his soldiers. He keeps for himself one very precious and priceless jewel (the *Lotus*) on his brow. However, seeing the loyalty and deeds of his soldiers, the king gives them the jewel too. Buddhahood is the only true *nirvana* and replaces, like the jewel, the earlier, less important, misconceived *nirvana* as the extinction of the self.

Chapter 11 of the *Lotus Sutra* tells of a miraculous event that is the most dramatic in the whole of the text and serves to divide the whole *sutra* into two. It describes how a magnificent Treasure Tower, a reliquary (Skt. *stupa*) appears in the sky. Flowers fall on it, music surrounds it, filling the earth and heavens; every sense is heightened by the whole effect. The Tower contains the complete body of Bodhisattva/Buddha Many Treasures, who had lived an interminably infinite time ago and had preached the *Lotus* then. This Buddha had vowed to return by way of the Tower if ever the *Lotus Sutra* were preached so that he could listen to it, and if all the emanations of the Buddha were present. Thus, the Tower emerges. The Buddha causes all his millions of emanations to emerge also, and when they fill the skies, he opens the Tower to reveal Many Treasures, perfect in body, within. Then the Buddha rises up into the Tower to sit beside him and lifts also the entire assembly into the air to be with him.

In Nichiren Daishonin Buddhism, the Treasure Tower is believed to be symbolic of the elevation in the self of the state of Buddhahood, and the Treasure Tower and the Ceremony in the Air have become the *Gohonzon*. Further, practice recreates that ceremony: "By exerting ourselves in faith, chanting daimoku and performing gongyo before the Gohonzon, we immediately become a part of the assembly in the air. Nothing could be more wonderful than this."[41] Practice is, thus, a method of bringing out the Buddhahood within, allowing it to surface and colour all around it. The Treasure Tower is seen as corresponding to *Myoho-renge-kyo* and to the *Gohonzon*. As Ikeda puts it: "In the mirror of the treasure tower (i.e., the Gohonzon) we see the treasure tower within ourselves. We perceive that we ourselves are the treasure tower."[42] Certainly there is a strong correlation between *Myoho-renge-kyo* and the Treasure Tower, because the latter will not appear without the former, but only in response to it. That is why Nichiren Daishonin Buddhism sees the chanting of *Nam-myoho-renge-kyo* as the means of bringing forth the Treasure Tower, the Buddhahood, that is within each self.

On the *Gohonzon*, *Nam-myoho-renge-kyo* is inscribed centrally and downward, and Shakyamuni Buddha and Many Treasures Buddha are placed either side of the inscription. As such, these two Buddhas represent the fusion, the oneness of Shakyamuni as wisdom, the true entity of all things and life itself, with Many Treasures representing reality, all phenomena and death. "When we pray to the Gohonzon, which depicts the Ceremony in the Air, we become one with the eternal and universal life in the present moment; and, right where we are, we manifest the vast state of life from which we can survey the entire universe."[43] The vastness of eternity is witnessed in each moment.

The fact that the Ceremony in the Air takes place in this world is indicative of the great potential for the beings that inhabit it. The Ceremony in the Air also serves to extol the *Lotus Sutra* through its marvellous imagery and symbolism. It also sheds immense light on the power of the Buddha who is able to summon forth all his emanations from every direction. All these countless lands he fuses as one with this *saha* (suffering) world as the centre, and unites Heaven and Earth by moving each toward the other. Then, too, the accepted idea that there can only be one Buddha in any age is challenged by the very presence of these two great Buddhas sitting side by side on a lion throne in the Treasure Tower.

In chapter 21 of the *Sutra*, a *bodhisattva* is mentioned who is called Superior Practices. He is important for Nichiren Daishonin Buddhism because Nichiren Daishonin is regarded as his reincarnation. In this chapter, Shakyamuni Buddha hands on the Law contained in the *Lotus Sutra* to Superior Practices and others to ensure that it is upheld when the Buddha is no longer present, in other words in what is called the Latter Day of the Law. Superior Practices is seen as the Buddha who totally transcends time by being a Buddha that has not become enlightened in the remote past, but who has always been and always will be a Buddha. It is the verse section of chapter 21 that is suggestive of such a Buddha, for example:

> One who can uphold this sutra
> has in effect already seen me,
> and likewise has seen Many Treasures Buddha
> and the Buddhas that are emanations of my body.
> And he also sees me today
> as I teach and convert the bodhisattvas.

One who can uphold this sutra
causes me and my emanations,
and Many Treasures Buddha who has already entered extinction,
all to be filled with joy.[44]

The verse section continues in the same vein suggestive of a person who will come after the Buddha:

As the light of the sun and moon
can banish all obscurity and gloom,
so this person as he passes through the world
can wipe out the darkness of living beings,
causing immeasurable numbers of bodhisattvas
in the end to dwell in the single vehicle.[45]

However, Ikeda makes it clear that Shakyamuni and Superior Practices are one Buddha not two. "They are two sides of the same Buddha."[46] The importance of Superior Practices for Nichiren Daishonin Buddhism lies in the belief that he does not seem to have had a beginning, and he has no end: therefore, he is simultaneously the cause of Buddhahood, *and at the same time*, its effect.

However Bodhisattva Superior Practices is viewed, it is clear that the unity of all through the medium of Buddhahood, and the Law, is always maintained. The *Gohonzon* expresses this unity with *Nam-myoho-renge-kyo* inscribed down the centre, the great *bodhisattvas* each side and the Ten Worlds, too, on each side representing all things. Everything in existence is the Law and is Buddhahood, and is intimately interrelated as the very life of the universe. Chappell aptly comments that "the main emphasis is not on an individual, group, or historical judgment, but on the individual as part of a cosmological process leading all beings toward ultimate buddhahood".[47] The message of Buddhahood in the *Lotus* is one of an approach to life, not a path to a goal. It is the *bodhisattva* approach that sees others as important as oneself.

While the life of the *bodhisattva* is one of good practice, people who live and teach the Law need not live in monasteries, erect towers or give alms (though they would probably accrue some benefit by doing so). It is true acceptance of the Law that is the speediest path to Buddhahood and not by ascetic denial, but by an ingrained joy in the participation in cosmic life. As was noted above, the word *Buddha-nature* does not appear explicitly in the *Sutra*, but the concept of it pervades the entire text. The potential to become a Buddha, to reveal one's Buddhahood, to have the wisdom of the Buddha, is to experience the *nature* of the Buddha – Buddha-nature. And just as the Buddha always remained a *bodhisattva*, assisting others to reveal their precious Buddha-nature that is the potential of all beings, so the *bodhisattva* life is the means to experience Buddha-nature in ordinary existence, for the self and for others, *but* rooted in the beliefs of the *Lotus Sutra*. For Nichiren Daishonin Buddhism, this is reflected in the *Gohonzon*.

The implications for humankind

The *Lotus Sutra* is thoroughly world-affirming. Its events take place in *this* suffering, *saha*, world, full as it may be with the difficulties and tribulations of humanity. The parables in the *Sutra* have their roots in worldly situations. The *bodhisattvas* come from their countless worlds to the assembly that takes place in this world; there will be plenty of scope for their salvific work in it, and plenty of opportunity for ordinary mortals to awaken their Buddha-nature. It is in the *saha* world that the Buddha acts as a *bodhisattva*, pervading all things and assisting all things on the path to Buddhahood. For Nichiren Daishonin Buddhism there is a possibility of transformation of the *saha* world into a perfect and pure land through the awakening of Buddhahood in all beings. The world may be transient, impermanent and changing, but it is nevertheless the world in which Siddhartha Gautama became enlightened and in which he works for the enlightenment of all. It is a *real* world in which Buddhahood in all things interrelates everything and transcends the distinctions between all things and the pluralities of them.

The *Lotus Sutra* depicts the world as *both* a world of suffering *and at the same time* a pure Buddha land (chapter 16). It will just depend on the outlook of each individual. Some individuals will be in a level of consciousness that will only see evil and suffering; others will be in a state of Buddhahood and will be joyful even though they may be suffering. Importantly, the latter will be the *bodhisattvas* who seek to end the suffering of others. Here, the Ten Worlds (which will be examined in CHAPTER SEVEN of this book) serve to explain why some are trapped in the lower worlds and cannot experience their own Buddhahood that is deep within. Others, who operate from the level of Buddhahood, transform their experiences of the lower worlds through the filter of Buddhahood. Since the other nine worlds are always present, they are integrated with Buddhahood: the Ten Worlds always exist mutually in all beings. Their existence is gleaned from chapter 19 of the *Lotus Sutra*.[48]

Ikeda described the entire universe as "like our own personal bank account".[49] But it depends on what we put in it. We can draw on what is needed according to the way in which we live our lives: the higher in the Ten Worlds we are, the greater the fortune we can see. Ultimately, however, the fortune is always there for anyone to draw on. The fortune is the same for each being; the Buddhahood of one is the Buddhahood of all and the lack of it, the lack in all. True benefits come from the realization of Buddhahood within and with *bodhisattva* practice in the world.

One problematic area of the *Lotus Sutra* is its ambivalence in relation to gender difference. The Buddha lived in an age when men were considered superior, and in early Buddhism it was widely held that women could not become enlightened. Early Buddhist texts tend, therefore, to very negative towards women. While the *Lotus Sutra* clearly says, as we have seen, that all beings have Buddhahood and all can be enlightened irrespective of gender –

indeed, this is a fundamental message of the *sutra* – there are many textual instances of discrimination against women.[50] Perhaps such derision of women stems from the traditional negativity of early, conservative Buddhism. In chapter 23 of the *Sutra*, we find that a woman who hears the *Lotus Sutra* and carries out its practices will be reborn in a Buddha land, but as a man, never having to be born as a woman again. In the same chapter there is a description of a Buddha land in which "there were no women, hell dwellers, hungry spirits, beasts or asuras [demons], and no kinds of tribulation".[51] Similarly in chapter 8, of another Buddha land, the text has: "There will be no evil paths of existence there, nor will there be any women."[52] Clearly, in such passages, women are linked with the lowest of beings and the lowest of life's paths. Lucinda Peach comments, not without justification, that "the text's prescription for removing the problems of sexual desire and reproduction is to remove the women!"[53] As she later points out, the *Lotus Sutra* is not as ready as other Mahayana texts to champion gender equality.[54] It needs to be said, however, that neither is it as negative as some texts.

A remarkable story occurs in chapter 12 of the *Sutra*, recounting the enlightenment by the great Bodhisattva Manjushri of an eight-year-old Dragon King's daughter. Shariputra, one of the Buddha's major disciples, says to the girl, "a woman's body is soiled and defiled, not a vessel for the Law".[55] What follows is the transformation of the girl into a true Buddha and, then, into male form – an event reflecting, perhaps, the idea contained in other Mahayana texts that women can attain Buddhahood, or be reborn in a Pure Land, after changing their form to male. The impression gained is that the account has more to do with highlighting the power of the *Lotus Sutra* to cause even a minor, non-human and a female to become a Buddha, and in record time, rather than there being any overt message for women. Perhaps it is a "compromising device", as suggested by Miriam Levering,[56] that found a pathway to enlightenment for women through a change of gender.

There are, however, many instances where the *Lotus* Sutra is positive with regard to the status of women. Women can, it seems, be reborn in a heavenly realm without having to change their sex. While it has to be admitted that all the great *bodhisattvas* who are mentioned are male, chapter 1 actually mentions some women who are on the path to enlightenment, or have attained it, by name. In chapter 13, too, there are predictions of full Buddhahood for women who are present, without any suggestion that they would have to change their sex for that to occur. Clearly, too, the text abounds with proof that there were many women present in the assembly. Ultimately, a true *bodhisattva* must be dedicated to helping all beings to enlightenment without distinctions. Buddhahood for a *bodhisattva* is impossible unless all others attain Buddhahood, too. If women were to be excluded, their mission would be worthless.

As far as Nichiren Daishonin Buddhism is concerned, Ikeda sees the story of the dragon girl's enlightenment as "a tale about how arrogant men are defeated by women",[57] and also a tale to show the power of the *Lotus Sutra*.

The *enlightenment* of the dragon girl occurred when she was in female form; it was then that her Buddhahood was completed. Her transformation into a male form merely serves as proof of her becoming a Buddha.[58] The speed at which this girl is enlightened also obviates the countless years of assiduous practice that was normally considered to be the only path to Buddhahood. Many of the great male *bodhisattvas* present must have been radically surprised by the overturning of such a principle as well as of the prohibition against a woman becoming a Buddha. To put the point in Ikeda's words: "The dragon girl's enlightenment in an oppressively discriminatory society amounts to a ringing declaration of human rights."[59] The *immediacy* of her enlightenment also decries the idea that a woman would have to be reborn as a male in a pure land as a stepping stone to enlightenment and Buddha status. In the end, it seems that the underlying message of Buddhahood for all in the *Lotus Sutra* must take precedence over minor inconsistencies that may reflect earlier concepts.

Immediately before her rapid Buddha status, the dragon girl gives the Buddha an exceptional and priceless jewel, claiming that she will attain Buddhahood in less time than it takes to offer it to the Buddha. For Nichiren Daishonin Buddhism, this jewel represents the Mystic Law both of the universe and of the essence of each individual being. Her offering is, therefore, one of utter devotion, like the *Nam* of *Nam-myoho-renge-kyo*, and the Buddha's acceptance of the jewel, the fusion of his own essence with that of the dragon girl.[60] The message to women in the *Lotus Sutra* is that such unity with the Buddha is the potential in every being regardless of age, sex, wealth or even animal or human form.

Because the *bodhisattvas* of the *Lotus Sutra* have the role of teaching and spreading the Law, and of aiding all beings on their paths to enlightenment, a certain social responsibility is endemic in the practical aims of the *Sutra*. Those Buddhist sects that base their teachings on the *Lotus* actively try to change society for the better, and Nichiren Daishonin Buddhism is no exception. The point is put rather well by David Chappell when he says:

> Lotus Sutra Buddhists are not passive hearers of a finalized message, but their capacities and needs and goals help to shape the flowering of the Dharma here and now. Thus, they are both receivers and cocreators of the message and participate in the process of manifesting the Dharma. Accordingly, part of the task of our lives is to help creatively to realize the Dharma in each situation, and to bring it into being in our lives and in the lives of those who are in need and for a world in need.[61]

Nichiren Daishonin Buddhists are actively engaged in the promotion of peace through Soka Gakkai International, which is affiliated to the United Nations. And the concept of active engagement in society and the world at large is a reciprocal one, the benefits one bestows on others yield benefits for oneself, and these in turn benefit all others because of the interconnectedness of all at the heart of the *Lotus Sutra*. "To believe in the great life force within oneself is at once to believe in the great life force existing within all people. Buddhism teaches that we should treasure the lives of others just as highly as we treasure our own."[62] The *Lotus Sutra* is not seen as a text appropriate only to its own context in time, for the Buddha was at pains throughout the *Sutra* to ensure that its teachings would be passed on, and made relevant in the ages that would follow. Masahiro Shimoda points out that: "Social movements grounded on the discourses of the Lotus Sutra are rooted in the fundamental idea of the sutra: the truth in the form of the Buddha's words should be repeatedly brought into the present situation by a preacher by skilful means (*upaya-kausalya*)".[63] SGI is dedicated to actualizing the Law of the *Lotus Sutra* in the present world, and to manifesting its teachings creatively in working for universal peace and harmony with the aim of transforming the world.

The implications of the *Lotus Sutra* for other faiths

It is held that the Buddha revealed his ultimate truth, ultimate *dharma* in the *Lotus Sutra* and that his earlier teachings were expedient means or provisional truths. These provisional teachings are often referred to as "the teaching of innumerable meanings". But the degree to which these earlier teachings are derived from the one truth is a delicate issue. Some consider that the *Lotus Sutra* accepts religious plurality or inclusivism in an ultimate religious unity,[64] and this may be a relevant consideration, given the number of disparate Buddhist factions at the time the *Sutra* was written. Similarly, Reeves points out the *unity* of the many worlds and the whole cosmos that the Buddha reveals. Yet, as he says, there is no attempt by the Buddha to lessen the reality and plurality of these many worlds: they are the many that are united by the one. He writes: "As the truth is ultimately one, i.e., without internal contradiction, so too the teachings of the Buddha who discovered the truth must be one. That is, finally there can be only one Buddha-way. But in the Lotus Sutra, the one does not destroy or denigrate the many."[65] Like the parable of the rain falling on the trees, herbs and plants in chapter 5 of the *Sutra*, there is recognition of the difference between them, even if the rain is the same rain, and each species will need varying amounts. In today's terms, the parable might suggest that all need the same source of nurturing and help, but according to their different needs. Thus, different religions are ultimately parts of the same unified truth.

The *Lotus Sutra* does not deny the importance of other religions, or of other religious teachings, but it does depict them as inferior, as skilful, expedient means suited to the levels of consciousness of their adherents. It is only the *Lotus Sutra* that combines and transcends them all as the *ultimate* teaching, the true teaching. Of course, such a doctrine raises a considerable challenge to the champions of religious pluralism. Chappell has an interesting way around the problem. In view of the fact that the *Lotus Sutra talks* of a *sutra*, but does not actually say: "And here it is", Chappell thinks it refers to the *content* of the ultimate teaching, but is not itself identified with it. He writes: "I would propose that the saving truth that is celebrated in the written text is in fact **beyond the written text**, is beyond the chanted words, and is beyond our ability to own, read, write, or fully express it, even though we may have access to this saving truth *through* the written words."[66] This, Chappell says, using a frequently stated analogy, is rather like the finger pointing to the moon, and would make the *Lotus Sutra* itself a means, the finger, like all other religions, that point to a higher truth, the moon.[67] Such a thesis, were it to be supported, would make other religions *inclusive*. But the thesis has its difficulties. It is easy to see that fundamental truths *are* purported by the *Sutra* – provisional teachings as opposed to the true teaching about the eternal nature of the Buddha, and the Buddhahood in all. However, the very fact that Buddhahood informs all things and all beings is itself an *inclusive* theory, irrespective of, and transcendent to, religious differences.

The universality of Buddhahood is described in the parable of the gem in the robe in chapter 9 of the *Sutra*. A poor man visits a friend, who provides him with food and drinks until, rather inebriated, he falls asleep. Then the friend has to leave in a hurry, but before he does, he sews a priceless jewel in the man's robe. When he wakes up, the poor man leaves the house of his friend and journeys from place to place, all the time becoming more destitute, and all the time completely unaware of the priceless jewel he carries. Such is Buddhahood and the "desire for comprehensive wisdom"[68] in all beings. Buddhahood is there all the time, we just don't see it. Eventually, the poor man comes across the friend, who explains about the gem. His delight at the discovery is like the rekindling of the "desire for comprehensive wisdom" that puts one on the path to revelation of one's Buddhahood.

Clearly the universality of Buddhahood is a fundamental premise of the *Lotus Sutra*. Despite the presence of those who commit unspeakable evils in the world, they, too, have the potential for Buddhahood within: Buddhahood is the means of salvation and it is open to all. Nevertheless, it is closer for those who hear and accept the teachings of the *Lotus Sutra*, while for those who do not hear it or want to hear it at all, expedient means may be necessary to change their lives. Many of the parables are geared to this end for they tell of means by which people are helped to embark on the right pathways. Again, it is Gene Reeves that puts this point rather well when he says: "What is intended primarily, I think, is that you and I understand that we can become Buddha-like because we have that capacity already within us simply by virtue of being alive. This capacity or potential is in everyone. It does not have to be earned and it cannot be taken away. But it does have to be developed."[69]

In his days on Earth as Siddhartha, the Buddha had a dire enemy called Devadatta, who had even made attempts on Siddhartha's life. However, in chapter 12, the *Sutra* explains that countless aeons previously, the Buddha had desperately sought the truth of the *Lotus Sutra*, eventually to be taught it by a seer to whom he then devoted his life. That seer, the Buddha says in this chapter, was Devadatta, and he, too, would become an enlightened Buddha responsible for the propagation of the *Lotus Sutra*. It is an interesting story in that it lends credence to the theory of the Ten Worlds, since Devadatta certainly had a post-seer fall from Buddhahood into a hellish state of mind, only later to recover his Buddhahood. Again, however, it is a message of salvation even for the evil-doers: if there is hope for Devadatta, there is universal hope for all. It shows that Buddhahood is never distanced from the world of Hell nor life in the state of Hell from the world of Buddhahood.

The Buddha is impartial in his *bodhisattva* mission to bring all to Buddhahood: "I am the father of living beings and I should rescue them from their sufferings and give them the joy of the measureless and boundless Buddha wisdom so that they may find their enjoyment in that."[70] Buddhahood always exists as a potential world within each being, and cannot exist without ordinary beings. The ordinary mortal is the Buddha and *vice versa*. While this may be true, Nichiren Daishonin Buddhism does not accept that *all* paths are true and that all teachings can be subsumed under the unity of the *Lotus Sutra*. Indeed, the Daishonin was adamant that other Buddhist sects were clearly on the wrong path if they believed such ideas.

Nichiren Daishonin held to an exclusivist doctrine that the *Lotus Sutra* alone could lead one to Buddhahood, especially and specifically, by chanting its title preceded by *Nam, Nam-myoho-renge-kyo*. He believed that other practices would be of no use and that *shakubuku*, the active refutation of other beliefs, was a social obligation in order to bring people to the true path of the *Lotus Sutra*. It was to be an exclusive stance that would set Nichiren Daishonin Buddhism apart from other strands of Mahayana Buddhism. The *Lotus Sutra* speaks of a time when persecution of those that preached it would come about: its words were certainly true in the case of Nichiren Daishonin. *Kosen-rufu*, spreading Nichiren Daishonin Buddhism widely, is the way in which SGI propagates the Mystic Law and encourages faith in the *Gohonzon*. However, if Nichiren Daishonin Buddhism believes that no text or philosophy other than the *Lotus Sutra* can portray the full, unified truth, and that other truths are only fragmentary, it has certainly evolved to the point where sincere respect for the religious beliefs of others is endemic, as was seen in CHAPTER THREE of this book.

The unique nature of the *Lotus Sutra*

The *Lotus Sutra* is an immensely positive and dynamic text that lifts life to a superbly enlightened level. Soothill says of it: "A magnificent apocalyptic, it presents a spiritual drama of the highest order, with the universe as its stage, eternity as its period, and Buddhas, gods, men, devils, as the dramatis personae",[71] (though it would have been better to include women in the list of characters). When first reading the *Lotus Sutra* as a text, it is tempting to see no *sutra* at all and only a good deal of talk about it. Burton Watson makes an interesting comment here when he says that the highest truth in Mahayana cannot be put into words, "since words immediately create the kind of distinctions that violate the unity of Emptiness. All the sutra can do, therefore, is to talk around it, leaving a hole in the middle where truth can reside."[72] Is this, then, what Chappell was saying above, that the words themselves cannot be ultimate? There is little on Emptiness, *shunyata*, the idea that nothing has any true and permanent essence, throughout the *Sutra*, which perhaps takes the concept as read. Yet, the major message is not so much the emptiness of all *dharmas* but their unity. The fact that the Buddha does not discriminate between all beings suggests that each is empty of "own-being", that each is simply the "suchness" of all things. But there is nothing on the tenet of loss of ego and the creation of equilibrium in order to experience "suchness", which pervades so much of Mahayana Buddhism.

The message for each individual who visits the pages of the *Lotus Sutra* is to become a practitioner of the *bodhisattva* path. For when this happens we are sharing the life of the Buddha, embarking on his mission in our own world, and blending our own lives with the cosmic flow of the Law. It is then that the *Lotus Sutra* becomes "a ceremony that takes place in our heart".[73]

CHAPTER SIX

The Practice

Nichiren Daishonin Buddhism is a *living* religion that concentrates on *this* world and not on supposition about an afterlife. Because it does not deny the world and is world-affirming, its beliefs and practices are related to daily life in a very pragmatic way. Soka Gakkai International has never wavered from Nichiren's position that there are three fundamental aspects to practice, a point well made by the inaugural Director of SGI-UK, the late Richard Causton:

> There are three essential aspects to Nichiren Daishonin's Buddhism: *faith*, which means to determine to attain enlightenment through practising to the Gohonzon for the whole of one's life; *practice*, for oneself and others, which means to perform *gongyo* twice a day and to chant *Nam-myoho-renge-kyo* "to your heart's content", while making efforts to teach others about this Buddhism and to work for their fundamental happiness, whether they practise Buddhism or not; and *study*, which means to read and try to understand the profundity of the teachings of Nichiren Daishonin.[1]

The practice itself is what provides the *actual proof* of Nichiren Daishonin's three proofs – documentary, theoretical and actual. In this chapter, the three dimensions of praxis – practice, study and faith – will be the rubrics for discussion.

Practice

Central to practice, and hence the path to salvation, are the "Three Great Secret *Dharmas*" (*San Dai Hiho*) – the *Gohonzon*, the *daimoku*, and the *kaidan*, entrusted by Shakyamuni to Bodhisattva Superior Conduct to assist those living in the Final *Dharma* Age. The *kaidan* was conceived as the "ordination platform of the origin teaching", an actual institution that would be established at some time in the future. When, for various reasons, this failed to materialize, the concept of an "ordination platform in actuality" was replaced by an alternative interpretation of an "ordination in principle", in other words the ordination platform is wherever one might chant the *daimoku*.[2] This is the interpretation of *kaidan* favoured by SGI today, as

President Daisaku Ikeda explains: "By exerting ourselves in faith, chanting daimoku and performing gongyo before the Gohonzon, we immediately become a part of the assembly in the air. Nothing could be more wonderful than this. Mr Toda often said, 'In the daily lives of us ordinary people, there is no place as sacred as the place where we practice gongyo and chant daimoku.'"[3] As proof of how such practice changes not only the lives of individuals but also the lives of those around them, the recounting of personal experiences is a very important part of group practice in Nichiren Daishonin Buddhism. At meetings, *Gohonzon* receiving ceremonies, special general meetings – indeed, any occasion – reading or relating an experience is an expression of how "exerting ourselves in faith" has direct results on the life-condition of adherents. Experiences are rational belief and faith put into practice through chanting, and the direct results thereof. So important is this aspect that members' experiences are often published in the SGI magazine, *Art of Living*, and the final chapter of this book, CHAPTER NINE, is devoted to reproducing some of them, as well as hitherto unpublished ones.

The daily practice, known as *gongyo*, takes about thirty minutes in the morning and in the evening, with a slightly different format for each session – five prayers in the morning and three in the evening. An excerpt from chapter 2, the "Expedient Means", *Hoben*, chapter of the *Lotus Sutra* is chanted. Also chanted is the *jigage* verse section of chapter 16, the "Life Span", *Juryo*, chapter, which is considered to encapsulate the whole of the *Lotus Sutra*. The chanting of *daimoku* (*Nam-myoho-renge-kyo*), is essential practice.[4] Pronounced according to Japanese phonetics and chanted in archaic classical Chinese, comprehension is not considered to be important, as the former Director of SGI-UK highlighted.[5] The *butsudan* housing the *Gohonzon* is opened and members sit or kneel in front of the *Gohonzon* holding a small string of prayer beads like a rosary called *juzu*. These are periodically rubbed together to aid concentration, though neither the symbolism of the beads themselves nor the accoutrements that adorn the *butsudan* are the focus of attention.

The "Distinctions in Benefits" chapter of the *Lotus Sutra*[6] identifies the five stages of practice as:

- to rejoice on hearing the *Lotus Sutra*
- to read and recite the *Sutra*
- to propagate the *Sutra* to others
- to practice the six *paramitas* while embracing the *Lotus Sutra*
- to perfect the six *paramitas*.

The SGI position, however, is that the twenty-sixth high priest, Nichikan, regarded as futile the recital of the entire twenty-eight chapters of the *Lotus Sutra* that had been proposed previously by Nisshin.[7] Ikeda reminds us that in his commentary on Nichiren's "The True Object of Worship", Nichikan affirms: "[If you have faith in this Gohonzon and chant Nam-myoho-renge-kyo even for a short while], no prayer will go unanswered, no offense unexpiated, no good fortune unbestowed, and all righteousness proven."[8] For similar reasons, apart from the formalized recitation of parts of the *Hoben* and *Juryo* chapters, which are said to contain the essence of the entire *Sutra*, members are not enjoined to make their focus of study the whole of the *Lotus Sutra*, though they do take the *Sutra* to be the final and complete teaching of the Buddha. The point at issue is that though the *Lotus* attests to Shakyamuni's personal experience of enlightenment, it makes no attempt to explain *how* this was realized.[9] Furthermore, though "The Life Span of the Thus Come One" chapter[10] seeks to reveal Shakyamuni's own mentor, it does not explicitly state that this was the Mystic Law of cause and effect (Jap. *myoho*) and nowhere does the *Lotus* define what exactly should be regarded as an object of worship.

Neither in Nichiren's lifetime, nor in his *Gosho* was the chanting of the *Hoben* and *Juryo* chapters given any precise format, and the structure of five prayers in the morning and three in the evening was a later development. SGI General Director, Eiichi Wada explains why these chapters are important: "Simply stated . . . the recitation of these two chapters serves to extol Nam-myoho-renge-kyo. We praise . . . the ultimate Law for attaining Buddhahood, with the unparalleled words of the Buddha, which comprise these two chapters."[11] On 1 January 2004, SGI-UK, following SGI world-wide, adopted the new format of chanting and prayer.

The new format of gongyo

- Facing the *Gohonzon*, sound the bell and chant *daimoku* three times in unison.
- Offer a silent prayer of appreciation to *Shoten Zenjin*, the guardian deities of Buddhism and Life's Protection Forces (morning *gongyo* only).
- When there is more than one member chanting, the group will have a leader. The leader alone chants *daimoku* three times.
- Sound the bell both before and after recitation of each of the relevant portions of the *Hoben* and *Juryo* chapters of the *Lotus Sutra*.
- Begin chanting *daimoku*.
- Sound the bell when *daimoku* is completed. The leader alone chants *daimoku* three times.
- Offer silent prayers of appreciation for the *Dai-Gohonzon*, as well as Nichiren and the high priests in his lineage.
- Offer silent prayers for the realization of *kosen-rufu* and appreciation and respect for the three founding presidents, Tsunesaburo Makiguchi, Josei Toda and Daisaku Ikeda.
- The leader alone chants *daimoku* three times.
- Sounding the bell continuously, personal prayers and prayers for the

deceased are offered in unison: "I pray to bring forth Buddhahood from within my life, change my *karma* and to fulfil my wishes in the present and future."

- The leader alone chants *daimoku* three times.
- Offer prayers for peace throughout the world and the happiness of all humanity.
- The bell is sounded and *daimoku* is chanted three times in unison to conclude *gongyo*.[12]

Prayer is central to the practice of Nichiren Buddhism. Its function is not to petition external sources for self-gratification: the purpose of prayer is to align the consciousness of the individual with the pulse of the universe, with the aim of expanding the individual consciousness: "Prayer is the process of realigning our individual lives (the lesser self, with all its impulses and desires) with the rhythm of the living cosmos (the greater self). In doing this we unleash previously untapped sources of self-knowledge, wisdom, vitality and perseverance."[13] Daisaku Ikeda's advice to members is that: "Prayers based on the Mystic Law are not abstract. They are a concrete reality in our lives. To offer prayers is to conduct a dialogue, an exchange with the universe".[14] Sixteen members from Wales and the Borders are of similar mind, since they associate chanting before the *Gohonzon* with an increased connection to the life-force of the universe, with commensurate results. Anny Pritchard from Swansea feels a "more powerful connection with the rhythm and meaning of *Nam-myoho-renge-kyo* within myself", while Josie Cousens from Cardiff speaks of feeling "connected to the experience, faith and wisdom (and struggles) of so many others".

Unsurprisingly, there was a wide range of responses from the 145 members who replied to the question, "How often do you chant and for how long? Are there any constraints on this?"[15] Answers ranged from one respondent who admitted that he chants only at meetings and on an *ad hoc* basis at home, and another who chants "ten minutes weekly" to members who chant "to their heart's content" up to two, three and even five hours daily (eleven say they chant "daily" without giving any timescale). Nevertheless, there were no surprises as to constraints imposed on the practice (apart from the fact that there were few), which include meeting the needs of small children and work pressures. Only one respondent met resistance from another member of the household. Forty-five per cent of members who responded chant for one hour daily and 10 of these say some of this time occurs while driving. For health reasons, two respondents prefer bouts of fifteen minutes chanting throughout the day, rather than the more favoured thirty-minute slot in the morning and then again in the evening. *Tozo* is the Japanese term used by SGI members for those who chant together for a specific time period, usually one hour; *domei* is chanting alone but at the same time as others.

The practice is not represented as being esoteric or ritualistic *per* se. Indeed, Nichiren was highly critical of the mystical and esoteric practices of other

Buddhist schools. Although modern scholarship has called into question the long-held view that the so-called Old Buddhism propounded by Tendai, Shingon and the Nara schools was unable to respond to the needs of a people facing the crisis of the age of *mappo*,[16] the Kamakura period (1185–1333) nevertheless saw the rise of Zen, Pure Land and Nichiren Buddhism in Japan. This was an age in which names such as Honen, Shinran, Eisai, Dogen, Ippen and Nichiren came to the fore, along with the new religious Buddhist movements they propounded. Given the vitriolic diatribe tirelessly launched by Nichiren against all schools of Buddhism other than Tendai, it is unsurprising that Japanese scholars of the Nichiren schools have not been inclined to scrutinize Nichiren's teachings for evidence of esoteric influence. Instead, through the mists of time has emerged the picture of a fierce, somewhat eccentric figure, combative in speech, confrontational in manner, an individual totally dismissive of any opinion other than his own. This view, depicted iconographically,[17] finds support in his unwavering insistence on the exclusive reliance on the *Lotus Sutra*, and in his specific condemnation of esoteric Buddhism. Modern scholarship has revisited the relationship between Nichiren and esoteric Buddhism (*mikkyo*), however, and Lucia Dolce, among others, has called into question previously held assumptions. As surely as early Buddhism was not conceived in a vacuum, neither was the Buddhism of Nichiren Daishonin. Jacqueline Stone believes that the influence of Pure Land thought is transparent in his teachings,[18] though exclusive faith in the *Lotus Sutra* was held to be the only means (through chanting) to realize the ideal Buddha land in this world, as she notes elsewhere.[19] In fact, the founder of the Japanese Jodo or Pure Land sect, Honen (1133–1212), was the first to deny the efficacy of traditional all-embracing Buddhist practices, and proclaim to the new Kamakura Buddhist movement that salvation in the evil age of the Final *Dharma* (*mappo*), was entirely dependent not on a plurality of practices, but on one single exclusive practice accorded universal status.[20]

There is no doubt that in the *latter* part of his career Nichiren railed against the esoteric teachings of both Taimitsu and Tomitsu traditions, attributing neglect of the *Lotus Sutra* and the consequent disasters befalling Japan to reliance on *mikkyo*, esoteric teachings, and neglect of the *Lotus Sutra*.[21] This is the only *Sutra* wherein the three bodies of the Buddha are presented as infinite – itself an esoteric concept. To fail to recognize that the Buddha is eternal, omnipotent and omnipresent, and regard this teaching as a metaphor misses the central issue of the *Sutra*, which emphasizes that Buddhahood can be realized through *practice*. Buddha-nature is not the preserve of a chosen people: as we saw in CHAPTER FIVE above it is present throughout all humanity – another esoteric concept. Consequently, everyone can attain salvation through practice, since this Buddha is immanent in every aspect of reality. What is often overlooked is the fact that criticism of other Buddhist schools was not unknown in the Buddhist tradition. Nichiren merely adopted a common practice of criticism that was well known in Buddhist circles – a self-legitimating strategy – and one that would have been recognized immediately and accepted as such by any audience.[22] On Dolce's view, though he put his own school forward by emphasizing the superiority of the *Lotus Sutra*, Nichiren was just as intent on formulating a new form of esoteric Buddhism as he was in criticising *mikkyo*, and the construction of a *mandala* as the central object of worship or *honzon* has obvious esoteric undertones.[23]

In response to the question, "Do you chant longer and more earnestly for matters you consider to be important? What sort of matters would these be?"[24], only two out of 141 respondents say "No", one is "unsure", while a fifth answers: "Not yet. It is all too new to me". Mushota Chipasha from Newport, South Wales, is one of two respondents who affirm "I give the same time to all matters." Fifty-eight per cent of members chant more earnestly for the health and the well-being of themselves and others, while a further five members chant for "life and death matters", and 3 for the strength needed to overcome a bereavement. Twenty-two members chant more earnestly for a resolution to unsatisfactory world situations and 23 for a solution to serious relationship problems. Teresa Kean from Lilleshall, Shropshire, encapsulates the mood of respondents precisely when she writes: "I chant to raise my life state. I chant about my relationships (at all levels) in my life. I chant about everything in order to approach my life from Buddhahood. Chanting affects our mindset in a positive way and alters our perception." Six members chant for *kosen-rufu*, five for Headquarter responsibilities and activities, with a further six seeking support for successful lectures or projects. Seven members honestly recognize faults in themselves that are causing suffering, and the subsequent need to change their *karma*, though, surprisingly, another term ubiquitous throughout mainstream Buddhism, *ego*, went unmentioned. Predictably, correspondents address stress levels and problems at work, money problems, and personal crises; unpredictably only one mentioned President Ikeda.

Although the *Gohonzon* is considered to be the main object of worship in Nichiren Buddhism, Jacqueline Stone demonstrates that in his other writings, Nichiren attests that the object of worship is, in fact, the *Lotus Sutra*, or the *daimoku* itself.[25] *Daimoku* is a term used throughout Chinese and Japanese by many Buddhist sects, and simply means "title", though SGI members use the word specifically to refer to the title of the *Lotus Sutra*. Nichiren was *not* the first to advocate chanting the *daimoku* of the *Lotus Sutra*, but he *was* the first to declare that this was *all* that was needed to reveal one's Buddhahood,[26] giving this single, exclusive practice a highly developed doctrinal foundation.[27] Nor is *mappo* an age that will be remembered for its enhancement of the literary skills of the common man; the few who had access to the *sutras* could not read them. Consequently, Nichiren remorselessly castigated those who advocated that faith with no understanding of the meaning of *daimoku* was useless.[28] Nevertheless, Nichiren never prohibited the worship of objects or deities inscribed on the various *gohonzon*; the expectation that each sect of Buddhism should have an *exclusive* unified object of worship post-dated the Daishonin's time on earth.[29]

Practice, as we have seen, traditionally consists of the assiduous recital of *gongyo* and *daimoku* before the *Gohonzon*. The original meaning of *gongyo* in Nichiren Buddhism was to chant *Nam-myoho-renge-kyo*, though today what are known as the primary practice and the secondary practice have developed, as SGI General Director Eiichi Wada explains:

> Gongyo is comprised of what is termed the "primary practice" and the "supplementary practice". The primary practice, of course, consists of chanting Nam-myoho-renge-kyo. Chanting daimoku represents the means by which we bring forth the Buddhahood inherent in our lives based on faith in the Gohonzon; it is the basic practice for polishing and forging our lives and achieving Buddhahood in this lifetime. It is also the core of our practice for realising kosen-rufu. The supplementary practice, meanwhile, consists of reciting the "Expedient Means" and "Life Span" chapters (of the *Lotus Sutra*).[30]

Nichiren created a religious practice based exclusively on the *Lotus Sutra*, with a philosophy that is complete in itself. As will be seen in CHAPTER SEVEN, the philosophy answers questions about life in general, the purpose of life and the ways in which life is interlinked with the wider cosmos. Total belief in the efficacy of the *Lotus Sutra* is a prerequisite, indeed the only prerequisite, to salvation in the age of *mappo*. All other *sutras* are not only inferior to the *Lotus* but ineffectual.

The true object of worship – the *Gohonzon*

Following the dutiful bestowal at a joyful but dignified ceremony,[31] new members take their individual *Gohonzon*, which are transcribed copies of the original printed on a small paper scroll, to their own homes. Enshrinement in a wooden *butsudan*, at another ceremony called *okuri*, follows only after a suitable room has been selected. Here, a senior practitioner will be in attendance and *gongyo* is recited. The *Gohonzon* is ceremoniously revealed only immediately before and during ritual practice, and photographs of the *butsudan* are permitted only when the doors are closed. Since the *Gohonzon* is believed to be a reflection of the life of the practitioner, voluntary offerings ostensibly made to the object of worship are, in fact, being offered to the practitioner, a point emphasized by Nichiren himself.[32] These include evergreen branches, which symbolize permanence and the eternal nature of life, as well as vitality. Incense represents the Buddha's compassion, and water and fruit, as well as the manifestation of light (from candles), represent the Buddha's wisdom. Other than the idea of symbolism, these items are not regarded in any way as essential to ritual, and neither the candles, nor the incense need to be lit. A gong is also struck to separate the sections of daily prayer.[33] Meetings held in the home of a local leader commence with the chanting of *gongyo*, followed by *daimoku* before the *Gohonzon*. It is usual to read the words for *gongyo* from members' personal copies of a *gongyo* book,[34] though experienced members may chant without recourse to the text. There is also an *omamori*, a very small *Gohonzon* kept in a plastic case and carried around the neck when travelling; it opens up like a little book.

The word *honzon* is used in both Japanese and Chinese languages as a general term for an object of worship; it is not specific to Nichiren Buddhism. *Go* is an honorific prefix meaning "worthy of honour". In his lifetime, Nichiren inscribed innumerable *honzon*[35] of different types, and there are more than 130 such *mandalas* extant. There is no evidence of standardization among the extant *honzon*, nor is any such intention attested anywhere in Nichiren's writings. Indeed, in the entire corpus, there are only two passages where he describes the *Gohonzon*. *Mandalas* have different layers of interpretation and some were sent to villages for specific reasons. Sometimes the name of the person to whom the *mandala* was given is found depicted in the *mandala* itself; these *gohonzon* are called *joju*, indicating that the recipient is "eternally dwelling" in the *mandala*. Kathy Aitken draws attention to the fact that there are differences between types of *gohonzon*: "Subsequently, a woodblock printing process was used . . . whilst nowadays Gohonzon are produced by advanced printing techniques. Both these types of Gohonzon are known as *okatagi*, meaning woodblock, to differentiate from those written by hand. The Gohonzon SGI now uses was inscribed by Nichikan Shonin, the 26th High Priest of Nichiren Shoshu . . . A slightly larger *okatagi* Gohonzon, known as *tokubetsu*, is sometimes conferred on leaders or other long-practising individuals within the SGI movement. This is generally as a means of encouragement to the recipient to continue their great contribution for *kosen-rufu*."[36] The chanting of the Mystic Law, as the phrase *Nam-myoho-renge-kyo* exemplifies, may be undertaken at any time in any place, but it is the *Gohonzon* that is said to reflect the Buddhahood within every individual.

In the Sado exile, Nichiren formulated the philosophical and doctrinal basis for the establishment of the *Dai-Gohonzon*. This Great *Gohonzon*, inscribed by Nichiren on 12 October 1279, from which all *Gohonzon* derive, was intended to become the true object of worship for the present age. In his letter, "The Real Aspect of the Gohonzon", Nichiren refers to the great Treasure Tower ceremony (which we have already met in CHAPTER FIVE), attested in chapter 15 of the *Lotus Sutra*.[37] A great jewel-encrusted tower emerges from the ground and soars into the sky. Hovering in the air, its doors open and the Buddha, Many Treasures, welcomes Shakyamuni inside, symbolically giving credence to Shakyamuni's teachings. The *Gohonzon*, explained Nichiren, is a representation of the Treasure Tower, which, in turn, is a representation of life itself, in all its glory and mystery: "It follows, therefore, that whether eminent or humble, high or low, those who chant Nam-myoho-renge-kyo are themselves the treasure tower, and, likewise, are themselves the Thus Come One Many Treasures. No treasure tower exists other than Myoho-renge-kyo. The daimoku of the Lotus Sutra is the treasure tower, and the treasure tower

is Nam-myoho-renge-kyo."[38] The point being made by this graphic representation is that, as surely as any life-conditions are, by definition, conditions for
life, so can they be brought under control in each individual by chanting the
supreme law, thus making practitioners authors of their own destinies by
revealing their Buddhahood. SGI's official position is that chanting before the
Gohonzon is the best way to change one's *karma*.

Formerly enshrined in the now destroyed Grand Main Temple (Sho-
Hondo) at Taiseki-ji, at the foot of Mount Fuji, and currently housed in a
temple building in the grounds, the *Dai-Gohonzon* is now inaccessible to those
who do not follow the priesthood, and hence out of bounds to all SGI
members. It is a plank of camphor wood bearing a carved inscription written
in black *sumi* ink. Bereft of pictures, it is written entirely in characters. The
inscription that runs down the centre of the *mandala* reads *Nam-myoho-
renge-kyo, Nichiren*, in a stroke fusing the Mystic Law of cause and effect with
the very Buddha whom the Nikko school believes to be the original Buddha,
Nichiren Daishonin. Two Buddhas, Shakyamuni and Many Treasures
(Prabhutaratna and Taho respectively) whom we met in CHAPTER FIVE, are
to be found flanking the central inscription at the top; these in turn are flanked
by four Bodhisattvas of the Earth. Shakyamuni represents the arising of
wisdom in practice, and ManyTreasures, ultimate truth. The Bodhisattvas
represent true self, eternity, purity and happiness, which members also believe
arise in practice, albeit over a period of time. A guardian deity is indicated at
each of the four corners of the *Gohonzon*, symbolizing the protective forces
of the universe. In the middle of each side are the characters Aizen Myoo
(Craving Filled) on the left, and Fudo Myoo (Immovable) on the right, their
names representing, respectively, the doctrines of "the defilements are *bodhi*"
and "*samsara* is *nirvana*"; in other words, Fudo and Aizen attest to the ability
of the power of chanting to overcome the opposites in life, including human
sufferings and negative impulses, and to recognize the unity of all things.
Nichiren was the first to depict Fudo and Aizen *together* on the same *mandala*,
their names being denoted by their "seed characters" written in Siddham, the
Japanese Sanskrit orthography.[39]

With the exception of Fudo and Aizen, each figure is represented by the
Chinese character for its name. Also represented are figures present at Eagle
Peak during the exposition of the *Lotus Sutra*. At either side of the inscription
are to be found characters that indicate each of the Ten Worlds of Tendai
philosophy. As was seen in CHAPTER FIVE, Nichiren followers believe in Ten
Worlds or life-conditions ranging from Hell to Buddhahood that are experienced with alarming regularity, but which can be transformed into positive
tendencies through practice. They will be dealt with in detail in CHAPTER
SEVEN. Graphic representations at the bottom of the inscription attest that the
Dai Gohonzon is not the preserve of esoteric worshippers, but *ichiembudai
soyo* – "bestowed upon the entire world" – the point being that the
Buddhahood of the Daishonin is embodied within the *Dai-Gohonzon*; this
was his eternal legacy. At the lower right of the inscription is Nichiren's signa-

ture and his declaration that: "This is the supreme mandala never known in all the world in the more than 2,230 years since the Buddha's passing."[40]

Nichiren gave the term *honzon* a twofold application, seeing it at one and the same time as a physical icon forming the focus of practice – the common view in his day – and as the embodiment of ultimate reality. When Nichiren claimed he saw his life reflected in a pond at Seicho-ji temple, he termed it "the great *mandala*". Consequently, the *Gohonzon*, which Nichiren followers take to be the true object of worship, is like a mirror not a god, an interpretation ubiquitous throughout responses from members in Wales and the Borders. In premodern Japan, icons and *mandalas* were understood to be *participatory* in acts of worship, not literally blocks of wood. Accordingly, for practitioners today, this object of worship is not only their focus of attention while chanting *gongyo* and *daimoku*, but it is believed to be instrumental in lifting depressing clouds and manifesting the Buddha-nature of the participants. Robert Harrap, Vice Chair, SGI-UK Study Department, puts the case well: "Observing the mind, then, is nothing other than faith to fight fundamental darkness, having confidence in the existence of the Buddha nature, and practising so that it will appear."[41] This absence of duality in subject–object differentiation is evidenced in one of the most frequently quoted Nichiren letters, "The Real Aspect of the Gohonzon":

> Never seek this Gohonzon outside yourself. The Gohonzon exists only within the mortal flesh of us ordinary people who embrace the Lotus Sutra and chant Nam-myoho-renge-kyo . . . What is most important is that, by chanting Nam-myoho-renge-kyo alone, you can attain Buddhahood. It will no doubt depend on the strength of your faith. To have faith is the basis of Buddhism.[42]

Information gleaned from the 134 members from Wales and the Borders who responded to the question, "What difference does it make chanting to the *Gohonzon* rather than without it?"[43] was very interesting. "John", from Hereford, says "my prayers seem to be realized more quickly when chanting to the *Gohonzon*. However, the *Gohonzon* is now all over the world, in all directions, so it does not matter." Perhaps Jodie Allinson from Cardiff has Nichiren's words above in mind when she observes: "You are always chanting to the *Gohonzon*, because it is in your heart. An actual *Gohonzon* reminds you of this." Ann Shabbaz, also from Cardiff, takes a similar, though slightly different, tack when she writes: "The *Gohonzon* is like looking into your own heart, and that's what it symbolizes for me, looking at my life." Jayne Timmins from Carmarthenshire offers an equally beautiful simili: "I practised for seven years without a *Gohonzon*. Having a *Gohonzon* is like having a magnifying glass, it amplifies the strength of the prayer. The sun is the same, but when you use a magnifying glass you can harness the sun's power to burn."

Seventy-two per cent of members use the word *focus* or *focal point* about the *Gohonzon*, saying that it concentrates the mind on the chanting. Eleven respondents say that they find chanting before the *Gohonzon* "visually stimulating", though nine respondents see this as its *only* function. Peter Hazle, from Glyn Ceiriog, gives a response that is typical: "Chanting to the *Gohonzon* gives you a specific focus for your thoughts and concentrates the mind on your beliefs." Thirteen respondents speak of the *Gohonzon* as a *mirror*, which reflects their life-state (16 respondents actually use the word *reflection*). Amy Milton, from Newport, South Wales, puts the case well: "The *Gohonzon* is an integral part of the practice: it's a mirror of your own life, and your life's focus. If someone is not focused on something, for example, let's say a map, they may take a direction that takes them twice as long, or leads them down the wrong road. They would just be guessing at their path in life. Having the *Gohonzon* present while you chant helps you not to guess, and makes clear well-thought determinations and goals for the future." Ilona Bailey from Fishguard adds a poetic touch when she writes: "It's rather like a musician without his instrument. The two make the music. The *Gohonzon* mirrors the best in me back to me. It reflects my inherent Buddhahood."

However, Stephanie Bond from Lampeter adds a note of caution to the mirror metaphor when she reminds us that there may be things about ourselves that we don't want to see, but that we cannot avoid noticing: "The *Gohonzon* is a mirror of ourselves. Being able to look at that mirror, there is no hiding place from yourself – you have to be true and honest to yourself, or there is no point to anything." Stephanie's point is an interesting one, for not everyone feels comfortable looking in a mirror, where there is no place to hide, and some members are happier *away from* anything or anyone that reflects the true self. Richie Turner from Cardiff makes this very point when he observes that "chanting without the *Gohonzon* is less focused and you can avoid bits of yourself". Roger Langford from Hereford, who has been chanting since 1994, is only now beginning to feel comfortable having his inner self revealed before his eyes: "I sometimes find it harder in front of *Gohonzon* than without it. Maybe this is because I chanted for 6–7 years without one, but I have recently started to let go and trust in front of *Gohonzon*, which has made a big difference."

Many members admit to chanting in natural surroundings – by the sea, like Suzanne Jenkinson from Cardiff, while commuting by car, or even driving a bus in Pembrokeshire, like Jonathan Davies, though they still face the *Gohonzon* when at home, where Jonathan doesn't get "funny looks from the passengers on the bus". Jenn Carter, who runs a smallholding near Whitland writes: "I prefer to chant as I work through the day, rather than sitting in front of the *Gohonzon*. I haven't noticed that the chanting is more meaningful when I do it in front of the *Gohonzon*." In fact, Richard Causton made this very point twenty years ago when he wrote: "Indeed, as we spend much more time in activities other than chanting, it only makes sense that the benefits we gain from the physical practice of this Buddhism must be applicable to all other areas of our lives. If this were not the case, the implication would be that we could only be happy in front of the *Gohonzon*, which is not what Nichiren

Daishonin teaches at all."[44] These responses from Wales and the Borders members clearly indicate that they live normal lives in society; there is no question of disengagement from friends and family. SGI does not advocate separation from society but engagement in it.

In fact, though three members are adamant that there is 100% difference chanting before the *Gohonzon*, with a further 22 describing its presence as making the practice "more powerful", not every respondent is convinced of the necessity of chanting before a *Gohonzon*. Robert Newis from Cardiff, admitting that: "This is something I've struggled with on an intellectual basis as a question", makes the salient point that: "Nichiren must have chanted *daimoku* without one." Nine respondents, conceding that the *Gohonzon* gives a focus to the chanting, insist that this is all it does. Fourteen say chanting with or without the *Gohonzon* made little or no difference; two respondents were unsure. Sriram Vaidyanathan, from Newport, South Wales, emphatically writes: "Because I have travelled extensively in the United Kingdom . . . for the last two years, I can say with great conviction that it does not make any difference whether you chant to *Gohonzon* or not, as long as you have deep faith." An article by Kathy Aitken in the *Art of Living* affirms: "The benefit one receives from practising depends ultimately on one's own faith, not whether the physical object known as the Gohonzon is enshrined in your home."[45] Sue Rogers from Penrhiwllan, appreciates that: "There is something special about chanting in front of the *Gohonzon*. I feel more focused on inner change, more hopeful", but, again, stresses that it is not essential to practice: "When I first started to practise we couldn't get *Gohonzon* because of the priesthood issue, yet I had *tremendous* benefit and proof chanting to my blank wall." Robert Cook from Pontfaen expresses similar sentiments when he writes: "I quickly connect with the inner reality of my Buddhahood when I am in front of the *Gohonzon*. Otherwise I have to imagine the *Gohonzon* is there. I am confident in both situations though." Clearly, there is no consensus of opinion from members with regard to this question.

Study

Nichiren Daishonin exhorted others to: "Exert yourself in the two ways of practice and study. Without practice and study there can be no Buddhism. You must not only preserve yourself; you must also teach others."[46] The teaching of others is known as *kosen-rufu*. Daisaku Ikeda has said that: "Study is the backbone of faith and action" and, on the SGI European Study website, he defines the purpose of study as being:

- To deepen our faith
- As a driving force to promote *kosen rufu*
- To establish a philosophy of new humanism.[47]

In this light, the term "study" as used in the Buddhism of Nichiren Daishonin warrants qualification, for it is claimed that it has nothing whatever to do with the acquisition of academic knowledge. Nor does it require committing to memory key verses of scripture that one normally associates with other religious movements. Richard Causton acknowledged that "at its simplest, study consists of reading a line or phrase of the *Gosho* each day in order to assimilate its profound meaning and further deepen our understanding of the spirit of Buddhist practice".[48] The *Gosho* is the collection of texts (*go* means "worthy of the greatest respect" and *sho* means "writings"), containing the teachings of Nichiren Daishonin. It comprises easy to understand personal letters from Nichiren, as well as difficult doctrinal treatises written in classical Chinese intended for a formal audience. Study involves not only reading the writings of Nichiren, but their daily application also. Alex Canfor-Dumas explains:

> Studying Nichiren Daishonin's Buddhism has little in common with academic learning and more to do with applying the principles of Buddhism to life. Intellectual comprehension is not the key to faith. What matters is what we do, not what we know. Study deepens our understanding of the issues that confront us in our day-to-day lives. Furthermore, it deepens our understanding of Buddhism itself. The fundamental source material that we have is the collected writings of Nichiren Daishonin, known as the Gosho. Many of these are letters to his disciples, who had written asking him to clarify how they could apply their faith to a certain problem. Reading the Gosho, it becomes clear that most problems are universal, whatever the time or place, and the key to solving them lies in these beautiful and compassionate verses.[49]

To this end, monthly chapter meetings are held wherein a *Gosho* excerpt is studied by members, as well as by any interested guests who may be present. The precise *Gosho* in question is published monthly in the *Art of Living* (sometimes in a supplement), and study is prescribed nationally as part of a formal programme. The same *Gosho* is studied by each chapter (though there is a different *Gosho* each month), with guidelines that mitigate against digression. The background to the letter is given, which explains its setting in life – its purpose and function and what is known of the recipient to whom Nichiren wrote. There follow several pages of commentary and explanation from a senior SGI member in which advice given in the *Gosho* is related to everyday life – help in coping with the pressures of living in a stress-filled society and to "help us to attain the supreme happiness of Buddhahood",[50] as Causton put it. Under the title "Inspiration for Discussion Meetings", the January 2008 issue of *Art of Living* adds as a rider to that month's *Gosho*, "The Izu Exile":

> The letter that we are studying this month highlights the humanity underpinning the teachings of Nichiren Daishonin. The SGI theme for

2008, The Year of Capable People and Development, also expresses the aim and spirit to nurture human potential, so creating a flow of ordinary human beings who can change the karma of humankind. What does this theme mean to us? What might it look like in our lives, our families and our community? Let's kick off the year sharing our experiences and vision together.

Thirty members from Wales and the Borders failed to say whether or not they receive the *Art of Living* on a regular basis.[51]. However, 83% of those that did reply answered in the affirmative. Ten say they do receive the magazine but irregularly, while several subscribe to two or three copies, which they distribute in order to promote *kosen-rufu*. The greatest preponderance of subscriptions to the magazine comes from the age range 51–60, where 100% of respondents subscribe. Next is the 41–50 age range with 97% subscribers, 31–40 year band with 88% and the 61–70 age range with 75% subscribers. Either side of these age bands there is a decreasingly proportionate readership. More than 79% of respondents from Wales and the Borders attend meetings on a regular basis;[52] several others would like to do so but are in poor health. Only six respondents admit to attending meetings infrequently without explanation. As was seen in CHAPTER THREE, courses are also available to members serious enough about their studies to travel to the European SGI Centre at Trets in the South of France while, in recent years, Buddhist scholars of world standing, such as Richard Gombrich and Lucia Dolce, have addressed both members and guests at the Institute of Oriental Philosophy European Centre at Taplow, Berkshire.

Considering Alex Canfor-Dumas' insistence that "intellectual comprehension is not the key to faith. What matters is what we do, not what we know", and Richard Causton's affirmation that study "has little in common with academic learning",[53] it is surprising that SGI offers members the opportunity to study in preparation for a knowledge-based examination. Nevertheless, the valiant efforts in 2004 of several members from Wales and the Borders who took the elementary examination, along with SGI-UK's General Director, Robert Samuels, are worthy of mention:

> Barbara (Anderson, 85 years old) lives in a village called Llanidloes in an isolated area of Mid Wales, but made a round trip of 200 kilometres on one of the coldest days of the winter to take the (elementary) exam. She made her own way to her local railway station, and then walked to the study venue . . . Ian Caulfield and his wife Marlene have been practising for more than 20 years in the market town of Hereford, where they are district leaders. Ian is totally blind and Marlene is almost blind. Ian took the exam via e-mail, making use of his "talking" computer . . . Alyn Webley, South and East Wales Young Men's division HQ Leader, who lives near Merthyr Tydfil said that taking the study exam was one of the most enjoyable experiences he has ever had.[54]

Such expressed sentiments are not what examiners are accustomed to reading, when sifting through course evaluations in the Further and Higher sectors of education, but there are notable differences here. To begin with, SGI candidates are given sight of all the examination questions long before the examination day itself, though they do not know the precise combination of questions that will be offered on the day of the examination. They are then encouraged to discuss these with other members (some of whom may already have been successful in the examination in question). All study material is also readily available on the SGI European Study website. [55]

Contrary to Causton's assertion that members do not study in order to "amass knowledge about Buddhism", [56] the elementary study course does, it would seem, prepare candidates for an examination that largely consists of testing their powers of recall. Although there have been questions on past and current papers that allow candidates freedom of expression in terms of critical analytical thought, such as "What does it mean to have the same heart as Nichiren Daishonin?" and "'The lion seeks no companion'. Explain what this means for President Ikeda and what can it mean for us today", the majority of questions are simply memory tests. The opening part of Section A of the Grade 1 Study Course 2007 is a case in point, and poses questions such as: "When and where was Nichiren Daishonin born?", " When was he first exiled and to where?", and " When and where did he die?"

The main difference between the SGI examination system and that found in other areas of education is that the object of the exercise for SGI is not the successful completion of an examination paper, but *preparation* for it by way of holding meetings between members in study discussion groups. Indeed, the SGI European Study website affirms that: "The main purpose of the Grade 1 study course is for members to meet together to study the topics and prepare the answers to ALL the questions." [57] In this light, SGI's warnings against the futility of amassing academic knowledge become clear. The tenor of meetings is one of open discussion rather than didactic teaching and there is no necessary intention of reaching a consensus of opinion. Although many chapter leaders are eminently capable of giving guidance on the writings of both Nichiren and President Ikeda, as well as on selected chapters of the *Lotus Sutra*, views are expressed freely, with no thought of attempting to stifle the challenging opinions of either members or guests. Comments on Nichiren's teachings as outlined in the *Gosho* are welcomed, dictatorial edicts on moral behaviour are not.

Despite a firm belief that happiness is the right of all individuals, Nichiren Buddhism has a pronounced ethical basis that is situational rather than prescriptive. It is the situation that should indicate what is right or wrong, and not the dictates of some legal code. This puts the onus for moral behaviour firmly on the shoulders of each individual. Nichiren Daishonin Buddhists are, therefore, very concerned about freedom of individual choice, and this is evident in study meetings, where frank experiences play an important part and are welcomed and shared openly. Hammond and Machacek's study of Soka

Gakkai in America concludes that: "Soka Gakkai members, therefore, not only believe that people should be given considerable freedom to make moral decisions, but they are also more likely to believe that people are worthy of this kind of liberty."[58]

Clearly, then, the main emphasis is not on the successful completion of an examination, but on the study meetings themselves, so while almost 80% of respondents from Wales and the Borders attend meetings on a regular basis (discussion meetings are held monthly by district, study meetings are held monthly by chapter), only 50 members have taken the examination at any level. Nevertheless, candidates must successfully complete the elementary examination before being allowed to approach the Grade Two Study Course. SGI's position is that the goal of study is the deepening of faith, and anything that does not fulfil that aim is not encouraged. In 1995, Kazuo Fujii, Vice-General Director SGI-UK, confirmed that: "Advanced study was discontinued because the leadership considered it led to disrespect for Chapter Study and that it did not help to deepen faith."[59] In a recent communication to the authors, he added: "Advanced study came to an end in order to allow people to focus on chapter study, where they can receive good grounding in the principles of Buddhism. The study preparation for study lecturers takes place to provide a training ground for chapter study lecturers, with the aim of making chapter study as effective as it can be."[60]

Causton affirmed that "mere 'expertise' is no more a guarantee of personal happiness in Buddhism than it is in law, medicine, or any other field. As Daisaku Ikeda says 'faith is like an axle, and practice and study are like the two wheels of a cart. No matter how much you know about Buddhist doctrines, if your practice is weak, your faith can be said to be crippled.'"[61] Given this faith, Nichiren Buddhism empowers individuals to make changes in their lives, in effect giving them authorship of their own destiny. SGI's position is that chanting before the *Gohonzon* is the only way to change one's *karma*, though several respondents express the opinion that it is foolhardy to rely solely on chanting; there is a need to make the effort to study more, in the hope of changing one's *karma* by doing "your share of the work", as several put it. No matter how hard you chant, change will only happen if it is *karmically* right for you, is the point they are making. Jenny Nicholson from Fishguard speaks for more than a dozen respondents when she writes: "I take a long-term view. I deepen my faith and increase my activities for *kosen-rufu* – that is more *daimoku*, support others, study more, speak to others – just make more effort in my Buddhist practice and read Sensei's guidance." Thirteen members recognize that changes do not happen because there are causes in their lives that are preventing what they are chanting for happening, a point that did not escape the attention of Helen Delingpole from Cardiff: "I struggle for a bit and then try honestly to reflect on what I am asking for. I have found recently that I am chanting less about the smaller things and more about the bigger picture, that is to open my heart to everyone I encounter and to see their Buddhahood." Robert Newis, among others, looks to the *Gosho*'s guidance when he writes: "'Worthy persons deserve to be called so because they are not carried away by the eight winds: prosperity, decline, disgrace, honour, praise, censure, suffering and pleasure.' It is necessary to understand that, just because I want something to happen, that doesn't necessarily make it the best thing for my happiness!"

Faith

We can again turn to the "Distinctions in Benefits" chapter of the *Lotus Sutra* for a definition of the four stages of faith, summarized here by President Ikeda:

- to produce even a single moment of faith in the *sutra*
- to understand the Buddha's teaching in the *sutra*
- to propagate this teaching widely to others
- to realize the truth expounded by the Buddha with deep faith.[62]

In the light of Nichiren's assertion that: "Without practice and study, there can be no Buddhism . . . Both practice and study arise from faith. Teach others to the best of your ability, even if it is only a single sentence or phrase",[63] though all three are interconnected, faith must be the most important aspect of Nichiren Buddhism. Faith in the power of *Nam-myoho-renge-kyo*, as embodied in the *Gohonzon*, accompanied by total conviction of the effectiveness of chanting, is germane to the practice, otherwise there would seem little point to practice. As with study, academic background has nothing whatever to do with faith, and may even prove to be an impediment.[64] Ikeda observes that Josei Toda went so far as to say: "The sutras are all that exist. Where there is no correct faith, there is no Buddhism. The sutras, just by themselves, are simply texts; they are not Buddhism." Ikeda added: "Faith should be manifest in living and not an intellectual game."[65] The teaching of Nichiren is that faith in *Nam-myoho-renge-kyo* and the chanting of *daimoku*[66] will evoke the same life-condition of Buddhahood found embodied within the *Dai-Gohonzon*. Faith involves a determination to become enlightened by having total belief in the efficacy of *Nam-myoho-renge-kyo*, and the trust that practice will bring about the life-condition of Buddhahood.

Some very interesting responses were elicited from the answers received to the question: "How do you respond to times when things you have chanted for have not been realized at all?"[67] *Redetermine* is a common response used by 37% of the 145 respondents, along with the necessity to be patient and continue, extending the strength and time of the chanting. One anonymous correspondent from Wales and the Borders throws more light on this when she writes: "I understand that my life is about learning patience, and so what I truly need does not always come to me immediately or even at all. It is not about physically receiving what I chant for but to use these things as fuel in order for me to understand my relationship to them." Twenty-seven respondents were confident that at the end of the day you will always know why what you were chanting for did not materialize, or as Sook Hun Lister from Bridgend says: "A more desirable outcome usually manifests itself". Several make the point that chanting is not magic or, as Sriram Vaidyanathan, from Newport, South Wales, arrestingly puts it: "Nichiren never claimed that if you chant for 10 days you will get a four-bedroom house and a blonde woman who says 'Darling' after every sentence! What Nichiren does say is that if the person who chants with the realization that his or her life is endowed with infinite potential uses the wisdom gained thereof and takes courageous action, no prayer will ever go unanswered. Accordingly, I have yet to meet something that I have not realized through chanting *Nam-myoho-renge-kyo*." Clearly, members from Wales and the Borders see Nichiren Buddhism as a practice that *works*. Whatever the life-condition an individual is in, it is said to be able to answer difficulties.

Bearing in mind that in premodern Japan, *gohonzon* were understood to be *participatory* in acts of worship, it is unsurprising that SGI regard faith, practice and study, not as isolated independent phenomena, but as interconnected and interdependent aspects of worship. Study increases faith, faith stimulates practice and practice fortifies faith. Faith without practice is considered to be vacuous, as meaningless as the person who claims to be a good cook, yet who never sets foot inside the kitchen, as Causton put it.[68] The interconnectedness does not end there, however, for the encouragement of others to do likewise, known as *kosen-rufu*, is believed to lead ultimately to world peace. World peace, along with human rights, care for the environment, equality, education and culture, is one of the fundamental altruistic goals of SGI. Ikeda affirms the SGI position: "The ultimate meaning of faith is to treasure Nam-myoho-renge-kyo even more highly than our own lives. It is to devote ourselves entirely to achieving the widespread propagation of the Mystic Law."[69]

It has been well said that eastern thought lies beyond the compass of the western mind, which tends to evaluate eastern beliefs through western eyes. Accordingly, the press has never been slow to criticise any faith that it deems to be failing to toe the party line. Once such a belief system is identified, in many instances, often-sensationalized newspaper accounts, even television documentaries purporting to report "the true facts", soon follow. The media has long found difficulty accepting faiths that break with the Christian tradition of "sacrificing oneself" for others, wherein the practitioner may be perceived to be seeking personal (sometimes, even material) gain. In the present survey, 42 out of 144 respondents from Wales and the Borders desire financial solvency and its ensuing rewards in terms of personal possessions (11 chant for a home, six for a car). However, it needs to be emphasized that Nichiren Buddhism sits firmly within a tradition of eastern thought that parts company with western thinking. The eastern mindset is more in keeping with the instructions given by airline cabin crews, who advise passengers that, in the unlikely event of oxygen being needed, passengers should first ensure that their own masks are fitted properly before attempting to assist others. Only when passengers are safe and secure in their own minds and bodies are they in a position to best be of assistance to others in need of help.

Richard Causton saw self-centred (*conspicuous*) goals to be essential to neophytes, since their realization is sure proof that the practice works. He added: "Once we have gained this proof, so our practice tends increasingly to turn outwards, towards practising for the happiness of other people or overcoming our weaknesses or failings."[70] Ostensibly, this observation is borne out by the responses received in the present study, where 83 of the 150 respondents have been chanting for more than a decade. In answer to the question "For what do you chant?"[71] Marc Lister from Bridgend makes an interesting point when he resolves "to ensure that the things that I want, I want for the right reason". Eighteen of the 144 respondents (13 of whom were male) chant for improved career prospects; of these, 15 had been chanting for less than ten years. James Rourke from Cardiff, admitting that he is now "doing a job that I've always wanted", adds weight to the theory of increased altruism when he states: "I've been chanting since 1983, so gradually what I chant for has shifted from personal benefit to the development and spread of *kosen-rufu* in Wales. I also chant to overcome arrogance, small mindedness, prejudice and apathy." Causton designated these last named "*inconspicuous benefits*" and to this end 21 respondents chant for increased courage, 17 for wisdom, and 10 to become more compassionate. 27 chant for SGI members (21 for local members), while 33 respondents chant for *kosen-rufu*.

Changing oneself through the "human revolution" is an inward process from which stems outward compassion and altruism directed towards the planet as a whole and all humanity. A happier and better-balanced individual can engage in world-wide issues. Damien Keown, moreover, strikes an apposite chord when he notes that not all personal desire is wrong; quite the contrary. Keown distinguishes between what he terms excessive or wrongly directed desire (*tanha*) and desire described in more positive terms (*chanda*):

> Whereas wrong desires restrict and fetter, right desires enhance and liberate. We might use smoking as an example to illustrate the difference. The desire of a chain-smoker for another cigarette is *tanha*, since its aim is nothing more than short-term gratification. Such a desire is compulsive, limiting and cyclic: it leads nowhere but to the next cigarette (and, as a side effect to ill health). The desire of a chain-smoker to give up smoking, on the other hand, would be a virtuous desire since it would break the cyclic pattern of a compulsive negative habit and enhance health and well-being.[72]

In this light, it comes as no surprise to learn that the vast majority of respondents from Wales and the Borders see the need to change the self first as the priority, an observation noted already in CHAPTER THREE. More than 100 respondents chant for their personal well-being, 12 wish to improve their relationship with others, with 10 hoping to find a partner. Seventy-one chant for family, and 39 for friends; 22 chant for the happiness of others. Unlike some religions, Nichiren Buddhism encourages happiness, and not suffering, as a human right. It has the firm belief that happiness is the right of all individuals; it encourages individuals to be happy without feeling guilty about it. Guests invited to occasions such as anniversary celebrations in both Wales and London invariably comment on the display of positive vibrancy and happiness that members exude. Twenty-five respondents chant for the revelation of their personal Buddhahood and one anonymous respondent poignantly expresses a desire to "see Buddhahood in people one has difficulty with".

David Harris from the Vale of Glamorgan makes a valid point when, in order to address negative personality traits, he says that his chanting is "different daily, because every day I have different issues." This is pertinent, because Buddhism teaches that circumstances change by the moment, like bubbles on the surface of a frothy stream. This is why several respondents replied that the things they chant for are too numerous to list, and why Josei Toda warned of the dangers of compiling lists of "must haves". Daisaku Ikeda records that: "Second Soka Gakkai president Josei Toda characterized those who chant with a laundry list of things that they want, as though it were the duty of the Gohonzon to supply benefit, as having 'beggar's faith'. And he urged that they should stand up with the determination: 'I will stake my life on the struggle for kosen-rufu.'"[73] Amy Milton from Newport, South Wales, makes the interesting observation that there are fundamental issues germane to whole batteries of problems. Accordingly, chanting need not consist of vast lists of concerns that need addressing:

> I chant for a few things, but things that will transform a wide number of challenges, not just a specific problem, be they emotional, physical, mental or spiritual, they are all interconnected, so chanting for one thing can cover a lot of other things. For example, one of the things I have been chanting for most recently is "not to look outside of myself for happiness in others, but to rely on the Law". The most fundamental thing I have learnt from the start about practising Buddhism is that you have to take personal responsibility for the things that happen around you or within your personal environment, and actually in doing so you then, without knowing it, inspire others to do the same, thus making them happier, more rounded people. So one prayer can cover a lot of prayers, such as I would like there to be order and tranquillity in the universe, and this could affect the geographical environment, say positive changes against rapid climate change, right down to tranquillity within yourself, to be your true self.

In answer to the question: "How do you think your personality has changed since becoming a Nichiren Daishonin Buddhist?",[74] all of the 136 respondents recognize positive changes in their personalities. Only one respondent sought to apportion blame for his/her own failings, all others recognize that it is folly to blame others for one's shortcomings, and 10 recognize the need to overcome their own negative personality traits. In this light, Liz Moulson from Cardigan identifies the so-called three Buddhist poisons of greed, anger and ignorance (delusion) in her personality and chants in order to transform them into value-creating aspects. Jane Robbins from Fishguard, Pembrokeshire, who has been chanting since 1989, writes: "I chant to reveal my positive, enlightened qualities and for others to have the opportunity to do the same. I am definitely more positive, confident and compassionate than previously. I also chant for specific changes in my circumstances where necessary, and this has never failed to work." Jane also frankly admits that she is now "less likely to tolerate behaviour I find unacceptable".

Few, either within or without SGI-UK, would argue that being of an agreeable disposition is not reciprocal, or that how we view our environment is not dependent on our present mindset. Thus, our surroundings may well *seem* to have improved by reason of our having the feel-good factor at any given moment. But Nichiren Buddhism goes much further than this. It is claimed that chanting *Nam-myoho-renge-kyo* can have a direct effect on the world in which we live. Causton, himself, acknowledging that this is more difficult to accept, maintained that the realization of ostensibly miraculous *conspicuous* benefits is "merely your environment reacting *directly* to your chanting".[75] Jenny Nicholson from Fishguard says that she is now more able to "embrace the lives of others . . . have good relationships . . . give to the world and to others and . . . *smile more.*" Liz Moulson adds that she no longer feels "like a leaf tossed by the wind". Ben Gaster from Brecon says he is now "earthed in the realities of daily life", while Kim Rees from Pembrokeshire poignantly observes: "I am now seeing who I am instead of seeing who I want to be".

When asked: "If for any reason you are unable to chant for a while do you notice any changes in your life?"[76], of the 118 respondents who answered this question, only one claims to notice no change in his life, though he qualifies this by adding "I am chanting to myself most of the time". More than half of respondents (56%) claim that they backslide, returning to their previous states of negativity, depression and criticism/self-criticism. Over a third (36%) say their life-condition deteriorates with ensuing problems. Twenty-nine per cent of members identify such symptoms as demonstrating anger and irritability, an increase in stress levels, accompanied by a decrease in tolerance and compassion. Of the 32 respondents who chose not to answer this question, 16 say that there has never been a time when they have not chanted. Lillah Cottier, from Cardiff, says that she would be afraid not to chant, while Robert Wilson Thomas from Ashbourne states categorically: "I have not taken a break from chanting in the last 22 years." An anonymous respondent adds: "When I was in hospital I had to stop chanting for a while, though I didn't notice any difference because the chanting is always in my mind." Nick Sherwood from Westhope doubts the validity of the question. He validly objects: "One is never *unable to chant* – it is always a decision one makes! But if my practice is weak, I almost always feel worse, and notice things going wrong, getting me down." Two respondents say that at the very least they would always perform *sansho* (three prayers), in other words three slow utterances of *Nam-myoho-renge-kyo*.

Almost a half (47%) of respondents say they feel "out of synch/disconnected" when they do not chant, or as Carole Gell from Newport, South Wales, aptly puts it: "It is like being disconnected from my battery charger." Adrienne O'Sullivan from Cardiff is equally eloquent: "The only way I can describe it is that when I chant correctly and regularly, my life seems strongly connected to that of others. I feel happy whether I'm in difficult circumstances or not. When I don't practise it feels like the world becomes further away and I feel more separate and disengaged. It's the difference between a technicolor film when I chant, and a black and white movie when I don't." Sriram Vaidyanathan, speaks from the heart when he writes: "As soon as I stop chanting, life drowns into a state of misery and hell. It is only then that you realize how you get used to a higher life-state and making decisions from a fount of inexhaustible wisdom within yourself. This has to be experienced and often cannot be defined in words."

Taking the advice that we should be extremely careful what we wish for in case we get it, others raise the salient point that since we don't always (perhaps seldom) know what it is that we want, it would be foolish in the extreme to have all our wishes granted immediately and unquestioningly. Accordingly, 16 respondents say that they would want to ask whether they are chanting for the right thing, for the right reason, or whether, in fact, the time is ripe for changes that should really take years to realize. When prayers are not answered, only six of the 118 members who responded to the question, "If for any reason you are unable to chant for a while do you notice any changes in your life?" say they become frustrated, despondent, miserable, complaining, want to question the validity of the practice or even "want to give up".

One hundred and thirty-eight respondents conflated their answers to the two questions, "What have been the benefits of Nichiren Daishonin Buddhism for you?" and "What changes have come about in your life since becoming a Nichiren Daishonin Buddhist?"[77] Several divided their responses into categories for, as Suzanne Jenkinson attests: "I recognize the truth of the idea expressed in Nichiren Daishonin Buddhism that there are conspicuous and inconspicuous benefits and I have felt and known results from both." Seven respondents attributed lack of received benefits so far to a need to change the dark side of their personalities responsible for their failings, and address their negative *karma*.

Well over a third (39%) of members say they are now happier than before they began to practise. They find life to be more satisfying and they like themselves more: one of the reasons for this is that they feel more contented within themselves. Some (16%) describe themselves as being more compassionate and some (20%) as being calmer and slower to anger. Others (29%) say they have more trusted friendships with like-minded people, both within and without SGI-UK. Over a third (38%), speak of a strengthened life-force within, enabling them to overcome previous problems of anxiety and depression and to face life's challenges with positivity, hope and energy. More than a quarter of respondents (28%) recognize a marked increase in self-esteem, identified by Liz Jenkins from Goodwick, Pembrokeshire as being the most important gain the practice has brought: "The main benefit is confidence. I was very shy and introverted and would not speak to anyone, whereas recently I had a small part in a TV Documentary/Drama with no nerves at all." Stephanie Bond gives meaning and reason to why the practice increases self-belief: "By revealing my Buddhahood from within I have realized that, no matter what obstacles are put in my way, I can recognize them as challenges and be happy about it no matter what. What matters more than anything else are the treasures of the heart." Claire Boland from Shropshire agrees: "I have developed a strong sense of self. I do not give up so easily. I am more respectful and less critical of others. I take more personal responsibility for my life and complain and attribute blame to others rarely." Peter Baker-Jones from Solva says he now has an "awareness of the suffering of others and a mechanism to influence their happiness by connecting to inner wisdom." In fact, almost a quarter of respondents (23%) speak of their being more respectful of others with a commensurate improvement in relationships. A further 17% identify improved family life or the formation of stable secure relationships to be the direct result of a change in attitude.

Some members (14%) describe experiencing an inner change from feeling fearful to being courageous, with six feeling better equipped to cope with severe health problems. Sixteen per cent see themselves as being more persevering and determined. A few (8%) find themselves to be more self-contained, masters of their minds, or as Nick Dowsett puts it: "It made (and makes) absolute sense to take responsibility for my life and my environment. It enables me to be pro-active rather than passive." Thus, members speak of having a deep sense of gratitude and understanding of the meaning of life. Luke Conlon from Awelfa, Pembrokeshire, is one of 10 members who attest that they are now more responsible for their actions. Luke says he no longer blames others for his problems but now sees his problems as an opportunity to grow.

Almost a third of members (32%) speak of now being financially secure, some with improved career prospects, though this is not the main thrust of thought. Contrary to critical opinion, the picture that evolves from answers to these questions is not one of a grasping membership, constantly desiring more. One anonymous respondent puts the position well: "I have not become hugely wealthy or more glamorous, and I do not have a posh car, but I do not care. I am feeling good within myself and I am not constantly attached to desires." A change in attitude, rather than material gain is what most see as the reason for their happiness and contentment, or as Terence Murphy from Treharris puts it: "I'm not better off financially, but that's not very important." Valerie Stewart from Newport, South Wales, throws similar light on a lessened emphasis on financial solvency when she writes: "I am very patient with other people and always find time to listen to what they have to say. I am no longer materialistic whereas before I was always out shopping and buying etc." In summation, it is clear that members in SGI-Wales and the Borders have developed profound faith in their practice, and believe that the results of that faith, and their regular chanting, are having an equally profound impact in their lives. Their faith, also, is in Daisaku Ikeda as *Sensei*, teacher and mentor, and it is to this important aspect of faith that we now turn.

The mentor–disciple relationship

The *Lotus Sutra* is set on a cosmic canvas of inconceivable proportions with myriads of characters assembled to listen to the words of the Buddha. He is about to reveal that all his prior teachings have been provisional, that the *Lotus Sutra* is the pre-eminent teaching and that he is the *eternal* Buddha, existent through all time past, present and future. But the greatest revelation is that the Buddhahood that he is exists, too, in all beings: they, also, are inherently Buddhas. There were some, however, that left the gathering believing that they were already enlightened, already had all the answers and had no more to which they needed to be awakened. Those who remained – albeit here and there with some doubts – were those who had *faith*, faith in the Buddha, and that what he was about to tell them was absolute truth.

It is with that same kind of faith that the words of the Buddha have been preserved. Accounts of his teachings begin with the words "Thus have I heard", a statement tantamount to saying that what is to be reported are the exact words of the Buddha, faithfully memorized and transmitted to the audience. This, indeed, was a major role of disciples. In chapter 16 of the *Lotus Sutra*, is the parable, noted in CHAPTER FIVE above, about the children of a physician, who, while he is away, drink poison. When he returns and finds an antidote for them, some take it; others do not. The former have faith in their father to cure them, but the rest have lost their minds, and the father has to feign death in order to bring them back to their senses. Having faith, however, is the shorter route to recovery. The Buddha, like the father, does not abandon anyone, but he has a special relationship with his disciples, teaching and guiding them in countless lifetimes even when their faith in him is lost. Indeed, the Buddha stresses how important it is that the teachings of the *Lotus Sutra* are passed on so that others can have the benefit of its message in ages to come – even in the darkest of ages. For Nichiren Daishonin Buddhism, the mentor-disciple relationship begins with the *Lotus Sutra*, begins with the message of Shakyamuni Buddha within it, with the disciples who heard his words and with their faith in what the Buddha taught. As mentor, Shakyamuni wanted the *same* Buddhahood, the *same* enlightened state to be realized by all his disciples. Like any good teacher, he wanted to guide and encourage all to realize what he himself had.

Thus, it is important that the *Lotus Sutra* is *transmitted* from mentor to disciples for the benefit of others to come. In all faiths, the transmission of teachings from teacher to disciples is what preserves the tenets of religion, albeit that they evolve as times change. Nevertheless, it is the essence of the faith that is the heart of what is passed on; it is the mentor that transmits it to disciples who, in their turn, will become the future mentors. In the "Entrustment" chapter of the *Lotus Sutra*, the Buddha says:

> In future ages if there are good men and good women who have faith in the wisdom of the Thus Come One, you should preach and expound the *Lotus Sutra* for them, so that others may hear and understand it. For in this way you can cause them to gain the Buddha wisdom. If there are living beings who do not believe and accept it, you should use some of the other profound doctrines of the Thus Come One to teach, benefit and bring joy to them. If you do all this, then you will have repaid the debt of gratitude that you owe to the Buddhas.[78]

The importance of accepting, upholding, reading, reciting, explaining, preaching, transcribing and practising the *Lotus Sutra* is paramount in the text.[79] In Nichiren Daishonin Buddhism this whole process is embodied in the title *Nam-myoho-renge-kyo*. It is *bodhisattvas* as much as Buddhas here, who are the medium of transmission – the disciples of the time and the mentors of the future. And the true disciple wishes to impart the same teaching, the correct doctrine, for the same purpose, the Buddhahood of all.

A mentor is essentially a teacher, one responsible for the guidance of others and a person whose teachings are accorded respect. The greater the mentor, the less the disciple is inclined to alter those teachings in any way with his or her own thoughts. Thus, the true disciple *protects* the words and teachings of the mentor, and *preserves* their integrity for others. While, normally, students outstrip their teachers and great disciples have excelled beyond their masters, there is, nevertheless, a distinct interconnection between the two. But, at the heart of the *Lotus Sutra* is the fundamental message of the supremacy of the *Sutra*, the eternal nature of the Buddha, and Buddhahood as the inherent nature of all. These are the tenets that are protected and preserved by the disciples of the *Sutra*, and which they agree to pass to others in the ages to come without distortion.

The mentor–disciple relationship is a reciprocally rewarding, complementary relationship, where the goals are mutual, the path the same, and there are no master–servant constraints. But a lot depends on the attitude of the disciple. Ikeda says that: "the mentor–disciple relationship is strict. Everything depends on how earnestly one can accept and act on even a single word of the mentor. A true disciple strives to actualize the mentor's vision – not by mimicking the mentor but by putting into action what the mentor has taught."[80] The relationship between mentor and disciple is, therefore dependent on the trust the latter has for the former and to what extent that disciple is prepared to put into practice the teachings of the mentor. In the *Lotus Sutra*, the Buddhas and Bodhisattvas of the Earth sit on lion thrones. In Chinese, the word "lion" is composed of two characters, one meaning "mentor" and the other "disciple". Thus, the strength of the lion is the combination of the two and Nichiren Daishonin Buddhism uses the analogy of a lion frequently to symbolize the inner strength and bond between mentor and disciple for the cause of *kosen-rufu* and the revelation of the Mystic Law in all human life.

Mentor and disciple are one because "the heart, spirit and teaching that each uphold . . . make them inseparable".[81] They are one, also, because the disciple practises what the mentor teaches, because he or she shares the same goal with the mentor. When the Buddha's disciples prefixed his words with "Thus have I heard", they were reiterating this devoted following of their mentor's teachings. They also put into practice the Buddha's words in order to be awakened to the same life-condition as their mentor – the ultimate aim of the disciple. Ultimately, too, if Buddhahood is the natural state of all beings, then all is one: the mentor and disciple are united by the Buddhahood that informs both. According to Nichiren Daishonin Buddhism, the Mystic Law that unifies all things also informs and unifies the mentor–disciple relationship. *Myo*, which is mystic, is the Buddhahood of the mentor, the ultimate result, the ultimate effect. *Ho* is the law, the disciple that contains both Buddhahood and the other nine worlds and the causes that make up reality. *Renge* is the lotus that combines both cause and effect as one, suggesting that the unity of the Mystic Law is also the unity of mentor and disciple.[82]

Nichiren Daishonin, as a disciple of the *Lotus Sutra*, became the Buddha for this age, according to Nichiren Daishonin Buddhist belief: he became the original mentor of the movement. His successor Nikko Shonin had the following to say about the mentor–disciple relationship: "In this teaching [of the Daishonin], the way to enlightenment is attained through correctly practising the path of mentor and disciple. If we err in the path of mentor–disciple, then, even though we might uphold the Lotus Sutra, we will fall into the hell of incessant suffering."[83] At a time when he believed Buddhism had lost its way – a point prophesied in the *Lotus Sutra* itself – Nichiren became the mentor who attempted to guide people to what he believed as the correct path.

Josei Toda accepted Tsunesaburo Makiguchi as his mentor and believed that both of them had been reborn time and again to study and further the *Lotus Sutra*. He said: "Our relationship as mentor and disciple is not limited to this lifetime alone. When I am the mentor, President Makiguchi becomes the disciple; and when President Makiguchi is the mentor, I become the disciple. We are inseparable companions in both the past and the future."[84] Together for a time in prison, Toda, as the disciple of Makiguchi, survived his mentor, and took on his mentor's goal to spread Nichiren Daishonin Buddhism. Without that aim, Soka Gakkai could not be where it is today. Similarly, Toda as mentor asked of his disciple Daisaku Ikeda: "Whatever your position, always protect the Gakkai."[85] Given the global manifestation of Soka Gakkai, it could certainly be claimed that Ikeda fulfilled his mentor's words.

Ikeda says that "Buddhism is about the disciple taking on the spirit of the mentor to aspire eternally for kosen-rufu. Without the mentor–disciple relationship, there can be no advancement. There can only be decline"[86] But for the wider discipleship, like the members of SGI throughout the world, the mentor–disciple relationship involves the acceptance of Ikeda's transmission of guidance about the correct pathway in life to those who are prepared to accept him as mentor. That wider circle of disciples needs to embrace the teachings of a mentor in order for the movement to survive, and that will necessitate *faith* in both the teachings and the mentor who has received and transmits them. The desire for the spread of Nichiren Daishonin Buddhism throughout the world, for world peace, and for the happiness of humanity is the same desire that all members as disciples share with their present mentor, Daisaku Ikeda. They refer to him as *Sensei*, "Teacher" because as mentor, he transmits the correct path and offers guidance. The objectives are common to all members and the ultimate goals the same. Members of SGI may never have met Daisaku Ikeda, but by striving to follow his ideals, they are participating in the mentor–disciple relationship and accepting the beliefs and praxis of Nichiren Daishonin Buddhism. The relationship of mentor–disciple is, then, foundational to the success of Nichiren Daishonin Buddhism, which would not and could not survive without it: teaching and transmission would be lost. As it is, however, both survive through the shared and unified spirit of the world-wide Gakkai.

CHAPTER SEVEN

The Philosophy of Nichiren Daishonin Buddhism

The Buddha once said that if you are pierced by a poisoned arrow, you don't wait to find out who shot it, from where, why, and with what kind of poison: rather, you get on with trying to save your life. Thus, putting beliefs *into practice*, rather than first philosophizing about them, has been a major route of much Buddhism. Nichiren Daishonin Buddhism, especially, focuses on the benefits of practice, and pegs its philosophy onto the living faith instead of teaching abstract truths first. It was the educator, Makiguchi Tsunesaburo, who particularly stressed the value of practice for its outcomes of beneficial human change. Therefore, a chapter devoted entirely to the philosophy of Nichiren Daishonin Buddhism is in some ways an artificial separation of two complementary aspects, especially because chanting *Nam-myoho-renge-kyo* and parts of the *Lotus Sutra*, study, and the dissemination of Nichiren Daishonin Buddhism to others are the three pragmatic *actions* by means of which ultimate truths are experienced rather than learned. However, as was seen in CHAPTER FOUR, it is the philosophy that was the main attraction to the members of Wales and the Borders. Then, too, Nichiren Daishonin Buddhism has a very cohesive, integrated and unified metaphysical system and can do considerable justice to itself when its components are drawn together in order to take their place alongside other philosophical systems. The philosophy of Nichiren Daishonin Buddhism provides, also, one of its three proofs of a correct teaching – theoretical proof based on reason and logic. The other two are documentary proof, which is the *Lotus Sutra*, and actual proof, exemplified in the previous chapter on praxis. What we have in this chapter, then, is Nichiren Daishonin Buddhism set out as a philosophical *system* – its beliefs about ultimate reality, causation; the nature of the self; the relation of the self to ultimate reality. But let us begin with the reality we know in the condition of ordinary, everyday life.

The life-condition

One of the questions we used to ask our students in their first year of Philosophy and Religious Studies at the University of Wales concerned their degree of happiness in life. The question went something like this: "Are you happy enough in this lifetime to want to be reborn in the same kind of existence in a future life?" Surprisingly, despite most of the students being fresh from school into the university experience, only a very small percentage (and usually those who had just fallen in love!), would want a shot at another life. What is it, then, that makes life seem too difficult to repeat – even for those in their prime of life? We all have different ideas of what happiness is – usually for students, financial security, a good job on leaving university and perhaps a stable relationship come top of the list. As we get older, we may want better health and more intangible things such as "a better quality of life" as many say, more "space" to enjoy life and time to pause to smell the roses or to "do our own thing". But for all of us, complete happiness is elusive simply because whatever moments or spells of happiness we have are *always* temporary. Time ensures that nothing can ever last, and that includes happiness.

The Buddha taught that all life is suffering. It is an idea that has often been criticized for its seeming pessimism. The word for suffering in Sanskrit is *duhkha* and if we think of this word as *dis-ease*, that is to say not comfortable, not easy, it will convey some of the nuances of suffering that we all experience. No one reading these words is at this moment *totally* in a state of harmony and ease – in health, physiology, mental attitude, well-being, personality, in psychological and social harmony and so on. We may have an idea of what such a condition of total ease might be, but experience of it will elude us. The Buddha, as was seen in CHAPTER TWO, identified four fundamental states of suffering that affect us all: all life has suffering, sickness, old age and death. But he did not leave us with such a negative thought, for he and subsequent Buddhism taught how to overcome the suffering inherent in all life through a profound philosophy that is *lived*. This is an important point, for Buddhism solves the problems of life by *action* not by philosophy alone.

Individual and communal life is about evolution, and evolution that is in the right directions for personal, environmental, societal and world harmony. If we cannot avoid dis-ease, suffering and disharmony at so many points of our lives, we can at least turn such times into positive outcomes. For example, Daisaku Ikeda wrote concerning illness that: "Buddhism views illness as an opportunity for us to attain a higher, nobler state of life. It teaches that, instead of agonizing about a serious disease, or despairing of ever overcoming it, we should use illness as a means to build a strong, compassionate self, which in turn will make it possible for our lives in this world to be truly fulfilling."[1] The manifestation of suffering in individual life is the result of many complicated factors as we shall see below when we look at the nature of the self. Suffice it to say here that, for life's sufferings we have only our own selves to blame, it is our own mental and psychological pathologies that cause us to act according to detrimental tendencies and that create the causes of our suffering. Illness is regarded by Buddhism as the outward manifestation of inward imbalances in the self – a point that some non-Buddhist medics are beginning to accept. What we are going to explore in this chapter is the philosophy put forward by Nichiren Buddhism that enables each individual to increase his or her inner and outer harmony with the environment and all things. The purpose of this chapter is to understand who and what we are in relation to the greater canvas of the world and the cosmos in which it is placed. We shall begin by examining what Nichiren Daishonin Buddhism accepts as *ultimate reality*.

Ultimate reality

Nichiren Daishonin Buddhism is atheistic. It accepts, not a personal God but a universal and impersonal Law as absolute and ultimate reality. Such ultimate reality is indescribable; it is neither this nor that and beyond anything of which we can conceive. It is invisible, eternal and unconnected with time and space. However, this Law, this ultimate reality, is not beyond life and matter, but is within all phenomena whether living or inanimate as *Buddha-nature* or *Buddhahood*. It is the eternal, changeless rhythm that is the underlying and permanent reality underpinning all the impermanent flux and change and becoming and dying of all things. Its rhythm of perpetual and alternate active and passive phases informs all things. Each individual is a part of that process. In Ikeda's words: "Every living being plays music in the rhythms of life."[2] The Law is life and death, evolution and involution, active presence and passive withdrawal, existence and non-existence. In short it is the changing processes of all life and the unchanging reality that makes them possible.

Importantly, as the permanent foundation of all existence, ultimate reality is that which *connects* all things, making every thing and every moment interrelated. Again, in Ikeda's words: "Every single moment transcends the bounds of space and time to be simultaneously one with the cosmic life force – the ultimate reality of the Universe. All forms of life interrelate endlessly in the vast totality of cosmic life, and yet none of them ever loses its uniqueness."[3] So ultimate reality pervades each moment and each moment pervades the whole universe: the two are integrated and interdependent aspects of the unity of reality. The interrelation and unity of all things in the universe is critical to the understanding of Nichiren Daishonin Buddhism, and will be a concept referred to many times through different theories in the pages that follow. Each entity in existence is like each moment, changeable and transient, but at the same time incorporating the unchanging eternal reality from one moment to the next from the beginning of life to its end and from life into death. The ultimate reality is the whole that links one moment to the next, one day to the next and one lifetime to another. It is the whole that unites myriad separate and unique parts. The goal of Nichiren Daishonin Buddhism is to experience that wholeness, that ultimate reality, and to live life fully informed by it in all dimensions.

The Mystic Law

Ultimate reality is the *Mystic* Law, Buddhahood or Buddha-nature. The whole point of Nichiren Daishonin Buddhism is to reveal that Law and to live life according to the harmony and rhythm of it. It is to the Mystic Law that the Buddha Siddhartha Gautama awakened and in the writings of Nichiren Daishonin we find the words: "Concerning the debt owed to the Law, the Law is the teacher of all Buddhas. It is because of the Law that the Buddhas are worthy of respect. Therefore, those who wish to repay their debt to the Buddha must first repay the debt they owe to the Law."[4] Everything that exists is a manifestation of this Law that links all the different parts of manifest existence together as one. While it allows for individuation and diversity, the Law as the ultimate reality ensures the interconnection of all manifest phenomena. Experience of such interconnection, of the oneness of all is concomitant with Buddhahood. The Law as ultimate reality is, thus, the original entity from which all transient things began in the past, begin in the present and will begin in the future. It is that constant, infinite, eternal process that generates the true pulse and rhythm of the whole universe and permeates everything from the vast expanses of space, to individual life and a tiny grain of sand. As such it is incomprehensible and unfathomable – it is *Mystic*.

What, then, prevents experience of the Mystic Law? This question will be answered in more depth when we look at the self later in this chapter. What needs to be noted here is that the causes individuals make in their lives ensure that they will have to reap the results of their thoughts, words and actions. It is these results, these effects, which cloud perspectives of reality, causing life to be lived in a deluded reality. Nichiren Daishonin explained: "The mystic principle that is the essential nature of phenomena possesses two aspects, the defiled aspect and the pure aspect. If the defiled aspect is operative, this is called delusion. If the pure aspect is operative, this is called enlightenment. Enlightenment constitutes the realm of Buddhahood. Delusion constitutes the realm of ordinary mortals."[5] Thus, there is a choice on how to live life – revealing the Law within or inhibiting it. Because the Law permits individuation and change, choices are always possible in both negative and positive directions. The point of Nichiren Daishonin Buddhism is to change through the aid of the Mystic Law within, and live according to the "pure aspect" noted in the Daishonin's words above. But both delusion and enlightenment are aspects of the one Law and are united by it. In the words of Nichiren Daishonin again:

> These two aspects, the deluded and the enlightened, are indeed two
> different phenomena, and yet both are the workings of the one principle,
> that is, the essential nature of phenomena, or the true aspect of reality. It
> is like a piece of crystal. If the crystal is placed in the sun's rays, it will
> attract them and produce fire. But if it is placed in the moon's rays, it will

produce water. The crystal is a single entity, but the effects it produces differ according to the circumstances.

The mystic principle of the true aspect of reality is like this. The mystic principle of the true aspect of reality is one, but if it encounters evil influences, it will manifest delusion, while if it encounters good influences it will manifest enlightenment. Enlightenment means enlightenment to the essential nature of phenomena, and delusion ignorance of it.[6]

The Three Truths (santai)

While ultimate reality is one, *Three Truths* inform it:

- The truth of the transient phenomenal existence called *ketai* or just *ke*.
- The truth of spiritual non-substantiality, or emptiness called *kutai* or *ku*.
- The truth of the Middle Way called *chutai* or *chu*, which is the binding force of the other two, *ke* and *ku*.

Ke, *ku* and *chu* are three perspectives of the same reality, and an enlightened person experiences their perfect unity.

Ke is the outward, physical, manifest aspect of something, let us say a person, for example. It is what is empirically verifiable either directly by the senses or by indirect methods and so includes the whole universe. As matter it is subject to decay and death or disintegration and so we can say that all existence is temporary. Whatever exists as *ke* is a temporary combination of causes that makes it what it is. When these causes dissipate, what is left is its non-substantiality or *ku*.

Ku is the non-physical aspect of something rather like its nature. In a person, this would be the character and personality that underpins the manifest, physical person. But it has much deeper meanings in that *ku* is the invisible, non-substantial *potentiality* that is neither existence nor non-existence. Buddhism has long taught the theory of *Dependent Origination*, that is to say that everything that comes into existence is dependent on something else, is dependent on other components. *Ku* is what binds these components together and provides the underlying nature of things that acquire a temporary reality: so it is present in all manifest phenomena, all *ke*. But when phenomena cease to exist they become the *potential* non-substance of *ku* – not lost, but existing in potential alone. Thus, from death we pass like all things from a state of *ke* to *ku*. It will be an important concept that we shall return to when we look at death under the topic of the self. *Ku* is sometimes called Void, Emptiness (Skt. *shunyata*) or latency, but none of these terms is meant in the sense of nothingness, or non-existence: rather, *ku* is that which is in a state of neither existence nor non-existence. When potentiality of *ku* is shifted by appropriate causes to *ke*, then some manifest object is born: when it dies or disintegrates the temporary existence of that object as *ke* reverts to its potential as *ku*. *Ke* and *ku* represent the manifest and non-manifest phases of all things.

Chu is the wider and deeper essence or entity that contains both *ke* and *ku* and that provides continuity to their existence. It is like the whole, continuous life of a person in which his or her physical and spiritual self are contained. *Chu* is the most important aspect, for it is that by which we can improve our *ke* and *ku*. It is the uniqueness of a phenomenon and that which links it with the cosmos. Both *ke* and *ku* are temporary, so ultimately they are neither substantial nor non-substantial. Only *chu* can make sense of reality because it is the Middle Way that makes *ke* and *ku* possible and integrates them, giving reality to the transient and temporary. While all things have temporary existence and non-substantiality, in fact they are fundamentally neither of these. As Ikeda points out, *chu* "can be thought of as the permanently unchangeable 'nucleus' of life".[7] *Chu*, then, is the truth of the Middle Way that all things are in nature temporary existence and non-substantiality combined, while *chu* itself provides their continuity and unites them.

As human beings, we live life according to balances between our physical and spiritual make-up, but neither can provide us with the correct perspective of reality. If we could transcend the two and see life as it *really* is, then we would be viewing things from the perspective of the Middle Way, from *chutai*. Then, life would become more balanced, more harmonious, and we would see into the truth of all things. But if we are blind to *chu*, to the Middle Way, then we live our lives under delusion and in ignorance. Through *chu* we can see the unity of *ke*, *ku* and *chu* and the true way in which they represent a unified reality. The Middle Way is ultimate truth, ultimate reality, the true nature of all things that is permanent and unchanging. In the words of the Daishonin: "Life is indeed an elusive reality that transcends both the words and concepts of existence and non-existence. It is neither existence nor non-existence, yet exhibits the qualities of both. It is the mystic entity of the Middle Way that is the ultimate reality."[8] That "elusive reality" is what can unify the self with the cosmic life-force.

The Three Truths have other interpretations too. In the life of the Buddha they represent the three enlightened properties or bodies (*Trikaya*) of his physical being and compassion (Skt. *nirmanakaya*, corresponding to *ke*), the spiritual wisdom of the blissful Buddha (Skt. *sambhogakaya*, corresponding to *ku*) and the essence of the Buddha that is the Law, the ultimate reality and the Middle Way (Skt. *Dharmakaya*, corresponding to *chu*). Like *ke*, *ku* and *chu* the three bodies or aspects of the Buddha are united as one. *Ke*, *ku* and *chu* also represent three virtues, freedom from the suffering of birth and death (corresponding to *ke*), the virtue of wisdom (corresponding to *ku*), and the ultimate truth of the Mystic Law, the Middle Way (corresponding to *chu*).

The interconnected universe

Since the Mystic Law as ultimate reality is the source and unifying factor of all phenomena, everything is interconnected and everything, since it has the Mystic Law within, is eternal. Reality could not be *ultimate* if it were transient. It is a truth and reality that pervades all for all time. Buddhism accepts that the world in which we live is not the only one in the cosmos and that there are countless worlds with life forms in other universes beyond our own. The Law remains the uniting factor in the whole of the cosmos, a pulse that makes the whole cosmos a unified and interconnected existence – a macrocosm in which are millions of microcosms and infinitesimal microcosms like the human self that are connected, through the Law, to the whole cosmos. That interconnection exists in every moment of time so that the whole cosmos is contained in each single moment of existence of any phenomenon. Because the Law is the *eternal* ultimate reality that pervades all things, each moment possesses eternity, both time and timelessness. The Mystic Law is *kuon ganjo*, time without beginning, beyond past, present and future. Each moment contains eternity and all the causes and effects of past, present and future.

The Indian, Hindu and Buddhist view of the universe has always been one of evolution and involution in repeated cycles. Whatever comes into existence has to die, but such "death" is not so much a total disappearance but a return to a latent and potential state, rather like the state of deep sleep before we wake to live another day. The universe, like living forms, sleeps and wakes and sleeps and wakes until the end of existence when a more pervasive sleep occurs, the "death" of the form. The existence of the universe is no different to that of the human in that it is born and goes through a stage, or *kalpa*, of evolution and formation. Then it has a stage of continuance, followed by one of decline and then one of disintegration, only to be reborn after a long period of quiescence. This is the Buddhist theory of eternal rise and fall of all world systems.

Buddhist *sutras* often mention the worlds of Buddhas and *bodhisattvas* in other universes. Even the *Gohonzon*, as was seen in CHAPTER SIX, has the names of deities, Buddhas and *bodhisattvas* inscribed on it. For Nichiren Daishonin Buddhism, such references are usually understood as imagery referring to the Buddhahood within oneself or that in the universe, and so are meant figuratively. Ikeda certainly suggests so, indicating that deities can be thought to "symbolize the powers of protection inherent in the natural phenomena of the Universe and in society, powers which are activated and strengthened by the individual's Buddhist practice".[9] Indeed, if all is interconnected and at one, this is a logical premise: whatever is in the cosmos is also within the self. These deities represent positive forces in the universe that the believer wishes to call forth in his or her self and may provide a focus for such.

From all that has been written so far, we would have to say that, according to Nichiren Daishonin Buddhism, nothing at all – no person, inanimate object, cosmic force, law – can be separated from our lives. Everything is permanently and eternally interconnected and interrelated. This is what ultimate reality is all about and to see such interrelation is to experience that reality. Ultimately, the entire cosmos exists within the inner self. In Ikeda's words: "Buddhism teaches that all people must pursue, in their own daily lives and throughout their entire lives, the knowledge of 'the identity of the Universe and life' – in other words, of the true aspect of the mutual activity, communication and sympathy of the macrocosm without and the microcosm within."[10]

The principle of oneness accepted by Nichiren Daishonin Buddhism is critical to the understanding of this branch of Buddhism. Oneness is indicative of unity between life and its environment, between mind and matter, between living and inanimate objects, between microcosm and macrocosm simply because everything is brought together as one by the cosmic force of the Mystic Law, by Buddhahood or Buddha-nature. The specific oneness between life and its environment is termed *esho funi*, the *e* of *esho* (short for *eho*), referring to the objective environment and *sho* (short for *shoho*), to subjective life. The relationship between the two is often explained as the body (life) and its shadow (the environment). *Funi* means "two in manifestation but not two in essence", that is to say, life and the environment are independent in one sense but inseparably unified in another.

Of course, our perspectives of the reality of the environment around us will differ according to our individual pathologies and states at a particular moment in time, and in general: the bottle is half empty for some and half full for others. Importantly, because of the inseparability of life and its environment, whatever takes place in the environment or whatever life comes into being does so because of the alignment of causes in the cosmos that link them at that moment, not by chance or by what appear to be immediate observable factors. Past *karma*, a concept that will be looked at in more detail below in the context of the self, brings about a life form *and* an inseparable and appropriate environment for that form. We could say that each person has a unique self, a unique environment and a unique perspective of that environment. Further, the inseparability between life and its environment is indicative of the radical influence that each has on the other, a point graphically stated in the following words: "An environment is a reflection of the inner life of the individual living within it; it takes on characteristics which accord with the life-condition of the individual in question. In other words, life extends its influence into the surroundings."[11] The implications of such a theory for the way in which we behave and relate to our environment and planet are self-evident; the environment will resonate to the same influences as the people who inhabit it.

What emerges from the examination of ultimate reality above is the non-dual nature of the cosmos, of the self and the cosmos, as well as the environment and the self. If we include the oneness of mind and body, the implications are an identity of the self with the whole universe.[12] Nichiren Daishonin Buddhism, therefore "teaches that the human being is essentially one with the Universe and clarifies the vastness of the human mind. Spatially the infinite expanse of the Universe in the ten directions and temporally the eternal flow of time spanning the three existences of past, present and future – all this is contained in a single moment of one's mind".[13] One of the doctrines to emerge as singular to all aspects of Buddhism is that of *ahimsa* "non-harm" or "non-violence". It is a concept intensified by the idea of the oneness of all things.

Nam-myoho-renge-kyo

Nichiren Daishonin Buddhism bases its concepts on the *Lotus Sutra* (Skt. *Saddharma-pundarika-sutra, The Sutra of the Lotus Blossom of the Wonderful Law*). The importance of this primary text of Mahayana Buddhism has been emphasized in CHAPTER FIVE. A few words are necessary here to remind us of some of the historical factors. It was T'ien-t'ai, the great Chinese teacher who studied and classified the teachings of the Buddha Shakyamuni. He concluded that the *Lotus Sutra* was the supreme teaching – a *Sutra* that stated that Buddhahood was available to all people. For Nichiren Daishonin, it was particularly the title, the *daimoku*, of the *Lotus Sutra* – *Myoho-renge-kyo* – that not only contained the whole essence of the *Sutra* but was the equivalent of ultimate reality. Nichiren Daishonin was later to state: "If you wish to free yourself from the sufferings of birth and death you have endured since time without beginning and to attain without fail unsurpassed enlightenment in this lifetime, you must perceive the mystic truth that is originally inherent in all living beings. This truth is *Myoho-renge-kyo*."[14] Because *Nam-myoho-renge-kyo* is the Mystic Law and ultimate reality, chanting it brings one in line with the rhythm and pulse of that Law, with the universe, the Buddha-nature inherent in it, with ultimate reality and with the oneness of all things. Nichiren Daishonin prefaced the title with the word *nam*, an abbreviated form of Sanskrit *namas* "devotion". What he indicated was that devotion to *Myoho-renge-kyo* reveals one's Buddhahood – the same Buddhahood to which all Buddhas are enlightened.

So *Myoho-renge-kyo* is the Mystic Law and ultimate reality. In Ikeda's words, *Nam-myoho-renge-kyo* "is the Law which enables all things and all phenomena to maintain perfect harmony and order. It is also the source of limitless energy for creation and revitalization. In a word, *Myoho-renge-kyo* is the Law which ensures that human beings and society continue to develop and progress".[15] And if *Myoho-renge-kyo* is the Law, then it is also *ke, ku* and *chu*, manifest phenomena, non-substantiality and the Middle Way: it is all life and inanimate matter. Let us turn now to look at each of the characters in the title.

Nam

Nichiren Daishonin placed the word *nam* in front of the title of the *Lotus Sutra*. It has the meaning "devotion" or, if translated into Japanese, *kimyo*, meaning verbally "to devote one's life". Richard Causton commented that: "The concept of *nam* is so important because the deepest meaning of this word encapsulates both the action we need to take, and the attitude we need to develop, if we are to attain Buddhahood in this lifetime."[16] Devotion is a strong and active word. Just thinking about *Nam-myoho-renge-kyo* is insufficient; *devotion* in an *active* sense is necessary in order to reveal Buddhahood. Devotion is needed in every dimension of one's being since devotion in terms of *Nam-myoho-renge-kyo* is devotion to, and fusion with, *ultimate* reality as the Law that pervades the whole of the universe, and with the truth that is the deepest aspect of our own selves. And in fusing with that Law and revealing it within the self, the wisdom of the Law becomes the inner experience through which an individual perceives life. It is such devotion that makes Nichiren Daishonin Buddhism an *active* rather than a fundamentally philosophically-focused faith.

Myoho

Myoho means "Mystic" or "Wonderful Law". *Myo* means "to open", "fully endowed", "mystic", "wonderful" and "to revive" and is *ku*, non-substantiality and the unseen essence that lies within all manifest phenomena. More than that, "fully endowed" suggests the perfection of containing all possibilities and truths, both latent and manifest, all of which are beyond the limits of conception by the mind, and so remain mystic. It is *ho*, "law", which refers to manifest phenomena and so is synonymous with *ke*. *Myo/ku* and *ho/ke* combined as *myoho* is the Mystic Law as *chu*. The three, *ke*, *ku* and *chu*, are three interdependent aspects of ultimate reality. Each entity in existence is a combination of both *myo* and *ho*, so in the human being, *myo* is the spirituality, nature and potentiality within, while *ho* is the physical being, along with the way the inner nature and potential is manifested exteriorly as good or evil.

Buddhahood and enlightenment are *myo* as aspects of ultimate reality that cannot be perceived. Their opposite would be phenomenal reality as seen through illusion and delusion, as *ho*. When combined, enlightenment and delusion are one as *myoho* or *chu*, for both *myo* and *ho* are interrelated and made possible by *chu*. *Myo* incorporates death as the latent and unseen state of *ku* that life passes into and from which new life comes forth in ever-repeated cycles – hence two of its meanings as "to revive" and "to open", indicative of that which opens up the unseen creative energy necessary for life to emerge. To open also suggests "to reveal" in the sense of revealing the secrets of ultimate reality and Buddhahood. Ikeda interprets "to revive" in the sense of personal evolution: "'To revive' means that, by embracing the Mystic Law, each person without exception can carry out a vibrant and boundless reformation of his or her life itself. This reformation forms the basis for the perfection of one's character and, moreover, provides the power to transform one's destiny."[17] *Ho* represents life and all manifestation that emerges, repeatedly, from the latent state of *ku*. That manifestation can be positive or negative, good or evil, for the latent, unseen and unmanifest state of *ku* contains all possibilities. Further, from what we have seen of the oneness of the nature of ultimate reality above, we know that each entity in existence, including the microcosm of the human self, has within it the entire cosmos, and that would include the potential for all things whether negative or positive.

Renge

The word *renge* means "lotus blossom" and refers to the flower that has become a powerful symbol in Buddhism. Many people are already familiar with the "lotus position" where, in meditation, a person sits with each upturned foot on the opposite thigh, spine erect and the body still and quiet. Here, the outstretched knees resemble the leaves of the lotus and the erect body the lotus flower. The lotus, too, is an exquisitely beautiful flower that grows in muddy swamps, rising dry above the wet flat leaves on which it is based. Such imagery is symbolic of the Buddhahood that can rise from the defilements of the world, or within ordinary life. The lotus is also symbolic of beauty, prosperity, longevity and fertility. It is important in Nichiren Daishonin Buddhism, too, because the prime teaching of the Buddha, the *Lotus Sutra*, purposefully uses the lotus to refer to Buddhahood. But the lotus is also unusual because its flower and fruit/seeds occur at the same time and that factor, for Nichiren Daishonin Buddhism, symbolizes the simultaneity and oneness of cause and effect, that is to say, when we create a cause, an effect, even though latent, *is created at the same time*.[18] Moreover, the fact that the flower and fruit appear simultaneously is also symbolic of the presence of Buddhahood at the same time as all other factors of life at any one moment. This will be seen when we examine the Ten Worlds below.

Nothing can escape the law of cause and effect; nothing can come into existence without a cause, and where there is a cause, then there must be an effect. Nor can anything happen by chance, for effects are related to their causes and cannot occur at random. Such a theory of causality excludes the possibility of a first cause, a creator of some kind, for everything – and that would include a first cause – must itself be an effect of a prior cause. Then, too, the seeds of the lotus can survive for thousands of years and still germinate[19] and this symbolizes the point that an effect of a cause can lie latent for a very long time before becoming manifest. In *Nam-myoho-renge-kyo*, the word *renge*, then, has immense significance, indicating that, like the oneness of flower and fruit of the lotus, ultimate reality is singular, and causes and their effects are simultaneous. In terms of practice, chanting *Nam-myoho-renge-kyo* is the excellent cause that will produce simultaneous excellent effects.

We should pause here to take a closer look at the theory of causality in

Nichiren Daishonin Buddhism. While effects are simultaneous and immediate with their causes, they may take lifetimes to emerge and so are *latent effects* of *inherent causes*, causes that are made, but neither causes nor effects are yet manifest. Then, particular circumstances occur that make the *inherent cause* manifest; in other words we have an *external cause*. It is that *external cause* that will bring about the *manifest effect*. So we have:

inherent cause(s) producing simultaneous *latent effect(s)* until
external cause(s) produce *manifest effect(s)*

Thus, causes for things that happen to us lie deep within until the right circumstances, the *external causes* bring them to the surface and create *manifest effects*. Importantly, two people can do the same action but will not always reap the same effects of it. That is because the *inherent causes* and their immediate *latent effects* deep within the self have not yet been triggered by the right *external causes*. Of course, if two men rob a bank and are caught, they are likely to have the same effect of being put in jail. Yet their experiences of robbery and jail are likely to be very different, depending on their unique natures and the *inherent causes* and *effects* for other experiences. Human beings have an instinctive habit of blaming everyone else for things that go wrong in their lives. But Buddhist belief is that the causes lie within their own selves: what happens in life is just the play-off of those *inherent causes*. We cannot experience the effects of someone else's causes, only the effects of our own. Causton put the point clearly when he wrote: "But until we learn to accept that we become angry or upset not because of any external cause, such as our relationships with other people or our circumstances, but ultimately because of something that already exists within our own lives – the inherent cause – we can never begin to change that innate tendency and so become fundamentally happy."[20]

Every time we react to something we immediately create another *inherent cause* that will store a *latent effect* that will emerge sometime in the future under the right circumstances. It will be seen how this has deeper meaning when the concept of *karma* is examined in the context of the self later in this chapter. Our thoughts, words and actions tend to form habit patterns and it is these from the past that produce innate tendencies to behave and think in a certain way: we are not as free as we think we are. Then, too, the innate tendencies we have incline us towards certain types of people, certain areas of life, into violence, into anger, into poetry, into science and so on. If we think we are suffering, then we have to examine what the innate causes of that suffering might be and seek to change them by laying down different, better *inherent causes*. According to Nichiren Daishonin Buddhism, chanting *Nam-myoho-renge-kyo* is an *external cause* that deposits beneficial *inherent causes* deep within the self, so changing the innate nature of the personality. Moreover, because all things are contained in one life moment, Buddhahood remains an *inherent cause* deep within the self; it just has to have the right conditions to manifest its effects: chanting *Nam-myoho-renge-kyo* is believed to effectuate this.

Causes should not be thought of singularly, that is to say *one* action producing *one* specific effect. The process of cause and effect is much more complicated, with multiple causes producing complex effects. The Buddha expressed this multiple-cause theory in his teaching of *Dependent Origination* that was mentioned above. What this theory suggests is that everything depends on something else; it is impossible to have a first cause that is itself uncaused. Birth necessitates death, and death necessitates birth. According to Shakyamuni Buddha, it is ignorance, desires and cravings that keep us within this cycle: losing ignorance and gaining knowledge about the true nature of the self as non-self, will bring an end to the desires and cravings that create fruitive *karma* and that bind the individual to countless rebirths. Nichiren Daishonin Buddhism is unique in that it accepts the principle of cause and effect *in perpetuity*: life is regenerated for ever and there is no final end effect of permanent release from life. Far from being a negative concept, revealing the Buddha-nature within and living life from that state within, means that humankind is in a position to help all others in life, in the true *bodhisattva* ideal.

Kyo

Kyo, literally the warp in cloth, the thread (Skt. *sutra*), refers to the teaching of a Buddha in its most dynamic sense of reverberation of the ultimate truth. To Nichiren Daishonin Buddhism this truth is that the whole of the universe is the manifestation of the Mystic Law. It is life reverberating in all things, the vibration of the central essence and ultimate reality of the universe. *Kyo* was extended in meaning to refer to the sound and voice of teaching – an appropriate extension given the fact that the Buddha taught not by the written but by the spoken word. It also came to indicate the eternal nature of what was taught as ultimate truth. According to Ikeda: "A Buddha's enlightenment, expressed in the voice of his preaching, is *kyo*, and the truth to which he has been enlightened is eternal, spanning past, present and future. When we awaken to this truth we realize the eternal aspect of our own lives, an aspect that transcends the changes of the physical world and the cycle of birth and death."[21]

Taken as a whole, *Nam-myoho-renge-kyo* is indicative of the ultimate reality that pervades the entire cosmos. It is resonant with the Buddha-nature in all things. And that reality in all things is the power by which it is possible for sentient beings to change – for they have the power to reveal it – but at the same time, to recognize that same reality in all things, in non-sentient, inanimate things with which they can interact with the wisdom of human Buddha-nature. Now it is necessary to turn from an analysis of ultimate reality in its cosmic sense to a more focused view of the human being his or her self, beginning with the *Ten Worlds*.

The Ten Worlds

The Ten Worlds (*jikkai*) were thought of in some strands of Buddhism as ten separate worlds into which people were reborn depending on their *karma*.[22] But in Nichiren Daishonin Buddhism they are ten *states of being* or *conditions of life*. The important point about them is that they *all exist at any one time in every thing*, for they are a facet of the unity of all reality. It is in the human being as part of that unified ultimate reality, however, that they are critically experienced and in which they are capable of being changed. These states or Ten Worlds are Hell, Hunger, Animality, Anger, Tranquillity, Rapture, Learning, Realization, *Bodhisattva* and Buddhahood. With the exception of the last two of these, we all know that we can experience hell at some time in our lives, just the same as we can feel we are experiencing heaven, say, when we're in love. We can also shift from one extreme to another fairly quickly in life, perhaps radiantly happy and in heaven, only for something dreadful to happen and reduce us to hell. These ten different states, then, at any moment in time, obtain in our personalities. The first three are called the *Three Evil Paths*, for they often appear hand in hand and characterize those who are bound by their own instinctive cravings. They tend to be associated with evil and wrong-doing and are the lowest of the Ten Worlds and carry considerable suffering.

Hell (Jap. *jigoku*) is the state we are in when we are suffering or when we impulsively cause suffering to others. It is the destructive tendency in life, as well as embodying the feeling, or causing, of total constraint and lack of freedom. It is the worst and lowest condition of life causing the greatest mental or physical suffering about which one feels helpless. Intense worry and anxiety are characteristic. It is also a myopic state because it is all its experiencer can think about and this affects attitudes to the external environment, often resulting in destructive rage.

Hunger (Jap. *gaki*) is the state of desires and cravings. It is a state that dominates most of our existence. Most people spend a large percentage of their lives working for things that are generally accepted as societal norms – a home, a family, a car, a better job, a holiday, and even basics like food, warmth and shelter. We also desire psychological support such as love, acceptance, social standing, approval, praise, pleasure and so on. Usually, we think that we will be happier when we have achieved these goals, but in the state of Hunger, satisfaction never occurs, and hunger for the next things, sometimes obsessively, always exists. Causton described it as "a kind of psychological condition characterized by a constant inner restlessness, an intense yearning for happiness and fulfilment which fixes upon various things in the vain hope that they will finally satisfy this all-consuming desire".[23] Greed and jealousy often ensue. However, desire is a facet of life, and to seek to eradicate it – as some strands of Buddhism do – is to deny humanity, according to Nichiren Daishonin Buddhism. Filtering desires through the life-condition of

Buddhahood or through the *Bodhisattva* condition makes them more altruistic, less egocentric and important for the well-being of humanity.

Animality (Jap. *chikuso*) is the state in which we allow our instinctive drives to come to the fore rather than our reasoning and moral consciousness. While we have to rely on some instincts for survival, if we prey on those weaker than ourselves, become aggressive or misuse power, or have no control over our behaviour, then the state of Animality exists. Fear is also a characteristic, a fear that drives a living being for instinctive survival. According to Ikeda: "Animality is a state of brute stupidity in which one is totally caught up in instinctual reactions to immediate affairs and makes no attempt to grasp what is most important or essential in life."[24] When we add the next state we have the *Four Evil Paths*:

Anger (Jap. *shura*[25]) is a state of conflict and aggression. But it has more subtle nuances of meaning than the word superficially suggests, for it connotes the kind of egoistic selfishness that makes a person feel he or she is better than all others. This sort of person harms the weak. In the state of Anger people display arrogance, conceit, self-importance, self-centredness and superiority. In fact, the greater the ego, the more the individual resides in the world of Anger. Causton described the state vividly when he wrote: "The person in the state of Anger cannot bear to lose. Quite simply, he must be the best. He must have the best job, the highest salary, the prettiest wife, in short, anything and everything which will separate him from, and place him above, the common herd of humanity."[26] Here, then, we have the competitive person, the patronizing one, the resentful one and the one who has to achieve at the expense of others, or who cannot bear others to achieve. Nevertheless, Anger can be a positive force if used altruistically to fight injustice. But, as Aristotle said: "Anyone can become angry – that is easy. But to be angry with the right person, to the right degree, at the right time, for the right purpose, and in the right way – that is not easy."[27] These four are the lowest states in which we can find ourselves. Then follow two more states that make us feel happy.

Tranquillity or *Humanity* (Jap. *nin*) is the state in which we experience peace, calm and quietude. It is the harmonious state when desires are under check and there is harmony with all that is around one and with others in the world. To achieve this humane state we need wisdom, discernment, rationality, good judgement and sound morality, for we can reason with ourselves and others. The contrast with the previous world of Anger is obvious and the experience of slipping from a pleasant calm state into one of the lower worlds is all too evident when a negative stimulus in the environment occurs. But while Tranquillity lacks the imbalances of the lower worlds, it can be negatively construed as apathy and lack of effort – taking the easy way out of things for a peaceful life. If it is too neutral it can lead to stagnation. Essentially, it is a restorative state, rather like sleep, but not one in which life should be permanently lived.

Rapture or *Heaven* (Jap. *ten*) is the state of happiness when our troubles have dissipated and our desires have been fulfilled. It is the state we want most in life – joyful, satisfied, and full of well-being. Of course, the degree of Rapture will depend on our desires. If fulfilled desires from the lower worlds make us happy, then it is likely not to last. But we also feel happy when we are fit and well – particularly after a long illness – for then we are better able to cope with whatever life brings to us. However, the best kind of happiness is that which bubbles up from within, that is part of our inner spiritual being and that is there even when life is difficult. This is the highest kind of Rapture. It is the Heaven on Earth that contrasts with the Hell on Earth, but can only be stable when it comes from within, not, from some transient and changing stimulus or person in the environment. Heaven and Hell are, thus, states of being of our own making – either from past *karma* or from present thought and action.

The six states from *Hell* to *Rapture* are called the *Six Paths* and are the states of life that we experience regularly in ordinary, day-to-day life. In the main, they are regulated by our environment, by people around us, and by our external experiences.[28] They are states concomitant with desires and aversions and reactions to the environments and cultures in which we live. In fact, these six worlds represent the full extent of life for many people, dictating how they shape their lives and their concepts of their own self identity. The transience of these states makes fulfilment in any real sense impossible, and delusion and suffering become the basic characteristics of life as individuals try to find happiness in a world of flux. In contrast, the last four worlds are called the *Four Noble Paths* or *Four Noble Worlds*. They are more internalized states that we have to work at in order to gain release from the lower life of the *Six Paths*. The self-effort here contrasts with the behaviour of the lower worlds in which we are swayed by external stimuli. The first two of the *Four*, *Learning* and *Realization*, are known as the *two vehicles* (Jap. *nijo*), because they are the vehicles, the means, by which one takes action to evolve to higher life-conditions. Here, the individual has more independence of thought than when trapped in the desires and aversions of the lower six worlds. The first three of the *Four Noble Paths* – Learning, Realization and *Bodhisattva*—are known as the *Three Higher Worlds*.

Learning (Jap. *shomon*) is the state of conscious expansion of knowledge about the impermanence of life, suffering, the self, and reality, through study, but mainly vicariously through the experience and teaching of others. It is a condition of seeking, of trying to evolve through learning. The Japanese word for it, *shomon*, means "voice-hearer", referring to those who heard the voice, the teachings, of the Buddha. These individuals were seeking enlightenment and were the disciples of the Buddha, but in Nichiren Daishonin Buddhism, Learning, as one of the Ten Worlds, suggests that everyone carries the potential for it – everyone can seek enlightenment. Learning is a positive process, but it can be intense enough to exclude other things, so becoming self-centred. It is all too easy for the knowledgeable to think they are superior to others, and degenerate into the condition of Anger.

Realization (Jap. *engaku*) is a more internalized knowledge of life. It is when we come to understand things about life from deep within and independently, rather than being told about something. The Sanskrit word for knowledge is *jnana*, while knowledge of ultimate reality that springs from an intuitive depth and understanding within, is *vijnana*. A similar kind of distinction obtains between Learning and Realization. Realization is the world, the life-condition that makes partial enlightenment possible. But, like the state of Learning, Realization can become an egocentric goal, so encompassing more of the world of Anger than of evolving forward to enlightenment. And with both Learning and Realization there is the danger of becoming so focused in study and knowledge that the rest of the world is excluded. If wisdom becomes myopic, fundamentalist and exclusive, the world of Anger emerges. Then, too, fear of failure and the opposite drive for success are all too often concomitant with erudition.

Bodhisattva (Jap. *bosatsu*) at its best is the state of universal compassionate care for others. Compassion (Jap. *jihi*[29]) is altruistic to the extent that hardship encountered through devotion to others is a joy, for personal self-centredness is absent. *Bodhisattvas* are those who seek enlightenment not only for themselves, but for all others also.[30] Since reality is a unity, then one's own happiness and those of all others is inevitably linked. However, should the ego come into play with self-praise and self-emulation for such deeds, then the state of *Bodhisattva* is tinged with those of the lower worlds. Thus, it is important to develop the wisdom and knowledge that occur in the two previous states of Learning and Realization in order to gain the kind of vital energy that is not dissipated by disillusion or sadness.

Buddhahood (Jap. *butsu*) is the outcome of the *Bodhisattva* state. It is the state in which we see everything such as it is without our own egos, desires and aversions colouring what we see. Causton described the state admirably when he wrote: "The Ten Worlds can thus be likened to ten different pairs of glasses. Nine[31] of those pairs, from Hell to Bodhisattva, can give a distorted view of reality, while only Buddhahood enables us to see our life as it really is."[32] In this condition, there is absolute freedom, experience of ultimate reality as a unity, and the ability to live life with total wisdom and compassion. What is important to realize about Buddhahood is that, since it is one of the Ten Worlds, it exists *in every living and every inanimate thing*. Thus, in terms of human beings, anyone can experience the same Buddhahood as the Buddha Shakyamuni or as any of the Buddhas. Ikeda calls it "the supreme jewel in the depths of our being".[33] For most, however, Buddhahood remains in the latent, non-substantial state of *ku*.

Importantly, too, Buddhahood is not a static state but a dynamic one, for once awakened it enables an individual to handle and deal with all the other nine states through its essential reality. Put simply, Buddhahood *transforms* all the experiences that occur in the other states. It is not separate from ordinary existence but dynamically involved with every moment of it. Buddhahood is enlightenment and is also everyday life. Causton's words are more than pertinent here when he said that "Buddhahood is not an ethereal or 'other worldly' state, but a quality which finds expression in the behaviour of ordinary people and the practicalities of everyday life. In short, we do not practice this Buddhism to become saints or superhumans but to become great human beings, capable of solving every human problem".[34] Suffering still exists, but is experienced differently in Buddhahood: Ikeda says that it is "possession of a vibrant, sturdy life force and the abundant wisdom to challenge and overcome all the sufferings and the difficulties that we may encounter".[35] Buddhahood involves self-wisdom and boundless compassion. The enlightened individual understands the true nature of the self, has knowledge of the eternity of life, has pure reason and wisdom that are independent of ego and is thoroughly happy and free. The other life-conditions still exist but are viewed differently through the filter of Buddhahood, the filter of knowledge of ultimate reality as a unity, infinite wisdom and infinite compassion.

Underpinning the Ten Worlds is the unity behind constant change and flux – a theory supported by the *mutual possession* or *mutual inclusion* of the Ten Worlds in each phenomenon in life. That is to say that each of the worlds includes the others too. But such mutual possession does not mean that everyone and every thing reveals *all* of the conditions; each simply possesses them, even inanimate objects. When not expressed, the different worlds are latent, and are in a state of non-substantiality – the state of *ku* that was dealt with above. In an individual, it is likely that he or she will live life mainly in a dominant state, a dominant condition and, even though at times in life flickers or longer manifestations of the other conditions may be evident, personalities are usually characterized by their own unique blends of traits. So two people in exactly the same environment, exactly the same situation, will see things differently, depending on which of the Ten Worlds, the life-condition, they are in at the time – the respective pair of glasses they are wearing, to use Causton's analogy above. The dominant condition will effect all the others, so if a person is angry, he or she is likely to bring that tendency to the fore in situations where perhaps the compassion of the state of *Bodhisattva* is needed, and feel angry instead of caring. Then, too, a person predominantly in the world of Anger will have a tendency to transform all the other worlds into situations of Anger. To give another example, contrast the Hunger experienced by a person dominated by Animality with that by a person dominated by *Bodhisattva*. The former will thirst to satiate basic drives and the latter to aid humanity. Because each of the Ten Worlds contains the nine others, a hundred different states, or life-conditions, exist at any one moment, in manifest (*ke*) or latent (*ku*) possibilities.

If we think of mutual possession in the context of the unity of reality, then what happens in one part of that unity has the propensity to affect the rest of reality. Thus, the life condition in which one lives – in whichever of the Ten Worlds one lives life – has the potential to affect everything else. Working towards living life in the condition of Buddhahood – albeit that the other nine states will always be present – has the possibility of creating positive changes in the other aspects of reality with which one is unified, for whatever state we are in will affect all the others. The condition of Buddhahood is present even in the world of Hell. Causton's comment here is pertinent: "Even if you have never actually experienced your Buddhahood, it exists, at this very moment, in the state of *ku*, and, just like flowers in the cherry tree, is simply waiting for the right conditions in order to appear."[36] So, dependent on the right kinds of causes in the environment, and on prior *karmic* causes, one or other of the Ten Worlds will come to the fore, while the others will remain in the latency of *ku*. But whatever life-condition is mainly manifest – be it Hell or Buddhahood – even the hellish person has the propensity for Buddhahood and a Buddha carries the same propensity for Hell: a Buddha and an ordinary person are really identical. Thus, the unity of reality is maintained at the level of all selves. The mutual possession of the Ten Worlds applies to everything in existence, not just to the human being. What needs to be explored now are human selves and just how they are facets of ultimate reality.

The self

It was seen from the nature of the Ten Worlds that most people operate in the lower six, in the worlds that are dictated by desires and responses to the external stimuli of the environment. Many strands of Buddhism believe that the path to enlightenment involves losing all desires and aversions, so creating an equilibrium of harmony and eliminating the acquisition of more *karma* – the causes that necessitate having to be reborn in order to reap their results. Nichiren Daishonin Buddhism, on the other hand, sees desires and aversions as essential in life, and the denial of them a denial of the vibrancy of life itself. It is not desire *per se* that is wrong, but the *kind* of desire. It is desires motivated by the lower six worlds that lead to fruitive *karma* and to suffering. Ikeda aptly refers to the "seething whirlpool of desires, drives and impulses, which give rise to vices and suffering",[37] and the word "whirlpool" describes rather well the complex multiplicity of stimuli to which we respond in our daily lives. Nichiren Daishonin Buddhism has two complementary aims, the revelation of Buddhahood in each human being and the channelling of the other nine worlds through that Buddhahood for the benefit of others. Thus, there is a conscious effort to direct desires in the right way – the desire for the well-being of others, for respect for all peoples, for peace, for the obliteration of poverty, and so on. These are good desires that are essential components of a global harmony and, indeed, are consonant with true, compassionate Buddhahood: desire and enlightenment is the same thing.

In ordinary life, however, most of our desires are governed by our needs for health, financial security, a good job, food on the table, a good life for the children and the fulfilment of cultural, societal norms. Buddhism reduces all our earthly desires into three categories known as the *three poisons* – greed, anger and delusion, ignorance, or stupidity. Greed makes us strive egoistically to fulfil extrinsic aims often through means that are not intrinsically valuable, and with no intrinsically valuable outcomes either. Nothing satisfies when greed dictates desires. Trying to fulfil these desires wears us out and, in Ikeda's words: "The fresh green land of our lives is transformed into the desolate, parched land of Hunger."[38] Anger, as was seen from the fourth of the Ten Worlds above, makes us strive to fulfil our desires at the expense of, or in competition with, others. Delusion, or stupidity – "dark, gloomy clouds squatting over our internal skies"[39] – traps us in our respective worlds and blindfolds us to the wider reality of existence. To be stupid is to be ignorant of the truth and to live life under delusion. The worst delusions are the grasping for permanence when all is transient and impermanent; the belief that we have ownership of things and people, when such possession cannot possibly last; belief in an eternal life in a paradisiacal land and the belief that there is nothing after death. Equally delusional is the refusal to accept that we shall reap what we sow and that there are results for all the causes that we make. Some delusions are learned through cultures and environments, others are pathological instincts and deep-seated character traits to which one is genetically (*karmically*) disposed. Once delusion is replaced by enlightenment then all desires manifest the enlightened state, the Mystic Law, the rhythm of the universe and reality.

In terms of the composition of the self, its mental and physical aspects are believed to be made up of mixtures of the energies of the same four elements, earth, water, fire and air or wind that are found in the external universe itself. The harmony between these elements in the body and between them and the elements of the immediate environment and universe is what creates harmony. Shakespeare wrote of Brutus in *Julius Caesar*: "This was the noblest Roman of them all . . . His life was gentle, and the elements so mixed in him that Nature might stand up and say to all the world *This was a man*."[40] To be fully human, the elements within have to be perfectly balanced, in perfect harmony, reflecting the harmony and balance of the enlightened individual and the Law within the universe. It is disharmony of the elements within and their imbalance with the universal elements that cause sickness and *vice versa*.

Buddhism accepts that the self is composed of five components (Skt. *skandhas*). These five components join together to form human life, and at death are scattered. The five components are form, sensation, perception, volition and consciousness. Nichiren Daishonin Buddhism defines these as form, perception, conception, volition and consciousness.[41] *Form* refers to the physical body and its sense organs, as well as the four elements. *Perception* refers to the functioning of the five senses and the mind (which in Buddhism is considered to be a sense organ). *Conception* is the process by which ideas about what we perceive are formulated, and *volition* accounts for our reactions to our conceptions. *Consciousness* is the functioning of thought in direct and abstract ways to allow for discernment and judgement. Take away these five components and there can be no self. They also operate interactively and holistically: take away one and the others cannot function. When conditions are right for an individual to come into existence, these five components come together to create the life form; hitherto, they would have been suspended in the non-substantial but potential state of *ku*. Thus, as Causton wrote: "Our individual life appears as it emerges from this state of *ku*, out of the great 'sea' of life-force that pervades the universe, and at death merges back into this life-force, in the state of *ku*."[42]

The Nine Consciousnesses

The component of consciousness is divided into nine levels in Nichiren Daishonin Buddhism. The first five levels correspond to the five senses of sight, hearing, smell, taste and touch and need not detain us, for they simply connect the external world with the internal consciousness processes. Similarly, the *sixth consciousness* is related to the phenomenal world, to *ke*, and is that which synthesizes the data relayed to us by our senses. The sixth consciousness is the mind, the sixth sense of Buddhism and, like the previous five levels, is purely concerned with external stimuli. It is the last three, the seventh to ninth, which are more critically important, for they are internalized levels that are not dependent on external stimuli, and need to be explored individually.

The *seventh (mano) consciousness* is concerned with the internal, spiritual or non-substantial world of *ku*. It is the thinking consciousness that permits abstract thought, imagination, philosophizing, reflection, differentiation, value judgements and more sophisticated thought processes. However, it is this level of consciousness that is most supportive to the ego and, therefore, to the delusions that were noted above. So the seventh consciousness can motivate the individual towards enlightenment or towards egocentrism. It creates a notion of self that permits identity after a period of unconsciousness, or coma, or after deep sleep, but also gives the individual a false sense of permanence.

The *eighth (alaya) consciousness* is a "store" consciousness – that which stores up all our experiences, our thoughts, words we have spoken and actions we have done. All these reside in a state of latent *ku* unless recalled by some stimulus or need. *Everything* reaches this eighth consciousness; nothing is lost, even though it may reach the very depths of the subconscious. And since nothing is lost in this level, all the thoughts, words and deeds of previous lives are also stored here, ready to influence the way an individual thinks, speaks and acts in his or her present existence. It is from the eighth consciousness that dreams take their content, at a time when the first seven consciousnessness are dormant during sleep. It is, then, our subconscious, containing all the *karmic* seeds that are causes waiting to blossom into effects at the appropriate time. At death, all the residue of *karmic* causes unique to each individual in this level of consciousness are stored in *ku* latency awaiting the right circumstances for regrouping of the five components in another life.

The *alaya* consciousness also contains the collective seeds, the collective *karma* of a family, a race, a whole culture, so dictating the kind of cultural existence into which one would be born for many lifetimes. The idea is similar to Carl Jung's theory of the collective unconscious in which, he believed, all human beings possess the collective psyche of all humanity. And according to Ikeda: "Indeed, it might be that the footprint of each and every step in our past evolution is recorded in the deepest level of our individual minds."[43] If reality is truly unified, then it has to be so throughout time, in the past, present and future. And if the *alaya* consciousness does contain all the footprints – whether good, evil or indifferent – of the past then it contains, too, the whole cosmic energy of all time, manifest and non-manifest.

The *ninth (amala) consciousness* is pure consciousness, ultimate reality and the Mystic Law. It is the very depth and life-force of the universe and is totally free from *karmic* residue. It is *chu* as the ultimate reality and Middle Way that underpins both *ke* and *ku*. It is Buddhahood and Buddha-nature; it is *Nam-myoho-renge-kyo* and the physical *Gohonzon* that represents it; it is the state of oneness with all reality. Revealing this ninth level of consciousness is revealing the Buddhahood deep within, bringing it from a non-manifest state into manifestation. Then, each level of consciousness below the ninth is affected by the universal power that pervades the whole of the self so that even the first six sensory consciousnesses are led by the discerning wisdom of Buddha-nature.

Oneness of body and mind (*shikishin funi*)

The theory of the interconnected universe examined earlier in this chapter put forward the principle of oneness that maintained unity between life and its environment, between macrocosm and microcosm and between living and inanimate objects, for every phenomenon is an expression of the Mystic Law of ultimate reality. The same unity exists also between the mind and the body, between the spiritual and the physical. The theory that each life is a unity in this way is known as *shikishin funi*. *Shiki* refers to the body and what is material and physical, *shin* to the mind, what is inward and what is spiritual, and *funi*[44] to their oneness. Body and mind may have different functions but are interconnected in such a way as to make them one. We experience this when we are ill and find our spirits low, or when our spirits are depressed we can become physically ill. It is the seventh level of consciousness that promotes the idea of ego, of a permanent and unique self that is separate from others and from the environment. In positing an "I" there is a tendency to see that "I" as superior to the body, so encouraging a dualistic perception of the two. But, in line with its unified reality, Nichiren Daishonin Buddhism does not accept such dualism. All the nine levels of consciousness exist in any individual: the higher ones may be latent in the state of *ku* but they are nevertheless parts of the integrated unity of the whole human being. Similarly, the individual is a unity of the five components.

Karma

Most people in the West are familiar with the concept of *karma*, the idea that present causes result in future effects, either in this world or the next: it is a law of causality, of action and reaction. *Karma* is created through any kind of action. That action might be *thought*, which is an action of the mind, *word*, which is the action of speaking, or *deed*, which is more overt action. So, while it might be said that a person is good because he or she does no harmful actions, what goes on in the mind is critically important to ascertaining whether a person is good or not. Whereas we might be able to control our actions, thoughts are a completely different matter, and it is the inner state of an individual that embodies all the tendencies and characteristics that are expressed through the states of the Ten Worlds. While the inner state may be the opposite of what is evident in the outer person, or may be expressed externally, thoughts, words and deeds are all laying down causes on causes, effects on effects, and tendencies on tendencies. Importantly, as was seen above in the context of the word *renge* in *Nam-myoho-renge-kyo*, effects occur *simultaneously* with causes, though they are likely to be latent for a long time – perhaps several lifetimes – before the right external causes bring them to fruition.

Some *karma* is like an arrow that has already left the bow; nothing can be done to avoid it. It is very strong personality tendencies that produce such immutable *karma* and constantly reinforce it. However, Nichiren Daishonin Buddhism believes that even some kinds of ostensibly immutable *karma* can be overcome through revealing one's Buddhahood. Other *karma* is still being formed, particularly that accrued by less intense personality traits, and so is capable of being changed, watered down or burnt away. Sometimes, the manifest effects of *karma* accrued in the present life materialize in the present life, too. Other *karma* will become manifest in the next life or even in a life in the distant future. All such causes and their latent effects are, as we saw above, stored in the eighth consciousness, the *alaya* consiousness. At every moment in life, new causes are being made, old causes are being reinforced – the more general tendency – and by right actions, negative *karma* is being modified. It is a process that, like the universe itself, is eternal for every living being.

Karma is also collective and associative. Since the right circumstances have to obtain before the latent effects to produce a living being become manifest, similarities in a collective number of *karmas* will place individuals together in a particular culture or society. This rather suggests that there should also be a collective, as well as individual, effort to overcome the residues of negative causes, especially since Nichiren Daishonin Buddhism accepts the oneness of all life. Many people "share" *karma*: that is to say the interaction between individuals links their *karmic* causes because of an ongoing similarity in life patterns. While it is their individual *karma* that places them in a specific life, the society into which they are born is by no means a chance event.[45] Associative *karma* occurs when there is resemblance between members of a family, or between very close friends. According to the theory of *kenzoku*, "relatives and followers", individuals are put together when their *karmas* are compatible. Individual *karma* will, again, make each person unique, but will also place those with similar *karmic* patterns associatively and collectively.

Whichever of the Ten Worlds in which an individual finds him or herself, that world, combined with desires in the world around, creates the inherent causes within. It is reaction to those desires – by thought, word or deed – that provide the inherent causes, and those inherent causes simultaneously create latent effects that lie dormant until the right moment in the future when circumstances combine for them to become manifest. This is how *karma* works. What is immediately obvious is that it is the respective world of the Ten Worlds that provides the foundation for the inherent causes as *karma*: the better the life-condition in which one is, the better the inherent causes of *karma*. The possibility for better *karma* in the future depends on living life in the highest of the Ten Worlds.

While every individual has innate tendencies that may dominate his or her personality, each always has the relative freedom to choose how he or she acts. Speech may be a little more difficult and thought even more so but, ultimately, choice always remains a possibility. In fact, in every situation there is usually the possibility of engaging with circumstances either positively or negatively. Positive and good choices are the source of evolution of the self. Raising the level of existence from the lowest of the Ten Worlds to the four noble worlds, to *Bodhisattva* and Buddhahood, creates the kind of inherent causes that free the individual eventually from negative *karma*. Experience of Buddha-nature brings about the four qualities of Buddhahood – eternity, the freedom of a true self, happiness and purity of living. The goal of Nichiren Daishonin Buddhism is to bring about a "human revolution" in the self by living life in the tenth world of Buddhahood, where only good *karma* accrues and negative *karma* is burnt up. Then, the great potential in each human life can be revealed. It is in this context that we can see how important practice is. Chanting, studying and teaching are the three branches of practice that effectuate individual and social change. *Practice* is the best possible action in life to bring about change in the present life-condition of the self and of others. Changing the self, and consequently one's *karma*, however, is no easy task, but remembering that any suffering encountered in life is entirely the result of one's own causes – however far back in time – should be an incentive for positive change. Conversely, while negative causes have been laid down in the past the freedom for positive actions is always there for the present and the future.

Death and rebirth

Life for Nichiren Daishonin Buddhism is eternal: even Buddhas are reborn. Death is but a pause in the continuous cycle of life forms. Because of the oneness of ultimate reality, each life form is identical to the cosmos and has the same eternal existence. While everything comes into being, matures, declines and passes out of existence into the cosmic life-force, all is renewed and re-emerges from that cosmos. Death is the means for renewal. Because causes produce related effects and not dissimilar ones, causality provides the links between one life and the next. *Karma* dictates the kind of personality one has – to put it another way, the genes – that inform individuality.

When an individual dies, the body disintegrates and the five components are dispersed, but all the internal causes made during life and past lives still exist in the latent state of *ku* in the eighth *alaya* consciousness. This latent state of *ku* is the same as that of the universe, so the latent *karmic* causes are suspended in potentiality and are merged in the cosmos as a whole. The essence of life exists in potentiality in the universe, but not in form. Thus, to use Causton's graphic words, the universe is "simply an infinite collection of harmoniously related life entities which similarly appear and disappear throughout eternity".[46] But whereas the living being as *ke* and the being in death as *ku* are both temporary states, *chu*, the deeper essence that contains both *ke* and *ku* is what provides the continuity not only in a life, but in the eternal cycle of life and death. Each being has the life entity of *chu* that remains constant through life and death. *Chu* provides the true existence of an entity, while each lifetime is but a temporary existence.

As in much Indian thought, Nichiren Daishonin Buddhism believes that the moment of death is important, for it encapsulates the whole life experience on the one hand and, on the other, points forward into the next existence taking with it its relative negativity or positivity. It is from the eighth, *alaya* subconsciousness that such negative and positive impressions arise at this time. Death is a distinct process in Nichiren Daishonin Buddhism. The first seven consciousnesses close down, first the five sensory consciousnesses, then the sixth and then the seventh, but all their impressions are stored in the eighth, along with all the *karmic* seeds that make up the psycho-emotional being, and the energies that are residues of the disintegrating physical being. The better the life lived, the better the death is likely to be, and the converse for a negative life. As the environment around fades, the dominant state of the Ten Worlds – the one that dominated the life – rises to the surface. As Ikeda puts it: "As life shifts from its manifest into its latent state, our power to influence the environment or to be influenced by it is lost and – just as fluid water becomes rigid ice – our basic tendencies become 'frozen'".[47] Death will be Hell for those who lived in the world of Hell, just as it will be human for those who lived in Humanity. In Buddhahood, death is a positive phase, faced with courage and without fear. So even death itself is dictated by the law of causality. Death absorbs life which slips into unity with the cosmos waiting for the time for individualization in a new birth. All things conform to this law. In Nichiren Daishonin's words: "No phenomena – either heaven or earth, yin or yang, the sun or the moon, the five planets, or any of the worlds from hell to Buddhahood – are free from the two phases of life and death. Life and death are simply the two functions of Myoho-renge-kyo."[48]

Thus, between death and rebirth is a spell of intermediate existence whose condition matches the dominant state of life in terms of the Ten Worlds. So an individual who lives life mainly in the world of Hell will experience the same after death before rebirth.[49] *Bodhisattvas*, however, are reborn immediately in order to help all sentient beings on the path to enlightenment. Mahayana Buddhism often accepts that the actions of the living in the form of rites and veneration can have a positive effect on the intermediate existence of individuals. Nichiren Daishonin Buddhism accepts that prayers by the living, particularly the chanting of *Nam-myoho-renge-kyo*, can, indeed, affect *karma* in the eighth consciousness of the deceased while in this intermediate state, as well as the condition of the next rebirth.

When conditions are right (like the right blend of chromosomes and genes between male and female at conception), they provide the external causes that permit the internal latent *karmic* effects to become manifest. Then, the life-force of the universe restores a life. That life is the manifestation of a unique entity, determined by its own intrinsic *karma* that shifts from latent to manifest existence. The five components of the last existence have completely disappeared and a new combination of them houses the *karmic* residues of the former existences. Thus, the "self" that is reborn is not the same as in a previous existence. The five components are different, a new self is born, but previous *karmic* residues are housed in the eighth consciousness of the new being, who is born according to his or her particular *karmic* causes.

The non-self and the true self

Buddhism in general has no belief in a "soul", an *atman*, some kind of *substance* that survives the body at death. It has instead a belief in *no-self*, which means that there can be no permanent *substance* as a self that survives death. There has always been a tension between what can be permanent and impermanent in most Mahayana Buddhist thought. Nichiren Daishonin Buddhism is clear that any *substance* is *ke* and cannot be permanent. It is *karma* that is the transmigratory factor in human life, not the ordinary self. What *is* permanent is the life of the universe and the true self as *chu* that transcends and unites *ke* and *ku*. Life is not just the expression of *ke* in a manifest existence, but is, in reality, the *whole* of the universe. Such a theory runs close to belief in a permanent self in so far as there is continuity of a life that stretches infinitely back in the past and equally infinitely forward into the future. Thus, Ikeda states that "the source of physical and spiritual functions is a nucleus called the self, or the atman, which, transcending life and death, survives. While being the nucleus of the individual life, the atman embraces the universal life force, or the greater self. I consider the notion of the atman's being at once the nucleus of the individual life and embracing the universal life as correct".[50] Such an *atman*, however, is in no way a *substance* sense of some Indian concepts of the word: it is *ku*, non-substanti~

The tension between permanence and impermanence is ob~ point that life is permanent because it is eternal, permeates ev~

exists as the unchanging essence in endless cycles of manifestation and latency of phenomena. But life is impermanent in that each life manifestation is transient. Ikeda writes: "Simply stated, our life – that is, the true nature of life at each moment – has neither beginning nor end, and shall not vanish from the world, or the universe at death. Life itself possesses an inherent reality or dimension that is eternal, transcending birth and death."[51] There is, then, a true self that *is* the cosmos that neither begins nor ends. Life is *kuon ganjo*, stretching into the infinite past (*kuon*) and with endless beginnings (*ganjo*). Time has no beginning and eternity no end; the true self is eternal and in each moment that eternity is present. The true self is that experienced in the ninth consciousness. It is Buddha-nature, Buddhahood and the Mystic Law that permeates all things as ultimate reality and that transcends both temporary existence as *ke* and non-substantiality as *ku*.

Ichinen sanzen

The theory of *ichinen sanzen* explains the oneness of ultimate reality as the Mystic Law pervading everything from a blade of grass and a particle of dust to the sophistication of a human being. The term means "three-thousand realms in a single moment of life". Components come together through *innen*, the internal and external causes that combine to make something what it is, and to make it manifest or *ke*. *Ichinen* means "one thought", or "one mind", or the entity of life. The addition of *sanzen* "three thousand", a figurative term for a multitude, is indicative of all the manifestation that emerges from *ichinen* as the foundational reality. It is a philosophical theory based on the *Lotus Sutra* to depict the unity of reality and was devised by T'ien-t'ai (538–97). The figure three thousand is reached in the following way:

- The *mutual possession of the Ten Worlds* means that there are a hundred possible variations in any given moment, for in any combination all the others are still extant. It is this theory that enables Buddhahood to be contained in all things.
- *Ten factors of existence* obtain in each of the Ten Worlds and are the means by which the Ten Worlds become manifest in life. So together with the Ten Worlds there are a thousand variations, again, with all the others always extant.
- There are *three realms of existence* in which the thousand variations of the Ten Worlds/ten factors of existence are manifest, and that makes three thousand ($10 \times 10 \times 10 \times 3 = 3,000$) varieties of manifestation.

The nature and mutual possession of the Ten Worlds have been dealt with already above; the other two areas of the theory of *ichinen sanzen* need exploration. First, the ten factors of existence (Jap. *junyoze*), some of which have ʳeady been met in the previous pages, are found in the second chapter of the

Lotus Sutra. Unlike the Ten Worlds, which deal with the *changing* aspects in life, the ten factors deal with the *unchanging* aspects of manifest life: they are *always* present in existence. Even though we change from one to another of the Ten Worlds in living life, these ten factors are modes of reality that are *constant* in every state. They exist in a Buddha as much as anyone or anything else in life, so they are as much in the state of Buddhahood as that of Hell. The first three of the ten factors denote the nature of existence.

Appearance (Jap. *nyoze*) is *ke*, the manifest world. It is what we can experience with our senses and so has form and colour and behavioural patterns.

Nature (Jap. *nyozesho*) is *ku* the non-substantial, non-visible aspects such as mentality, personality, character, disposition, spirituality, mind, consciousness.

Entity (Jap. *nyozetai*) is *chu*, the essence that permeates and unites *ke* as physical appearance and *ku* as hidden nature, and also transcends them. *Entity* is the source of appearance and nature.

The next six factors depict the functioning of life in terms of its actions, its causes and resultant effects.

Power (Jap. *nyozeriki*) is the kind of *potential* energy necessary for action, both mental and physical.

Influence (Jap. *nyozesa*) is the physical or mental action that occurs when power releases potential or latent energy. It is thought, word and deed.

The following four are to do with causality, which have been discussed already in the context of *renge*.

Internal cause (Jap. *nyozein*) is a cause that contains at the same time a latent effect of the same nature.

External cause or *relation* (Jap. *nyozeen*) is that which modifies the internal cause to produce a new latent effect that is relevant both to the cause and to the external surroundings. It is also that which makes a latent effect become manifest. It is neatly described as "the intermediary connecting the potential with the manifest".[52] Its function is therefore dual – the producing of a latent effect and its later manifestation of that effect.

Latent effect (Jap. *nyozeka*) is what results when the external cause or relation modifies the internal cause. If good it will produce good manifest effects, if evil, evil ones.

Manifest effect (Jap. *nyozeho*) is the materialization of the original cause at whatever point in the near or distant future.

Consistency from beginning to end (Jap. *nyoze hommatsu kukyoto*) provides the holistic continuity to all the other factors. It is described as consistency from beginning to end because it links the first three *physical* factors which are the necessary beginnings for action with their ends, the functioning and end products of action. Also, in whichever of the Ten Worlds an individual is, all the other worlds will be consistent with that state from beginning to end. Thus, it is impossible to experience all the worlds at the same time, they will all be channelled through, or latently concealed in, whichever state happens to be dominant at the time. Equally so, if Buddhahood is the dominant state, then all the other worlds, even Hell, have to be consistent with Buddhahood. Consistency ensures that every cause, effect, and condition of life is synchronized and harmonized.

So far, then, there are Ten Worlds, each of which possesses all the others (= 100) and ten factors of life that are all constantly present in each of the Ten Worlds (= 1000). To these aspects of reality are added the three realms (Jap. *san seken*) of existence and all the Ten Worlds and the ten factors exist in these three realms (1000 × 3 = 3,000), thus making up the three thousand realms of existence. These three realms account for all the individuation in life; they account for differences in people, in cultures and in geographical locations. They are as follows:

- *The five components* (Jap. *go'on seken*) were dealt with above in the context of the nature of the self. They are defined by Nichiren Daishonin Buddhism as form, perception, conception, volition and consciousness and they will differ from one individual to another as they temporarily combine to make up a human being. No two individuals can ever be the same or react identically to every aspect of the environment.
- *Sentient beings* (Jap. *shujo seken*) is the realm of animate, living beings who integrate and function alongside each other and with each other in societal interaction. The world of creatures is also included here, each according to its own habitat.
- *The environment* (Jap. *kokudo seken*) is the insentient, inanimate world – land, sea, mountains, hills, air and the like. While the land is inanimate, it reflects the life-conditions of those who inhabit it and is not only viewed negatively by those in the lower life-conditions, but can itself become a Hell, can reveal Anger, become a Heaven, and so on. How a culture reacts to its environment determines which of the Ten Worlds is manifested by it. The environment possesses qualities that have a negative or positive effect and that can repel or inspire.

The whole theory of *ichinen sanzen* expresses the unity of reality on the one hand and yet the diversity and difference between all entities. Everyone and everything possesses exactly the same ingredients of existence and so is unified and inseparable, but as far as living beings are concerned, the way in which those ingredients are revealed means that each being will respond to life differently, will prefer one habitat or environment to another, will congregate with some and not others, will have a specific view of others, of the environment and of reality – all dependent on the manifestation of the dominant one of the Ten Worlds in which that being lives, and on the individual and collective *karmas*.

Those in whom Buddhahood is dormant cannot experience the unity of *ichinen sanzen* and, according to T'ien-t'ai and the second chapter of the *Lotus Sutra*, the principle of *ichinen sanzen* must then be a theory only. But for the enlightened Buddha, Shakyamuni, the unity of the three-thousand was actual, not theoretical – a view upheld by the sixteenth chapter of the *Lotus Sutra*, according to T'ien-t'ai. Nichiren Daishonin went further and said that the ultimate, unified reality of *Nam-myoho-renge-kyo* was the cause of the Buddha's enlightenment and that of any enlightened being past, present and future. It is this that is represented on the object of worship in Nichiren Daishonin Buddhism, the *Gohonzon*, and that indicates Buddhahood for anyone.

The theory of *ichinen sanzen* is a way of saying that there are multitudinous ways (*sanzen*, three thousand) in which manifestation can occur, but that they are all unified in one unchanging foundation. At any moment in time, all these variations – the whole three-thousand, or the whole universe – exist. A single moment encapsulates the whole universe and the whole universe permeates a single moment. Each animate and inanimate object is unified at every moment with the cosmos, contains that cosmos and permeates that cosmos. In each moment, too, are past, present and future. Ikeda writes: "Our lifetime is an accumulation of myriad such miniscule moments, which flow without interruption from the past through the present to the future. Therefore, because eternity consists of moments, and because each moment is the condensation of an entire lifetime, the most important thing is our state of life in each moment. Our state of life from moment to moment determines the overall course our life takes."[53] Ultimate reality is the unchanging essence that links moment to moment and that pervades each moment, making reality and all manifestation an interrelated and coexistent unity. *Ichinen* is that ultimate reality, and *sanzen* the multiple manifestations of existence. Not only is one individual in unity with all others, but he or she is in unity also with the entire environment and the entire universe. Whatever that individual is will have an effect on the whole reality pervading every moment of life.

Enlightenment

According to the theory of *ichinen sanzen* everything and everyone in life has enlightenment as one facet of its manifest existence. Enlightenment or Buddhahood is not something for which to reach or for which to search. It exists already within each entity, in the midst of ordinary life and in the cycle of repeated birth and death. It exists alongside suffering and underneath the veil of ignorance. Even inanimate objects can be used in an enlightened way. To be enlightened is to awaken to the unity of reality and to the rhythms of the universe. But Buddhahood is not easy to realize and demands constant effort, wisdom and the means to achieve it. Nichiren Daishonin Buddhism believes that chanting *Nam-myoho-renge-kyo* supplies the means and heightens the life-condition to reveal it. However, Nichiren wrote: "To attain Buddhahood is difficult indeed, more difficult than the feat of placing a needle atop the Mount Sumeru of this world and then casting a thread from atop the Mount Sumeru of another world directly through the eye of this needle. And the feat is even more difficult if it must be done in the face of a contrary wind."[54] Given the theory of causality in Nichiren Daishonin Buddhism, chanting *Nam-myoho-renge-kyo* is deemed to be the excellent cause that lays down the kind of *karma*, the kind of causes that assist in the realization of the goal of Buddhahood. Buddhahood is the truth to which a Buddha becomes enlightened, the means to enlightenment by those who embrace it, and the means to inner peace and a peaceful and harmonious world.

CHAPTER EIGHT

Special Occasions

Every culture has its special occasions, its times for celebrations that are religious and secular, and times when individuals celebrate the important occasions in their lives. Religious occasions are usually celebrations of the birth and important times in the lives of founders, of incidents from stories and legends in the hagiography of deities, and times to remember important historical religious people who feature in the respective religions. At a more secular level, rites of passage have always been important in every culture, so important, in fact, that they are often linked with religious praxis. Death, for example, is the one rite that most often involves religious ritual, though birth and marriage, too, may be either religious or secular. Nichiren Daishonin Buddhism, however, has no celebrations of a religious nature. It does not set aside occasions to mark the birth, enlightenment and final *nirvana* of Shakyamuni Buddha, for example. Nor does it celebrate the birth and death of the Daishonin, or the deaths of its presidents. What it does have are "Commemorative Days" throughout the year. On these occasions, "commemoration" is during *gongyo*, not extraneous to it. Devotion in Nichiren Daishonin Buddhism is devoid of ritualistic celebration added on for special occasions. "Celebration" on such days, then, is simply a focus of attention during normal praxis.

On the first of January is New Year's *Gongyo*. In 2008 at Taplow Court, families gathered together to celebrate the day, and the Centre's Ikeda New Century Hall was entirely full. On this day, too, in 2008, SGI-UK celebrated reaching a target of 10,000 members in the UK. Later in the same month, on 26 January, is Soka Gakkai International Day. *Kosen-rufu* Day is celebrated on 16 March. It is a day when commitment to the promotion of world peace and happiness is reiterated. April 28 each year commemorates the Declaration of Invocation by Nichiren Daishonin, which took place on the same day in 1253: it was the day on which *Nam-myoho-renge-kyo* was first declared by the Daishonin. May 3 is Soka Gakkai Day. On that day in 1951, Josei Toda became president and vowed to increase membership of the Soka Gakkai from 10,000 to 750,000 before he died – a goal he realized by the time of his death in 1958. The third of May is also the day when Daisaku Ikeda took over the presidency in 1960. It is a day that has become something like the New Year; a time for new beginnings and a time for setting targets for the coming year and chanting to achieve them.

SGI-Europe celebrates 6 June, commemorating the beginning of the *kosen-*

rufu movement in Europe. President Ikeda named this day Europe Day in 1981. June 6 was also the day, in 1871, when Tsunesaburo Makiguchi was born. Members from Wales and the Borders, as throughout the UK, celebrate the day with a commemorative *gongyo*. Later in the year, 12 October, is the day that commemorates the inscribing of the *Dai-Gohonzon* by Nichiren in 1279. *Gongyo* and *daimoku* are the main activities of these commemorative days, accompanied by addresses appropriate to the occasion. SGI also has quite spectacular *cultural* events in which its members participate fully. Although mainly amateurs, SGI members often take to the stage themselves in dance and song. On other occasions, more professional musical concerts are held at Taplow Court. In May 2008, for example, Saint-Saëns' *Carnival of the Animals* was performed, the proceeds of which were donated to UNICEF. February 2008 saw, also, the eightieth birthday of Daisaku Ikeda, which was celebrated by members everywhere.

The Nichiren Daishonin Buddhist is also able to marry and celebrate the life of someone who has died in ways that are special to his or her beliefs. But how do individuals from Wales and the Borders view the festive occasions that are part of the wider religious and cultural traditions in which they live?

Attitudes to religious festivals

Asked whether there are festivals of other religions in which they participate, such as Christmas[1]– a religious festival that would be difficult to avoid in the West – only 10% of Nichiren Daishonin Buddhists in Wales and the Borders say they do *not* celebrate any non-SGI religious festivals at all. The vast majority *do* celebrate Christmas. "I love Christmas!" says Hannah Chivers, and many others echo her sentiments, mainly because it is an important time for the family to gather together. Amy Milton from Newport puts this point rather well when she writes: "Of course I participate because I don't want to alienate anyone from me because of my practice; that would be wrong. I don't believe what they believe, but it's important to communicate and understand other people or there will be no peace." Like Amy, Bridget Keehan from Barry celebrates Christmas "out of respect for family and work colleagues".

It would have to be said that, for many non-Buddhists, Christmas has become a secular celebration, and this is exactly how many Nichiren Daishonin Buddhists in Wales and the Borders see it. Ben Davies from Cardiff says, for example, that he participates "not in a 'religious' way, but I gather with my family for Christmas and Easter, mainly because of the cultural holidays." Thus, many adherents engage in Christmas and regard it as a *cultural* occasion for the sake of the family and for the children in particular. They send cards, exchange gifts, "indulge in it a bit", enjoy singing carols, and see it as a time of social festivity: "Any excuse for a party!", writes Carol Brown of Swansea, "but only on a cultural, social level. I don't celebrate anything religiously that is not Nichiren Buddhism." So it is on such a cultural rather than religious level that Christmas is enjoyed by Nichiren Daishonin Buddhists. Linda Owen Hicks from Splott in Cardiff says, for example, that she celebrates Christmas "for our daughter, as we want her to have the experience of our culture" – a splendid example of the open-mindedness of Nichiren Daishonin Buddhists in Wales and the Borders.

Linda's open-mindedness is expressed by others from Wales and the Borders, too. Stephanie Bond from Lampeter says: "Yes, of course I celebrate other festivals. No occasion for joy should be ignored. I love Christmas with my family. Should any of my friends of other religious backgrounds invite me to any festivals, I would gladly go to share the experience of joy and happiness." Similarly, Karen Silk from Chepstow writes: "I celebrate Christmas, not as a religious festival but just as a time of love and friendship." Nicky Delgado from Cardiff says that he is "most happy to attend all festivals as celebrations of life. I will accept invitations to any religious ceremony gladly". However, Nicky adds, like a few others: "While they pray, I chant silently: you only see the lips moving if observant."

The willingness to share in *any* festivals is perhaps related to the considerable knowledge Nichiren Daishonin Buddhists in Wales and the Borders have of other religions. Ann Shabbaz of Cardiff, says that she is happy to celebrate festivals of any religion because they are "celebrations of life, or of people's faith". Mark Medcalf from Newport says that he does not participate in festivals of other religions constantly, "but I have been to Shinto festivals, the Turkish Muslim festival of Bayram, Diwali, and I have been blessed by Buddhist Sri Lankan monks and Hindu Holy men" – a truly open-minded range of experience! Another anonymous writer says: "I feel comfortable in other religious groups, places of worship or celebrations, when invited." When asked whether he would participate in other festivals, Desmond Connell from Shrewsbury replies that he would go to "all and any I am allowed to. I love a festival!" And Debra Blakemore from Senghenydd writes: "Because I teach English as a second language, I quite often celebrate Diwali and Eid with my students. I go to church at Christmas to watch my nephew's nativity play and also go to Christian weddings and funerals." Sriram Vaidyanathan from Newport writes: "I participate in all festivals, including all Hindu festivals, Ramadan, and celebrate Christmas with great cheer with my friends and colleagues. Last year, in particular, I really enjoyed a traditional Cornish Christmas."

For some, Christmas is more a pagan or mid-winter festival that has no real religious significance, and for a minority (7%), their Christmas celebrations are more reluctant and nominal. Far fewer Nichiren Daishonin Buddhists in Wales and the Borders joined in Easter celebrations – a fact that probably reflects the decline of Easter celebration amongst the general populace, apart from the traditional giving of Easter eggs to children. A few say they celebrate the solstice and equinoxes, the change in the seasons and harvest. Some Chinese respondents celebrate Chinese New Year, and some Hindu festivals are also celebrated. Broadly speaking, then, there is no exclusivity of Nichiren Daishonin Buddhists from the general cultural festivities, even when they are overlaid with strong religious traditions.

Finally, Wales and the Borders has its oldest member in Lillah Cottier from Cardiff. Lillah began chanting in 1967. She was eighty-nine when she responded to the questionnaire and is now ninety. A fellow SGI member helped her fill in the questionnaire. Lillah remembers one occasion very special to her. She says:

> I enjoyed the day Daisaku Ikeda came to Taplow Court. I still have the hat he gave me! I dressed a hundred Welsh dolls and sent them to Japan, and I have been in contact with some of the Japanese members since. I sent the dolls as a gift to Daisaku Ikeda to put something back into Buddhism. I wanted to say thank you with some appreciation for what Buddhism has given me and to send some Welsh appreciation to Japan.

Life-cycle rites

There are no official ceremonies in Nichiren Daishonin Buddhism that mark the arrival of a baby into the world. One anonymous member of SGI-Wales and the Borders comments: "I wish there were some ideas for children's naming ceremonies but I haven't come across them. All I have done is to nominate two friends to be 'Buddmothers' for my two girls."[2] Sometimes, non-Buddhists approach Nichiren Daishonin Buddhists to invite them to conduct such a naming ceremony. Peter Baker-Jones had such an experience: "A non-Buddhist friend asked me if I could perform a ceremony to celebrate the birth of a child. I told her 'I am not a priest' and suggested she make her own ceremony using poetry she loved in surroundings that she found inspiring." Jane Robbins from Caerphilly says, too: "My partner and I conducted a naming ceremony for some friends' child. They are not Buddhists but wanted the positive influence of our practice." The official position, however, is that birth events are not marked by any ceremony.

Nevertheless, while there may not be official ceremonies for birth, chanting is often part of the occasion. Martine Branford from Aberaeron highlights one such incident: "A friend asked me to chant with them for their sister while she was in labour (I didn't know her). She put me at ease by saying I should enjoy the experience and introduced me to a *Gosho*, 'Easy Delivery of a Fortune Child'[3] and 'The Birth of Tsukimaro'[4]. The *Gosho* mentions a 'protective agent', which I found had been in my pocket throughout – a rainbow giraffe that my daughter had drawn. I gave it to the parents afterwards." Lynette Rowlands from Cardiff writes " I have heard of couples chanting throughout childbirth (or listening to a tape of chanting)" and Steven Harris says: "I chanted to my daughter the moment she was born!" Thus, while there are no specific ceremonies for birth, chanting, which is so integral to the daily life of Nichiren Daishonin Buddhists is likely to be a particular feature of the occasion.

Marriage

While many (42%) had no experience whatever of marriage and funerals in Nichiren Daishonin Buddhism, a higher percentage had attended such occasions, with 21% having had a Nichiren Daishonin Buddhist wedding ceremony. Marriages can now take place at Taplow Court without the necessity of an additional civil ceremony. There are four SGI-UK officiants who are sanctioned by the Home Office to conduct ceremonies at Taplow. If the Nichiren Daishonin Buddhism marriage takes place anywhere else, however, then it is not recognized as legal: a civil ceremony is necessary for that. For those who do not wish to marry at Taplow Court, then, the civil *and* SGI ceremonies are the norm. Phil Luffman from Usk and Wye district was married at Taplow in 1993, but at that time needed a civil ceremony too: "My partner and I were 'married' at Taplow Court. This ceremony we experienced as far more important than the legal registry office marriage we underwent two days before." On the other hand, an anonymous respondent says: "We invited around a hundred people, including non-members of SGI-UK members and families. We hired a local community centre and asked the SGI-UK leader to come and conduct the ceremony."

Before a marriage takes place, a *butsudan* is set up and the *Gohonzon* placed on it. The bride and groom make their entry as in a civil or church wedding in the UK, though they are free to choose any format. It is also up to the bride whether or not she wears a traditional white dress. The ceremony begins with *gongyo* and *daimoku*. The central rite is the ceremony of the cups, *sansankudo*, which is a very old Japanese custom of uncertain origin. The rite involves three cups, small, medium and large, each containing a little of the well-known Japanese drink called *sake*. The bride and the groom each take a little from the small cup, then from the medium-sized cup and, finally, from the large one. The increasing size of the cups symbolizes the growth and development of the couple – the expansion of their lives into harmonious living and an unending relationship. A short address follows, particularly including words from Nichiren's "Letter to the Brothers":

> You are like two wings of a bird, or the two eyes of a person. . . Women support others and thereby cause others to support them. When a husband is happy, his wife will be fulfilled. If a husband is a thief, his wife will become one, too. This is not a matter of this life alone. A husband and wife are as close as a form and shadow, flowers and fruit, or roots and leaves, in every existence of life. Insects eat the trees they live in, and fish drink the water in which they swim. If grasses wither, orchids grieve; if pine trees flourish, cypresses rejoice. Even trees and plants are so

closely related. The hiyoku is a bird with one body and two heads. Both of its mouths nourish the same body. Himoku are fish with only one eye each, so the male and female remain together for life. A husband and wife should be like them.[5]

The wedding couple is able to include any personal contributions, or contributions from their family and friends, at any point during the ceremony. Best man at a Buddhist wedding of two friends, Robert Newis from Cardiff writes of the ceremony:

> The ceremony of the cups is very beautiful in its elegance and simplicity. The person who was presiding was wonderful. I was particularly impressed with his explanation of the Buddhist view of relationships. Marriage is about two people working out their issues together so that they can become stronger individuals, rather than a marriage being viewed as a merger and suppression of the individual. It makes far more sense than the modern, rather naïve view of relationships that most people seem to have when they get married.

Some respondents find the Nichiren Daishonin Buddhist marriage ceremony similar in tone on occasions to the Christian ceremony, but, as Tarquin Richardson from Tregynon writes, having attended one Buddhist wedding, it was "less formal, more relaxed but solemn. The ceremonial part was attractive and moving but seemed to be based in reality and a comfortable 'normality'". An anonymous respondent from Cardiff echoes Tarquin's words when he says the three weddings he has been to were "very joyful, but also quite profound, grounded in reality; not 'happy ever after' but the start of something difficult yet rewarding'"

An action team of members often take on the responsibility for organizing a wedding. In Cardiff member Ann Shabbaz's experience:

> I was really impressed at how a wedding was truly a group experience. The action teams worked really hard to ensure that it went well for all and reduced the stress and strain for the wedding couple. People organized food, the venue, the music and looked after the guests, and they also cleared away. It was fantastic organization. Care was taken in helping and yet being a part of a great celebration. And the ceremonies are beautiful, simple and powerful.

The idea of support from other SGI members has been mentioned so often in the previous pages, and it is no less a facet of occasions like weddings. Judith James from Cardiff had a Nichiren Buddhist wedding that she and an action team planned together. "We did a lot of *daimoku* and a lot of planning", she writes. "The Buddhists brought a lot of the food and a team of young Buddhists looked after all the arrangements. I had 164 guests and it was a fantastic day. People loved the chanting, the ceremony and the entertainments. It was a fantastic celebration." Antony Owen Hicks from Cardiff also comments on the "high level of support from fellow SGI members". He says, too: "Weddings are very celebratory with an equally high level of joy and appreciation. The ceremony is solemn and profound but very joyful. Guests can take an active part in the ceremony and there is a great sense of community."

With the exception of just one individual, all those who had experienced a Nichiren Daishonin Buddhist wedding ceremony found it a rewarding experience. Ilona Bailey from Fishguard writes of her experience: "My sister had a Buddhist wedding. She was eight months pregnant and dressed in red velvet. The ceremony took place in a field under a canvas canopy. All the guests who attended chanted together; though a lot of them weren't Buddhist." After witnessing the ceremony of the cups, Ilona says: "I seem to remember the couple wound ribbons around each others' wrists. The whole ceremony was full of symbolism and very moving. The most important aspect of a Buddhist marriage is *respect* for each other. This need is stressed more than love, which I found difficult to grasp at the beginning of my practice, but now I believe it to be the essential element in a marriage." Nick and Mani Dowsett from Dinas Cross were married at Taplow Court in 1992 "in front of the UK *Gohonzon*", says Mani, in "a wonderful experience of deep significance", says Nick, "a very simple ceremony but 'loaded' with importance".

Nichiren Daishonin Buddhist marriage, says an anonymous respondent, "is about support of the other person, drawing out the poison in their lives to turn to medicine." Ben Gaster from Brecon summarizes rather well the impression many members have of a Nichiren Daishonin Buddhist marriage ceremony: "It is a profound but simple ceremony to mark the union of the lives of two people and their support for the development of Buddhahood in each others' lives and its positive influence in society." Finally, a happy thought from Anny Pritchard of Swansea, who, with her partner, is contemplating her own wedding. She says in the light of their plans "the concept of expanding our lives to include the other makes more sense than 'two joined as one'."

Funerals

As in marriages, so in the case of funerals, a *butsudan* is set up with an accompanying *Gohonzon*. It is up to the family how it wishes to begin the ceremony, perhaps with the coffin already in place, or brought in when the mourners are assembled. Ministers of ceremony (male or female) normally conduct the proceedings. There is a standard pattern of service that is usually followed. *Gongyo* and *daimoku* are the central aspects, but there is also a rite using ceremonial incense. Here, while *gongyo* is recited, a tray of special incense is carried around, usually by a woman, so that mourners may take a pinch of incense and hold it to their foreheads with thoughts about the deceased. They then drop the incense onto burning incense on the tray. The use of incense is an old Japanese tradition that symbolizes the eternity of life. In the funeral service it is used as a means to focus on the life of the deceased person. The address that follows *gongyo* explains the Buddhist views about life and death and praises the deceased for what he or she has been in life and will become in the next life. Death is not the end; it is a new beginning. At this point, contributions by family and friends may be included. Most members who die are cremated, but burial sometimes occurs. At Taplow Court, there is a Garden of Remembrance for those who wish to scatter the ashes of the deceased there.

Well over a third of the members in Wales and the Borders have attended a Nichiren Daishonin Buddhist funeral. Only one individual found it a negative experience. An anonymous Japanese member gives a warm and detailed account of her father's funeral in Japan:

> My father's funeral was conducted according to Nichiren Daishonin Buddhism, ten years ago in Japan. Unlike other Buddhist ceremonies, there was no priest dressed up, but one of the SGI leaders led *gongyo* and *daimoku* instead. There were about a hundred members chanting all through the ceremonies and people who were non-members naturally joined in the chanting, which made the big hall full of the beautiful harmony of *Nam-myoho-renge-kyo*. We did ceremonies for 7-day, 49-day, monthly and yearly anniversaries likewise. We didn't pay for the ceremonies except for the charge for the hall, though usually you have to pay priests more than £10,000 for their visits. Some visitors and relatives who attended the funeral were impressed with the atmosphere and the sincere way it was conducted by Soka Gakkai members.

Now living in Wales, this anonymous member of SGI Wales and the Borders supplies both a moving account of a personal funeral and an interesting insight into the differences the schism between the Nichiren priesthood and SGI has made, with the aggrandizement of the priests on the one hand, and the supportive financial aid of the separated SGI on the other. By way of contrast, the following is an equally sensitive account of a Nichiren Daishonin Buddhist funeral in Wales from Jo Ogilvie of Parcllyn:

> In November 1992, my husband died suddenly at home. I knew you have to chant immediately and continue to for some time. I contacted my HQ leaders by 7.00 a.m. and they contacted my nearest members, who then came to support me and my children. A close SGI friend put her children in school and then drove the one and a half hours to my house to help with *daimoku*. This support happened over many days. The funeral was held in the crematorium and officiated over by SGI-UK. We did *gongyo* and chanted, offering incense. My men's division HQ leader then talked about my husband – it must have been very difficult for him as they were

close friends. Because my husband was well-respected both within SGI-UK and in his local community, about two hundred people attended. Although it was a grief-stricken day, it was also very joyful.

Just as the anonymous writer above found SGI support in Japan, so Jo also writes very clearly of the importance and availability of SGI support here in Wales and the Borders.

Members' impressions of such funerals are very positive. Douglas Angus from Meidrim writes of the funeral he attended: "It wasn't morbid in any way or seriously confusing like some funerals I've been to before," and Edward Thomas of Swansea says: "I attended a Nichiren Buddhist funeral in which we chanted. It was the most uplifting, upbeat funeral I have ever attended. Many non-Buddhists who attended remarked how uplifting it was." All deaths are tragic, but that of a baby is especially so. Yet Jenny Bartlett of Leominster is able to say of such a sensitive occasion: "I went to the funeral of my friend's baby. I felt more hope at this funeral for his future than I have at funerals conducted in the Church of England. Life and death felt more tangible, that is to say, the cycle of life."

For most of those who have had experience of a Nichiren Daishonin Buddhist funeral, it is one of *celebration* of life rather than mourning. Peter Baker-Jones puts this very well, along with related Buddhist teachings, in the following words:

> The talk at the funeral is a celebration for the life of the dead one. The understanding that life is eternal is implicit and usually supported by a reading from the *Gosho* (the Writings of Nichiren Daishonin). It is therefore uplifting rather than solemn. Life and death is a natural cycle that must happen to all phenomena; humans are no exception. The tendency to see death as a tragic mistake is why Shakyamuni called it one of the four sufferings. Of course, we are human and will miss the departed deeply. But, while we feel this, we are happy that the person embraced *Nam-myoho-renge-kyo* in life and therefore made the best cause for joy both in *ku*[6] or Eagle Peak and in future existences.

It is the fact of a life *continuing* that is important in the Nichiren Buddhist understanding of death. Thus, in the words of Chris Bradbury from Newtown: "I always feel that Buddhist funerals are a celebration of the deceased person's life – a joyful occasion – with the hope that he or she is moving on to something even better." Some members attended the funeral of the past General Director of SGI-UK, Richard Causton. Mani Dowsett was one and she says: "I remember the spontaneous applause as the hearse took the coffin out of the gates of Taplow Court." And Mani's husband, Nick Dowsett writes of his experiences:

> I have been to, perhaps, a dozen or so Buddhist funerals and have

officiated at many of them on behalf of SGI-UK. The emotions surrounding someone's passing are many and various, depending on the nature of the passing. The Buddhist ceremony in the tradition of the SGI is, again, 'simply profound', promoting, as it does, the celebration of life and the certainty of continuation through the cycle of birth/death/ rebirth. I have always felt uplifted – and without exception. Family and friends of the deceased have approached me later with gratitude for the hopeful view that the ceremony promotes.

Mairead Knell from Baschurch also found the funeral she attended, like weddings, a joyous occasion: "The funeral celebrated the person's life, though it was sad to say goodbye to a friend as we knew her. There was also the knowledge that death is just another side of life and not final. Everything changes: nothing stays the same as it is. So it is with life and death – different sides of the same coin."

Some members felt keenly the differences in experience between Christian and Buddhist funerals. Anny Pritchard remarks: "I've been to three Buddhist funerals. The concept of eternity of life is a strong comfort, and Buddhist funerals are far more a celebration of a person's life. I've been to many Christian funerals and thought the sermons nonsensical, especially the one about preparation of the place in my father's mansion etc." Jayne Timmins from Glanaman's experience is similar. "I have been to a Nichiren Daishonin Buddhist funeral and an Anglican funeral within three weeks. The Buddhist ceremony left *everyone* feeling as though they had been a part of really cele-brating someone's life, and we all felt uplifted. In contrast, the Anglican funeral left me feeling miserable and mournful." As one anonymous person says succinctly about funerals in Nichiren Daishonin Buddhism: "They are serious but not depressing. They are hopeful, extraordinary really, with a real sense that life continues."

CHAPTER NINE

Experiences

Birth of Strong Faith
Claire Boland

I always claim that all my friends chose me, except for one. I went out of my way to create a friendship with her. That was in 1977 in Rome. Eleven years later, in London, she introduced me to Nichiren Daishonin's Buddhism. It had an instant impact on my life. I felt I was re-establishing a connection with my life that had been broken for a very long time. From the beginning, my practice was strong and consistent.

About eighteen months into my practice, I had an experience that seemed like a miracle. I was chanting strongly to see what my life really needed to grow. I became aware through my chanting that I wanted to be in a committed relationship. I was 37 at the time and had never been in any relationship for longer than six months (and there were only two of those). Being young in my practice, and very enthusiastic, I gave myself ten days of chanting. Through this chanting I understood a lot about my fear around relationships. On the tenth day I met David and fell deeply in love.

However, the relationship then became very stormy and difficult and we split up three times over the next five years. Throughout, I kept chanting for the success of our relationship, taking all my pain and sadness and huge anger to the *Gohonzon* at all hours of the day and night, even though there were times I was so angry or depressed that chanting was the last thing I wanted to do. There were times when I felt like destroying my *Gohonzon* in rage and frustration. But I used this energy to chant even more and truly succeeded in turning poison into medicine. In 1995, we were married at a Buddhist ceremony at Taplow Court, despite my husband's previous hostility to the practice.

As soon as we got married we decided to try for a baby. This had been a great desire of mine. I was 42. After a year, when the longed-for pregnancy did not materialize, I was told I was no longer ovulating and that my only chance of getting pregnant was to have egg donation. I was completely prepared to try this, despite the cost, the long waiting lists, the only one-in-four chance of success and the ethical dilemmas involved. However, I felt I wanted guidance about it, which I sought. As usual with this wonderful practice, there are no rules. If the technology is available, if it is value-creating, then I as an individual need to chant about what is right for my husband's life and mine. The guidance was very focused on taking my husband's wishes into account, something I wasn't very good at!

We put ourselves on a waiting list. After one year we had a letter saying the waiting list had been cancelled, as there were no donors coming forward. But I could not give up now. We got information about other fertility centres around the country, and put ourselves on other waiting lists, and waited. Of course I continued to chant strongly, but even I was wondering if we should try other possibilities. I was now 45.

Another year later when nothing had happened, we started investigating adoption. One weekend, when visiting my husband's mother, we were looking at pictures of him as a baby and I felt an overwhelming desire to have my husband's baby. I did not want to adopt. When I got home that Sunday night, there was a message on the answering machine asking me to call one of the fertility clinics. We had come to the top of the waiting list! I was reading President Ikeda's book on the mysteries of birth and death while awaiting my treatment. In this, he says for conception to occur, in addition to the egg and the sperm, life in the state of intermediate existence with a *karma* that corresponds with the parents must also be present. Whilst undergoing my treatment, I chanted to connect with the life out there in the universe whose *karma* matched mine, who was waiting for me as a mother. Two weeks later I found out I was pregnant with twins!

The pregnancy went like a dream. At four months I attended a course at SGI's European training centre at Trets. Two weeks before the babies were due to be induced, my friend in my district and chapter had organized all-day chanting to support me. Somewhere, the Mystic Law was working. I needed all the *daimoku* I could get during the experience that was to follow. During my long labour I was buoyant, telling the midwives about my experience and *Nam-myoho-renge-kyo*.

At 12.23 and 12.28, on 10 December 1999, my daughter Ruth and my son Thomas were born. Thomas had had to be helped out rather abruptly with forceps to avoid being suffocated by the cord, which had prolapsed. Both babies, however, appeared to be fine. Two hours later I was still in theatre, bleeding profusely. I was given about five or six pints of blood. Eventually they told me they would have to give me a general anaesthetic and consider an emergency hysterectomy.

Several hours later, I woke up in the Intensive Care Unit, in what seemed like a scene from the TV series *ER*. There were lines coming out of every orifice and monitors blaring all over the place. In my semi-conscious state, the only thing that kept going around and around in my head was the quotation from Nichiren Daishonin's writings, "a sword will be useless in the hands of a coward". I eventually found out that I had not had a hysterectomy, that I had given all the staff a big scare because they thought "they were going to lose me", but I could leave ICU that afternoon, though I was not yet well enough to be with my babies who were "lodging" in the special baby care unit, or so I thought.

I then found out that Thomas had been put in an incubator because he had "problems". Later, this turned out to be a brain haemorrhage as a result of the forceps delivery. On the third night after the birth I was allowed to have Ruth with me. At 6 a.m., after a sleepless night, I accidentally overheard a doctor on the phone to the special care unit saying that Thomas was having some kind of fit. I begged to go to him, but the ward was so busy that no one could take me, and they said I was not well enough to go alone. I waited for three hours and during that time I chanted the most powerful *daimoku* of my life. Eventually, when I saw Thomas I felt a most powerful connection to him that seemed to have been there for centuries.

Although he had had something that appeared like a fit, at 6 a.m. when I had overheard the doctor, he did not have another one. I placed a card with *Nam-myoho-renge-kyo* printed on it in his incubator with a message saying how Thomas had responded to chanting when he was in the womb (by kicking vigorously!) and suggesting that any nurse who felt like it could repeat those words to him as I could only be with him for short periods of time every night. Several did ask me about my practice as a result of this.

Thomas was allowed home in time for Christmas, but on 4 January we were rushed to Great Ormond Street Children's Hospital because Thomas had developed hydrocephalus as a result of the haemorrhage. They thought he would need an emergency operation to put in a valve to drain off the fluid that was collecting on his brain. Throughout, I had tremendous support from my friends in SGI, who were all chanting for Thomas. He did not need to have this operation, and in ten weeks this condition had spontaneously arrested.

However, Thomas's development was delayed because of his early difficulties, and the doctors could not tell us how he would progress. But, when pushed, the consultant said he thought Thomas would have "moderate" handicaps. I was too scared to ask what this meant. He was floppy, his head was not developing as it should and he could not focus his eyes. When I eventually realized that if he did not develop head control he would never learn to walk and that he might be cognitively impaired, I had to face all my fears about having a disabled child.

Selfishly, perhaps, I started organizing *daimoku* rotas for one day each month for Thomas's complete recovery. Sometimes, other members organized the chanting rota for me. Thomas continued to improve, and everyone took a keen interest in his progress. Even President Ikeda responded to letters from me on two occasions, telling me he was praying for Thomas. I am incredibly grateful for the amazing support I have had. By August, at eight months, Thomas was doing very well, though he was behind with some of his milestones. A leader told me it was more important and would bring Thomas benefit if, instead of organizing *daimoku* specifically for him, I committed my energies to chanting to expand the numbers of people who knew about this wonderful Buddhism, and encouraging others to do the same. I was a bit taken aback about this at first but committed myself to wholeheartedly supporting *daimoku* on a chapter-wide basis for the growth of the membership. Needless to say, Thomas continued to progress and said his first words and took his first steps!

It was not easy as a 47-year old mother of twin babies to continue a strong and consistent practice over the last year, but I have had such amazing results that I can heartily recommend it to anyone. Please fight for your dreams. They won't come easily always, but the effort and the ups-and-downs create a stronger, more confident you, who can prove to others that *Nam-myoho-renge-kyo* really works.

Art of Living, October 2001

Thomas and Ruth are now eight years old, and Thomas is hoping to play the clarinet at the twenty-fifth anniversary of the beginning of SGI in Wales and the Borders in Swansea on 2 November 2008. Claire also had further fertility treatment, another experience – of being pregnant at fifty! She now has Billy, who is five years' old.

The Benefits of Illness
Robert Cook

In May of 2006, I was told that I have Hepatitis 'C'. This is a virus that lives in the blood, causing damage to the body, especially the liver. I have probably had this virus for over thirty years. I used to find it hard to understand my life or my world. I had spiritual experiences but no grasp of their meaning or significance. My life was crying out for vitality and understanding. In 1977, I was practising meditation with another Buddhist group. I was approached by someone and told that I should be chanting *Nam-myoho-renge-kyo*. I was dogmatic and convinced that he was wrong. In 1983, I went to Art School at Falmouth in Cornwall. My life, though outwardly creative and passionate, was still dominated by a pervasive sadness. My environment was also sad with cruise missiles being deployed in our countryside.

The third of May 1985, I chanted with someone for the first time. Within twenty minutes, I knew with absolute certainty that *Nam-myoho-renge-kyo* was the absolute truth of life. I experienced a happiness that I had never known before. For the first time since I was a child, I saw the world with joy. Absolute freedom welled up from within my life. This was greater than any government or any threat of nuclear war. I came home to the ultimate truth of life.

In 1995, my health started to deteriorate. I had a heart scare and developed arthritis. Maybe this was to be expected as my working life has always involved physical labour and I was working long hours as a French polisher when this occurred. At this time, our Buddhist organization was also encountering difficulties. We were experiencing persecution and slander from the

Nichiren Shoshu priesthood. Our General Director, Dick Causton, died in 1995, and we entered a period of "reassessment" which, though healthy, was difficult. These challenges had a profound effect on us all and confused many people. The slander that arose from Nikken was undoubtedly the devilish nature of Sansho Shima, and this fundamental darkness tried to arise in our own lives to cause disunity and disrespect. I was being attacked from within by the devilish nature of illness and, at the same time, I encountered slander and persecution in my environment. I was very concerned. I chanted many hours of *daimoku* to protect Sensei and my fellow members. I poured all my faith into the *Gohonzon*.

We moved to Pembrokeshire in 2000 and, in 2005, to the Gwaun Valley, which is one of the most beautiful places in the world. Because of the move, I registered with a new GP and was given routine blood tests. At first, there were questions about my liver's health, but this was not investigated further until I developed what I thought was another very bad 'flu infection that I had difficulty overcoming. I was feeling more and more exhausted. I visited the doctor again and was given further blood tests. On 2 May 2006, I had an appointment to see a specialist at my local hospital. It was he who explained to me for the first time that I had an active Hepatitis 'C' virus. 3 May was the twenty-first anniversary of my first chanting *Nam-myoho-renge-kyo*. I had finally found the cause of my health problems. Since November of last year, I have received anti-viral treatment and am confident that I will overcome all these health difficulties very quickly. In fact, I was told recently that there is no longer any detectable virus in my blood.

I have grasped a deepening sense of my own mission as I have continued to practise this Buddhism. Since moving to Wales, I have had many great benefits. I have immense gratitude for having faced all my struggles and feel that this illness is the greatest opportunity I have so far had to change everything from deep within my life. I believe that I vowed to be born at this time in order to reveal how great life really is. One aspect of this was that I chose to have such an illness. I vowed to show what it means to be a human being. I promise to do so in every way that I can including through illness. We are all great, and we can reveal such greatness just as we are.

In June 2008, Robert received the news that he had overcome the Hepatitis C virus.

Treasures of the Heart
Jonathan Davies

I've always felt out of synch with the world. Why? Fear! A deep-rooted fear of everything has pervaded my life for the longest time. This fear led to anger.

Together, these emotions led me to close my heart and have caused me, and loved ones, to suffer tremendously.

Five to six years ago I got a job driving buses. At first I enjoyed it. But after four years I had come to despise everything about it: the passengers, the management, my colleagues, everything! In those four years, I'd also amassed a lot of debt. I had a mortgage and a loan for a motorcycle. My overdraft and credit card were over their limits. It got to the point when I was scared to go home, fearing what the postman had delivered. So, about two months before Easter last year I found myself in a very dark place. The debts were still growing. I'd had an accident that had kept me off work for over a year, involving two painful operations on my arm. I was deeply depressed. And things were about to get worse!

My anger was out of control. One night, out of belligerence, I carried a couple beyond their village stop. On the same run a young man tried to tell me what he thought of my attitude. I wasn't having "some arrogant young fool with no knowledge of the stresses of my job" tell me anything. I interrupted him with a rude hand gesture, and he retorted with a verbal obscenity. I saw red and switched the engine off and jumped from the cab, leaving the bus unattended – an act that is illegal. He ran into a supermarket car park as I thundered after him, calling for him to come back so that I could hurt him. I vowed that it wouldn't happen again. But two weeks later I was interviewed by the police and suspended for three days, having been involved in a similar incident. Both times I'd cried as I had tried to justify my actions by blaming others.

I went back to work on a Thursday late shift. Half way through the shift my mate phoned. He'd had an argument with his wife and asked if he could have a bed for a couple of nights. He and I had similar backgrounds. We carried the same fears and anger. That night he told my parents that I was his mate; the only one he could turn to. The following Tuesday his body was found in his car. He had gassed himself by attaching a hose to his exhaust and feeding it through the window, using a bottle of whisky and some pills to put himself into a stupor. We cremated him and scattered his ashes. After this, though still depressed, I still decided to go back to work because of the debt.

The Wednesday before Easter I was signed back to work on Easter Sunday, which meant I would also have to work Easter Monday. That Wednesday, a friend gave me about £20 worth of dope. I had smoked it socially in Australia when travelling there, but had used it almost continuously since having the accident. Two days later, on the Friday, the police called. They had been told that I had "substantial" amounts of dope and class A drugs, and that I was dealing. This wasn't true. I was devastated; I could have coped with being stopped in the street, but someone I knew and trusted had informed on me. Not only that, but they had exaggerated the amount I used and what I did with it.

I spent Friday afternoon crying, wondering what I had done to deserve all this. Thoughts of suicide, that had been around before my mate came to me, surfaced, and with a vengeance. I began to seriously contemplate the act, seeing his "solution" as the best way to free myself of this burden. I tried to swap duties. I just didn't want to work; but nobody could, or would, which was unusual. That afternoon I wrote a note: "To whom it may concern." In it, I detailed the arrangements for my funeral. The writing sobered me and I decided to do the work and put off killing myself until I'd seen my three-week-old niece. I was still weeping though, and as I lay on my settee, I cried aloud for release; to be free of this pain. I didn't care if that were by my own hand, or if I was killed at work, or if I just didn't wake up in the morning.

I did wake up though, and went to work, leaving the note on my desk. I wore my sunglasses, hoping that they would hide the tears that flowed all day. On Easter Monday, I woke again; again disappointed that I had. The day was bright and I wore the glasses again, barely talking to any of the passengers that travelled with me. I had my break and started the 16:30 service back into town. Ten minutes later I stopped in a village and carried a woman to the town's train station. It takes five minutes to get from that village to the next. In that time, this woman had told me that she was a Buddhist and I had asked her how she had got into that. By the time we got to town, she had told me part of her story and I had told her that I wasn't very happy at all. I think I told her of the note, but maybe not. She felt my pain though, I'm sure, and as we neared her stop, she told me what she chanted and how she chanted it. She then made me repeat it as she readied to catch her train. Then she told me: "If you chant this for ten minutes every morning, I promise you it will change your life." And then she was gone.

I had nothing to lose. But, too embarrassed to go to my flat, I chanted that evening in the empty depot. The next morning I chanted again, and again over the next few days. By then, I was smiling more. So, too, were the passengers. That Thursday, I had to present myself at the police station to be formally arrested and charged. Memories of my last visit flooded back, but they didn't affect me as before. I told the officer concerned to tell whoever had informed on me that I forgave them.

A couple of days later, wanting to get in contact with Buddhists in Pembrokeshire, I phoned SGI-UK's headquarters at Taplow Court. As it happened, the local leaders were at reception, having just arrived for a course: fate! A week later I went to a men's meeting and felt so welcome! I was given some beads, a *gongyo* book and a copy of a letter that Nichiren Daishonin had sent to one of his closest friends and disciples called "The Three Kinds of Treasure". It could have been written to me. I kept chanting, learning how to recite the *Lotus Sutra*; chanting to see the Buddhahood in my passengers. It went against the grain, but hey! I was feeling good, so I gave it a go. I came to realize that these people don't get up in the morning specifically to annoy me! So, I tried smiling more, thinking about their problems. I started to hear things like: "I wish there were more bus drivers like you!" I began to accumulate my own Treasures of the Heart.

Before my mate came to me, I had considered selling my flat to clear my debts. After his funeral, I decided to go ahead with the sale as the chanting was clearing my head enough to see that this was the wisest thing to do. I phoned an estate agent to make an appointment, telling her that I wanted a quick sale, which I also chanted for. It turned out that a girl from her office was interested. The flat was never actually on the market, but I joke that it was for half an hour. Because of the state of the market, I sold the flat for twice the value I paid for it; enough to pay all my debts and leave some. The day I left the flat I chanted for half an hour, partly for the new occupant, but mainly to determine that I would never be in debt again.

Since I started chanting and practising Buddhism, four letters have been added to my personal file at work. Three of them have been commendations. One of them is from the firm's business manager (the same guy who imposed my suspension). He states: "Thank you for your efforts in operating the Tenby 'Park and Ride', in what I know were difficult circumstances. Feedback from passengers and the council indicate that you have been a credit to the company." The last letter is from my immediate manager. In this one she says that, so impressed is she with my improved attitude to passengers and colleagues, she would like to offer me the position of 'mentor'" This means that all new drivers to our depot will be put in my care. I will be responsible for teaching them how to be a bus driver in our depot. From maniac to mentor in nineteen weeks! I was offered this position on Friday, 5 September. Two days later, on the Sunday, I received *Gohonzon* and became a member of SGI-UK. I cried; in gratitude I cried.

Since I started chanting I've learned that I'm a Bodhisattva of the Earth, and that I chose to suffer in order to help people, because I can identify with their pain. When I read this I laughed and laughed. I was laughing because it made sense. It gave my life meaning. It gave me purpose. I am no longer out of synch with the world. I have a voice. Most of all I'm opening my heart, opening it to all. I'm learning to trust others, to trust myself, to trust my faith! I chant *Nam-myoho-renge-kyo*.

I was going to leave things there, but I wrote this experience in October 2003, when things were going magnificently for me. Since then I have allowed deep sadness to enter my life again. These last six months have been extremely hard for me. Great doubts spring up from within me, as the fear and anger I thought vanquished, prove that my human revolution is an ongoing, every day (every moment) battle. Indeed, at times my practice suffers, as old delusions frenziedly fight for control. I don't want to go back to the shell I was. I can't go back! So if that means embracing responsibility – responsibility for my life and within the SGI – then I determine to do so! I'm also determined to help build SGI-UK's male membership, especially in Wales. This is because I need as many hugs as I can get at the men's courses!

Will I be worried? Yes!

Will I have doubts about my abilities? Yes!

Will I conquer? Yes!

Why? Because what I'm still learning is that taking responsibility for your own life is not always easy, especially when you've shirked it as I have done. But, in the darkness I have known one thing, and that has brought me time and again back to my *Gohonzon*: for a man such as me there is only one way to transform my *karma* and find the true freedom and happiness I seek; the way of the *Lotus Sutra*; the Buddhism of Nichiren Daishonin.

Hey though! It's not all doom and gloom. I have laughed and grown; I try to appreciate and recognize my victories and have seen glimpses of the Buddha I am. I am learning that Rome was *not* built in a day. I am learning that "winter always turns to spring"! That is why I chant *Nam-myoho-renge-kyo*.

Art of Living, September 2004

From Hell to Eternity
Nicky Delgado

On my tenth wedding anniversary I was overcome with trepidation. My favourite *Gosho* quotation for many years: "Regard your survival as wondrous" (*Major Writings of Nichiren Daishonin*, vol. 1, p. 246), has always brought a grin (or was it a grimace?) to my face. My second wife and I had survived twelve years together, battling tremendous problems that always returned in new and complicated forms. Her family history, coupled with my background of self-neglect and self-disrespect, proved a heady concoction. Indeed, many who knew us wondered if our relationship would last.

One year later, my fears proved true. My wife made it clear that she could not continue to remain married to me. Eighteen months after that we were living in separate homes. Our marital break-up sent shock waves to families and friends that always echoed with a bang back to the epicentre – us. Many struggled to come to terms with what had happened to the perfect couple, as we had sometimes been described. As we struggled to understand it ourselves, others, unable to find a satisfactory reason, drew their own incorrect conclusions. Often they sided one way or the other, causing further pain to all concerned, especially the three children, one of whom became painfully cold towards me.

Months after separating, I slid deep into a slick, oily pit of retreat in my new home. At the beginning of the fourth month I found myself, eyes glazed, saying: "Do you realize where you are? You're wallowing in Hell and enjoying it!" At work, my manager, whom I later introduced to Buddhism, saw my strain in my strange behaviour, lack of concentration and my low performance. For two months, my Buddhist practice consisted mainly of going through the motions.

Confiding with two friends over many beers, we each revealed that our first long-term partner was already mentally ill and our latest long-term partner we had "driven mad". At first we believed that this was our fate, then we realized that we were the "mad" ones to accept it. For me, this became the start of a continuing course in the "opening of the eyes" to the true grit of men's *karma* – masking our pain behind imposed social standards and conditioning.

Yet another friend suggested that I needed to re-establish my connection with Africa: I realized I had a deep spiritual need to do that. The first and only time I touched base there was seventeen years previously, the benefits of this appearing for the next ten years. One of many examples was writing my first musical for a Buddhist show. For two months I wrote every night until the early hours, with only one day off each week. Chanting a little to refresh me when tired, I wrote much of this in a strange style that I later realized was an expression of my genetic heritage as an African born in Wales.

When my wife spoke about ending our marriage, we had tremendous difficulty in finding out what had gone wrong. During many months of deep and sincere chanting, I began to focus on some prime realizations – I did not want us to split up; what could I change to prevent the break-up; I was the family man no more; I always carry things on my shoulders; I was facing the demons inside me. These demons were my own self-disrespect and destructive tendencies hidden deep within me. Perhaps these had existed in my past lives too, but now I was aware of their strength. I felt weak and disempowered. All hell was breaking loose in my life. I had a battle on my hands that seemed huge. I thought I had done away with such stuff before, but now I knew I had dealt only with the tip of the iceberg. This was to be a long and bloody battle, and it still continues, and will do so until I am victorious in turning poison into medicine – the cure. When I subdue my demons once and for all, I will bring forth deeper compassion, wisdom and courage to help others, and reveal my true, happier self.

One month before my fiftieth birthday, I was strongly considering giving up leadership responsibilities within SGI-UK. I had no idea why, but I felt an overwhelming need to start practising from the beginning again. I struggled and struggled to do this, then the words *hon'nin myo* appeared like a beacon from nowhere. This is a Buddhist term, "starting from now", summoning up the deep conviction based on faith that you will start afresh, overcome and win through. Again and again I tried to do this. My concerted struggle developed my life-force and, eventually, the freshness of my practice came to the fore, bringing joy and benefits (and more struggle).

Finally, I underwent a tremendous change. It was the morning after my fiftieth birthday party and one month after climbing out of my pit of retreat. I had been aided by many members in Wales, who chanted to support me after I gave an experience about my problem. I was sitting in the bright sunshine that Sunday, 17 January, with three fellow Buddhists, all of whom I had introduced to the practice. They were all Young Men's division leaders, one of them my youngest brother. I began to realize that each and every difficulty we face is part of our own carefully concocted "potion" that we choose to "drink", *only to make us stronger*. The sooner we "drink" this, absorb this realization into our lives, the sooner we can use it as fuel for growth, not as baggage to hold us back. Each personal weakness is one more bitter (urghh) herb we add to the pot to finally create the sweet taste of victory. It is a bit like a homoeopathic remedy where you take highly diluted portions of what you are allergic to, to help build up immunity. Then, when the allergic substance itself appears in your life, you are stronger than it is.

Shortly afterwards, a question arose; not a doubt this time, but a question. Since childhood, I'd had an intuitive feeling that I would make it when I was fifty. But now I'd reached fifty, and nothing seemed to be happening. After more chanting, the answer appeared. I began to open my eyes and realize my true achievements. Four of the five determinations that had led me back to Cardiff were being realized: creating value in culture, education, youth/children, and the arts. With great struggles and disappointments I had been attempting to gather these elements into a force to help develop Cardiff into being a culturally progressive city. At last, the fruit was blooming. I now work on several projects that combine successfully to form brand new supportive partnerships. These involve youth, children, government, private bodies and arts groups working successfully together for the first time. It's a hard battle getting them to trust, but I feel I'm on a winner.

The fifth determination – linking these same elements in Africa, Wales, and the UK – is the next mountain I intend to climb, which is already in my grasp. Currently, I am assisting a project which is taking young people on an expedition to do development work in Ghana. On their return, they will support Cardiff-based community projects. I know I need to visit Ghana myself to help establish cultural developments and create mutually beneficial exchanges with Wales. For various reasons, I have been unable to go there during the last two years. Now I can see that the young people on the project I'm assisting are, in a way, ambassadors who are going there on my behalf. They will live and work there for three months, establishing contacts and communications that will benefit my own future visits.

Despite, or rather due to, tremendous obstacles and, at times, utter despair, I am achieving my life-purpose, sometimes chanting tearfully, angrily, threateningly, before the *Gohonzon*. But I can be really happy, when I allow myself, by practising deeply and sincerely. My ex-wife, the three children and I now get on marvellously. People are noticing our happiness and mutual support and are often affected by it. Now I'm looking forward to meeting my next partner, and enjoying more adventures on my journey to create happiness for myself and others.

UK Express, December 2004

Why I Chant
Hope Dowsett

I have written this experience for all my brilliant friends. 2004 was a big year for me, and I encountered lots of changes in my life. One of the biggest changes was starting high school. My first days there were extremely challenging. I found high school very daunting. At first it seemed so big and all the people seemed so big and there seemed so many of them. I had decided to go to a different high school to that of my two best friends. I only knew five girls well when I started high school and, at that time, I didn't feel particularly close to any of them. For the first few days, I felt extremely alone. I tended to cry a lot and just felt low all the time. I didn't want to feel like this, and so my Mum and Dad told me to chant. I chanted for thirty minutes, and during that time, I made a determination to make at least two new friends at the high school the next day.

The next day, I set out for school on a mission to make new friends, half wanting to go, and half wanting to stay at home and hide away. But I knew that that would mean that I was a coward, so I decided to be strong and go. That afternoon, I came home feeling on top of the world. That day, I had made eight!!! They were all really nice and kind and all seemed to understand me. Four of these new friends I am now extremely close to, and I have also strengthened my friendship with two of my older friends. I have still managed to keep in contact with my two best friends, which was another thing that I was worried about. I have even made friends in other countries – I have a pen-pal from America now, too! It just shows that, with chanting, you can change a bad situation into a good situation. I am now happier than I have ever been in my life.

I have been going to SGI-UK meetings and activities for as long as I can remember, and I still love going to them. They are great! You can learn new things about Buddhism and you are always guaranteed to have fun. When I was younger, I always enjoyed painting pictures and listening to the chanting, but now I'm thirteen, I like to join in with the chanting and help the younger children.

Going to activities is also a fantastic way to make some great friends. I met one of my best friends at a meeting. We have been on courses together, written experiences and even sang together in the children's choir at the big meeting held at the Royal Albert Hall last year. We now go to the same high school, and are in the same group of friends. In the future we hope to go on Future Group courses. I really urge everybody who has never been to an activity to go to one. You can learn a lot, make some great friends and, most of all, have loads and loads of fun.

I guess I've grown up with Buddhism as I was born into a Buddhist family. It's something that's always been there. I've been going to SGI-UK activities and meetings for as long as I can remember and I've been chanting all my life, too. However, until recently I never realized just how blessed I was to grow up with this great Buddhism. Sometimes, when you've grown up with *Nam-myoho-renge-kyo*, you can take it slightly for granted and think it's just something to "pick up on" every now and then. Recently, though, I decided to stop doing this and now I'm chanting every day.

This is a great victory for me. At the beginning of 2006, I made a determination to chant at least once a week. Now I'm doing it every day! My life has improved so much since doing this. Although I had an OK life beforehand, I now have a great life-condition, which is improving all the time. My school life, in particular, has got better, and I'm now socializing and making friends with people that I wouldn't have done before. As well as having a much better life-condition, I now have a greater understanding of Nichiren Buddhism, and I'm constantly learning more about it.

I understand how to attain Buddhahood and how there is Buddhahood in everything and anyone if I can bring it out. I used to think that Buddhism was really complex, but now I've realized the true meaning and essence of it, I've discovered that it's not really that complicated at all! Now I feel ready for any obstacles that I come across and rather than viewing them as a problem, I will view them as a challenge. I believe that absolutely nothing is impossible.

Art of Living, March 2005, May 2006, November 2006

My Experience
Tirion Dowsett

My name is Tirion (although most people call me Tiz). I am nine years old and I am Hope's sister. We live in a little village called Dinas Cross in West Wales and I go to school nearby where we all speak Welsh. This experience is about making friends. When I was younger, I made lots of friends but, unfortunately, one of my best friends moved away to live in England. I was a bit upset about this. Sometime after she left, I started to feel that there was something missing in our group and I couldn't understand why this was. I liked all the people and we all got on well. I didn't tell any of my friends about this. But I did decide to chant in my head in bed that something would happen to fill the gap.

Nothing happened for a while, but one day in class, something did! My friend was there, and she said she was moving back to Pembrokeshire! Now we play, muck about, work and do all sorts of things in our gang. The gap has been filled and we are all happy that she has come back. I am really glad I believed in the *Gohonzon* at that time, and I still do now and always will. These words from Nichiren Daishonin's *The Writings of Nichiren Daishonin*

(p. 750), remind me of this: "If you believe in this sutra all your desires will be fulfilled in both the present and the future."

When I was seven years old, I had a bad dream. Normally, I always chant before I go to sleep to make sure that I only have nice dreams, but one night I forgot to. Because I forgot to, I had a bad dream. It was all about a fire in my house and how I was stuck inside it. I woke up from the bad dream feeling very scared. However, I chanted, and then went back to sleep very happily. I haven't had a bad dream since because I've chanted every night not to have one. This shows that chanting really works, and that it makes us feel good in whatever situation.

Also when I was seven I wrote the following about friends in the *Art of Living* (February, 2005). I have three special things that explain one of my best friends. All these things are very special. First, I have this pot that she painted and stuck jewels on. Secondly, I have a card she gave to me. Thirdly, I have this skirt that I'm wearing. The pot is special because she gave it to me on my birthday. I put special things into this pot. The card reminds me of her, and I will always treasure it. And last, but not least, I have this skirt, which I wear for celebrations, and when I go to see her. I'll never forget her.

═══ ❖ ═══

Daimoku is Powerful beyond All Imagination
Kate Evans

I attended my first discussion meeting in January 2006. It was there that I first heard the words *Nam-myoho-renge-kyo* and felt the power of *daimoku*. I listened to experiences of how and why Buddhism was part of people's lives and I thought to myself: "Wow! How awesome, how powerful, I've got to give this a go!" And I was quite humbled actually, as my problems at that time seemed so small and insignificant compared to what others had faced. Anyway, I went away that day inspired by everyone, and I started to chant.

I was unemployed at the time and so I chanted for the capacity to have faith and confidence in myself to get a job. Now, I'd say that at that point, on a scale of one to ten, my *daimoku* was six to seven, and I must admit that I was fairly sceptical about this "proof" of which everyone had spoken. In a period of about three weeks, I applied for about seven different jobs and I wrote some kick-ass application forms. I attended five interviews and was successful in four of them – I was offered four jobs! Proof, I thought! Then I kind of slipped off the chanting wagon. I attended a few Monday night sessions and practised perhaps twice a week at home; then things started to go downhill fast.

My relationship, which had been on the rocks anyway, was dying by the day. We were both very depressed and ill and, to top it all, my mum was in hospital with severe pain – pain that she's lived with for over twelve months.

I was at an all-time low one rainy, dark evening. I was exhausted and felt like I had to escape, so I ran away– to Tesco! As I walked through the doors, I literally walked into a fellow SGI member, who asked me if I was OK? Little did I know the powers of protection at work when I said no! She sat me down by the café and I poured my heart out; I was completely overcome with grief. She held my hand, listened, gave me a quick-fix Reiki, and told me to go home and chant, for it would give me strength. So I walked home thinking: "I will chant, I will be strong, I will have strength for her and for my mum."

As I got through the front door, my dad rang my mobile. He had been at the hospital all weekend with my mother and as I'd had 'flu, I hadn't been to see her. I asked for an update: was there any news? Did they know what was wrong? Why was she in so much pain? My dad went very quiet, and then told me that there was some news but that he didn't want to tell me over the phone. However, I forced him to tell me that they had found a tumour on her lung and that they really didn't think there was anything that they could do. They actually told my mum and dad that she would only have a couple of months to live. I came off the phone and a text message came through from the SGI friend: it read *Nam-myoho-renge-kyo* × 3. I got on my knees that night and did some serious *daimoku*, ten out of ten. I chanted for my mum to be able to cure herself of cancer, and for the strength of my family to support her: I haven't stopped chanting since.

The week that I received *Gohonzon* in November, we had the news that the treatment had done as much as it possibly could, that her tumour had shrunk so much that all that was visible on the scan could even just be scar tissue – amazing proof again, I thought. Doctors at the hospital told her that they would see her the following February and every three to four months for a scan to make sure the cancer wasn't growing or spreading, though they said they might never really be able to get rid of the cancer completely. Mum asked about the possibility of surgery but the doctor said that was not possible due to the position of the tumour being close to the spine. But Mum asked for a referral to a doctor in London that she had learned about. She wanted a second opinion, but the hospital said that would not be likely. So that was that, and we were all happy with the "go away and come back in February" decision.

Then, in December, a week before I was due to be Master of Ceremonies for my first discussion meeting, where I gave this experience for the first time, Mum received a letter from the London hospital asking her to attend a meeting with the consultant that she'd heard about. So my chanting changed to: "Please let my mum have the best possible outcome." Mum saw the specialist and he said he couldn't see a problem with removing the top lobe of her lung, removing the cancer totally. Oh my God! PROOF again! And in the second week of February, my mum had her cancer removed and was home in ten days. Just this week she has had the all clear and was told she wouldn't need to be seen again for six months.

And that is my experience, PROOF, absolute proof, that *daimoku* and faith are absolutely powerful beyond imagination.

Fortune Child
Linda Owen Hicks

In March 1996, I was three months pregnant. Even though we hadn't consciously decided to have our daughter at this particular time, she decided it was absolutely the right thing for all our lives. Physically I was feeling very fit and healthy and spiritually I felt in control. I was the master of my own ship. I was about to start a new job with a Cardiff-based theatre company, which would last for four months. As I had had a miscarriage a year before, I wanted to wait three months before I told people about this new pregnancy. But when I phoned my employer about our surprise, the response was totally unexpected; I was told they didn't want a pregnant woman on board, it wasn't right for the show, and I lost my job. I felt totally helpless and had to chant through gritted teeth for my ex-employer's happiness.

My faith took a little bit of a nosedive, up until I was four and a half months pregnant. I went to the hospital for another routine scan, but the specialist found a "problem" with our little fortune child. She had talipes (two club feet), which unless operated on meant she wouldn't be able to walk. We were devastated, but deep in our hearts we knew we would be protected. Some close friends had just had a baby with the same condition, so we knew what to expect. Now we had to muster our faith more than ever. When we arrived home we had an overwhelming desire to name our baby (we knew she was a girl from the scan). So we called her Seren Eirian, which is Welsh, and means "a shining star". A great friend, sent us a *Gosho* quotation from "Reply to Kyo'o" after hearing the news. This quotation has proved invaluable and we took it to the hospital with us when Seren was born:

> Wherever your daughter may frolic or play, no harm will come to her; she will move about without fear like the lion king. Among the ten demon daughters, the protection of Kunti is the most profound. But your faith alone will determine all these things . . . Kyo'o's misfortune will change into fortune. Muster your faith, and pray to this Gohonzon. Then what is there that cannot be achieved? (*Writings of Nichiren Daishonin*, p. 412)

If I said it was easy, I would be lying. As a consequence of finding the talipes, the doctor told us there was a possibility that Seren could also have Down's syndrome. I decided to have an amniocentesis so that we could know for sure and be able to prepare ourselves and our families. We were determined to have Seren, no matter what. I realized that not doing the theatre job was real protection because I wouldn't have been physically able to perform after the amniocentesis and needed to rest for several days. We determined to exert ourselves in plentiful *daimoku* every day leading up to the results of the test. It was during this time we realized that Seren really was our great good fortune and our fear and heartache lessened, to be replaced with courage and hope. She was already making us chant and challenge our negativity and she hadn't been born yet! Two weeks later, we received the results confirming that Seren did not have Down's syndrome.

When I was eight months pregnant and very healthy, I was working hard organizing our band's trip to Lorient in Brittany for ten days. This trip was a great success and on the last night we performed to ten thousand people. Even though I was very pregnant and many people were concerned, I was full of energy and really enjoyed performing and transmitting the power of my Buddhahood to our audiences. I think Seren also enjoyed the concert because she kicked and danced for hours afterwards!

One week before Seren was due, we went to the hospital for a check-up. I ended up staying in with high blood pressure. The doctor was also concerned about Seren's size; she was quite small for full term. I wanted the real birth experience but, after five days of induction, increasing pain, and every drug available, I got what I had been chanting for; the easy delivery of a fortune child – easy for her that is! Seren was born by caesarean section on 24 September 1996, weighing 5lb 3oz.

I remember asking a senior leader in Wales the significance of the term "fortune child". I naïvely thought Seren was fortunate to be with us, her Buddhist parents, but the opposite was true. Our fortune child was helping *us* to deepen our faith. We went through two major operations on her feet when she was five months and nine months old and countless visits to the hospital for plastering. This was a very challenging and heart-breaking time. There were further complications but both operations were very successful and we really proved the power of our faith to ourselves and to our families.

I feel I've had great victories overcoming and challenging my fear of dealing with Seren's condition. I can now view every supposed problem as a real opportunity to develop my life, and create value. Since having Seren, I've really started to respect my life and role as a parent. Through this change in my attitude, my dreams have become realities. We've toured the United States with our band five times since Seren was born, and made two CDs. I've had acting work at the right moments, and now I'm broadening my horizons and retraining to work with children and special needs, using the Welsh language. To sum up, my faith had been stagnant and having Seren, our "universal star", has really made me open my life. It is an everyday struggle, but with my hand on my heart I absolutely respect my life in front of the *Gohonzon*.

Seren is now six and loves to dance and run. She's a very active little *bodhisattva*, and like it says in the *Gosho*, she does frolic and play and she is free from fear like the lion king.

Art of Living, October 2002

=== ❖ ===

Transforming the Fear Within
Mairead Knell

I have been chanting now for about twenty years. I received *Gohonzon* on 16 October 1988 and it was enshrined in my home on the twentieth. This was a very special date for me, special because I was receiving *Gohonzon*, but also special because of another anniversary – the anniversary of the death of my identical twin sister, Iseabal, who had died on this date thirty-five years earlier, in October 1953. I didn't connect with this at the time – in fact, it didn't even register with me that this was the date on which she had died. When people asked if I remembered her, I used to say "no", after all, I was a young child of six when this happened. I now know, however, why I had forgotten the date, and everything connected with our short life together. It was to save myself from pain. I never really wanted to acknowledge her death or her life.

Iseabal had developed polio in the September of 1953 and, after a very sudden and short illness, died. It was devastating for my parents. My mother never really got over it. I remember clearly being so very careful not to mention Iseabal's name, and I avoided any reminders of her because I knew it would make my mother cry, which I found unbearable. So I grew up not having come to terms with her death.

Events in childhood play such an enormous part in our emotional development. Even though I was in a loving family, I remember terrible nightmares and being very fearful and insecure. It's so often the case that it is those deep-seated patterns in our lives that make us unhappy. As an adult, I kept finding myself in the same difficult situations, making the same mistakes. My life was constantly dominated by fear. Sometimes I was aware of a great unease, a darkness that, oddly enough, I could sometimes smell, but – and this is the point – it was safely "out of reach". I knew this something was there, but I didn't ever want to go near it.

It was only after I started practising that I began to realize that this deep-seated fear was controlling much of my life. I worried about everything, was so afraid of criticism and failure that I ended up missing many opportunities – and this was when I was a supposedly mature woman! I had met Nichiren Daishonin's Buddhism around the 1980s through my sister. I could see how she was able to face her problems head on in a way in which, a few years earlier I would have said, would have been impossible! She had changed many aspects of her life for the better, and though I was very sceptical, decided to follow her advice of: "Stop complaining and have a go!" I did! Through chanting, I began to have a greater insight into my life, and could step back and look at the way I reacted to situations. I began to know myself better, and it began to dawn on me that perhaps I didn't really want to be happy. I was far more comfortable complaining and feeling sorry for myself. If happiness came too near, I literally panicked. Why? Because I felt I didn't deserve it. Why should I have life and be happy? Why had I survived and she had died?

I remember going to my first meeting in Wales and being told: "In this Buddhism, rather than asking help from without, we summon up courage and wisdom from *within* our own lives in order to confront and overcome any problem we may have." To hear this was so liberating, so I decided to give it a go, and started chanting regularly. I wanted to face up to, and change, the things that were making me unhappy, and take responsibility and control of my life. Once I realized that I had this power within myself, that I could face my fear, it was liberating. It took time, but each day I chanted to reveal my Buddhahood, and slowly I began to change. I realized that I don't *have* to suffer. The fear no longer controlled my life: I was entitled to be happy! The guilt of surviving and my twin sister dying left me. I had Buddhahood!

Each and every one of us has Buddhahood, and once you realize this, it's fantastic! At last, I had a tool to help me counteract and challenge the negative tendencies in my daily life. I remember at a discussion meeting being told to seek joy in every situation just like the sun: it is always there behind the clouds. Even when, at times, I couldn't see it, by doing my daily practice of *gongyo*, and chanting to the *Gohonzon*, I believed that the right outcomes or decisions would happen. So, at last, I began to reach out and accept myself.

Much happened over the years and, at times, it hasn't been easy. However, with the support of other members in my district, whom I treasure, looking back, I realize just how much *I* have changed. The longer I have been practising, however, the more I realize that faith in the *Gohonzon* is a continuous process: it's a gradual awareness that we make the choices, every day, every moment, that decides what sort of lives we want to live. I have literally grown up, and I am so grateful to have met this practice, where I have the opportunity each day to thank the *Gohonzon* for the simple, yet wonderful fact of being alive!

Transforming the Heart
Elisa Lewis

I received *Gohonzon* in 1998 and I practise in Cardiff, South Wales. This experience is about my relationship with my daughter Alice, who is eighteen years old. Alice has Down's syndrome, a genetic disorder that affects every cell of her body and was present from the moment of conception. Down's syndrome often has associated physical and intellectual symptoms, such as learning difficulties and heart problems. At the moment, Alice attends a special school in Cardiff.

When my daughter was born, both her father and I were totally unpre-

pared. As first-time parents in our twenties, Alice's condition affected our relationship badly. We didn't have the words to express our grief and sense of loss
when the perfect child we had planned for was born with such challenges
ahead of her. When she was five years old, Alice's father left us, giving only
one week's notice, and went to live abroad. We haven't seen him since. When
her father left, I moved into a period in which I struggled more than I could
ever have imagined. I drank too much alcohol during lonely evenings and was
very, very angry. I was like a "people repellent" and relationships of all kinds
came and went, each time leaving me feeling abandoned, with the weight of
the huge responsibility of caring for Alice alone.

Even though I felt immense love for her, in my heart I felt I was being
punished. I couldn't get away from the thought that somehow we had both
done something evil in another life and that our circumstances were some kind
of retribution. I often dreamt that I had been unable to save her from some
terrible fate. My love for her was conditional and tinged with resentment. The
prejudice people with disabilities suffer is immense and unrelenting.
Sometimes I just wanted to run away like her father had. But I am made of
stronger stuff than that, as I was about to discover.

When I met the practice, I was just coming out of my second marriage. I
had achieved certain things in my life such as going back to university as a
mature student, getting my degree and training as a social worker. I had also
had another child, Oscar, my precious boy, who loves his sister so much.
However, I was still very unhappy. During the first few years of my practice,
I experienced many changes. I chanted strongly about lots of different things,
attended courses, and spent a week as a volunteer in the SGI-UK National
Centre at Taplow Court. My personal circumstances changed beyond recognition: I got a house, a car, a job, and fantastic Buddhist friends. I also began
to study for an MSc in Systemic Psychotherapy. Despite all of these benefits,
I still felt like I was holding back. I could never chant for my own happiness
with sincerity. Nichiren Daishonin said: "Suffer what there is to suffer, enjoy
what there is to enjoy." (*The Writings of Nichiren Daishonin*, p. 681). In my
case, I became fabulous at *enjoying* what there was to suffer and *suffering*
what there was to enjoy!

However, there was one area of my life which I found impossible to chant
about. In fact, it hadn't even occurred to me that it was impossible because I
was so deeply entrenched in misery I had never challenged it. That was – Alice.
Coincidentally, as I began to chant about Alice, she moved into puberty. There
were temper tantrums, slamming doors, silence and verbal abuse – that was
just from me! Outwardly, I was becoming stronger; inwardly, I didn't want
to challenge my deepest sorrow. However, you can't chant to be indestruc-
tibly happy and not expect things to change. Gradually, with much
encouragement and chanting, the ice in my heart began to melt. On one
course, I asked a leader how to change my learning disabled child's *karma* and
he simply said "chant to see her Buddhahood". Next I took Alice to a Mimosa
course (the gathering of girls aged seven to twelve who meet together to learn

about Nichiren Buddhism), where an eleven-year-old child told me that she knew why I was so happy – it was because of Alice; she was my benefit. Guidance from President Ikeda gave me confidence that finding my own dignity was the key to both our happiness. I began to chant to have the same heart as President Ikeda and to become extraordinarily happy.

I held these thoughts as I continued to struggle to see Alice's and my own Buddhahood and realized that I was turning my deepest sorrow into my greatest joy. On another SGI course, I experienced a profound turning point. First, I learned how the first General Director, the late Richard Causton, had once said he chanted to be reborn not into ease and good circumstances, but into adversity and suffering so he could show the power of this practice with his life and help those suffering the most. Secondly, I realized that I had a mission to stand on the front line of *kosen-rufu* with SGI President Daisaku Ikeda. Only this time, someone else was there standing side by side with President Ikeda holding hands as equals. It was Alice.

I had never been so happy. Over the next few days, I chanted about Alice and became overwhelmed with gratitude for the life-force and compassion she has shown in this lifetime. I began to realize that she has been instrumental in helping me to challenge my deepest fears. Alice shares my mission for *kosen-rufu* but my negativity had been blocking her path as well as my own. I determined to make my role as her mother the cause for our happiness, not an obstacle to it. I couldn't wait to get home and the joy of my reunion with Alice this time felt like the exciting next chapter of our extraordinary lives.

Not long after my return, a discussion meeting was held in my house. Alice came out of her room at the end and, rather than the sullen teenager who normally roams my house, this incredible, engaging young woman appeared. She went round to everyone in the meeting, looked into their eyes and, with a smile and a handshake said: "Thank you, nice to meet you." Everyone was amazed! And I'm amazed that I was too blind to see her Buddhahood before, but so grateful that I can now see it every day.

This change has also been reflected in our environment and support has been pouring in from all directions. Alice now has a team of "personal assistants" to help her become more independent, one of whom has started chanting. She is the first person Alice has introduced to this practice and to SGI! I have a feeling there will be more. When I recently took her to an interview at college, she answered the question: "What does your family like to do together?" by putting her hands together and saying "chanting". Alice is now preparing to receive SGI membership.

These words from Nichiren Daishonin have sustained and encouraged me:

> But your faith alone will determine all these things. A sword is useless in the hands of a coward. The mighty sword of the Lotus Sutra must be wielded by one courageous in faith. Then one will be as strong as a demon armed with an iron staff. I, Nichiren, have inscribed my life in sumi ink, so believe in the Gohonzon with your whole heart . . . Kyo'o's

misfortune will change into fortune. Muster your faith, and pray to this Gohonzon. Then what is there that cannot be achieved. (Nichiren Daishonin, "Reply to Kyo'o", *The Writings of Nichiren Daishonin*, p. 412)

Art of Living, April 2005

Now, in 2008, Alice has just finished three years in college and is planning to live independently in a shared house with support. She's so amazing, and chants regularly, but not every day. My life is going well. I've just been offered a two-day post as Senior Lecturer in systemic psychotherapy. I've also started a private practice. I know without a shadow of a doubt that we couldn't have achieved any of this without the practice, and the wonderful guidance in faith that Daisaku Ikeda offers us. My success is the way to repay the immense debt of gratitude I owe my teacher. For me, this is the essence of the mentor–disciple relationship.

The Glory of the Flower
Claire Mason-Green

My *Gohonzon* receiving ceremony was on a cold, but beautifully sunny, day. I had been practising for about six months before I felt ready to receive, feeling that it was the right time for me. I remember being very excited in the days leading up to the ceremony and I was looking forward to it immensely. There was a feeling of almost relief, or completion. Of course, all that changed on the actual day.

As we pulled into the drive at Taplow Court, a feeling of abject terror washed over me. This was it, my faith. There was no turning back, and I was committing myself to one faith for the rest of my life. That was almost completely overwhelming. I'd always classed myself as agnostic, bordering on atheist, so I'd never experienced an actual belief structure; in fact, I'd done my level best to shy away from any kind of institutionalized religion. But then I sat down and thought about it, really thought about it.

I realized that I wasn't committing myself to anything or anyone but me. The whole point of chanting – whether it be to your wall or your *Gohonzon* – is to tap into your own energy, your own self-worth. It's ultimately about respecting yourself, believing in yourself and using that belief and strength to enhance your own life and the lives of people around you. That's what first attracted me to Nichiren Buddhism; the buck stops with you. Your thoughts and actions determine the outcome of your endeavours, of the obstacles you face.

I remember being told that obstacles would come my way before and after receiving, and I thought: "Oh great, I commit myself fully and it rewards me by throwing obstacles and problems at me from all directions!" But those obstacles would have been there to trip me up, whether I was chanting or not. Chanting to the *Gohonzon* and believing in the teachings of Nichiren Daishonin have given me the strength to deal with those obstacles in a calmer, clearer way than I would have before. It helps me to tap into that part of me that can work it out, can make it better, without panicking or worrying myself into a grey head of hair. For that, I'm incredibly grateful.

Nichiren Daishonin Buddhism has also helped me find the strength to deal with a side of my sexuality that I had previously ignored. Most of my friends are middle-aged, married, Christian women; so you can imagine my reluctance to come out to them. Through chanting and growing in inner strength, I realized that my sexuality was a part of myself I had come to be almost afraid of. A hidden part of me was hoping it would go away if I ignored it. I think this was due largely to my son. I was bullied mercilessly through my school years and I was/am so afraid of my child experiencing the same thing. As horrible as it seems, I just wanted to be normal for him.

Of course, that's never going to happen, so I thought: "Sod it!" I bit the bullet and grandly announced: "I'm gay!" to my friends. The general reaction was: "Well duh!", and that was it. All the fretting, all the panicking, all the worry culminated in a very soggy damp squib. I can't adequately explain the intense feeling of relief.

So, my experience with Nichiren Buddhism so far has been, and continues to be, quite a journey. I still have moments of: "Is this right for me?", but there's nothing wrong with adding a little sand of doubt to the oyster of your faith. The fact is, I feel better after *gongyo*; my day goes smoother because it brightens my outlook and clears my head.

The title of my Experience, "The Glory of the Flower" is taken from the poem "Ode on the Intimations of Immortality from Recollections of Early Childhood" by William Wordsworth. The passage reads:

> Though nothing can bring back the hour
> Of splendour in the grass, of glory in the flower;
> We will grieve not, rather find
> Strength in what remains behind.

The words mean a lot to me because of the journey I've had since losing my mum eight years ago. I clung to the grieving for a long time, and it blinded me to so much joy in the present. I've grown tremendously since then, and this poem means a lot to me because it reminds me that taking joy in what I have now doesn't mean letting go of the joy that's gone.

From Failure to Success
Liz Moulson

Practising Nichiren Daishonin's Buddhism with SGI has redirected my life in ways I could never have imagined. I have not had a particularly easy life, but in actual fact feel that tackling the difficulties I've encountered with this practice as a foundation, I've been able to develop a richness and depth in myself, which I feel wouldn't have been otherwise possible – a bit like finding a seam of gold in a dark, underground mine.

I initially viewed my problems in a negative light when I started practising. Maybe my Catholic upbringing influenced my attitude, I don't know. I would feel I was failing in some way and not showing enough proof of the practice to inspire others to start or continue. Or else I felt I must have done something awful in a past life and was receiving my *karmic* retribution. However, through reading Buddhist material, asking questions, and being guided by some wonderful Buddhist leaders, I gradually came to understand Nichiren Daishonin's teachings on *karma*.

I saw that there are two types of *karma*. One is straightforward cause and effect. The other is when we choose certain challenges in order to fulfil our mission in life. But how do we know which is which, I wondered. Even Nichiren Daishonin says in one *Gosho* that it is impossible to fathom one's *karma*. One day, I was talking to Kyoko Gibson about this, when she said that someone had suggested she had bad *karma* to have been born in Hiroshima shortly after the war and to have suffered from the effects of radiation all her life. She replied that she didn't know what she had done in the past. All she did know is that everything that had happened to her had made her the person she is today. And I can unequivocally say that she is what I call the Buddhist mother of Wales. Her wisdom and compassion have inspired and guided not only myself, but many of us in Wales. When she told me this story, it was as if she had shone a light into a dark part of my mind.

I suddenly realized that, instead of dwelling on what we might have done in the past, it's how we act now in the present that's most important: it's how much value we can create both for ourselves and for others from whatever happens to us. It's the causes we make from now that will create a whole new future. Buddhist practice gives me the power to break out of old *karmic* patterns that are destructive or detrimental and form new, positive ones. Of course, some patterns are so deeply ingrained that they take longer to change than others, but the ongoing challenge is, in itself, a great learning curve for my growth. The lotus blooming out of a muddy pond perfectly pictures this process.

My old feelings of failure may have also stemmed from a sense of not living up to my family's expectations. A few years ago, I apologized to my father for not having achieved the academic hopes and career he would have liked for me. He'd also wanted me to marry late, but I jumped into marriage at nineteen, and am now divorced. He cut me short by saying: "Stop it Elizabeth! Enough! Your compassion is so vast I want no more of that." I was stunned. As time has gone by, my criteria for judging success is now based on how much I can develop the treasures of the heart, how many people I can help become happy and encourage, and how much I can treasure others in the same way as Sensei.

People may wonder how I can call myself an independent, thinking woman and yet call Daisaku Ikeda my mentor in life. However, he has sincere respect for women and consistently praises the qualities they possess. He even calls the twenty-first century the century for women. By chanting to support him and doing my best to develop the same heart and spirit, I feel my own life has been empowered and expanded. In Buddhism, a mentor is someone that connects you to the same source of enlightenment, and this relationship is embodied in the principle called the oneness of mentor and disciple. While Nichiren Daishonin is my ultimate mentor, Daisaku Ikeda, along with the first two Presidents, is my mentor for *kosen-rufu*. Through his life and example, and his prolific writings, in which he makes the teachings of both Shakyamuni and Nichiren Daishonin clear and understandable to people in the present age, he demonstrates what it is to be an outstanding disciple of not only these great men but also of his two predecessors in the Soka Gakkai.

=== ❖ ===

Here and Now
Sue Rogers

In November 2001, we held a Wales General Meeting for SGI-UK members. SGI President Daisaku Ikeda sent a message of congratulations to the meeting and in it he said: "In one of his writings, Nichiren Daishonin teaches, 'I entrust you with the propagation of Buddhism in your province'. It is stated that 'the seeds of Buddhahood sprout as a result of conditions . . . '" (*The Writings of Nichiren Daishonin*, 1117)

I am grateful for the opportunity for personal growth that the SGI-UK's "awareness campaigns" have given us. My house stands in its own little valley on the outskirts of the small village of Penrhiwllan in West Wales. To reach the house one goes down a long steep drive; to the back of the house is small woodland, set back up the steep hill and stretching to either side, and fields stretch out to either side at the front. I am surrounded by ten acres of my own land. Although I have neighbours, in the fourteen years I have lived here I have barely met them. Last year I plucked up courage (using a lot of *daimoku*!) to do a collection for Dr Barnardo's, having rashly said 'yes' when asked on the telephone.

I posted the envelopes through letter-boxes one day, but when I went to collect them, knowing I would have to knock on doors, I was so nervous I didn't know how to force myself to walk up my drive. However, I had already decided to make it an activity for *kosen-rufu*, and to speak with everyone, which I did. I was a bit embarrassed that my next-door neighbours on both sides didn't recognize me! In doing this activity I realized how afraid I was of being known by them. Many years ago (forty in fact!), when I was a teenager, a woman whom I had never met made an unpleasant and untrue comment about me to our next-door neighbour. I decided there and then that I would never again care what people said about me. I had put up a shield of indifference, and tried to maintain anonymity ever since. After all, if people didn't know me, they couldn't talk about me, could they? Doing the Dr Barnado's collection, and talking to my neighbours for the first time was a small step in the other direction.

This year, I took a step further. In March I decided that, every day, I would chant for the happiness of every person in Penrhiwllan. I start, in my mind, with the man down the road, and work up the road, along the next road and back down again. At first it was very difficult. At each household I came to in my mind I found I was judging or slandering them or myself . . . "that man was so negative, I wouldn't want him to come to my house", "that woman is way too scary!", "that couple have loads of friends – why would they be interested in me?" and so on and so on. Over the next few days this changed and I started to wholeheartedly chant for each person's happiness.

As part of the SGI-UK awareness campaign, our local members planned an open women's meeting on 3 May at my house, and I decided that I would somehow pluck up the courage to invite some of my neighbours. I made a mental list of those I would ask. One woman wanted to come, but her family were arriving just at the time of the meeting, and though she said she probably wouldn't come, I felt at least I was making her aware that I am a Buddhist. A third person did not want to come to a "religious" gathering but was friendly enough to ask me a few days afterwards how the meeting had gone.

After inviting a few people, I decided I had made enough effort. But as I continued to chant for the happiness of everyone in my village, I began to picture in my mind each one of them chanting in front of his or her own *Gohonzon*. Then I realized I didn't want to give up on my original determination, so I chanted again to find the courage to invite my other neighbours. And I did! The girls next door were so friendly to me. They would have liked to come but they had a prior engagement. The others that I invited were also friendly. My last visit was to an elderly lady whom I had known ever since I moved here, because I used to play the organ in the tiny church on the hill, and she was one of the stalwart few in the congregation.

Well, in the end, she was the only guest to come, but it was a wonderful meeting. My friend recalled how terribly badly affected I had been for the six months after my father had died in 1991 (she had met him several times – he was a priest and had taken a couple of services at the little church when he visited me). She said how differently I had reacted when my mother died, two years later, after I had met this practice. She said how much she had enjoyed the meeting and she has invited me to a couple of Women's Institute events: a definite first for me!

A few years ago, I was worried that I might have to sell my house. My mind was constantly chopping and changing about whether or not to sell, and I thought I would go crazy if I couldn't reach a definite conclusion. I decided to seek guidance from a senior leader, then I remembered I would have to wait a few days to be able to see anyone. So, in desperation, I told the *Gohonzon* that I needed guidance from President Daisaku Ikeda now, I couldn't wait. I glanced at a book lying beside me – I discovered afterwards that a friend had left it by mistake. It was volume two of *Conversations and Lectures on the Lotus Sutra*. I picked it up, and it fell open on this passage:

> From the perspective of the true entity of all phenomena, here and now are the true and eternal sphere of activity. It is the actual stage on which we perform our mission. "There is no need", the Daishonin writes, "to leave this place and go elsewhere". (Daisaku Ikeda, *Conversations and Lectures on the Lotus Sutra*, SGI-UK, Vol. 2, p. 62)

I still feel the same overwhelming emotion when I recall this guidance, which I feel was personal guidance from my mentor in life, President Ikeda. Since that time, my mind constantly comes back to this passage. Although it has taken these few years for me to act on it, I was aware from that moment that my mission is "here (in this place) and now". Now I know I can draw up the courage for anything, and I am determined to realize *kosen-rufu* in all my local community.

Art of Living, October 2002

Using My Practice for My Health
Joanne Roxburgh

I started chanting *Nam-myoho-renge-kyo* four years ago. Since I have been chanting, I can honestly say that it has helped me overcome illnesses that I have suffered from over a number of years. I used to have a tendency to suffer from anxiety and depression. More recently, I suffered from a stress-related illness and high blood pressure. A month ago, I underwent major surgery.

Chanting *Nam-myoho-renge-kyo* has become for me a Buddhist medicine that treats the causes of my illness. I used to feel helpless to do anything about my tendency towards depression and anxiety, but now I don't. I still have problems like I did before I started to chant, but chanting has fundamentally changed my attitude to life. I have discovered that, however many obstacles and struggles I face in life, by chanting and taking action in daily life I can be fundamentally happy whatever my circumstances.

Buddhism has also taught me to take full responsibility for my own life and not to blame other people or my circumstances. Before I chanted, I used to wallow in self-pity and my weaknesses but now I transform them. Nichiren Daishonin's Buddhism has taught me that happiness comes from within me and not from external influences. Buddhism also teaches that *both* suffering and happiness come from within us. Buddhism has also taught me that the fundamental cause of suffering lies in negative impulses, delusions and ignorance of the true nature of life. Buddhism teaches that this fundamental cause of suffering lies hidden in our lives, below the level of our conscious minds.

I have personally experienced that, by chanting *Nam-myoho-renge-kyo*, I have broken through my negativity and drawn out all the positives in my life. The good thing is that I have never been made to feel guilty about my weaknesses, or those aspects of life that I don't like. Buddhism understands that without negatives you can't have positives. The challenge is to transform the negatives into positives. Buddhism has taught me that, through honestly chanting *Nam-myoho-renge-kyo*, I can totally transform my negative impulses. Buddhism, in fact, can only exist because we have a negative side that can be transformed into a positive, enlightened side.

As I began to chant, I came to see which of my actions create true value for me and for others and which cause me suffering and illness. This has been the biggest change in me, which has resulted in my general happiness and improvement in my health. Buddhism is the law of cause and effect. So when I pray strongly, and then take action based on my prayer, I know I will see results without fail. I have experienced this in recovering from illness. Nichiren Daishonin said in one of his letters, "Happiness in the World":

> Suffer what there is to suffer, enjoy what there is to enjoy. Regard both suffering and joy as facts of life and continue chanting *Nam-myoho-renge-kyo* no matter what happens. How could this be anything other than boundless joy of the Law.

Chanting for a Husband
Jayne Timmins

In September 2000, I found myself finishing yet another unsatisfactory relationship in which I was not being treated with respect. I had realized that there was something in me that was attracting this disrespect, and decided that I was going to change whatever it was. I had a profound feeling that it was the fact that I did not respect myself as much as I should that was manifesting itself in my environment.

I embarked on a three-million *daimoku* campaign and set about my transformation. I didn't want to get involved with anyone, but once again found myself falling in love with someone who was unsuitable: luckily, he lived over a hundred miles away, which meant that a relationship in his eyes was a nonstarter. I then nearly became involved with a man whom I found out at zero hour was married and, again, the relationship never got off the ground, despite mutual attraction. I felt much protected by my practice and continued to chant to resolve my relationship *karma*.

On the HQ course in June, I met a woman who gave me her experience of writing a list for a partner, and then, two weeks later, he arrived at her front door – literally! Once home, I tentatively started on my list. It began with "must want me for who I am", and it went on, and on, and on, and on . . . I included things like being good at DIY, doing the washing up voluntarily, enjoying gardening, how much he should earn, how tall I wanted him to be, that he must have children – some things may seem trivial, but they were important to me.

So, I continued to chant, and waited for my "partner for *kosen-rufu*" to knock at my door, or beam, Star Trek fashion, into my front room, which, of course, did not happen. By November, I realized that I was going to have to take action, and on the advice of a friend, joined "Date-line" on 1 January 2002. For weeks and weeks, I had *nothing*, and then a letter dropped onto my doormat from a man who lived five miles from me. I decided to be polite and answer, though he didn't seem to me to be exciting enough! I think I had my heart set on a man a bit younger than me, and he was two years older.

After a few weeks, we decided to meet. To test his mettle and suitability, I took him on the longest and muddiest walk I could find. He loved it! Strangely, I knew within minutes of our first meeting that we were going to marry, which we did in July 2003. Some months after I had finished my three-million *daimoku*, I found my husband-shopping list – and was able to tick off every one of my requests! Here, now, in 2007, I can truly say that I have the man I deserve. The self-worth I now have is reflected in the relationship we have, which is respectful and supportive.

As to proof of the practice, in 2004, my husband, Julian, was made redundant, but after a few weeks he got a job working for a shipping company in the Caspian Sea. The ship he was on had none of the usual forms of regular communication I was used to, such as satellite telephone, and computer e-mail, and though he had a local SIM card for his mobile, the reception was virtually impossible once they were more than four miles from the port. At this point in time, I had not spoken to, or had any form of communication from Julian for about three to four weeks because he was out at sea all the time. I was not worried, and kept up my regular practice of twice-daily *gongyo* and *daimoku* for thirty minutes each time. However, there were some important things I needed to tell him, so one morning, while doing my *daimoku*, I demanded proof of my practice from the universe. My demand was that there would be enough of a signal for him to speak to me with clear reception for no longer than five out of thirty minutes not long after I had finished my morning chanting. Forty-five minutes later, the phone rang; it was Julian, and we spoke for exactly five minutes! He was amazed to find that his mobile was suddenly showing full reception bars, so he phoned me instantly. He was so surprised; I wasn't, but was very grateful.

Me and My Hiccoughs
Robert Wilson Thomas

This is an experience about hiccoughs, an experience about hiccoughs and about practising until the final moment of your life. I am fifty-four years old, and I have practised the Buddhism of Nichiren Daishonin for over twenty-one years. You'd think by now I'd have learned a thing or two about the practice and how to "do" it properly. But no, I have had to learn the hard way – again!

In March 2006, I was diagnosed as suffering from a primary cancer of the tongue, with secondary cancer in the lymph node in my neck. Radical neck surgery got rid of the lymph glands and then the cancer of the tongue was treated with radiotherapy and chemotherapy in St Luke's Hospital, Dublin. After several weeks as an in-patient at St Luke's, I started to suffer with acute attacks of hiccoughs. They were few, at first, and went away if I held my breath, but over a couple of weeks, they had built up to, typically, forty, fifty, or even more attacks in a day. During the attacks, the hiccoughs came at intervals of six or seven seconds, so it was vexing rather than painful and frustrating that something like a hiccough should suddenly visit me with such frequency and, once here, should issue at such short intervals. Eating was a challenge in itself, as you might imagine.

There was nothing that the doctors were able to do about it. I suppose that the bewildering combination of pills and elixirs that were taken for the cancer, and to counter the side-effects of the radiotherapy and chemotherapy, must have had some adverse effects or contra-indications rattling about in there somewhere. Then, the hiccoughs came with an additional threat: instead of the regular coughs, my stomach heaved in a succession of gulps, as though my body was trying to make me vomit. The motion of the coughing settled into a pattern of single hiccoughs leading up to multiple spasms when it felt like my throat was being forced into my windpipe, effectively stopping my breathing, choking me.

On one evening during *gongyo*, I got desperate. I was on a nebuliser for my breathing, and the choking sensation was getting to me. I would retch six, eight, ten, a dozen times, becoming more distressed with each cycle. I got to the stage when I couldn't breathe until the retching subsided. The cycles of retching were getting longer and, to my horror, I realized that I was getting to the stage when the cycle was so long that I was in danger of choking to death. In "The Fourteen Slanders" of the *Gosho*, the *Writings of Nichiren Daishonin*, Nichiren Daishonin directs us:

> To chant *Nam-myoho-renge-kyo* single-mindedly . . . [and] to continue our practice without backsliding until the final moment of your life.

With the spasms threatening to choke me, I was very possibly near to the "last moment" of my life, or at least as near as I want to be for a while yet. What was more, even at this stage, I was chanting *Nam-myoho-renge-kyo* single-mindedly, albeit single-mindedly yearning to get rid of my hiccoughs!

I have always been able to chant for big things and, when I see or am told what they are, the necessary things. I have difficulty with the obvious and immediate, like my hiccoughs. I didn't realize that I was the only person who could have stopped them. Yet it didn't occur until later on what I should do. So between the spasms, I chanted to be rid of the hiccoughs:

> *Nam-myoho-renge-kyo*
> I no longer want these hiccoughs
> *Nam-myoho-renge-kyo*
> By the time I finish this *gongyo*
> *Nam-myoho-renge-kyo*
> I want the hiccoughs to go
> *Nam-myoho-renge-kyo*

I finished *gongyo* a few minutes later. The hiccoughs had stopped. Apart from the odd "hic" as a reminder of what they had been, they stopped!

I celebrated by telling the three or four nurses on duty what I had done! *Nam-myoho-renge-kyo* – like a lion! I was like the Boy Snow Mountains, wanting to tell everyone about the practice and how I had cured my hiccoughs with *Nam-myoho-renge-kyo*! An extract of guidance from Vice-President Tsuji reminds me of the truly awesome power of *daimoku*:

> When you chant daimoku, *Nam-myoho-renge-kyo* explodes in your life. There is not one part of your life which it does not affect. The important thing is to realise this and attack the area of your life that is causing you suffering – whether it is physical or spiritual sickness. The important thing is that you attack the specific area with your daimoku, remembering that its effect will be like the roar of a lion on other beings. Daimoku is not begging or asking; it is attacking the cause of your suffering. You must attack, attack not beg.

Before that night, when I believe I had been chanting "at the final moment of my life", my *daimoku* had actually been begging or asking. Then, I attacked and saw the proof of the practice immediately! But of course, I knew this in theory already. In the *Gosho* "Reply to Kyo'o" of the *Writings of Nichiren Daishonin*, it says:

> Believe in this mandala with all your heart. *Nam-myoho-renge-kyo* is like the roar of a lion. What sickness can therefore be an obstacle?

Eighteen months later, not only am I cancer free but the surgeon who removed my lymph glands stated that my throat was "very clean". I now see that the hiccoughs were simply the cause for me to chant strongly, but the effect of that was that I was attacking not the hiccoughs, but the cancer itself. That was when I beat the cancer.

Chanting to Win
Sriram Vaidyanathan

I started practising Nichiren Buddhism in India amidst a deluge of difficulties. I was recovering from a torrid relationship, had a visa rejection to the United States – despite excellent marks in their medical licensing examination – and had consequently taken to drinking and smoking too much. All I used to do after getting up was curl up in the foetal position, smoke cigarettes and feel sorry for myself.

Thus started my search for a spiritual pillar that would guide me through this mess. I became increasingly aware that all the money in the world could not bring me happiness. I became disillusioned because praying to deities, going to temples, churches, mosques and *gurdwaras* did not bring me any more happiness. I started going to astrologers and soothsayers only to find that this fuelled my anxiety even more. I could not see beyond the page of zodiac signs of the newspaper, and I was still desperate to find any means by which I could be happy. Of course, in my mind, happiness meant going to America and getting back with the woman with whom my relationship had failed.

After much spiritual window shopping, in 2003, I started doing a popular yoga-based meditation technique. Here, I found interesting and practical ideas of total self-responsibility, *karma* and inner peace. However, I didn't like the passive attitude to life and found the insistence on quitting non-vegetarianism, smoking and drinking very distressing. I found meditation very fragile, in that it was difficult to sustain such a life-state in daily life. I cannot describe the helplessness and absolute desperation to find a profound religion or philosophy that would change my life. I had come to realize that entreating stone statues, begging external beings, or meditating to achieve tranquillity did not seem to provide any answers.

At this stage, the aunt of one of my friends, who knew me very well, suggested that I should meet with her cousin, who was chanting. She said that her cousin claimed that with this chanting one could remove obstacles. She also said that, while her cousin had said many things about this practice, she felt that the crux of it was that it restored one's disordered rhythm with the universe. I was immediately interested, and went to see her cousin. I couldn't wait to hear more about this. It was like an inexhaustible thirst that had to be quenched as soon as was possible. I met with the middle-aged woman living in a posh colony in Delhi. She said that this Buddhism had changed her life. She told me a lot about the practice; however, it was her sincerity and absolute conviction that changed my heart. I started chanting immediately, much to her delight, and she taught me how to do *gongyo* as well.

I was asked to attend a district discussion meeting in Soka Bodhi Tree Garden, the Buddhist centre in Delhi. There were two hundred people there. Most of the meeting is a haze, but three things really made a deep impression on me. First, was the sound of everybody chanting together, and somehow I knew in the depths of my life that this was something I would continue forever. Second, was the absolute conviction of members that they were winning and could win every day. I heard a woman chanting, sweating, entreating *Gohonzon* with her whole being. She was like a lion, which contrasted with my impression of Buddhism as a quiet, meditative, serene practice. I remember thinking; "What is she chanting for? She must want it so badly." The third thing I remember is being told that chanting activates our Buddha-nature: like a tap that hasn't been opened for a long time, sometimes muddy water comes out first. I remember its being very practical, based in daily life – relationships, work, home, job, car, society. It was world-grounded, non-intellectual, non-theoretical. Instead of sympathy, everybody seemed to smile and congratulate me on feeling awful! I was reassured. I chanted intermittently for some time, never really completely believing in the power of *Nam-myoho-renge-kyo* at first. But things started to change; the wheels were in motion.

My main prayers were to go to America and get back together with the person with whom I had just broken up. I was also chanting for absolute happiness and victory. One of the earliest benefits I received was to slow down the speed of my motorbike through the crowded streets of Delhi. I often used to chant while riding my motorbike. I had some close shaves, which immediately made me slow down and drive sensibly. Of course, I was too depressed to realize these benefits. I couldn't go to America as I had my second visa rejection: I was rejected as a high-risk applicant, post 9/11, and, after some encouragement by friends and relatives, I came to the United Kingdom in 2004 to pursue my postgraduate training in medicine. I was full of begrudging and complaining. All I could do was write e-mails to my friends saying how sad and unhappy I was in this country, where I didn't have any friends. At this stage, I wasn't attending Buddhist meetings. I had quite a deep problem with authority and, consequently, I had great suspicion regarding SGI. I thought their traditions antediluvian and anachronistic. I consequently misunderstood people's sincerity as nosy behaviour. I spent five months in unemployment and cooped up in a room in East London with five other people. I hated every moment of my life, and was too embarrassed to return back to India.

I consistently applied for jobs in medicine, and even took postgraduate exams that were much above my level and passed them. However, for some reason, I never managed to get a job in medicine. I then proceeded to apply for unpaid observerships with various medical consultants. I managed to secure one such post on an observership in Hull-upon-Kingston. However, to my chagrin, after six weeks my consultant said that he would not be able to give me a reference as he did not feel that I had sufficient experience to be able to function safely at a senior house officer level. This was a big blow to me and I felt angry with him, particularly because he could have told me this earlier.

All the time, I continued to chant intermittently and to tell others about this Buddhism. My friends would often make fun of me at this stage, as my life was no big success story. However, I continued to chant. Surprisingly, surgical jobs that I applied for seemed to give me a more positive response. Another blow struck me when a job in the Isle of Wight, for which I had been consistently trying for months, materialized in an interview. However, the person who was receiving my e-mails forgot to tell me in time and I missed the interview. I was full of hatred, rage and blame, but I continued chanting.

Mystically, I got an observership in the casualty department in East London. This meant that I would have to return to the same place in East Ham – that rat-infested, overcrowded and undignified ghetto of unemployed medical professionals from India. This time, I was more positive, and I really enjoyed my observership. Particularly, what really amazed me was the absolute encouragement that I received from everybody in that hospital. Until today, I am grateful to the consultant for having helped preserve my dignity at a time when it was in danger of extinction. She consistently praised my surgical skills. This was a big surprise for me because, since childhood, I had always been under-confident of my dexterity and hand–eye coordination. I was constantly the focus of ridicule for being very poor at these skills. I was often made fun of among friends when I was not able to participate in sports activities. Even my parents had often called me "Monkey Hands". Therefore, to be praised for my surgical skills was completely astonishing because this was an opportunity for me to change very deep *karma*. Surgery was a great challenge; it seemed like I had to face up to my worst fears. To my surprise, I discovered that I loved it and had a great aptitude for it too. I realized that it wasn't coincidence that I came here to the UK. When I realized this, I chanted in gratitude.

Within two weeks I had been offered a job there as a senior house officer – the very level for which I had not been considered a month before. They were happy to keep me there until I was able to get more permanent training posts. By August 2004, there were fifteen days left for my visa to expire. Then I was invited for an interview at Chesterfield. I was very tense, but I knew at the interview I would get the job. I started it in August. By November, I had met my wife-to-be. We were pleasantly astonished after a month of courting when we realized that we each had been chanting *Nam-myoho-renge-kyo*! We were each other's first benefit of the practice. Since then, I have had many benefits and many challenges. I have had to brave deep prejudices, nepotism, not being one of the boys. But determination, effort, and deep encouragement from President Ikeda, who, when I wrote to him for guidance, not expecting to hear back, personally replied to address my problems, have made me strong.

My biggest lesson was to understand the power of *Nam-myoho-renge-kyo*, the power of chanting for *kosen-rufu*. The simplicity of this practice has never been clearer to me. We chant and we chant to win, not to theorize or intellectualize or to divide, but to include everybody; to join hearts. We chant to win, nothing else.

The Gauntlet

I challenge you
To dream the dream
and make it true
Fight as a drowning man
For the drifting wood
that comes in view.

Never in your lifetime
to just accept regress.
Nor fearful of your doubt
to go without – til then.

I charge you now
to courageously attune
What mankind seeks
With fullness of potential
that strides the inner city streets.

Remould thyself
with human revolution.
Stride yea! Ever struggle
to livicate evolution.

I challenge you to,
with just thyself compete
In justice name
and not in justification.

Confront the slanderous
shadows that you cast.
Lead through the
sea of suffering
strapped to the mast.

I charge you now
in battle to engage
Face ever forwards
to conquer thine own rage.

    Rejecting naught but
    the selfishness inside.
    That doth prevent
    the turning of the tide.

I dare you to inspire
with steadfast
determination
The family
the very hub, of the nation.

    Rejecting that dis-
    order of the day:
    That only through
    individualism
    Will we find the way.

To seek and reveal
the jewel of truth
so rare.
This is the gauntlet
courage alone
can wear.

        From *Silence of the Raised Voice*
        Nicky Delgado, Cardiff

Appendix A
The Questionnaire

Name (optional)

Age (please tick)
Under 10   10–20   21–30   31–40
41–50   51–60   61–70   71–80   80
plus

Contact details (optional)

Marital or non-marital status (please tick)

married   living with partner   divorced
separated   widowed   single

Male   Female   (please tick)

Occupation

Nationality

Qualifications

City/town/village

County

Ethnicity

Chapter/District

Please tick the division of which you are a member
Young Eagles   Mimosa   Future Group
Young Men's   Young Women's
Men's   Women's

1. What were your religious beliefs, if any, before you encountered Nichiren Daishonin Buddhism?

2. Give details of ways in which you were familiar with other eastern religions, if any, before you encountered Nichiren Daishonin Buddhism.

3. Are you a Nichiren Daishonin Buddhist *as well as* being a member of another faith? If so, what is that faith?

4. What was the approximate date of your first encounter with Nichiren Daishonin Buddhism?

5. How did you first hear about Nichiren Daishonin Buddhism?

If you heard through a person, please supply the following information about him or her:

Gender   Nationality   Ethnicity   Age   City/town/village   County
Chapter/District

6. Explain any contacts you may have had with Japan or Japanese apart from SGI.

7. When did you first begin chanting?

8. When did you become a member of SGI-UK?

9. Have you received Gohonzon and, if so, when was that?
   If you haven't received Gohonzon, is that because another member of your household has, in which case, who?

Which other members of your family, if any, practise Nichiren Daishonin Buddhism? If any, please indicate if they are SGI-UK members or not.

Which other SGI-UK members, if any, actually live in your household?

10. For how long were you practising before joining SGI-UK?

11. How often do you chant and for how long? Are there any constraints on how often and how long?

12. For what do you chant? Please also tick which of your responses you think were directly realized and comment on those that may have been indirectly realized.

13. How do you respond to times when things you have chanted for have not been realized at all?

14. What difference does it make chanting to the Gohonzon rather than without it?

15. If for any reason you are unable to chant for a while, do you notice any changes in your life?

16. Do you chant longer and more earnestly for matters you consider very important?
   What sort of matters would these be?

17. How frequently do you attend the monthly Chapter/District meetings?

18. In what ways do you engage in *kosen-rufu*?

   What do you understand by *shakubuku*? In what ways do you put it into practice?

19. Specify any voluntary service you have undertaken outside SGI.

20. Apart from monthly meetings, what SGI collective cultural events have you attended:
In Wales/Borders?

Outside Wales/Borders?

At SGI-UK National Centre at Taplow Court?

21. What links do you have with districts outside Wales and the Borders?

22. Have you taken the Study Exam?   No   Grade 1 Pass/Fail   Grade 2 Pass/Fail
                                                                     (please tick)

23. What are your views on:

Human rights:

Environmental issues:

Abortion:

Euthanasia:

Homosexuality:

Other religions:

24. What do you personally understand by the term "human revolution"?

25. Which do you think are the major areas of social and worldwide concerns that need urgent attention?

How do you think you, yourself, make a difference in these areas?

26. How do your friends, relatives and associates react to your beliefs and practices?

27. What attracted you first to Nichiren Daishonin Buddhism, and why do you remain attracted?

28. What have been the benefits of Nichiren Daishonin Buddhist practice for you?

29. What changes have come about in your life since becoming a Nichiren Daishonin Buddhist?

30. How do you think your personality has changed since becoming a Nichiren Daishonin Buddhist?

31. Do you have a Testimony/Experience already published in the *Art of Living*? If so, please specify: month year issue number

Would you agree to part(s) of it being included in the book? Yes No (please tick)

Do you regularly receive the *Art of Living*?

32. Are there any festivals of other religions in which you participate, e.g. Christmas?

33. Please outline any formal experiences you have of wedding or funeral ceremonies conducted according to Nichiren Daishonin Buddhism, and outline any informal experiences you may have had of birth or naming occasions.

If you wish to make any additional comments on any of the questions, please attach separate paper, indicating the number of the question to which you are responding. Thank you all for your help.

Appendix B
Charter of the Soka Gakkai International

Preamble

We, the constituent organisations and members of the Soka Gakkai International (hereinafter called 'SGI'), embrace the fundamental aim and mission of contributing to peace, culture and education based on the philosophy and ideals of the Buddhism of Nichiren Daishonin.

We recognise that at no other time in history has humankind experienced such an intense juxtaposition of war and peace, discrimination and equality, poverty and abundance as in the twentieth century; that the development of increasingly sophisticated military technology, exemplified by nuclear weapons, has created a situation where the very survival of the human species hangs in the balance; that the reality of violent ethnic and religious discrimination presents an unending cycle of conflict; that humanity's egoism and intemperance have engendered global problems, including degradation of the natural environment and widening economic chasms between developed and developing nations, with serious repercussions for humankind's collective future.

We believe that Nichiren Daishonin's Buddhism, a humanistic philosophy of infinite respect for the sanctity of life and all-encompassing compassion, enables individuals to cultivate and bring forth their inherent wisdom and, nurturing the creativity of the human spirit, to surmount the difficulties and crises facing humankind and realise a society of peaceful and prosperous coexistence.

We, the constituent organisations and members of SGI, therefore, being determined to raise high the banner of world citizenship, the spirit of tolerance, and respect for human rights based on the humanistic spirit of Buddhism, and to challenge the global issues that face humankind through dialogue and practical efforts based on a steadfast commitment to non-violence, hereby adopt this Charter, affirming the following purposes and principles:

Purposes and principles

One *SGI shall contribute to peace, culture and education for the happiness and welfare of all humanity based on Buddhist respect for the sanctity of life.*

Two *SGI, based on the ideal of world citizenship, shall safeguard fundamental human rights and not discriminate against any individual on any grounds.*

Three *SGI shall respect and protect the freedom of religion and religious expression.*

Four *SGI shall promote an understanding of Nichiren Daishonin's Buddhism through grass-roots exchange, thereby contributing to individual happiness.*

Five *SGI shall, through its constituent organisations, encourage its members to contribute towards the prosperity of their respective societies as good citizens.*

Six *SGI shall respect the independence and autonomy of its constituent organisation in accordance with the conditions prevailing in each country.*

Seven *SGI shall, based on the Buddhist spirit of tolerance, respect other religions, engage in dialogue and work together with them towards the resolution of fundamental issues concerning humanity.*

Eight *SGI shall respect cultural diversity and promote cultural exchange, thereby creating an international society of mutual understanding and harmony.*

Nine *SGI shall promote, based on the Buddhist ideal of symbiosis, the protection of nature and the environment.*

Ten *SGI shall contribute to the promotion of education, in the pursuit of truth as well as development of scholarship, to enable all people to cultivate their characters and enjoy fulfilling and happy lives.*

Glossary of Terms

bodhisattva   a Sanskrit term in Mahayana Buddhism for one who has delayed enlightenment until all other beings are enlightened too. In Nichiren Daishonin Buddhism, those who spread the teachings and help all to reveal their Buddhahood.

butsudan   a kind of altar or cabinet that houses the *Gohonzon*, the object of devotion.

chutai/chu   one of the Three Truths and the Middle Way; it is the force that binds together transient, phenomenal existence and spiritual, non-substantiality.

daimoku   literally, "title", in the Buddhism of Nichiren Daishonin, it refers specifically to the title of the *Lotus Sutra*, and to the chanting of *Nam-myoho-renge-kyo*.

esho funi   the principle depicting the oneness of all – life and its environment, mind and matter, living and inanimate, and microcosm and macrocosm.

gohonzon   an object of devotion in the form of a *mandala*. The *Gohonzon* in Nichiren Daishonin Buddhism embodies the Mystic Law of the universe, the summation of the whole of the *Lotus Sutra*, and the Buddhahood within the devotee.

gongyo   literally, "to exert oneself in practice". In Nichiren Daishonin Buddhism, this refers to chanting selected portions of the *Lotus Sutra*, namely parts of the "Expedient Means" and "Life Span" chapters.

Gosho   the writings of Nichiren Daishonin.

Hoben   "expedient means", Sanskrit *upaya*: the means devised as steps to Buddhahood, which are discarded when ultimate truth is realized. *Hoben* is the title of a chapter in the *Lotus Sutra* that forms part of the daily chanting of Nichiren Daishonin Buddhists.

ichinen sanzen   the theory of the oneness of all reality that exists in every single moment of life; literally, "three-thousand realms in a single moment."

Juryo   the "Life Span" chapter of the *Lotus Sutra*.

ketai/ke   the truth of transient, phenomenal existence, one of the Three Truths making up unified reality.

kosen-rufu   literally, "to declare and spread widely"; the aim of creating world peace and harmony through the spread of Nichiren Daishonin Buddhism.

kuon ganjo time without beginning or end, a reference to the uncreated and eternal Mystic Law.

kutai/ku the truth of spiritual non-substantiality, one of the Three Truths making up unified reality.

kyo literally, the warp in cloth, the thread, corresponding to the Sanskrit word *sutra*. *Kyo* is the final word in the Nichiren Daishonin Buddhist chant, *Nam-myoho-renge-kyo* that, like a thread, connects all.

mappo the Latter Day, when the teachings of Shakyamuni and the practices of true Buddhism will decline.

nam devotion, to devote one's life; the first word of the Nichiren Daishonin Buddhist chant, *Nam-myoho-renge-kyo* that summons the Mystic Law in the universe and the self.

myoho mystic; wonderful law; the second word of the Nichiren Daishonin Buddhist chant, *Nam-myoho-renge-kyo* that summons the Buddhahood within.

Nam-myoho-renge-kyo the title of the *Lotus Sutra*, prefixed by -*nam*. It is inscribed on the object of worship, the *Gohonzon*, and chanted twice daily as *daimoku*.

obutsumyogo the union of worldly matters and Buddhist teaching.

renge lotus blossom, the third word of the Nichiren Daishonin Buddhist chant, *Nam-myoho-renge-kyo*. Like the flower and fruit that appear at the same time on the lotus, *renge* symbolizes the creation of an effect at the same time as a cause.

Rissho Ankoku Ron "On Establishing the Correct Teaching for the Peace of the Land", one of the major writings of Nichiren Daishonin.

saha world the present world of suffering.

santai the Three Truths that reality is one and incorporates the truth of transient phenomenal existence, the truth of spiritual non-substantiality or emptiness, and the truth of the Middle Way, the binding force between the two.

shakubuku refutation of the views of others in order to bring them to the true doctrines of Nichiren Daishonin Buddhism.

Shakyamuni the Buddha, Siddhartha Gautama.

shikishin funi the theory of the unity of body and mind.

shoju a non-aggressive way of introducing people to Nichiren Daishonin Buddhism without refuting their attachments to other religious teachings.

Soka Gakkai Society for the Creation of Value.

sutra a Sanskrit term, literally meaning "thread", originally referring to short statements that were gathered together to form a text.

upaya kaushalya expedient means, skilful means, skill-in-means.

zadankai small group discussion meetings.

Notes

Introduction

1   Daniel A. Métraux, *The Lotus and the Maple Leaf: The Soka Gakkai Buddhist movement in Canada* (Lanham, New York, London: University Press of America, 1996).

2   Phillip E. Hammond and David W. Machacek, *Soka Gakkai in America: Accommodation and Conversion* (Oxford: Oxford University Press, 1999).

3   Bryan Wilson and Karel Dobbelaere, *A Time to Chant: The Soka Gakkai Buddhists in Britain* (Oxford: Clarendon Press, 1994).

4   See Maria Immacolata Macioti, "Buddhism in Action: Case Studies from Italy", in David Machacek and Bryan Wilson (eds), *Global Citizens: The Soka Gakkai Buddhist movement in the world* (Oxford: Oxford University Press, 2003 reprint of 2000 edn), pp. 375–401.

5   Daniel Métraux, "The Expansion of Soka Gakkai into Southeast Asia" in Machacek and Wilson (eds), *Global Citizens*, pp. 402–30.

6   Peter Clarke, "Buddhist Humanism and Catholic Culture in Brazil" in Machacek and Wilson (eds), *Global Citizens*, pp. 326–48.

7   Wilson and Dobbelaere, *A Time to Chant*.

8   Helen Waterhouse, *Buddhism in Bath: Adaptation and authority* (Monograph Series Community Religious Studies (Leeds: Department of Theology and Religious Studies, University of Leeds, 1997), pp. 91–134.

9   Appendix A: "SGI's Initiatives for Peace" in Daisaku Ikeda, *For the Sake of Peace: Seven paths to global harmony, a Buddhist perspective* (Santa Monica, CA: Middleway Press, 2002 reprint of 2000 edn), pp. 213–14.

CHAPTER ONE   Prologue

1   See <http:en.wikipedia.org/wiki/Atomic_bombings_of_Hiroshima_and_Naga-saki>, 29/09/ 2007>, p. 3. Population figures vary considerably and cannot be ascertained accurately because many labourers were drafted in by the military and because of evacuations.

2   *Ibid.*, p. 4.

3   *Ibid.*, pp. 4–5.

4   Kyoko Gibson, "Passion Born of War", *Art of Living*, no. 75, September 2007, p. 7 (Taplow, Maidenhead: SGI-UK).

5   Kyoko Gibson, in a speech given at the SGI-UK South London National Centre in Brixton, 8–16 September 2007, as part of a conference entitled "Life: Truth, Justice, Dignity" to commemorate the fiftieth anniversary of Josei Toda's speech to the youth division in Japan on the abolition of nuclear weapons.

6   *Ibid.*

7   *Ibid.*

8 Kyoko Gibson, "Passion Born of War", p. 7.
9 *Ibid.*
10 *Ibid.*
11 Les Gibson, in a speech given at the SGI-UK South London National Centre in Brixton 8–16 September, 2007, as part of a conference entitled "Life: Truth, Justice, Dignity".
12 *Ibid.*
13 *Ibid.*
14 Nichiren Daishonin, "On Attaining Buddhahood in This Lifetime", *The Writings of Nichiren Daishonin* no. 1, translated and edited by The Gosho Translation Committee (Tokyo: Soka Gakkai, 1999), p. 3.
15 Les and Kyoko Gibson, "A Lifetime Commitment", *UK Express*, no. 345, March 2000, p. 33.
16 Les Gibson in personal correspondence with the authors. We are grateful to Les Gibson for supplying a detailed historical account of the growth of Nichiren Daishonin Buddhism in Wales: much of what follows is taken from that account.
17 Judith Allan, "The Land of Song Celebrates", *Art of Living*, no. 30, December 2003, *News*, p. 1.
18 *Ibid.*

CHAPTER TWO   **The Buddhism of Nichiren Daishonin: Historical Perspectives**

1 Asvaghosha, *The Buddha-Karita or Life of Buddha*, edited from a Devanagari and two Nepalese manuscripts with variant readings. Translator Edward B. Cowell (New Delhi: Cosmo, 1977, first published in 1894), Book V: 12.
2 *Ibid.*, Book V: 29.
3 The conventionally accepted dates for the Buddha's life are 566–466 BCE, though Gombrich has assigned the Buddha's death to the last decade of the fifth century BCE. See Richard F. Gombrich, "Dating the Buddha: A Red Herring Revealed" in Heinz Bechert (ed.), *The Dating of the Historical Buddha*, Part 2 (Göttingen, 1992), pp. 237–59. Cf. Richard F. Gombrich, *How Buddhism Began: The conditioned genesis of the early teachings* (London: Athlone, 1996), p. 76, note 11.
4 Richard Gombrich, "The Evolution of the Sangha" in Heinz Bechert and Richard Gombrich (eds), *The World of Buddhism* (London: Thames and Hudson, 1984), p. 77.
5 David J. Kalupahana, *Buddhist Philosophy: An historical analysis* (Honolulu: University of Hawaii Press, 1976), p. 113.
6 Philip B. Yampolsky (ed.), "The Recitation of the *Hoben* and *Juryo* Chapters", *Letters of Nichiren*, no. 28, translated by Burton Watson *et al.* (New York: Columbia University Press, 1996), p. 2.
7 *Ibid.*.
8 *Ibid.*, p. 3.
9 Nariyoshi Tamaru, "Soka Gakkai in Historical Perspective" in David Machacek and Bryan Wilson (eds), *Global Citizens: The Soka Gakkai Buddhist movement in the world* (Oxford, New York: Oxford University Press, 2000), p. 22.
10 Yampolsky (ed.), "Letter from Sado" *Letters of Nichiren*, no. 3, p. 57.
11 Yasuji Kirimura, *The Life of Nichiren Daishonin* (Tokyo: Nichiren Shoshu International Center, hereafter NSIC, 1980), p. 12. The revised, 1993, second edn curiously omits the author's name.

12 *Nembutsu* is both a term meaning to meditate on a Buddha, or invoke his name (in later use it came to mean the recitation of Amida's name), and a generic term for those sects that seek to attain rebirth in the Pure Land by worshipping Amida Buddha. See Tomohiro Matsuda (ed.), *A Dictionary of Buddhist Terms and Concepts* (Tokyo: NSIC, 1983), pp. 287–8.

13 John S. Strong, *The Experience of Buddhism: Sources and interpretations* (Belmont, California: Wadsworth, 1995), p. 336.

14 Watanabe Hoyo, "Nichiren" in *Encyclopedia of Religion* (hereafter *ER*), edited by Mircia Eliade (New York: Macmillan, 1987), vol. 10, p. 426.

15 "Letter to Jakunichi-bo" in *The Major Writings of Nichiren Daishonin*, vol. 1, edited and translated by the Gosho Translation Committee (Tokyo: NSIC, 1979), p. 236.

16 *The Writings of Nichiren Daishonin*, no. 1, translated and edited by the Gosho Committee (Tokyo: Soka Gakkai, 1999).

17 Kirimura, *The Life of Nichiren Daishonin*, p. 25 footnote.

18 *The Writings of Nichiren Daishonin*, no. 2.

19 "The Four Debts of Gratitude" in *The Major Writings of Nichiren Daishonin*, vol. 5, edited and translated by the Gosho Translation Committee (Tokyo: NSIC, 1988), pp. 6–7.

20 *Daishonin* literally means "great sage", an honorific title bestowed on Nichiren by the School of Nikko to imply that Nichiren is the original Buddha and not simply another great *bodhisattva*. An account of what happened when priests in the Nichiren Shoshu tradition saw what they considered to be an attack on this doctrine will be examined in CHAPTER THREE.

21 "On the Buddha's Behaviour" in *The Major Writings of Nichiren Daishonin*, vol 1, p. 180.

22 *Ibid.*, p. 181.

23 *The Writings of Nichiren Daishonin*, no. 30.

24 "The True Object of Worship" in *The Major Writings of Nichiren Daishonin*, vol. 1, pp. 45–88.

25 For an outline of Nichiren's activities on Sado, see Hoyo, "Nichiren", *ER* 10, p. 426. See also "Letter from Sado" in Yampolsky, *Letters of Nichiren*, pp. 53–8.

26 "Reply to Kyo'o" in *The Major Writings of Nichiren Daishonin*, volume 1, p. 120.

27 For a full account, see The SGI-USA Study Department, *The Untold History of the Fuji School: The true story of Nichiren Shoshu* (Santa Monica, California: World Tribune Press, 2000).

28 Yampolsky, *Letters of Nichiren*, p. 548.

29 Tamaru, "Soka Gakkai in Historical Perspective", p. 27.

30 This is true also of Zen Buddhism. Commonly thought to have originated in Japan, in fact it has its roots in Chinese Ch'an Buddhism. See Merv Fowler, *Zen Buddhism: Beliefs and practices* (Brighton, Sussex and Portland: Sussex Academic Press, 2005).

31 Ruben L. F. Habito, "Bodily Reading of the *Lotus Sutra*: Understanding Nichiren's Buddhism", *Japanese Journal of Religious Studies*, vol. 26, nos 3–4 (Nagoya: Nanzan Institute for Religion and Culture, Fall 1999), pp. 281–306.

32 Tamaru, "Soka Gakkai in Historical Perspective", p. 26, especially note 1.

33 Robert Kisala, *Prophets of Peace: Pacifism and cultural identity in Japan's new religions* (Honolulu: University of Hawaii Press, 1999), p. 76.

34 Jane Hurst, "A Buddhist Reformation" in Machacek and Wilson (eds), *Global Citizens*, p. 73.

35 Dayle M. Bethel (ed.), *Education for Creative Living: Ideas and proposals of Tsunesaburo Makiguchi*, translated by Alfred Birnbaum (Ames, Iowa: Iowa State University Press, 1989), p. 6.

36 Dayle M. Bethel, *Makiguchi. The Value Creator: Revolutionary Japanese educator and founder of Soka Gakkai* (New York and Tokyo: Weatherhill, 1973), p. 53.

37 Tsunesaburo Makiguchi, *A Geography of Human Life*, edited by Dayle Bethel, and translated from Japanese by Katsusuku Hori *et al.* (San Francisco: Caddo Gap Press, 2002, first published as *Jinsei chirigaku* in 1903).

38 Bethel (ed.), *Education for Creative Living*, p. 6.

39 Makiguchi, *A Geography of Human Life*.

40 Koici Mori, *Study of Makiguchi Tsunesaburo: The founder of Soka Gakkai* (Ann Arbor, Michigan: University Microfilms International, 1977), p. 202.

41 Alvin Toppler, cited by Dayle M. Bethel in Tsunesaburo Makiguchi, *A Geography of Human Life*, p. xviii.

42 <http://www.barefootsworld.net/seattle.html>.

43 Jerry L. Clark, "Thus Spoke Chief Seattle: The story of an undocumented speech", <http://www.archives.gov/publications/prologue/1985/spring/chief-seattle.html>.

44 It will not have escaped rugby fans' attention that a plate for the winners of the Triple Crown was introduced in 2007.

45 Makiguchi, *A Geography of Human Life*, p. 21.

46 *Ibid.*, p. 139.

47 Signed in 1992 by 102 Nobel laureates in science and 1,600 scientists from seventy countries. See Dayle M. Bethel, "The Legacy of Tsunesaburo Makiguchi: Value creating society and global citizenship" in Machacek and Wilson (eds), *Global Citizens*, p. 47.

48 Bethel, *Makiguchi. The Value Creator*, p. 90.

49 *Ibid.*, p. 151.

50 Kisala, *Prophets of Peace*, p. 76.

51 See the section on The Mystic Law in CHAPTER SEVEN below.

52 Tamaru, "Soka Gakkai in Historical Perspective", p. 36.

53 Shin'ichi Yamamoto, "President Makiguchi's Gosho" *Art of Living*, no. 61, July 2006 (Taplow Court, Berkshire: SGI-UK), pp. 15–18.

54 Daniel A. Métraux, *The History and Theology of Soka Gakkai: A Japanese new religion* (New York: The Edwin Mellin Press, 1988), p. 22.

55 *Ibid.*, p. 29.

56 Daisaku Ikeda, *The Wisdom of the Lotus Sutra*, vol. 4 (Santa Monica, CA: World Tribune Press, 2002), p. 273.

57 "The Life Span of the Thus Come One." See *The Lotus Sutra*, translator Burton Watson (New York, Chichester: Columbia University Press, 1993), pp. 224–32.

58 H. Neill McFarland, *The Rush Hour of the Gods: A study of new religious movements in Japan* (New York: Macmillan, 1967).

59 Richard Hughes Seager, *Encountering the Dharma: Daisaku Ikeda, Soka Gakkai, and the globalization of Buddhist humanism* (Berkeley, Los Angeles, London: University of California Press, 2006), p. 53.

60 *Ibid.*, p. 54.
61 Tamaru, "Soka Gakkai in Historical Perspective", p. 37.
62 Bethel, *Makiguchi. The Value Creator*, p. 104.
63 Kisala, *Prophets of Peace*, p. 80.

CHAPTER THREE   **The Human Revolution for a Universal Humanity**

1 Daisaku Ikeda in Johan Galtung and Daisaku Ikeda, *Choose Peace: A dialogue between Johan Galtung & Daisaku Ikeda*, translated and edited by Richard L. Gage (London and East Haven, CT: Pluto Press, 1995), pp. 88–9.
2 Daniel A. Métraux, *The Lotus and the Maple Leaf: The Soka Gakkai Buddhist movement in Canada* (Lanham, New York, London: University Press of America, 1996), p. 125.
3 Richard Hughes Seager, *Encountering the Dharma: Daisaku Ikeda, Soka Gakkai, and the globalization of Buddhist humanism* (Berkeley, Los Angeles, London: University of California Press, 2006), p. 1.
4 Robert Kisala, *Prophets of Peace: Pacifism and cultural identity in Japan's new religions* (Honolulu: University of Hawaii Press, 1999), p. 74. While this estimate is not a recent one, growth in numbers of members in Japan has slowed down in recent years. It is elsewhere in the world that the increases are so evident. It should be borne in mind, too, that numbers in Japan are estimated by *households*, so if one member of a household has a *Gohonzon*, it is assumed that all others are practising members too: see Hiroshi Aruga, ""Soka Gakkai and Japanese Politics" in David Machacek and Bryan Wilson (eds), *Global Citizens: The Soka Gakkai Buddhist movement in the world* (Oxford: Oxford University Press, 2000), pp. 100–1, notes 5 and 6.
5 *Ibid.*, p. 2.
6 Daisaku Ikeda, *Soka Education: A Buddhist vision for teachers, students and parents* (Santa Monica, CA: Middleway Press, 2001), p. 149.
7 Seager, *Encountering the Dharma*, p. 87.
8 *Ibid.*, p. xv.
9 Komeito has, for example, supported the deployment of UN Self-Defence Forces. See Kisala, *Prophets of Peace*, pp. 83–4. As for Soka Gakkai members, according to Kisala, a very high percentage of Japanese Soka Gakkai members support UN peacekeeping involvement, see p. 89.
10 It is now impossible for an individual to hold a position of responsibility in both the political party and Soka Gakkai. In 1994 Komeito joined a new party, Shinshinto, which itself dispersed in 1997–8. At this point, the New Komeito party was formed from previous Komeito members.
11 See Daniel Métraux, "The Changing Role of the Komeito in Japanese Politics in the 1990s" in Machacek and Wilson (eds), *Global Citizens*, p. 129.
12 Chandra Wickramasinghe and Daisaku Ikeda, *Space and Eternal Life: A dialogue between Chandra Wickramasinghe and Daisaku Ikeda* (London and Sterling, VA: Journeyman Press, 1998), pp. 152–3.
13 For a full discussion of the media scandal, see Adam Gamble and Takesato Watanabe, *A Public Betrayed: An inside look at Japanese media atrocities and their warnings to the West* (Washington DC: Regnery Publishing, 2004), chapter 6, "Smearing a Buddhist Leader", pp. 211–51, and Bryan Wilson, "The British Movement and its Members" in Machacek and Wilson, *Global Citizens*, pp.

370–1. For a full, balanced account of the issues causing the schism, see Seager, *Encountering the Dharma*, pp. 127–30.

14 See Wilson, "The British Movement and its Members" in Machacek and Wilson, *Global Citizens*, p. 371.

15 Daniel Métraux, *The Soka Gakkai Revolution* (Lanham, Maryland and London: University Press of America, 1994), p. 150.

16 Responses to question 12 of the questionnaire, see Appendix A, p. 247.

17 Kazuo Fujii, "Q&A: Why Should We Be Interested. The Priesthood Means Nothing to Most People in the UK", *UK Express*, no. 347, May 2000, p. 15.

18 *Ibid.*, p. 16.

19 Seager, *Encountering the Dharma*, pp. 204–5.

20 SGI-USA Study Department: *The Untold History of the Fuji School: The true story of Nichiren Shoshu* (Santa Monica CA: World Tribune Press, 2000), p. 271.

21 Gamble and Watanabe, *A Public Betrayed*, pp. 219–20.

22 Seager, *Encountering the Dharma*, p. 125.

23 Ikeda, in Galtung and Ikeda, *Choose Peace*, p. 8.

24 *Ibid.*, p. 9.

25 Daisaku Ikeda, *A Youthful Diary: One man's journey from the beginning of faith to worldwide leadership for peace* (Santa Monica, CA: World Tribune Press, 2000), p. 500.

26 Métraux, *The Lotus and the Maple Leaf*, pp. 124–5.

27 Akemi Baynes, "In Rhythm with our Movement for Peace", *Art of Living*, no. 23, May 2003, p. 21.

28 Daisaku Ikeda, in the Preface to Daisaku Ikeda and Majid Tehranian, *Global Civilization: A Buddhist–Islamic dialogue* (London and New York: British Academic Press, 2003), p. xii.

29 Daisaku Ikeda, "Peace, Culture and Education: The Great Path of Soka!" President Ikeda's speech at the twenty-sixth Soka Gakkai Headquarters Leaders Meeting, Tokyo, 5 March 2003, *Art of Living*, no. 23, May 2003, p. 38.

30 Daisaku Ikeda, *For the Sake of Peace: Seven paths to global harmony. A Buddhist perspective* (Santa Monica, CA: Middleway Press, 2002 reprint of 2001 edn), p. xxi.

31 Majid Tehranian, in the Introduction to Ikeda and Tehranian, *Global Civilization*, pp. xv–xvi.

32 Daisaku Ikeda, "Dialogue: Opening the Way to Global Civilization", *Art of Living*, no. 13, July 2002, p. 17.

33 Wickramasinghe and Ikeda, *Space and Eternal Life*.

34 Hazel Henderson and Daisaku Ikeda, *Planetary Citizenship* (Santa Monica, CA: Middleway Press, 2004), p. 76.

35 Ikeda, in Wickramasinghe and Ikeda, *Space and Eternal Life*, p. 139.

36 Daisaku Ikeda, *A New Humanism: The university addresses of Daisaku Ikeda* (New York and Tokyo: Weatherhill, 1996), p. 173.

37 "On the Buddha's Prohecy" in *The Writings of Nichiren Daishonin*, no. 43, translated and edited by The Gosho Translation Committee (Tokyo: Soka Gakkai, 1999), p. 401.

38 For a list of Ikeda's lectures at institutions outside Japan from 1974 to 1997 and for Honorary Doctorates and Professorships awarded between 1975 and 1997, see Daisaku Ikeda, *Peace Builder* (Tokyo: Soka Gakkai, 1998), pp. 167–9.

39   Ikeda, *For the Sake of Peace*, p. 109.
40   *Ibid.*, p. 141.
41   *Ibid.*, p. 168.
42   Kindergartens have been established in Hong Kong, Singapore, Hokkaido, Malaysia and Brazil. In Tokyo and Kansai, high schools have been founded, and universities in Southern California and Hachioji.
43   See Karel Dobbelaere, *Soka Gakkai: From lay movement to religion*, translated by Olivier Urbain (USA: Signature Books, 1998, first published in Italian 1998), p. 61.
44   Ikeda, *Soka Education*, p. 35.
45   Ikeda, *For the Sake of Peace*, pp. 82–3.
46   Ikeda, in Wickramasinghe and Ikeda, *Space and Eternal Life*, p. 208.
47   Ikeda, in Galtung and Ikeda, *Choose Peace*, p. 23.
48   "The Wealthy Man Sudatta" in *The Writings of Nichiren Daishonin*, no. 157, p. 1086.
49   Ikeda, in Henderson and Ikeda, *Planetary Citizenship*, p. 149.
50   *Ibid.*, p. 150.
51   In response to question 20 of the questionnaire, see Appendix A, p. 248.
52   Ikeda, *A New Humanism*, p. 4.
53   Daisaku Ikeda, in René Huyghe and Daisaku Ikeda, *Dawn After Dark*, translated by Richard L. Gage (New York and Tokyo: Weatherhill, 1991), p. xiii.
54   For a detailed summary of SGI work for peace and disarmament, see Ikeda, *For the Sake of Peace*, pp. 214–16.
55   Ikeda in Wickramasinghe and Ikeda, *Space and Eternal Life*, p. 147.
56   *Ibid.*, p. 165.
57   *Ibid.*, p. 219.
58   For a list of these from 1983 to 2000, see Ikeda, *For the Sake of Peace*, pp. 225–6.
59   *Ibid.*, p. 17.
60   See Kisala, *Prophets of Peace*, pp. 85–6.
61   Daisaku Ikeda, *A Lasting Peace*, vol. 1 (New York and Tokyo: Weatherhill, 1985), and vol. 2 (New York and Tokyo, 1987).
62   Space does not permit a detailed analysis of Ikeda's suggestions for future peace, though they are extensive. The interested reader might look at his comments in *For the Sake of Peace*, pp. 199–212 and Henderson and Ikeda, *Planetary Citizenship*, pp. 124–31, in relation to the Earth Charter.
63   Responses to question 25 of the questionnaire, see Appendix A, p. 248.
64   Responses to question 12 of the questionnaire, see Appendix A, p. 247.
65   Responses to the second part of question 25 of the questionnaire, see Appendix A, p. 249.
66   "The Opening of the Eyes" in *The Writings of Nichiren Daishonin*, no. 30, p. 220.
67   SGI's Initiatives for Peace, in Ikeda, *For the Sake of Peace*, p. 213.
68   Ikeda, in Ikeda and Tehranian, *Global Civilization*, p. 25.
69   Ikeda, *For the Sake of Peace*, p. 67.
70   Responses to question 23, see Appendix A, p. 248.
71   A definition usually placed in the Glossary on the inside cover of the *Art of Living* magazines.
72   Daisaku Ikeda, *Songs from my Heart* translated by Burton Watson (New York: Weatherhill Inc., 1990), pp. 21–2.

73 Kazuo Fujii, *UK Express*, no. 347, May 2000, p. 20.
74 The English Buddhist Dictionary Committee, *The Soka Gakkai Dictionary of Buddhism* (Tokyo: Soka Gakkai, 2002), p. 580.
75 See Seager, *Encountering the Dharma*, p. 101, Kisala, *Prophets of Peace*, p. 80 and Gamble and Watanabe, *A Public Betrayed*, pp. 215–16.
76 Jane Hurst, "A Buddhist Reformation in the Twentieth Century: Causes and Implications of the Conflict between the Soka Gakkai and the Nichiren Shoshu Priesthood" in Machacek and Wilson, *Global Citizens*, p. 90.
77 Daisaku Ikeda in dialogue with members of SGI's Study Department, "The Practice of Respecting Others", *Art of Living*, no. 28, October 2003, p. 37.
78 *Ibid.*, p. 38.
79 *Ibid.*, p. 41.
80 Responses to question 18 of the questionnaire, see Appendix A, p. 248.
81 Métraux has recorded these sorts of reasons for people joining the movement in Japan, see Daniel A. Métraux, *The History and Theology of Soka Gakkai: A Japanese new religion* (Queenston, Ontario: The Edwin Mellen Press, 1988), pp. 59–62.
82 Helen Waterhouse, "Soka Gakkai Buddhism as a Global Religious Movement" in John Wolf (ed.), *Global Religious Movements in Regional Context* (Aldershot, UK and Burlington, USA: Ashgate in association with The Open University, 2002), p. 148.
83 See the second part of question 18 of the questionnaire, Appendix A, p. 248.
84 Ikeda, in Galtung and Ikeda, *Choose Peace*, p. 73.
85 Question 24, see Appendix A, p. 248.
86 Ikeda, in Ikeda and Tehranian, *Global Civilization*, p. 141.
87 Daisaku Ikeda, "Peace and Human Security: A Buddhist perspective for the twenty-first century", lecture delivered at the East–West Center, Hawaii, USA, 26 January 1995, translated by the SGI Public Relations Bureau, p. 9.
88 Ikeda, *A New Humanism*, p. 50.
89 Responses to question 19 of the questionnaire, see Appendix A, p. 248.
90 Daisaku Ikeda, *Humanity and the New Millennium: From chaos to cosmos*. 1998 Peace Proposal (Tokyo: Soka Gakkai, 1998), p. 41.
91 Ikeda, *For the Sake of Peace*, p. 60.

CHAPTER FOUR **Nichiren Daishonin Buddhism in Wales and the Borders**

1 Figures are based on statistics supplied by StatsWales Report 002534: Components of Population Change by Local Authority. Statistics are only currently available up to 2006. The authors are grateful to Richard Matthews of the Welsh Office for supplying source data.
2 Les Gibson, in a personal e-mail to the authors, 11/02/2008.
3 Thanks to the additional information to the questionnaire responses supplied by the area leaders, Kyoko and Les Gibson, numerical proportions in this section and those that follow are calculated from almost 96% of Wales/Borders members.
4 Compare here, for example, the situation in Hong Kong, where, according to Métraux, SGI attracts "alienated people living in an urban industrial environment". See Daniel Métraux, "The Expansion of the Soka Gakkai into Southeast Asia" in David Machacek and Bryan Wilson (eds), *Global Citizens: The Soka*

Gakkai Buddhist movement in the world (Oxford, New York: Oxford University Press, 2003 reprint of 2000 edn), p. 425.

5   In the South, for example, less Welsh is spoken, and that which is, has differences from the Welsh language of the North. People of the North are often critical of the more cosmopolitan South and are more fervent about using the Welsh language even with non-speaking Welsh visitors to the North. Unity of outlook is still perhaps confined to the national game of rugby!

6   The authors are grateful to SGI-UK General Director, Robert Samuels, for supplying the details here.

7   David W. Chappell, "Socially Inclusive Buddhists in America" in Machacek and Wilson (eds), *Global* Citizens, p. 324.

8   *Ibid.*

9   Bryan Wilson and Karel Dobbelaere, *A Time to Chant: The Soka Gakkai Buddhists in Britain* (Oxford, New York: Oxford University Press, 1994), p. 225.

10 Figures in this section are calculated on information based on 84% of the total number of members. Since some people travel to the Cardiff chapters from elsewhere, the percentage of members in the chapters is greater than the number of members actually resident in Cardiff.

11 See the questionnaire, Appendix A, p. 246.

12 Helen Waterhouse, *Buddhism in Bath: Adaptation and authority*. Monograph Series Community Religious Studies (Leeds: Department of Theology and Religious Studies, University of Leeds, 1997), p. 127.

13 Wilson and Dobbelaere, *A Time to Chant*, p. 39.

14 Phillip E. Hammond and David W. Machacek, *Soka Gakkai in America: Accommodation and conversion* (Oxford, New York: Oxford University Press, 1999), p. 49.

15 Maria Immacolata Macioti, "Buddhism in Action: Case Studies from Italy" in Machacek and Wilson, *Global Citizens*, p. 395.

16 See Atsuko Usui, "The Role of Women" in Machacek and Wilson (eds), *Global Citizens*, p. 154.

17 *Ibid.*, p. 168.

18 Percentages are based on fractionally below 100% of the members (99%).

19 See Daniel Métraux, *The Lotus and the Maple Leaf: The Soka Gakkai Buddhist movement in Canada* (Lanham, Maryland: University Press of America, 1996), p. 84.

20 Calculations are given from 96% of the members' profiles.

21 While asked for nationality and ethnicity as two separate questions, it is clear that many respondents confused both. Here, then, it has been necessary to conflate the two.

22 1 South American, 1 North American, 4 European, 1 Canadian, 3 African/South African, 1 Australian, 1 Middle Eastern, 4 Chinese, for example.

23 See Métraux, *The Lotus and the Maple Leaf*, p. 62.

24 Chappell, "Socially Inclusive Buddhists in America", p. 300.

25 Bryan Wilson, "The British Movement and its Members" in Machacek and Wilson (eds), *Global Citizens*, p. 360.

26 Wilson and Dobbelaere, *A Time to Chant*, p. 43.

27 *Ibid.*

28 Daniel Métraux, "The Expansion of the Soka Gakkai into Southeast Asia" in Machacek and Wilson (eds), *Global Citizens*, pp. 404–5.

29 Wilson and Dobbelaere, *A Time to Chant*, pp. 94–5.

30 The percentage here is based on questionnaire responses only, that is to say, approximately half of the members.

31 Hammond and Machacek, *Soka Gakkai in America*, p. 152.

32 Macioti, "Buddhism in Action", p. 375.

33 Métraux, "The Expansion of Soka Gakkai into Southeast Asia", p. 40.

34 Métraux, *The Lotus and the Maple Leaf*, p. 123.

35 See Waterhouse, *Buddhism in Bath*, pp. 124–5, and Wilson, "The British Movement and its Members", p. 367.

36 See David Machacek, "Organizational Isomorphism in SGI-USA" in Machacek and Wilson (eds), *Global Citizens*, p. 293.

37 See David Machacek and Kerry Mitchell, "Immigrant Buddhists in America" in Machacek and Wilson (eds), *Global Citizens*, pp. 262–4.

38 *Ibid.*, pp. 270–4.

39 Métraux, "The Expansion of the Soka Gakkai into Southeast Asia", p. 408.

40 Wilson, "The British Movement and its Members", p. 368.

41 Wilson and Dobbelaere, *A Time to Chant*, p. 116.

42 Statistics here are based on questionnaire responses and on information supplied by Les Gibson. The professions of a few people were not known so the data is based on 94% of the total membership.

43 See Wilson, "The British Movement and its Members", p. 368.

44 Welsh Office Annual Population Survey July 2006–June 2007: Persons Aged 16+ in Employment in Wales by Occupational Code. The authors are grateful to Martin Griffiths of the Welsh Office for supplying the data corresponding to the occupational codes.

45 Nine per cent, see Wilson, "The British Movement and its members", p. 368, but, curiously, the figure seems to be almost 19% elsewhere, see Wilson and Dobbelaere, *A Time to Chant*, p. 120.

46 Welsh Office Annual Population Survey July 2006–June 2007: Persons Aged 16+ in Employment in Wales by Occupational Code. The authors are grateful to Martin Griffiths of the Welsh Office for supplying the data corresponding to the occupational codes.

47 Martin Griffiths, in a private e-mail to the authors, 05/02/2008.

48 See Wilson, "The British Movement and its Members", p. 368, and Wilson and Dobbelaere, *A Time to Chant*, p. 120.

49 During October–December 2007, rates are for persons aged 16+. The source is *National Statistics*, Labour Force Survey, Labour market statistics, February, 2008. The authors are, again, grateful to Martin Griffiths of the Welsh Assembly Government for supplying the data.

50 Statistical Directorate, Welsh Assembly Government, *Statistical Bulletin SB 52/2007*: The Levels of Highest Qualification held by Working Age Adults in Wales, 2006. Comparisons with SGI-Wales/Borders members are calculated from 146 responses to the questionnaires.

51 A percentage that is quite unlike the national trend where it is the 25–34 age range that has the highest rate of qualifications in NQF levels 4–6.

52 Wilson, "The British Movement and its members", p. 368. However, in Wilson and Dobbelaere, *A Time to Chant*, almost 24% are recorded as having attended university, p. 122. Clearly, there is some odd discrepancy here between attendance

and degree status, suggesting an almost 50% drop-out between university entry and graduation.

53 Wilson, "The British Movement and its Members", p. 368.

54 Hammond and Machacek, *Soka Gakkai in America*, p. 52.

55 Wilson and Dobbelaere, *A Time to Chant*, p. 114.

56 Hammond and Machacek, *Soka Gakkai in America*, p. 48.

57 Karel Dobbelaere, *Soka Gakkai: From lay movement to religion* (USA: Signature Books Publishing, 1998), p. 33.

58 Thirty-nine per cent in 2004/5 is the most recently available published statistic, the source being *National Statistics* series FM2 no. 32, Marriage, Divorce and Adoption Statistics. The authors are grateful to Richard Matthews of the Welsh Office for the data provided on marriage and population.

59 Seventeen per cent, source *ibid*.

60 The remaining 7–8% are separated or widowed.

61 Percentages are based on exactly half of the members (150), who responded to the questionnaires. The information here is gleaned from responses to question 1 of the questionnaire concerning previous religious beliefs, see Appendix A, p. 246.

62 Wilson, "The British Movement and its Members", p. 362.

63 See *ibid*., pp. 350 and 352.

64 *Ibid*., p. 350.

65 Wilson and Dobbelaere, *A Time to Chant*, p. 79.

66 Métraux, *The Lotus and the Maple Leaf*, p. 83.

67 See Hammond and Machacek, *Soka Gakkai in America*, p. 143.

68 *Ibid*, p. 140.

69 *Ibid*., p. 147.

70 Question 2 on the questionnaire, see Appendix A, p. 246.

71 Waterhouse, *Buddhism in Bath*, p. 100.

72 Wilson and Dobbelaere, *A Time to Chant*, p. 92.

73 Hammond and Machacek, *Soka Gakkai in America*, p. 154.

74 *Ibid*., p. 154.

75 Question 3 on the questionnaire, see Appendix A, p. 246.

76 Les Gibson, in a private e-mail to the authors 26/05/2008.

77 Responses to question 5 on the questionnaire, see Appendix A, p. 246.

78 Percentages are based on the 150 responses to the questionnaire and represent approximately half of the total number of members.

79 Not so pronounced in Canada or the UK, see Métraux, *The Lotus and the Maple Leaf*, p. 85, Wilson, "The British Movement and its Members", p. 361, also Wilson and Dobbelaere, *A Time to Chant*, p. 50, though much more so in the USA, see Hammond and Machacek, *Soka Gakkai in America*, p. 105. Wilson states that 90% became members through partners, relatives, friends and colleagues, a much higher percentage than in our survey of Wales and the Borders members.

80 Métraux, *The Lotus and the Maple Leaf*, p. 85.

81 Wilson, "The British Movement and its Members", p. 362.

82 Hammond and Machacek, *Soka Gakkai in America*, p. 151.

83 Métraux, "The Expansion of Soka Gakkai in Southeast Asia", p. 409.

84 Dobbelaere, *Soka Gakkai*, p. 40.

85 See Métraux, *The Lotus and the Maple Leaf*, pp. 59–60.

86 See Wilson, "The British Movement and its Members", pp. 361–2, and Wilson and Dobbelaere, *A Time to Chant*, pp. 53–9.

87 See Wilson and Dobbelaere, *A Time to Chant*, p. 63.

88 *Ibid.*, p. 69.

89 Responses to question 26 of the questionnaire, see Appendix A, p. 249, amounting to 140 of the total of 150.

90 Hammond and Machacek, *Soka Gakkai in America*, p. 161.

91 Calculated from comparisons between responses to questions 4 and 7 of the questionnaire, see Appendix A p. 246–7, and the 89 women and 54 men who responded to these questions.

92 though of the women here, a far higher percentage than the men started to chant after two years, in which case, more men (22%) than women (17%) took longer to take up chanting.

93 Responses to questions 7, 8 and 10 of the questionnaire, see Appendix A, p. 247.

94 Thirty-three per cent, with an additional 13% who have a non-SGI practising member of the household.

95 Twenty-seven per cent, plus 8% with a practising non-member.

96 Thirty-nine per cent men, 24% women.

97 See Métraux, *The Lotus and the Maple Leaf*, p. 81.

98 See Wilson and Dobbelaere, *A Time to Chant*, p. 98.

99 Responses to question 23 of the questionnaire, see Appendix A, p. 248. Several respondents declined to comment on these issues, some indicating that the topics were too emotive. 134 responded to the question on abortion, 131 on euthanasia and 136 on homosexuality: percentages in each case are based on these respective numbers.

CHAPTER FIVE **The *Lotus Sutra***

1 *Lotus Sutra* 21, translator Burton Watson, *The Lotus Sutra* (New York, Chichester, West Sussex: Columbia University Press, 1993), p. 276. All following quotations from the *Lotus Sutra* are taken from this text.

2 Ruben L. F. Habito, "Buddha-body Theory and the Lotus Sutra: Implications for Praxis" in Gene Reeves (ed.), *A Buddhist Kaleidoscope: Essays on the Lotus Sutra* (Tokyo: Kosei Publishing Co., 2002), p. 311.

3 See Watson, *The Lotus Sutra*, p. ix, and for a succinct survey of the translations and transmission of the text, see W. E. Soothill, *The Lotus of the Wonderful Law or The Lotus Gospel* (Richmond, Surrey: Curzon Press, 1994 reprint, first published 1987), pp. 7–10.

4 The Chinese title of it is *Miao-fa-lien-hua-ching* from the Sanskrit *Saddharma-pundarika-sutra*.

5 See Einosuke Akiya, "On the Steps Leading up to the Publication of Lotus Manuscripts", *The Journal of Oriental Studies*, 7(1997), pp. 59–61, and *passim*; also Liu Guangtang, "Concerning Sanskrit Lotus Sutra Fragments from the Lüshun Museum Collection", pp. 59–61.

6 Watson, *The Lotus Sutra*, p. xxi.

7 Daisaku Ikeda, in Daisaku Ikeda, Katsuji Saito, Takanori Endo and Haruo Suda, *The Wisdom of the Lotus Sutra: A discussion*, vol. 1 (Santa Monica, CA: World Tribune Press, 2000), p. 14.

8 *Lotus Sutra* 10, Watson, p. 164.

 9 Daisaku Ikeda, in Daisaku Ikeda, Katsuji Saito, Takanori Endo and Haruo Suda, *The Wisdom of the Lotus Sutra: A discussion*, vol. 2 (Santa Monica, CA: World Tribune Press, 2000), p. 26.

10 *Lotus Sutra* 10, Watson, p. 161.

11 *Ibid.*, p. 167.

12 Daisaku Ikeda, in Daisaku Ikeda, Katsuji Saito, Takanori Endo and Haruo Suda, *The Wisdom of the Lotus Sutra: A discussion*, vol. 6 (Santa Monica, CA: World Tribune Press, 2000), pp. 256–7.

13 Malcolm David Eckel, "By the Power of the Buddha" in Reeves, *A Buddhist Kaleidoscope*, p. 138.

14 *Lotus Sutra* 1, Watson, p. 22.

15 Soothill, *The Lotus of the Wonderful Law*, p. 35.

16 Ikeda, *The Wisdom of the Lotus Sutra*, vol. 2, p. 53.

17 As was seen in CHAPTER TWO of this book, the best known Theravada teachings are the *Four Noble Truths*. These are that all life is suffering; suffering is caused by desires; ceasing desires ends suffering; the way to cease desires is to follow the *Noble Eightfold Path*. This last consists of eight moral precepts – right views, thoughts, speech, action, living, endeavour, mindfulness and meditation.

18 *Lotus Sutra* 4, Watson, p. 94.

19 Presumably as taught by other Mahayana texts. The *bodhisattva* of the *Lotus Sutra* is distinguished from others by becoming a *mahasattva* with the goal of Buddhahood and the salvation of all, and by acceptance of the superiority of the teachings of the *Lotus Sutra*.

20 See Ikeda *et al.*, *The Wisdom of the Lotus Sutra*, vol. 1, pp. 152–3, and for the contrary view of carriages for each son, Watson, *The Lotus Sutra* 3, pp. 57–8.

21 *Lotus Sutra* 3, Watson p. 62.

22 David W. Chappell, "Organic Truth: Personal Reflections on the Lotus Sutra" in Reeves, *A Buddhist Kaleidoscope*, p. 60.

23 *Lotus Sutra* 2, Watson, p. 35.

24 *Ibid.*, 2, Watson, p. 32.

25 *Ibid.*, 7, Watson, pp. 141–2.

26 *Ibid.*, 2, Watson, p. 36.

27 Gene Reeves, "The Lotus Sutra as Radically World-Affirming" in Reeves, *A Buddhist Kaleidoscope*, p. 194.

28 Yoichi Kawada, "The Lotus Sutra as a Doctrine of Inner Transformation", *Journal of Oriental Studies* 6(1996), p. 34.

29 *Lotus Sutra*, 16, Watson, p. 226.

30 Daisaku Ikeda in Daisaku Ikeda, Katsuji Saito, Takanori Endo and Haruo Suda, *The Wisdom of the Lotus Sutra: A discussion*, vol. 4 (Santa Monica, CA: World Tribune Press, 2000), p. 26.

31 Another interesting point about the eternal nature of the Buddha is made by Ikeda when he says that even though the Buddha may have become enlightened in an immeasurable past, there must have been a time when he was not enlightened, and that may suggest that the Buddha is inferior to the Law, even though he awakens to it in his intensely remote past. He thinks this hints at a *perfectly* eternal Buddha that really is one with the Mystic Law. This status he gives to all human beings. See Daisaku Ikeda, in Daisaku Ikeda, Katsuji Saito, Takanori Endo and Haruo Suda, *The Wisdom of the Lotus Sutra: A discussion*, vol. 5 (Santa Monica, CA: World Tribune Press, 2000), pp. 214–15.

32 *Lotus Sutra* 16, Watson, p. 226.

33 See Ikeda *et al.*, *The Wisdom of the Lotus Sutra*, vol. 4, pp. 34–5.

34 *Lotus Sutra* 5, Watson, p. 102.

35 In the Theravada tradition there is only one *bodhisattva* and that was Shakyamuni before he became enlightened, so here a *bodhisattva* is a Buddha-to-be.

36 For a detailed account, see *Lotus Sutra* 14, Watson pp. 196–8.

37 Daisaku Ikeda, in Daisaku Ikeda, Katsuji Saito, Takanori Endo and Haruo Suda, *The Wisdom of the Lotus Sutra: A discussion*, vol. 3 (Santa Monica, CA: World Tribune Press, 2000), p. 215.

38 Daisaku Ikeda, in Daisaku Ikeda, Katsuji Saito, Takanori Endo and Haruo Suda, *The Wisdom of the Lotus Sutra: A discussion*, vol. 5 (Santa Monica, CA: World Tribune Press, 2000), p. 158.

39 Burton Watson (translator), *The Record of the Orally Transmitted Teachings* (Tokyo: Soka Gakkai, 2004), p. 124.

40 Ikeda, in Ikeda *et al.*, *The Wisdom of the Lotus Sutra*, vol. 4, pp. 22–3.

41 Ikeda, in Ikeda *et al.*, *The Wisdom of the Lotus Sutra*, vol. 1, p. 96.

42 Ikeda, in Ikeda *et al.*, *The Wisdom of the Lotus Sutra*, vol. 3, p. 11.

43 *Ibid.*, p. 25.

44 *Lotus Sutra* 21, Watson, pp. 275–6.

45 *Ibid.*, p. 276.

46 Ikeda, in Ikeda *et al.*, *The Wisdom of the Lotus Sutra* vol. 5, p. 189.

47 Chappell, "Organic Truth", p. 66.

48 See Watson, *The Lotus Sutra*, pp. 252–3 and Ikeda *et al.*, *The Wisdom of the Lotus Sutra*, vol. 4, pp. 102–3.

49 Ikeda, in Ikeda *et al.*, *The Wisdom of the Lotus Sutra*, vol. 4, p. 187.

50 For a full discussion of the issue see Lucinda Joy Peach, "Social Responsibility, Sex Change, and Salvation: Gender Justice in the Lotus Sutra" in Reeves, *A Buddhist Kaleidoscope*, pp. 437–67, and Miriam Levering, "Is the Lotus Sutra 'Good News' for Women" in the same source, pp. 469–91.

51 *Lotus Sutra* 23, Watson p. 281, author's parentheses.

52 *Ibid.*, 8, Watson, p. 145.

53 Peach, "Social Responsibility, Sex Change, and Salvation", p. 441.

54 *Ibid.*, p. 457.

55 *Lotus Sutra* 12, Watson, p. 188.

56 Levering, "Is the Lotus Sutra 'Good News' for Women?", p. 478.

57 Ikeda, in Ikeda *et al.*, *The Wisdom of the Lotus Sutra*, vol. 3, p. 93.

58 *Ibid.*, p. 102.

59 *Ibid.*, p. 122.

60 *Ibid.*, p. 98.

61 Chappell, "Organic Truth", p. 66.

62 Ikeda, in Ikeda *et al.*, *The Wisdom of the Lotus Sutra*, vol. 4, p. 29.

63 Masahiro Shimoda, "How Has the Lotus Sutra Created Social Movements?: The Relationship of the Lotus Sutra to *Mahaparinirvana-sutra*" in Reeves, *A Buddhist Kaleidoscope*, p. 328.

64 See Schubert M. Ogden, "The Lotus Sutra and Interreligious Dialogue" in Reeves, *ibid.*, p. 108.

65 Reeves, "The Lotus Sutra as Radically World-affirming", in Reeves, *ibid.*, p. 183.

66 David W. Chappell, "Global Significance of the Lotus Sutra", *Journal of Oriental Studies*, 6 (1996), p. 3.

67 *Ibid.* pp. 3–4.

68 *Lotus Sutra* 9, Watson, p. 151.

69 Gene Reeves, "Appropriate Means as the Ethics of the Lotus Sutra" in Reeves, *A Buddhist Kaleidoscope*, p. 384.

70 *Lotus Sutra*, 3, Watson, p. 59.

71 Soothill, *The Lotus of the Wonderful Law*, p. 13.

72 Watson, *The Lotus Sutra*, p. xx.

73 Ikeda, in Ikeda *et al.*, *The Wisdom of the Lotus Sutra*, vol. 6, p. 21.

CHAPTER SIX **The Practice**

1 Richard Causton, *The Buddha in Daily Life* (London: Rider, 1995), p. 243. The work was originally published in 1988, under the title, *Nichiren Shoshu Buddhism*, prior to the schism with the priesthood.

2 Jacqueline I. Stone, *Original Enlightenment and the Transformation of Medieval Japanese Buddhism* (Honolulu: University of Hawaii Press, 1999), p. 290.

3 Daisaku Ikeda, *The Wisdom of the Lotus Sutra: A discussion*, vol. 1 (Santa Monica, CA: World Tribune Press, 2000), p. 96.

4 For a full account of daily practice, see Eiichi Wada, "Gongyo. Our Daily Practice", *Art of Living*, no. 31, January, 2004 (SGI-UK: Taplow, Berkshire), pp. 23–6.

5 See Richard Causton, "Daily Practice Gongyo", in Jim Cowan (ed.), *The Buddhism of the Sun* (Richmond: Nichiren Shoshu of the United Kingdom, 1982), p. 76.

6 See *The Lotus* Sutra, translated by Burton Watson, (New York and Chichester: Columbia University Press, 1993), pp. 233–44.

7 SGI-USA Study Department, *The Untold History of the Fuji School: The true story of Nichiren Shoshu* (Santa Monica, CA: World Tribune Press, 2000), p. 70.

8 Daisaku Ikeda, *The Wisdom of the Lotus Sutra: A discussion*, vol. 5 (Santa Monica, CA: World Tribune Press, 2003) , p. 17.

9 Bryan Wilson and Karel Dobbelaere, *A Time to Chant: The Soka Gakkai Buddhists in Britain* (Oxford: Clarendon Press, 1994), p. 27.

10 See *The Lotus* Sutra, translated by Burton Watson, pp. 224–32.

11 Eiichi Wada, "Gongyo. Our Daily Practice", pp. 23–6; also *The Liturgy of Nichiren Daishonin Buddhism* (SGI: no further details).

12 See Eiichi Wada, *ibid.*

13 "Prayer in Nichiren Buddhism", SGI Quarterly in *Art of Living*, no. 26, August 2003, p. 28.

14 Daisaku Ikeda, in *ibid.*, p. 29.

15 Question 11 on the questionnaire, see Appendix A, p. 247.

16 Jacqueline I. Stone, "Placing Nichiren in the 'Big Picture': Some Ongoing Issues in Scholarship", in *Revisiting Nichiren: A Special Issue Commemorating the Fiftieth Anniversary of Nanzan University* (Nanzan: *Japanese Journal of Religious Studies*, vol. 26, nos 3–4, September 1999), pp. 383–421.

17 As in the 183 cm bronze statue of Kaiketsu Nichiren (Wondrous Nichiren) that today stands in Inokashira Shizen Buka-en, Musashino City, Tokyo. See frontisplate in *Revisiting Nichiren, ibid.*

18 Stone, *Original Enlightenment and the Transformation of Medieval Japanese Buddhism*, pp. 290–5.

19 Jacqueline I. Stone, "When Disobedience is Filial and Resistance is Loyal: The

Lotus Sutra and Social Obligations in the Medieval Nichiren Tradition" in *Revisiting Nichiren*, p. 263.

20 *Ibid.*

21 *Ibid.*, p. 265.

22 Lucia Dolce, "Nichiren and Esoteric Buddhism"; lecture given at Taplow Court, 6 November 2004.

23 Lucia Dolce, "Criticism and Appropriation: Nichiren's Attitude towards Esoteric Buddhism", in *Revisiting Nichiren*, p. 349.

24 Question 16 on the questionnaire, see Appendix A, p. 247.

25 Stone, *Original Enlightenment and the Transformation of Medieval Japanese Buddhism*, p. 272. Elsewhere, Stone states that Nichiren "did not initially argue the potency of the *daimoku* in this way, see "Placing Nichiren in the 'Big Picture'", p. 400.

26 Dolce, "Nichiren and Esoteric Buddhism"; lecture given at Taplow Court, 6 November 2004.

27 Jacqueline I. Stone, "Chanting the August Title of the *Lotus Sutra: Daimoku.* Practices in Classical and Medieval Japan" in Richard K. Payne (ed.), *Re-visioning "Kamakura" Buddhism* (Honolulu: University of Hawaii Press, 1998), p. 154.

28 Laurel Rasplica Rodd, *Nichiren: Selected Writings* (Honolulu: University of Hawaii Press, 1980), p. 83.

29 Stone, *Original Enlightenment and the Transformation of Medieval Japanese Buddhism*, p. 276.

30 Eiichi Wada, "Gongyo. Our Daily Practice", pp. 23– 6.

31 *Gojukai* is the priests' expression, meaning "initiation ceremony". The term is no longer used by SGI, who prefer "*Gohonzon* receiving ceremony". On 24 May 2008, the present authors attended such a ceremony in Abergavenny, Monmouthshire, South Wales. Such ceremonies now take place regularly in Wales.

32 Nichiren Daishonin, "On the Treasure Tower", *The Writings of Nichiren Daishonin*, no. 31, edited and translated by The Gosho Translation Committee (Tokyo: Soka Gakkai, 1999), pp. 299–300.

33 It should be emphasized that symbolism should not be the centre of attention. For a detailed description of the various symbols and their meaning, see Ted Morino (SGI-USA Study Department senior advisor), "What is the significance of the accessories traditionally placed by the Buddhist altar?" *UK Express*, no. 343, January 2000 (SGI-UK: Taplow, Berkshire), pp. 40–4.

34 *The Liturgy of Nichiren Daishonin's Buddhism.*

35 In academic writing, the Japanese language does not use the plural form.

36 Kathy Aitken, "The Gohonzon", *Art of Living*, no. 4, October 2001, p. 21.

37 See "Emerging from the Earth", *The Lotus Sutra*, translated by Burton Watson, pp. 212–23.

38 "On the Treasure Tower" in *The Writings of Nichiren Daishonin*, no. 31, p. 299.

39 Dolce, "Nichiren and Esoteric Buddhism"; lecture given at Taplow Court, 6 November 2004.

40 Tomohira Matsuda (ed.), *A Dictionary of Buddhist Terms and Concepts* (Tokyo: Nichiren Shoshu International Centre, 1983), p. 143. An excellent account of the *Gohonzon* is to be found in Stone, *Original Enlightenment and the Transformation of Medieval Japanese Buddhism*, pp. 27–88.

41 Robert Harrap, "Embracing the Gohonzon is in itself Observing One's Own Mind", *Art of Living*, no. 41, November 2004, p. 9.

42 "The Real Aspect of the Gohonzon" in *The Writings of Nichiren Daishonin*, no. 101, p. 832.

43 Question 14 on the questionnaire, see Appendix A, p. 247.

44 Causton, *The Buddha in Daily Life*, p. 245.

45 Kathy Aitken, "The Gohonzon", p. 22.

46 "The True Aspect of all Phenomena" in *The Writings of Nichiren Daishonin*, no. 40, p. 386.

47 Shoichi Hasegawa, Chairman, SGI-Europe, http://www.guidestud.org, 26/04/2008.

48 Causton, *The Buddha in Daily Life*, p. 265.

49 Alex Canfor-Dumas, "Faith, Practice and Study" *UK Express,* no. 310, April 1997 (Taplow Court, Berkshire: SGI-UK), p. 33.

50 Causton, *The Buddha in Daily Life*, p. 265.

51 Responses to question 31 on the questionnaire, see Appendix A, p. 249.

52 Responses to question 17 on the questionnaire, see Appendix A, p. 247.

53 Causton, *The Buddha in Daily Life*, p. 265.

54 *Art of Living*, no. 34, April 2004, p. 3.

55 <www.guidestud.org>.

56 Causton, *The Buddha in Daily Life*, p. 265.

57 <www. guidestud.org>.

58 Phillip E. Hammond and David W. Machacek, *Soka Gakkai in America: Accommodation and conversion* (Oxford, New York: Oxford University Press, 1999), p. 121.

59 In an interview with Helen Waterhouse, 30 March 1995. See Helen Waterhouse, *Buddhism in Bath: Adaptation and Authority* (University of Leeds, 1997), p. 112, note 56.

60 E-mail received 16 May 2008.

61 Causton, *The Buddha in Daily Life*, p. 265.

62 Daisaku Ikeda, *The Wisdom of the Lotus Sutra*, vol. 5, p. 24.

63 "The True Aspect of all Phenomena" in *The Writings of Nichiren Daishonin*, no. 40, p. 386.

64 Daisaku Ikeda, *The Wisdom of the Lotus Sutra*, vol. 5, p. 220.

65 Daisaku Ikeda, *ibid.,* p. 102. See also, Takanori Endo, "The Lotus Sutra and the Philosophy of the Soka Gakkai", *The Journal of Oriental Studies*, vol. 6 (Tokyo: The Institute of Oriental Philosophy, 1996), p. 54.

66 For an excellent article on *daimoku*, see Stone, "Chanting the August Title of the *Lotus Sutra: Daimoku*", pp. 116–66.

67 Question 13 on the questionnaire, see Appendix A, p. 247.

68 Causton, *The Buddha in Daily Life*, p. 245.

69 Daisaku Ikeda, *The Wisdom of the Lotus Sutra: A discussion*, vol. 3 (Santa Monica, CA: World Tribune Press, 2001), p. 146. See especially p. 136.

70 Causton, *The Buddha in Daily Life*, p. 248.

71 Question 12 on the questionnaire, see Appendix A, p. 247.

72 Damien Keown, *Buddhism: A very short introduction* (Oxford: Oxford University Press, 1996), p. 53.

73 Daisaku Ikeda, *The Wisdom of the Lotus Sutra: A discussion*, vol. 5, p. 155.

74 Question 30 on the questionnaire, see Appendix A, p. 249.
75 Causton, *The Buddha in Daily Life*, p. 125.
76 Question 15 on the questionnaire, see Appendix A, p. 247.
77 Questions 28 and 29 on the questionnaire, see Appendix A, p. 249.
78 *The Lotus Sutra* 22, "Entrustment", translated by Burton Watson, p. 278.
79 See, for example, 21, "Supernatural Powers", *ibid.*, p. 274.
80 Ikeda, *The Wisdom of the Lotus Sutra*, vol. 5, p. 234.
81 Daisaku Ikeda, *The Wisdom of the Lotus Sutra: A discussion*, vol. 6 (Santa Monica, CA: World Tribune Press, 2003), p. 259.
82 See *ibid.*, p. 241.
83 Cited in *ibid.*, pp. 259–60.
84 Josei Toda, *Wakaki hi no shuki–Gokuchuki*, translated by and cited in Daisaku Ikeda, *The Wisdom of the Lotus Sutra: A discussion*, vol. 2 (Santa Monica, CA: World Tribune Press, 2003), p. 140.
85 Ikeda, *The Wisdom of the Lotus Sutra*, vol. 6, p. 237.
86 *Ibid.*, p. 259.

CHAPTER SEVEN **The Philosophy of Nichiren Daishonin Buddhism**

1 Daisaku Ikeda, *Unlocking the Mysteries of Birth and Death: Buddhism in the contemporary world* (London and Sydney: Macdonald & Co., 1988), pp. 65–6.
2 Daisaku Ikeda, in Chandra Wickramasinghe and Daisaku Ikeda, *Space and Eternal Life* (London and Sterling VA: Journeyman, 1998), p. 7.
3 Ikeda, *Unlocking the Mysteries of Birth and Death*, p. 113.
4 "The Four Debts of Gratitude" in *The Writings of Nichiren Daishonin*, no. 6, translated and edited by The Gosho Translation Committee (Tokyo: Soka Gakkai, 1999), p. 44.
5 "The Entity of the Mystic Law" *ibid.*, no. 47, p. 417.
6 *Ibid.*, pp. 417–18.
7 Daisaku Ikeda in conversation with Masayosh Kiguchi and Eiichi Shimura, *Buddhism and the Cosmos* (London and Sydney: Macdonald & Co., 1986 reprint of 1985 edn), pp. 261–2.
8 "On Attaining Buddhahood in This Lifetime" in *The Writings of Nichiren Daishonin*, no. 1, p. 4.
9 Ikeda, *Unlocking the Mysteries of Birth and Death*, p. 196.
10 Ikeda, in Wickramasinghe and Ikeda, *Space and Eternal Life*, p. 14.
11 Nichiren Shoshu International Center, *Fundamentals of Buddhism* (Tokyo: Nichiren Shoshu International Center, 1993, first published 1977), p. 71.
12 In fact there are ten onenesses or non-dualities. They are: body and mind; internal and external; inherent Buddha-nature and Buddhahood experienced in practice; cause and effect; pure and impure, in other words enlightenment and delusion; life and environment; self and others; thought, word and deed; provisional and true teachings of the Buddha; benefit of Buddhahood for the Buddha and all people. These ten non-dualities were promulgated by Miao-lo (711–82), the sixth patriarch of the Chinese T'ien-t'ai school in China.
13 Ikeda, in Wickramasinghe and Ikeda, *Space and Eternal Life*, p. 6.
14 "On Attaining Buddhahood in This Lifetime" in *The Writings of Nichiren Daishonin*, no. 1, p. 3.
15 Ikeda, in Ikeda, Masayosh Kiguchi and Eiichi Shimura, *Buddhism and the Cosmos*, p. 263.

16 Richard Causton, *The Buddha in Daily Life: An introduction to the Buddhism of Nichiren Daishonin* (London, Sydney, Auckland, Johannesburg: Rider, n.d., first published as *Nichiren Shoshu Buddhism: An introduction* in 1988), p. 212.

17 Ikeda, in Ikeda, Masayosh Kiguchi and Eiichi Shimura, *Buddhism and the Cosmos*, pp. 211–12.

18 In Hindu philosophy this theory that effects are latent in their causes and therefore exist prior to their manifestation is known as *satkaryavada*.

19 See Ikeda, *Unlocking the Mysteries of Birth and Death*, p. 184.

20 Causton, *The Buddha in Daily Life*, p. 170.

21 Ikeda, *Unlocking the Mysteries of Birth and Death*, p. 192.

22 Hell is self-explanatory as a separate world, as is Heaven. Humanity would be life on Earth, and Animality life as a creature. The higher worlds would represent different kinds of heavenly realms.

23 Causton, *The Buddha in Daily Life*, p. 44.

24 Ikeda, in Ikeda, Masayosh Kiguchi and Eiichi Shimura, *Buddhism and the Cosmos*, p. 46.

25 Compare Skt. *ashura*, the word for demon.

26 Causton, *The Buddha in Daily Life*, p. 52.

27 Aristotle, *The Nicomachean Ethics*.

28 The *Six Paths* are those that were believed in Indian thought generally to lead to rebirth. And even if one were to be reborn in Heaven, as soon as the good *karma* by which one had arrived there was used up, then rebirth in mortal state would follow.

29 *Ji* means to eradicate suffering and *hi* to give happiness.

30 This is the view of Mahayana Buddhism generally. Theravada Buddhism, which accepts only one Buddha in one aeon understood the term to refer to Shakyamuni Buddha before he became enlightened.

31 Termed the *Nine Worlds* in order to distinguish them from *Buddhahood*.

32 Causton, *The Buddha in Daily Life*, p. 122.

33 Ikeda, *Unlocking the Mysteries of Birth and Death*, p. 10.

34 Causton, *The Buddha in Daily Life*, p. 94.

35 Ikeda, *Unlocking the Mysteries of Birth and Death*, pp. 11–12.

36 Causton, *The Buddha in Daily Life*, pp. 81–2.

37 Ikeda, *Unlocking the Mysteries of Birth and Death*, p. 188.

38 *Ibid.*, p. 76.

39 *Ibid.*

40 William Shakespeare, *Julius Caesar*, Act V, scene 5.

41 See *Art of Living*, no. 84, June 2003, p. 32.

42 Causton, *The Buddha in Daily Life*, p. 144.

43 Ikeda, *Unlocking the Mysteries of Birth and Death*, p. 164.

44 *Funi* is actually an abbreviation of *nini-funi* "two but not two", that is to say having two integrated functions but unified all the same.

45 Inanimate forms have a shared *karma* but not an individual one.

46 Causton, *The Buddha in Daily Life*, p. 145.

47 Ikeda, *Unlocking the Mysteries of Birth and Death*, p. 168.

48 "The Heritage of the Ultimate Law of Life" in *The Writings of Nichiren Daishonin*, no. 29, p. 216.

49 Buddhist funeral rites in Japan are repeated at seven-day intervals after death for

up to forty nine days. It is believed that the deceased has the opportunity to be reborn on such days, so the family performs rites to aid the process.

50 Daisaku Ikeda, in René Huyghe and Daisaku Ikeda, *Dawn after Dark*, translated by Richard L. Gage (New York and Tokyo: Weatherhill, 1991 reprint of 1980 edn), pp. 392–3.

51 Ikeda, in Ikeda, Masayosh Kiguchi and Eiichi Shimura, *Buddhism and the Cosmos*, p. 34.

52 Nichiren Shoshu International Center, *Fundamentals of Buddhism*, p. 59.

53 Ikeda, *Unlocking the Mysteries of Birth and Death*, pp. 110–11.

54 "The Three Obstacles and Four Devils" in *The Writings of Nichiren Daishonin*, no. 77, p. 637.

CHAPTER EIGHT **Special Occasions**

1 Responses to question 32 of the questionnaire, see Appendix A, p. 249.

2 The expression "Buddmother", if correct, does not seem to be a well-known one, according to Kyoko Gibson.

3 "Easy Delivery of a Fortune Child", in *The Writings of Nichiren Daishonin*, no. 19 (Tokyo: Soka Gakkai, The Gosho Translation Committee, 1999), pp. 186–7.

4 "The Birth of Tsukimaro" *ibid.*, no. 20, p. 188.

5 Nichiren Daishonin, "Letter to the Brothers", *ibid.*, no. 61, pp. 501–2.

6 See CHAPTER SEVEN for an explanation of this concept.

Further Reading

The major primary sources of interest to the reader would be the works of Nichiren Daishonin, and the *Lotus Sutra*. The former have been collected, edited and translated into English by The Gosho Translation Committee. Published in two volumes in 1999 and 2006 by Soka Gakkai (Tokyo), they are entitled *The Writings of Nichiren Daishonin*. The same material, though edited by Philip B. Yampolsky, is to be found in *Letters of Nichiren*, translated by Burton Watson and members of the Gosho Committee (New York: Columbia University Press, 1996). As to the *Lotus Sutra*, a number of texts are available. The main one used in this book is Burton Watson's translation, *The Lotus Sutra* (New York: Columbia University Press, 1993). Apart from being an excellent translation, Watson's text has the advantage of being one favoured by Soka Gakkai. Also by Burton Watson is a recent translation of the *Ongi kuden* of Nichiren Daishonin, entitled *The Record of the Orally Transmitted Teachings* (Tokyo: Soka Gakkai, 2004). This text not only contains the *Lotus Sutra* but also Nichiren Daishonin's comments on it. Daisaku Ikeda, along with Katsuji Saito, Takanori Endo and Haruo Suda have recorded their conversations on all chapters of the *Lotus Sutra* in a highly readable six-volume work, *The Wisdom of the Lotus Sutra: A discussion* (Santa Monica, CA: World Tribune Press, 2000). For academic essays on the *Lotus Sutra*, an excellent edited work by Gene Reeves, *A Buddhist Kaleidoscope: Essays on the* Lotus Sutra (Tokyo: Kosei Publishing Company, 2002), contains scholarly articles on a range of issues related to the *Sutra*.

For the historical perspectives of Buddhism, Edward B. Cowell's rendition of Ashvaghosha's *The Buddha-Karita or Life of Buddha* (New Delhi: Cosmo, 1977, first published in 1894), edited from a Devanagari and two Nepalese manuscripts with variant readings, still supplies a vibrant and readable primary source for the life of the Buddha. The work by Edward Conze, *Buddhist Scriptures* (London: Penguin, 1959), contains primary texts from both the Theravada and Mahayana traditions. Richard Gombrich deals with early Buddhism in *How Buddhism Began: The conditioned genesis of the early teachings* (London: Athlone, 1996), as well as in his earlier work, *Theravada Buddhism: A social history from ancient Benares to modern Colombo* (London and New York: Routledge and Kegan Paul, 1988). Another excellent source for the foundation of Buddhism is Walpola Rahula's *What the Buddha Taught* (Oxford: Oneworld, 1998, first published 1959). For readers interested in understanding the basics of Buddhist philosophical and religious thought, Paul Williams' and Anthony Tribe's work *Buddhist Thought: A complete introduction to the Indian tradition* (London: Routledge, 2000) is recommended; the book is not confined to early Buddhist thought, and more then half of it considers the Mahayana tradition.

Paul Williams' *Mahayana Buddhism: The doctrinal foundations* (London: Routledge, 1989), remains a standard work in the field. Merv Fowler's *Buddhism: Beliefs and practices* (Brighton, Sussex and Portland, Oregon: Sussex Academic Press, 1999) is a very readable approach to the four main Mahayana schools of Buddhism including Tibetan. *A History of Japanese Buddhism*, edited by Kazuo Kasahara and translated by Paul McCarthy and Gaynor Sekimori (Tokyo: Kosei Publishing Co., first English edn 2004), has comprehensive articles on the schools of Nichiren, Tendai and many others, and is a veritable mine of information on Japanese religions.

For the life of Nichiren, Yasuji Kirimura's *The Life of Nichiren Daishonin* (Tokyo: Nichiren Shoshu International Center, 1980), is a concise source. Two works edited by Dayle M. Bethel are essential sources for the life and work of Tsunesaburo Makiguchi – *Education for Creative Living: Ideas and proposals of Tsunesaburo Makiguchi* (translated by Alfred Birnbaum (Ames, Iowa: Iowa State University Press, 1989), and *Makiguchi. The Value Creator: Revolutionary Japanese educator and founder of Soka Gakkai* (New York and Tokyo: Weatherhill, 1973). The work of Tsunesaburo Makiguchi himself, *A Geography of Human Life*, has been edited by Dayle Bethel and translated from Japanese by Katsusuku Hori *et al.* (San Francisco: Caddo Gap Press, 2002, first published in Japanese in 1903). For a full account of the history of the Nichiren Shoshu school, readers are referred to The SGI-UK Study Department's work, *The Untold History of the Fuji School: The true story of Nichiren Shoshu* (Santa Monica, CA: World Tribune Press, 2000).

Daisaku Ikeda's *The Human Revolution* (Taplow Court: Soka Gakkai International, 1994, revised English translation, first published in Japanese in 1965), is an eight-volume work in the style of a novel, charting the life of his mentor, Josei Toda and the history and development of the Soka Gakkai. Then, there is the nine-volume sequel, *The New Human Revolution* (Santa Monica, CA: World Tribune Press, 1995), which recounts the legacy of Josei Toda in the life and work of Ikeda himself. A diary of Ikeda's early years in the Gakkai is to be found in his *A Youthful Diary: One man's journey from the beginning of faith to worldwide leadership for peace* (Santa Monica CA: World Tribune Press, 2000).

There have been a number of studies undertaken throughout the world that have examined Soka Gakkai mainly from a sociological perspective. A sound summary of these can be found in David Machacek and Bryan Wilson (eds), *Global Citizens: The Soka Gakkai Buddhist movement in the world* (Oxford, New York: Oxford University Press, 2003 reprint of 2000 edn). Three perhaps need special mention: Daniel A. Métraux, *The Lotus and the Maple Leaf: The Soka Gakkai Buddhist movement in Canada* (Lanham, New York and London: University Press of America, 1996), Phillip E. Hammond and David W. Machacek, *Soka Gakkai in America: Accommodation and conversion* (Oxford, New York: Oxford University Press, 1999), and the study done in the United Kingdom by Bryan Wilson and Karel Dobbelaere, *A Time to Chant: The Soka Gakkai Buddhists in Britain* (Oxford, New York: Oxford University Press, 1994). The whole development of Soka Gakkai is treated in Richard Hughes Seager's *Encountering the Dharma: Daisaku Ikeda, Soka Gakkai, and the globalization of Buddhist humanism* (Berkeley, Los Angeles, London: University of California Press, 2006). Daniel Métraux' *The Soka Gakkai Revolution* (Lanham, Maryland and London: University Press of America, 1994), also deals with the development of the Gakkai.

The publications by President Daisaku Ikeda are too numerous to mention here. He is a comfortable writer who is able to put across difficult concepts with an ease of style. Of his many dialogues with other thinkers, *Choose Peace: A dialogue between Johan Galtung & Daisaku Ikeda* (translated and edited by Richard L. Gage, London and East Haven, CT: Pluto Press, 1995), is notable for the theme in its title, which is so important a feature of Ikeda's policies. The same theme, too, is the topic of *For the*

Sake of Peace: Seven paths to global harmony. A Buddhist perspective (Santa Monica, CA: Middleway Press, 2002 reprint of 2001 edn). His thoughts on education are also prolific, and crystallized in *Soka Education: A Buddhist vision for teachers, students and parents* (Santa Monica, CA: Middleway Press, 2001). His passion for scientific study is exemplified in his dialogue with the astronomer Chandra Wickramasinghe in *Space and Eternal Life: A dialogue between Chandra Wickramasinghe and Daisaku Ikeda* (London and Stirling, VA: Journeyman Press, 1998). In dialogue with René Simard and Guy Bourgeault is *On Being Human: Where ethics, medicine and spirituality converge* (Santa Monica, CA: Middleway Press, 2003), which, as its title suggests, deals with the challenges of medical health and science in the twenty-first century. Ikeda's university addresses throughout the world have been gathered together in one volume, *A New Humanism: The University Addresses of Daisaku Ikeda* (New York and Tokyo: Weatherhill, 1996).

For the serious reader, volume 26 of the *Japanese Journal of Religious Studies* (Nagoya: Nanzan Institute for Religion and Culture, 1999) is a must, with outstanding articles by Jacqueline I. Stone and Lucia Dolce, among others. Stone's work, *Original Enlightenment and the Transformation of Medieval Japanese Buddhism* (Honolulu: University of Hawaii Press, 1999) is similarly acclaimed, as are articles by Stone and others in Richard K. Payne's edited work, *Re-visioning "Kamakura Buddhism"* (Honolulu: University of Hawaii Press, 1980).The major comprehensive study of Nichiren Daishonin Buddhism is still the outstanding work by the late Richard Causton, *The Buddha in Daily Life: An introduction to the Buddhism of Nichiren Daishonin* (London, Sydney, Auckland, Johannesburg: Rider, 1995, first published as *Nichiren Shoshu Buddhism: An introduction* in 1988). This text covers all aspects of Nichiren Daishonin Buddhism, dealing extensively with praxis. Wilson and Dobbelaere's *A Time to Chant*, mentioned above, is also an excellent source for practice.

Richard Causton's book is also concerned with the philosophy that underpins Nichiren Daishonin Buddhism. Several works by Daisaku Ikeda are also invaluable for the philosophy. These are: *Unlocking the Mysteries of Birth and Death: Buddhism in the contemporary world* (London and Sydney: Macdonald & Co., 1988), Ikeda in conversation with Masayosh Kiguchi and Eiichi Shimura, *Buddhism and the Cosmos* (London and Sydney: Macdonald & Co., 1986 reprint of 1985 edn), and the dialogue between Daisaku Ikeda and Chandra Wickramasinghe, *Space and Eternal Life*, noted above.

The reader interested in all aspects of the SGI-UK, including details of every aspect of faith, practice and study, is referred to the movement's magazine, *Art of Living* published monthly at Taplow, Maidenhead, Berkshire. Details of the *Art of Living* are available on the website www.sgi-uk.org. The magazine also contains details of the basic principles of Nichiren Daishonin Buddhism, extracts from the works of its President, Daisaku Ikeda, study material and experiences of members and contemporary topics. Global websites are as follows:

USA	<www.sgi-usa.org>
Australia	<www.sgiaust.org>
Canada	<www.sgicanada.org>
Ireland	<www.sgi-ireland.org>
Italy	<www.sgi-italia.org>
UK	<www.sgi-uk.org>

Index